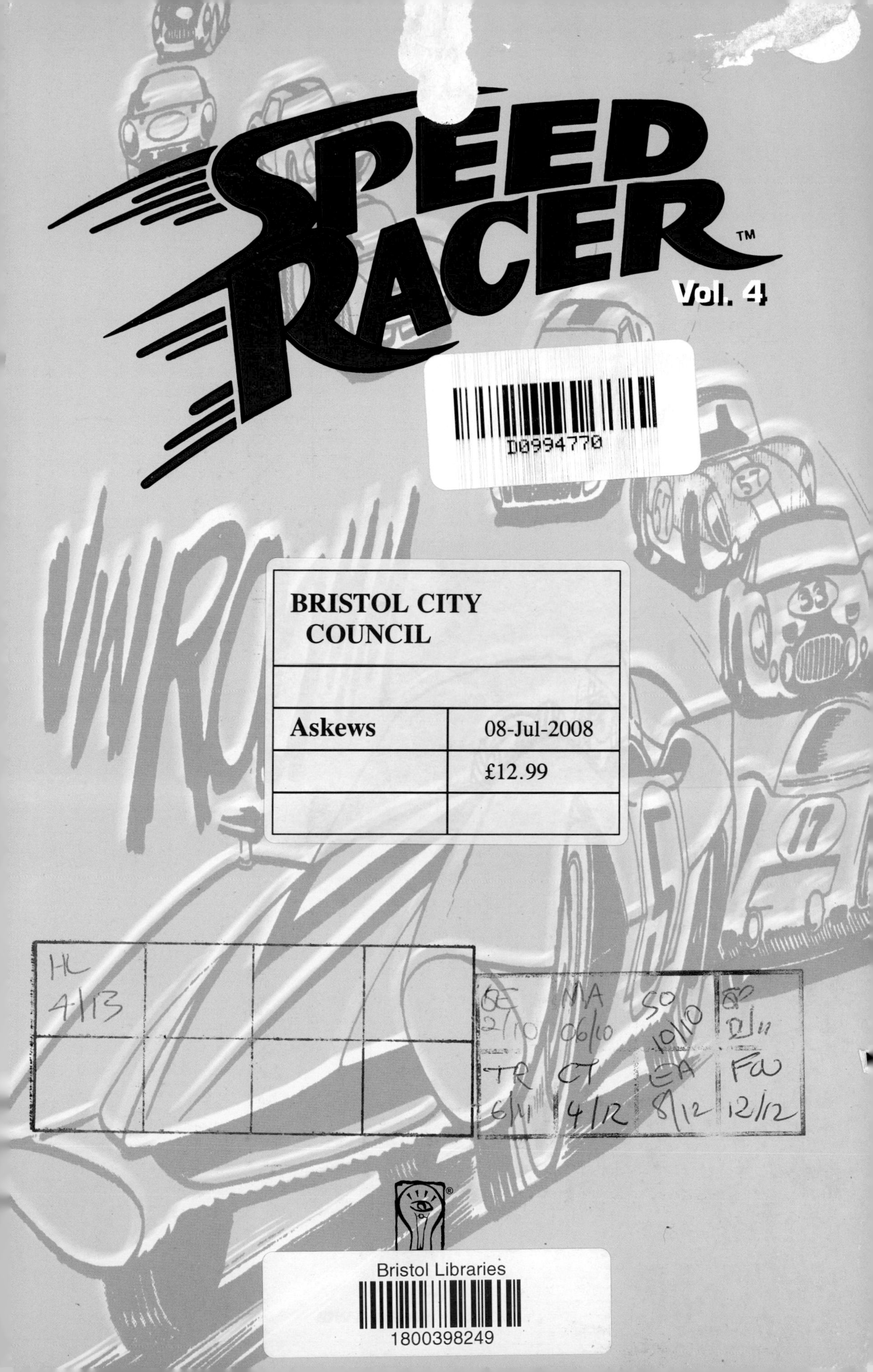
SPEED RACER™
Vol. 4

Speed Racer Vol. 4 TPB

Cover by **Ken Steacy**
Edited by **Dene Nee**
Design and Remaster by **Tom B. Long**

IDW Publishing is:
Ted Adams, President
Robbie Robbins, EVP/Sr. Graphic Artist
Chris Ryall, Publisher/Editor-in-Chief
Clifford Meth, EVP of Strategies/Editorial
Alan Payne, VP of Sales
Marci Kahn, Executive Assistant
Neil Uyetake, Art Director
Tom Waltz, Editor
Andrew Steven Harris, Editor
Chris Mowry, Graphic Artist
Amauri Osorio, Graphic Artist
Dene Nee, Graphic Artist/Editor
Matthew Ruzicka, CPA, Controller
Alonzo Simon, Shipping Manager
Kris Oprisko, Editor/Foreign Lic. Rep.

www.idwpublishing.com
www.speedracer.com

ISBN: 978-1-60010-177-9
11 10 09 08   1 2 3 4 5

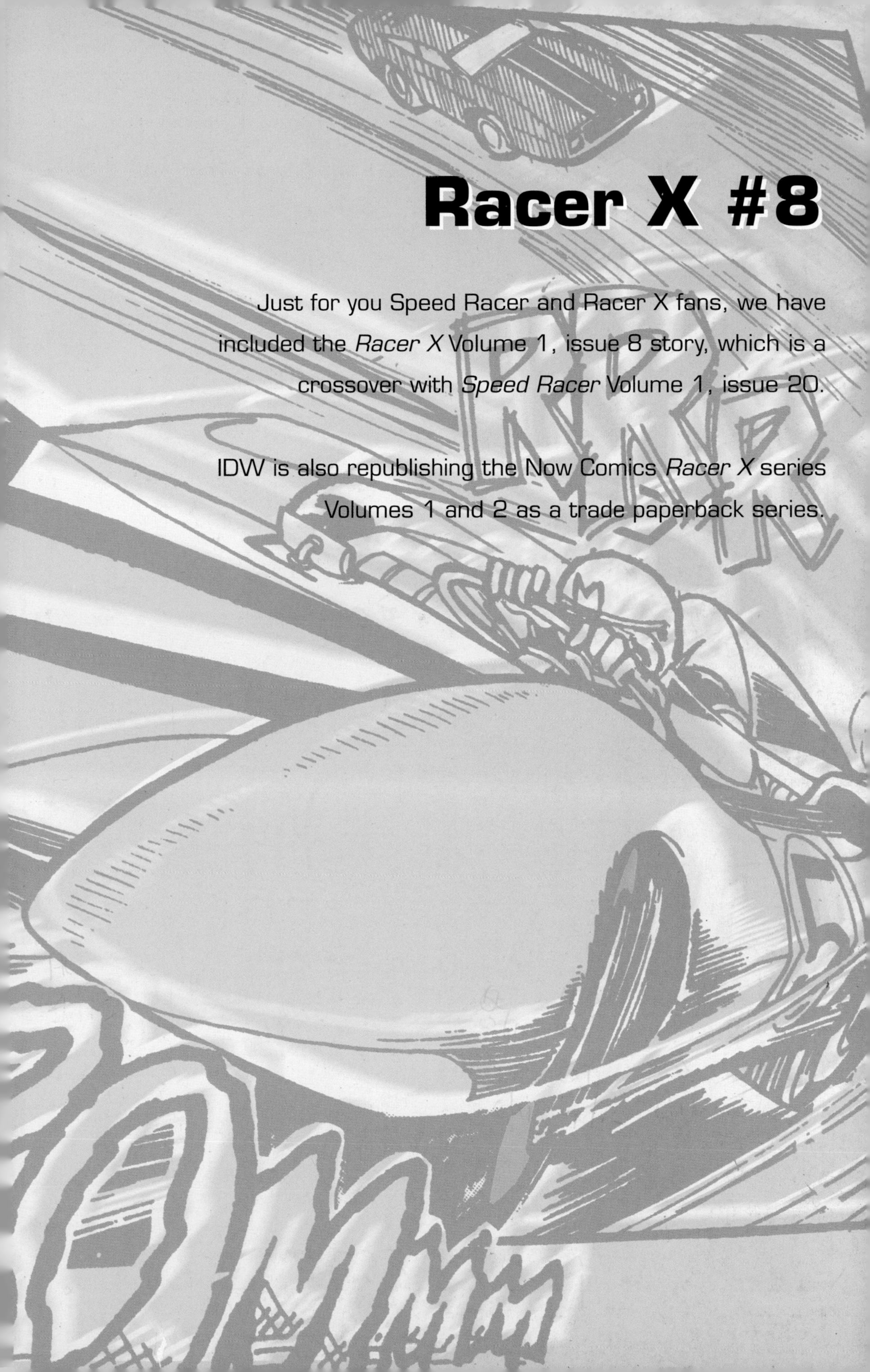

Racer X #8

Just for you Speed Racer and Racer X fans, we have included the *Racer X* Volume 1, issue 8 story, which is a crossover with *Speed Racer* Volume 1, issue 20.

IDW is also republishing the Now Comics *Racer X* series Volumes 1 and 2 as a trade paperback series.

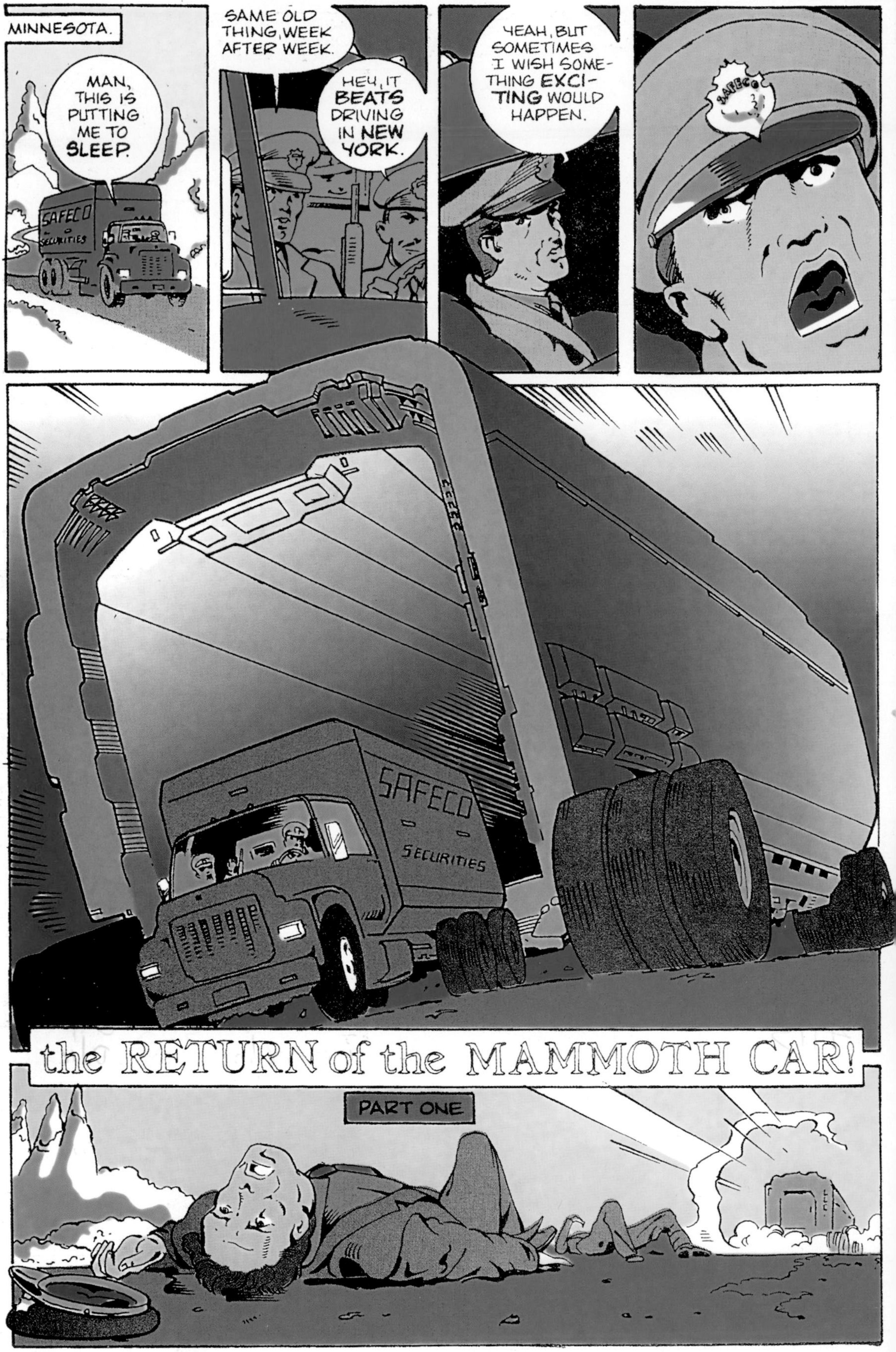
MINNESOTA.
MAN, THIS IS PUTTING ME TO SLEEP.
SAME OLD THING, WEEK AFTER WEEK.
HEY, IT BEATS DRIVING IN NEW YORK.
YEAH, BUT SOMETIMES I WISH SOMETHING EXCITING WOULD HAPPEN.
SAFECO
SAFECO SECURITIES
the RETURN of the MAMMOTH CAR!
PART ONE

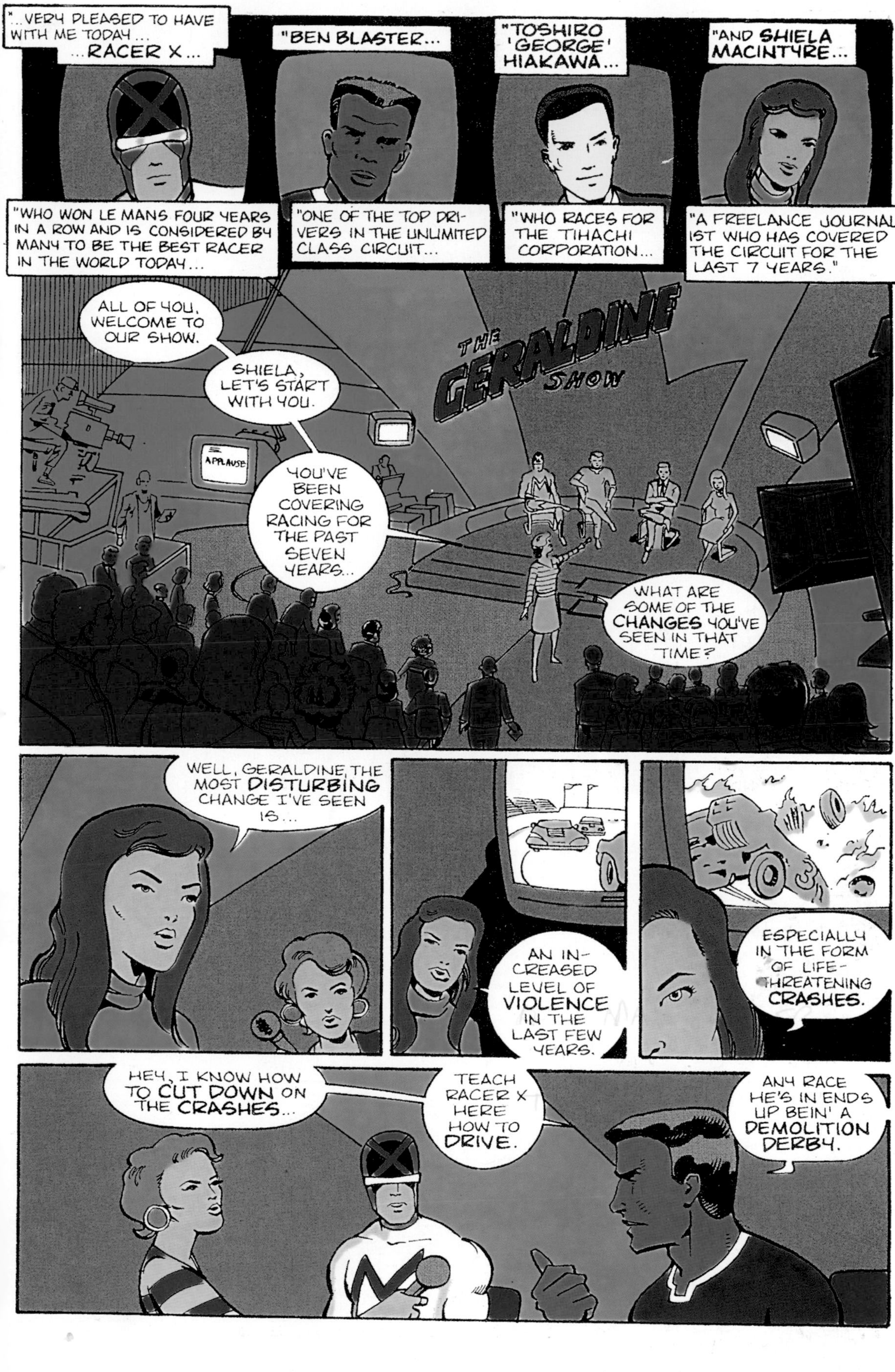
"...VERY PLEASED TO HAVE WITH ME TODAY... ...RACER X...
"WHO WON LE MANS FOUR YEARS IN A ROW AND IS CONSIDERED BY MANY TO BE THE BEST RACER IN THE WORLD TODAY...
"BEN BLASTER...
"ONE OF THE TOP DRIVERS IN THE UNLIMITED CLASS CIRCUIT...
"TOSHIRO 'GEORGE' HIAKAWA...
"WHO RACES FOR THE TIHACHI CORPORATION...
"AND SHIELA MACINTYRE...
"A FREELANCE JOURNALIST WHO HAS COVERED THE CIRCUIT FOR THE LAST 7 YEARS."
THE GERALDINE SHOW
APPLAUSE
ALL OF YOU, WELCOME TO OUR SHOW.
SHIELA, LET'S START WITH YOU.
YOU'VE BEEN COVERING RACING FOR THE PAST SEVEN YEARS...
WHAT ARE SOME OF THE CHANGES YOU'VE SEEN IN THAT TIME?
WELL, GERALDINE, THE MOST DISTURBING CHANGE I'VE SEEN IS...
AN INCREASED LEVEL OF VIOLENCE IN THE LAST FEW YEARS.
ESPECIALLY IN THE FORM OF LIFE-THREATENING CRASHES.
HEY, I KNOW HOW TO CUT DOWN ON THE CRASHES...
TEACH RACER X HERE HOW TO DRIVE.
ANY RACE HE'S IN ENDS UP BEIN' A DEMOLITION DERBY.

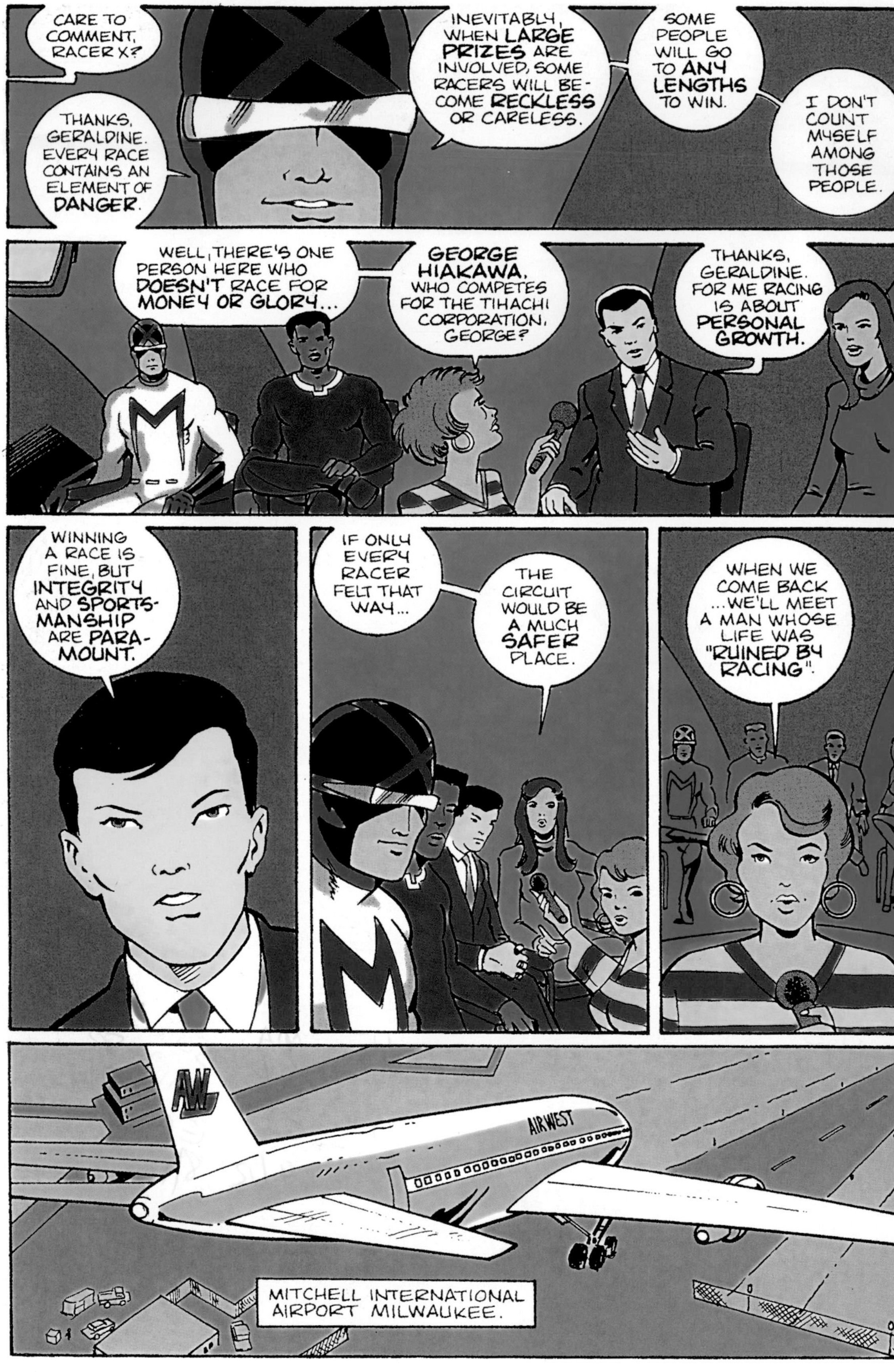
CARE TO COMMENT, RACER X?
THANKS, GERALDINE. EVERY RACE CONTAINS AN ELEMENT OF DANGER.
INEVITABLY, WHEN LARGE PRIZES ARE INVOLVED, SOME RACERS WILL BE-COME RECKLESS OR CARELESS.
SOME PEOPLE WILL GO TO ANY LENGTHS TO WIN.
I DON'T COUNT MYSELF AMONG THOSE PEOPLE.
WELL, THERE'S ONE PERSON HERE WHO DOESN'T RACE FOR MONEY OR GLORY...
GEORGE HIAKAWA, WHO COMPETES FOR THE TIHACHI CORPORATION. GEORGE?
THANKS, GERALDINE. FOR ME RACING IS ABOUT PERSONAL GROWTH.
WINNING A RACE IS FINE, BUT INTEGRITY AND SPORTS-MANSHIP ARE PARA-MOUNT.
IF ONLY EVERY RACER FELT THAT WAY...
THE CIRCUIT WOULD BE A MUCH SAFER PLACE.
WHEN WE COME BACK ...WE'LL MEET A MAN WHOSE LIFE WAS "RUINED BY RACING".
AW
AIRWEST
MITCHELL INTERNATIONAL AIRPORT MILWAUKEE.

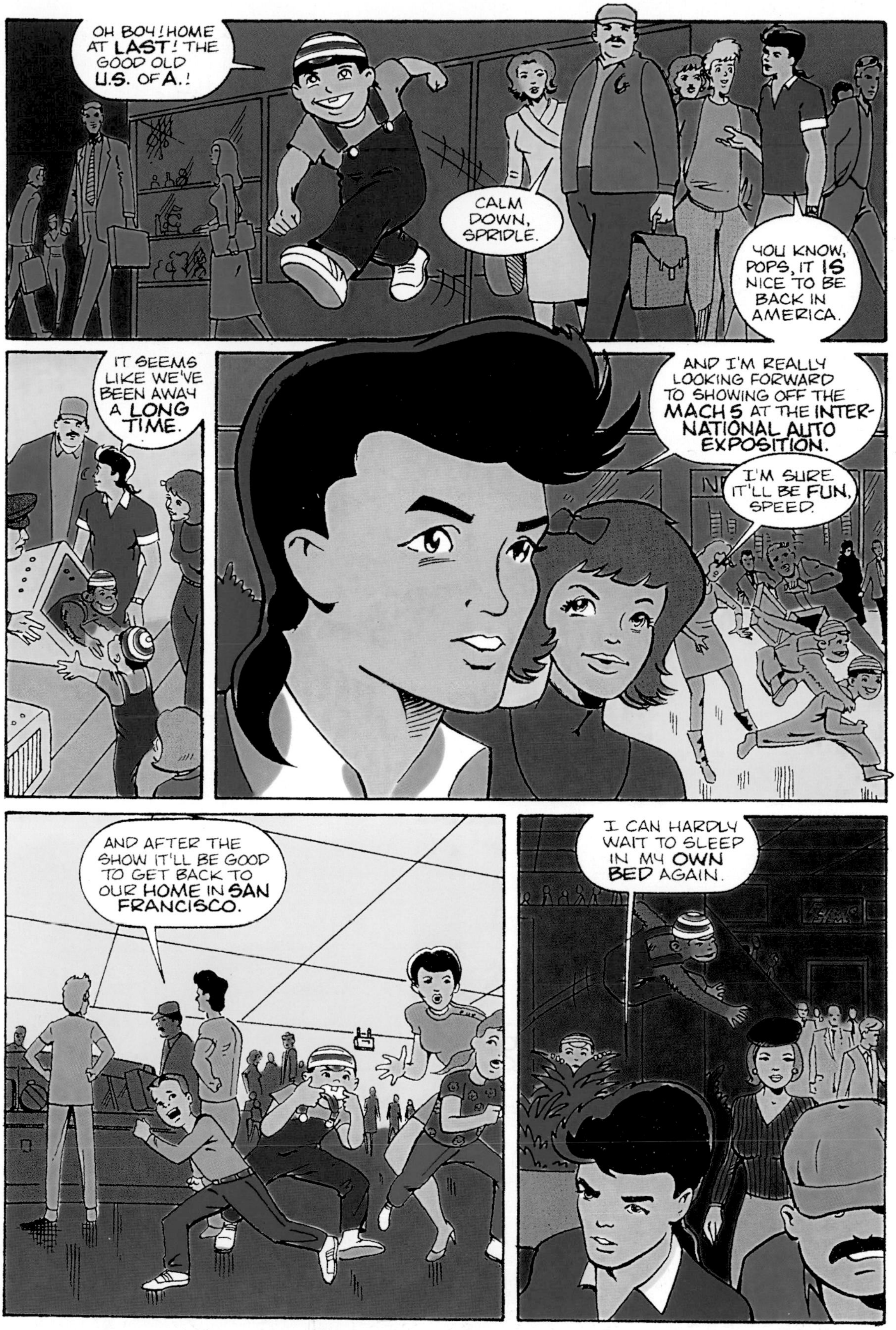
OH BOY! HOME AT LAST! THE GOOD OLD U.S. OF A.!
CALM DOWN, SPRIDLE.
YOU KNOW, POPS, IT IS NICE TO BE BACK IN AMERICA.
IT SEEMS LIKE WE'VE BEEN AWAY A LONG TIME.
AND I'M REALLY LOOKING FORWARD TO SHOWING OFF THE MACH 5 AT THE INTERNATIONAL AUTO EXPOSITION.
I'M SURE IT'LL BE FUN, SPEED.
AND AFTER THE SHOW IT'LL BE GOOD TO GET BACK TO OUR HOME IN SAN FRANCISCO.
I CAN HARDLY WAIT TO SLEEP IN MY OWN BED AGAIN.

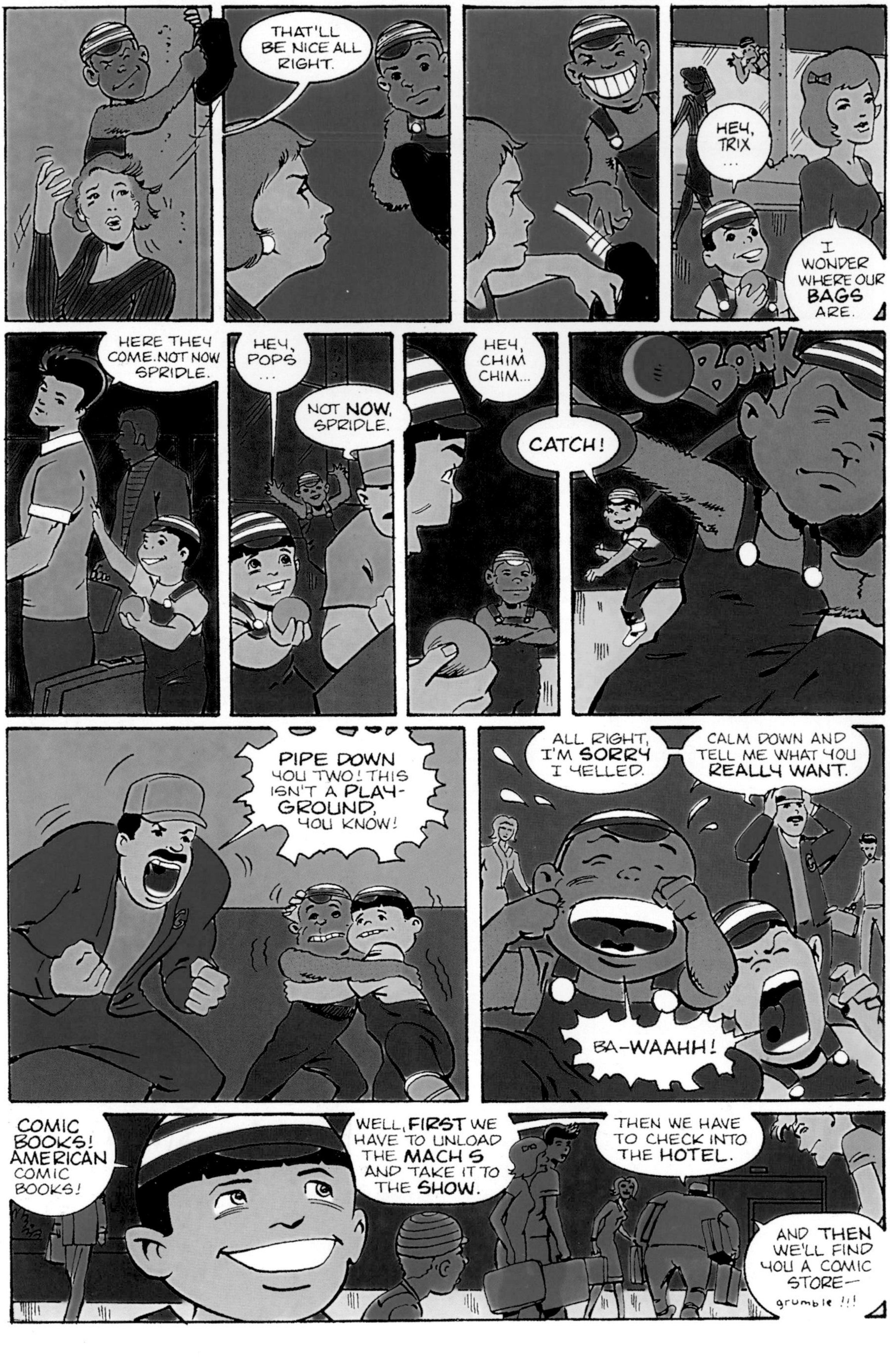
THAT'LL BE NICE ALL RIGHT.
HEY, TRIX ...
I WONDER WHERE OUR BAGS ARE.
HERE THEY COME. NOT NOW SPRIDLE.
HEY, POPS ...
NOT NOW, SPRIDLE.
HEY, CHIM CHIM...
CATCH!
BONK
PIPE DOWN YOU TWO! THIS ISN'T A PLAYGROUND, YOU KNOW!
ALL RIGHT, I'M SORRY I YELLED.
CALM DOWN AND TELL ME WHAT YOU REALLY WANT.
BA-WAAHH!
COMIC BOOKS! AMERICAN COMIC BOOKS!
WELL, FIRST WE HAVE TO UNLOAD THE MACH 5 AND TAKE IT TO THE SHOW.
THEN WE HAVE TO CHECK INTO THE HOTEL.
AND THEN WE'LL FIND YOU A COMIC STORE—
grumble !!!

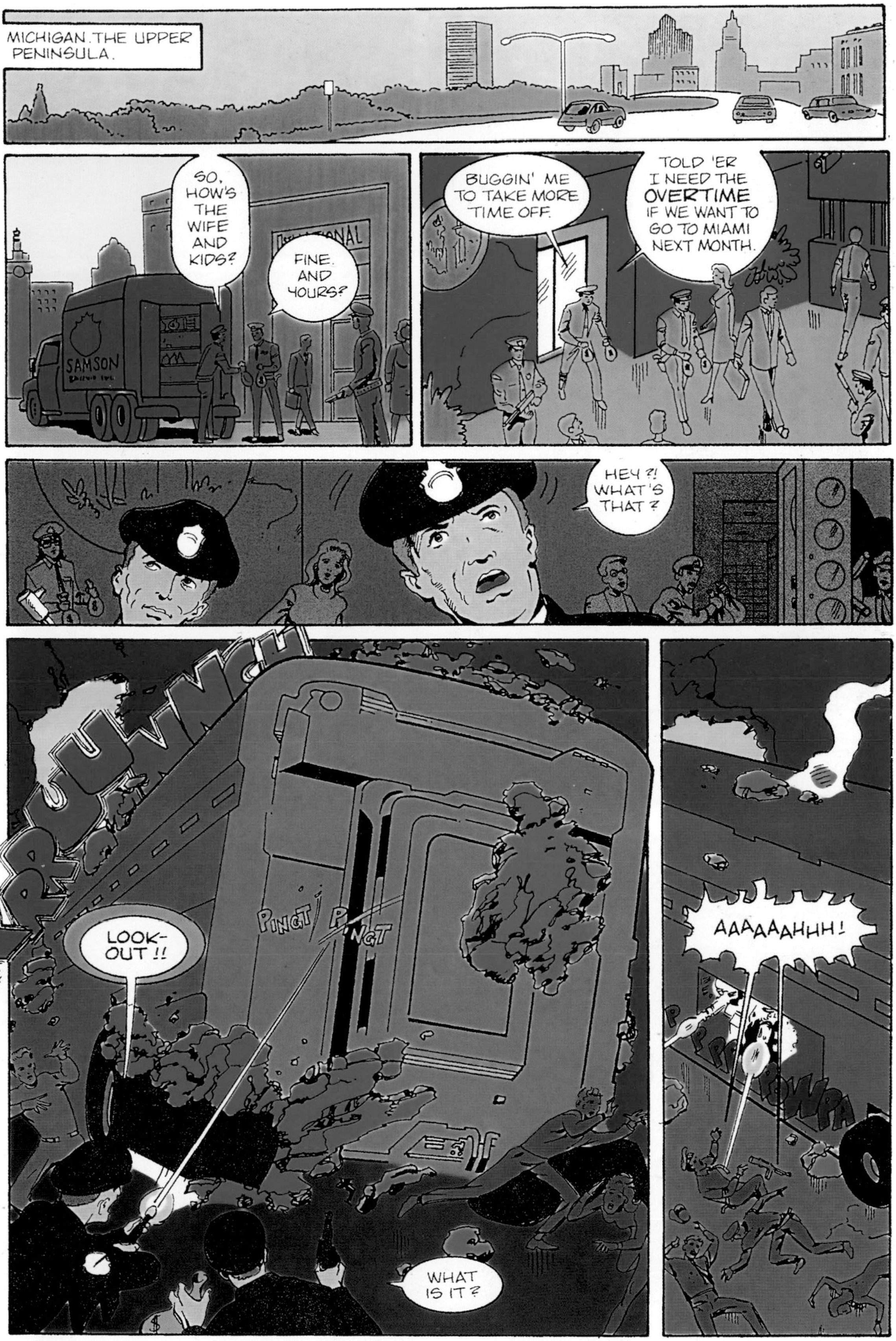
MICHIGAN. THE UPPER PENINSULA.
SO, HOW'S THE WIFE AND KIDS?
FINE. AND YOURS?
SAMSON
BUGGIN' ME TO TAKE MORE TIME OFF.
TOLD 'ER I NEED THE OVERTIME IF WE WANT TO GO TO MIAMI NEXT MONTH.
HEY ?! WHAT'S THAT ?
KRRUUNCH
PINGT PINGT
LOOK-OUT !!
WHAT IS IT?
AAAAAAHHH!

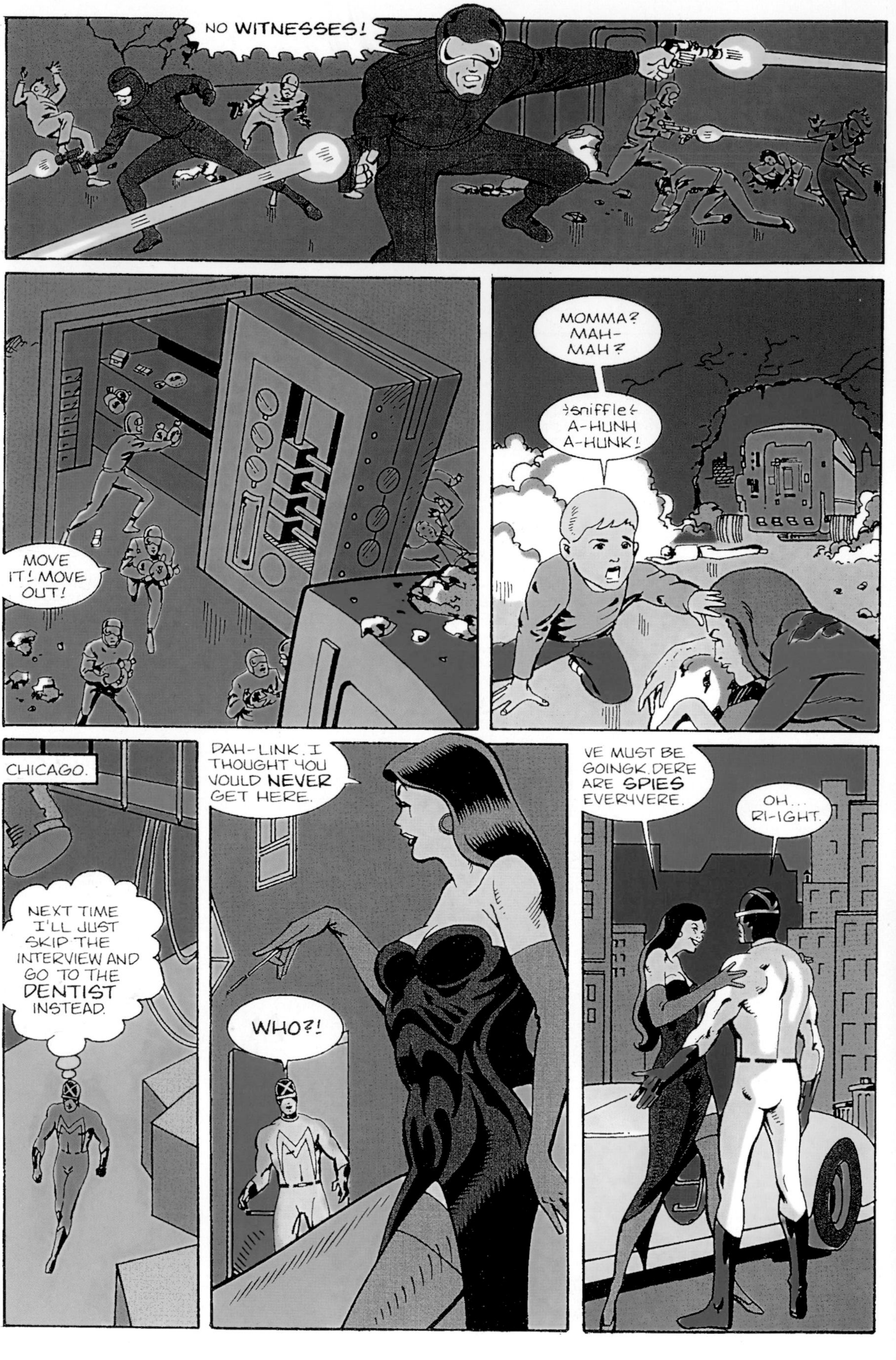
NO WITNESSES!
MOVE IT! MOVE OUT!
MOMMA? MAH-MAH?
sniffle A-HUNH A-HUNK!
CHICAGO.
NEXT TIME I'LL JUST SKIP THE INTERVIEW AND GO TO THE DENTIST INSTEAD.
DAH-LINK. I THOUGHT YOU VOULD NEVER GET HERE.
WHO?!
VE MUST BE GOINGK. DERE ARE SPIES EVERYVERE.
OH... RI-IGHT.

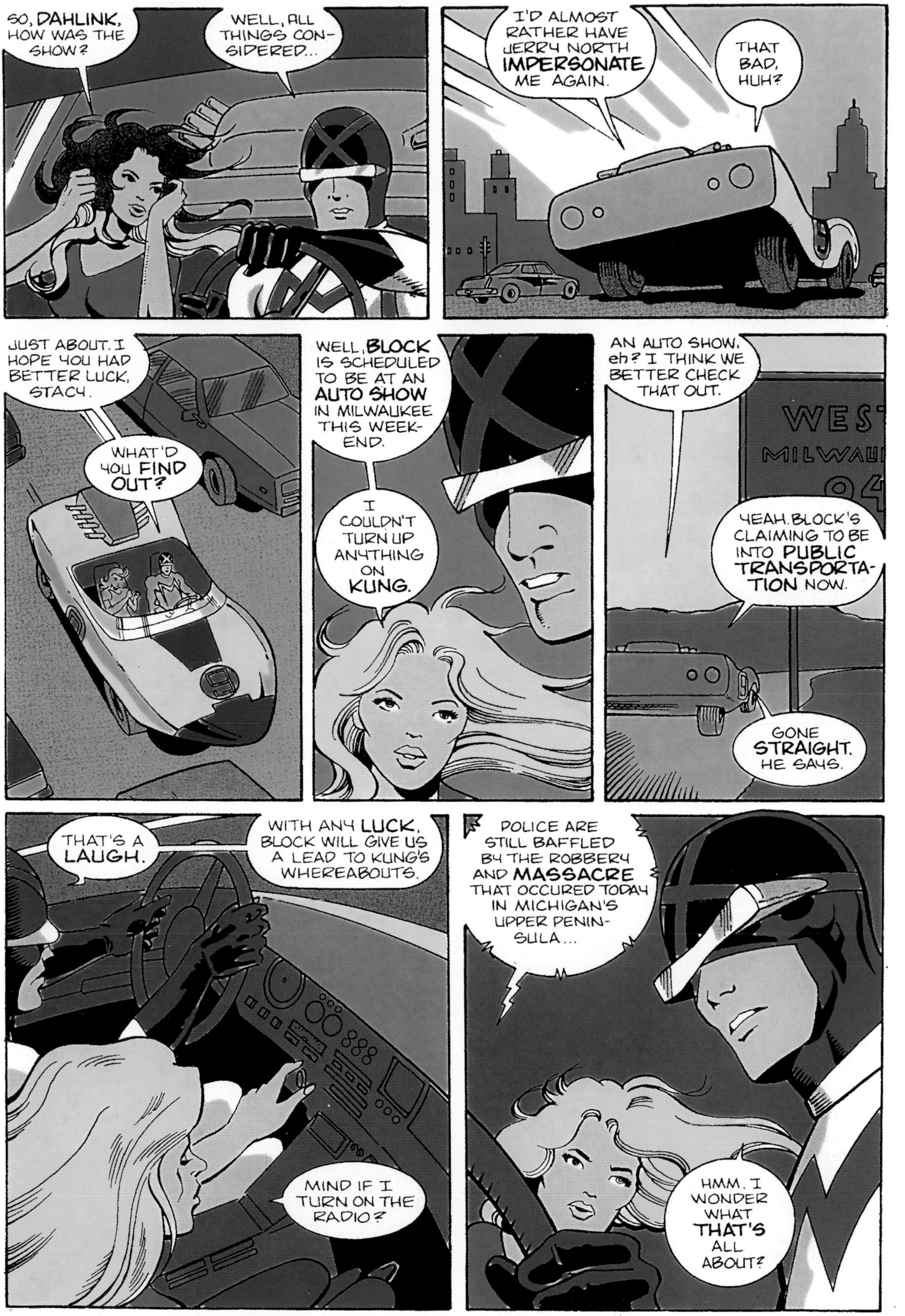
SO, DAHLINK, HOW WAS THE SHOW?
WELL, ALL THINGS CONSIDERED...
I'D ALMOST RATHER HAVE JERRY NORTH IMPERSONATE ME AGAIN.
THAT BAD, HUH?
JUST ABOUT. I HOPE YOU HAD BETTER LUCK, STACY.
WHAT'D YOU FIND OUT?
WELL, BLOCK IS SCHEDULED TO BE AT AN AUTO SHOW IN MILWAUKEE THIS WEEKEND.
I COULDN'T TURN UP ANYTHING ON KUNG.
AN AUTO SHOW, eh? I THINK WE BETTER CHECK THAT OUT.
WEST
MILWAU
94
YEAH. BLOCK'S CLAIMING TO BE INTO PUBLIC TRANSPORTATION NOW.
GONE STRAIGHT, HE SAYS.
THAT'S A LAUGH.
WITH ANY LUCK, BLOCK WILL GIVE US A LEAD TO KUNG'S WHEREABOUTS.
MIND IF I TURN ON THE RADIO?
POLICE ARE STILL BAFFLED BY THE ROBBERY AND MASSACRE THAT OCCURED TODAY IN MICHIGAN'S UPPER PENINSULA...
HMM. I WONDER WHAT THAT'S ALL ABOUT?

ELSEWHERE...

MASTER, ALL GOES ACCORDING TO PLAN.

THE ATTACKS PROVIDE AN EXCELLENT DIVERSION FOR OUR TRUE PURPOSE.

GOOD. AND BLOCK?

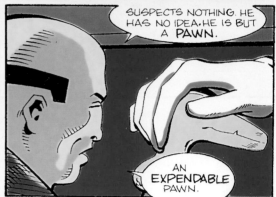

SUSPECTS NOTHING. HE HAS NO IDEA. HE IS BUT A PAWN.

AN EXPENDABLE PAWN.

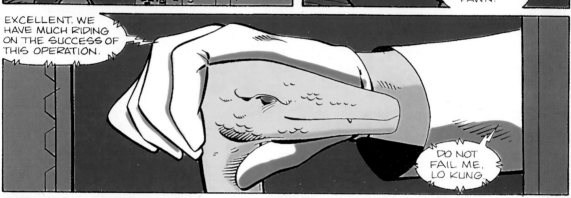

EXCELLENT. WE HAVE MUCH RIDING ON THE SUCCESS OF THIS OPERATION.

DO NOT FAIL ME, LO KUNG.

I WILL NOT, SUPREMO.

YOU CALLED MASTER?

HAVE YOU READIED THE MEN?

YES, GREAT ONE.

GOOD. I WILL BE TRAVELING TO MILWAUKIEE TO OVERSEE THE OPERATION PERSONALLY.

TAKE CHARGE UNTIL I RETURN.

I AM HONORED.

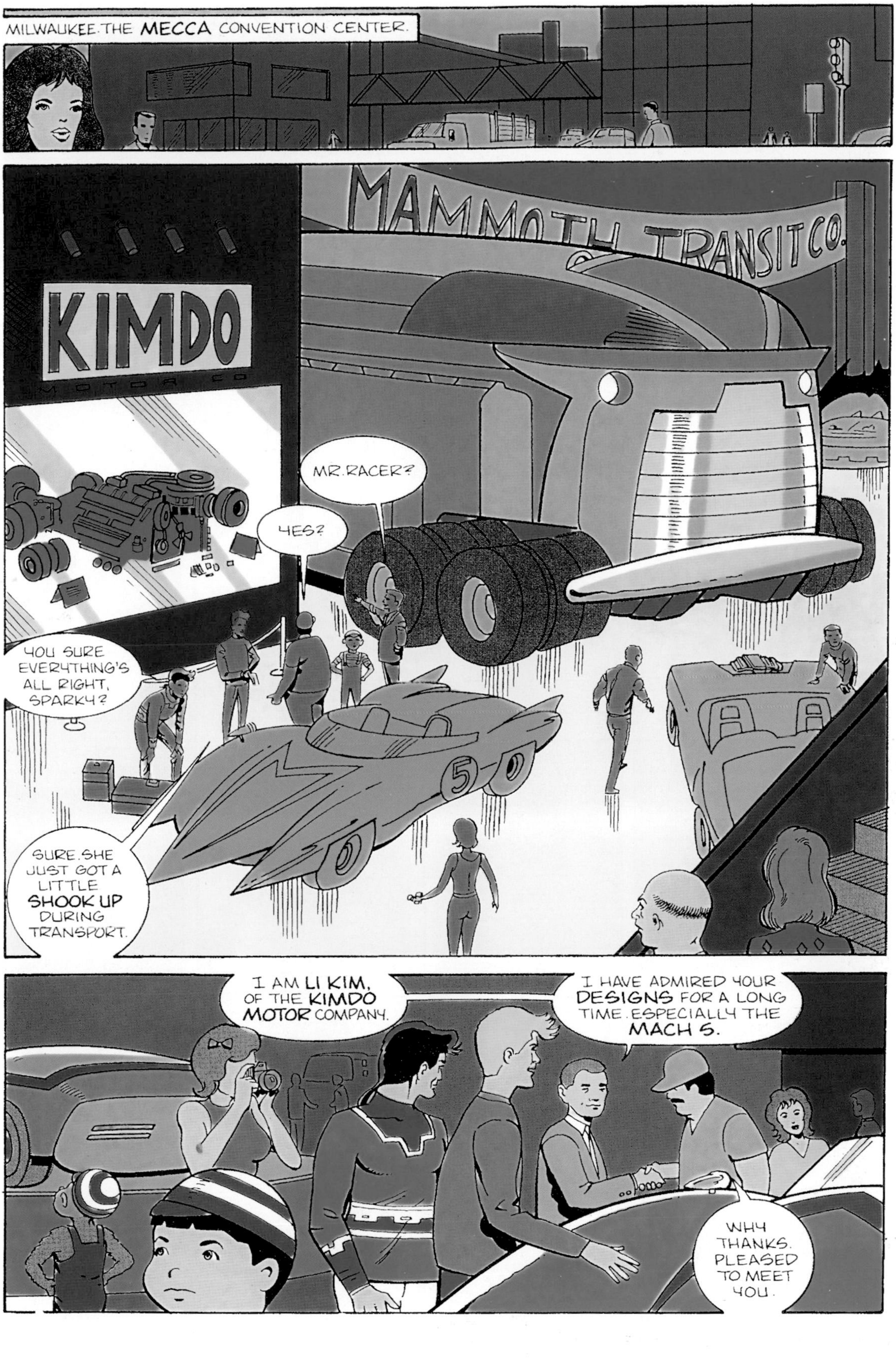
MILWAUKEE. THE MECCA CONVENTION CENTER.
KIMDO
MAMMOTH TRANSIT CO.
MR. RACER?
YES?
YOU SURE EVERYTHING'S ALL RIGHT, SPARKY?
SURE. SHE JUST GOT A LITTLE SHOOK UP DURING TRANSPORT.
I AM LI KIM, OF THE KIMDO MOTOR COMPANY.
I HAVE ADMIRED YOUR DESIGNS FOR A LONG TIME. ESPECIALLY THE MACH 5.
WHY THANKS. PLEASED TO MEET YOU.

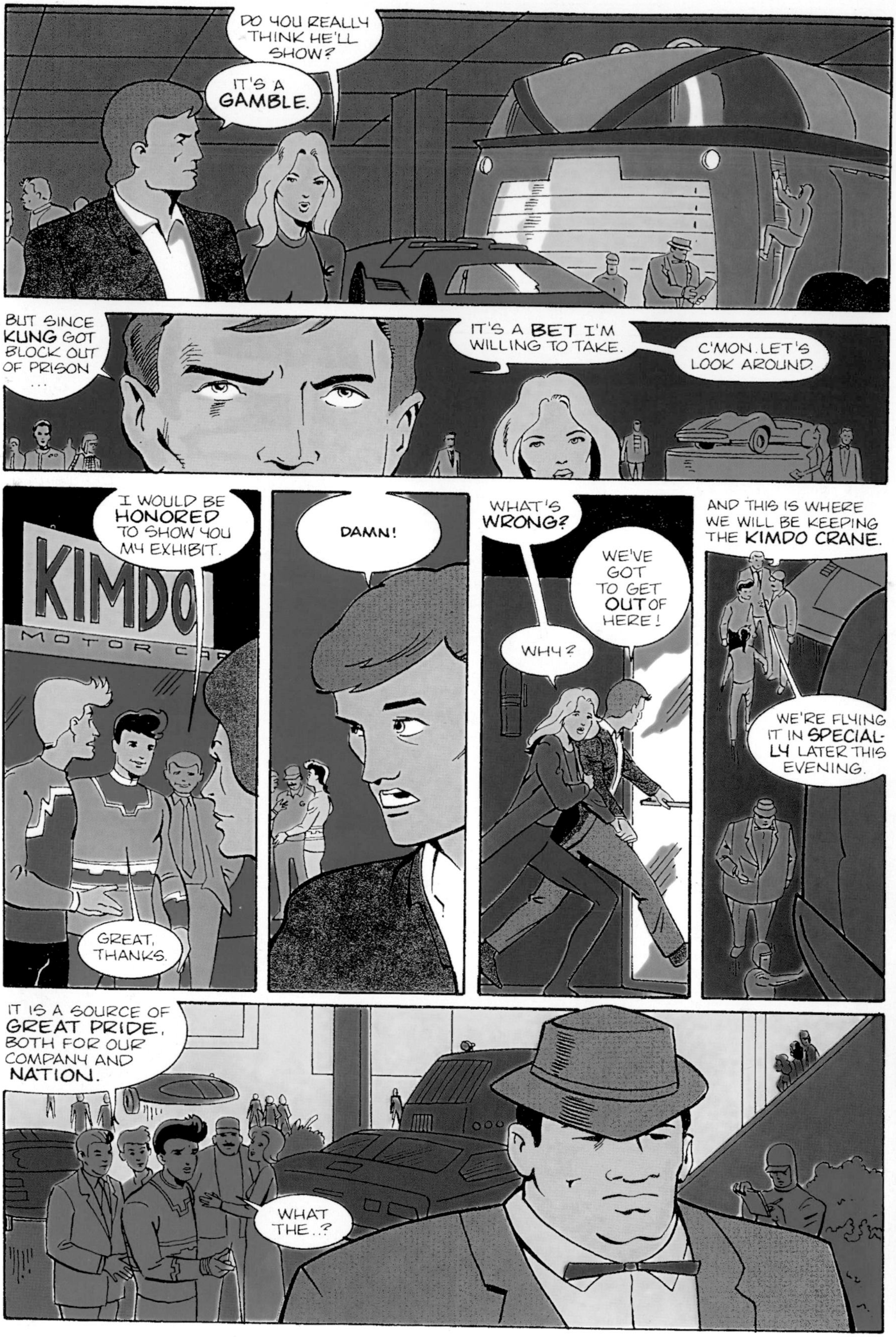
DO YOU REALLY THINK HE'LL SHOW?
IT'S A GAMBLE.
BUT SINCE KUNG GOT BLOCK OUT OF PRISON . . .
IT'S A BET I'M WILLING TO TAKE.
C'MON. LET'S LOOK AROUND.
I WOULD BE HONORED TO SHOW YOU MY EXHIBIT.
KIMDO
MOTOR CA
GREAT, THANKS.
DAMN!
WHAT'S WRONG?
WE'VE GOT TO GET OUT OF HERE!
WHY?
AND THIS IS WHERE WE WILL BE KEEPING THE KIMDO CRANE.
WE'RE FLYING IT IN SPECIALLY LATER THIS EVENING.
IT IS A SOURCE OF GREAT PRIDE, BOTH FOR OUR COMPANY AND NATION.
WHAT THE..?

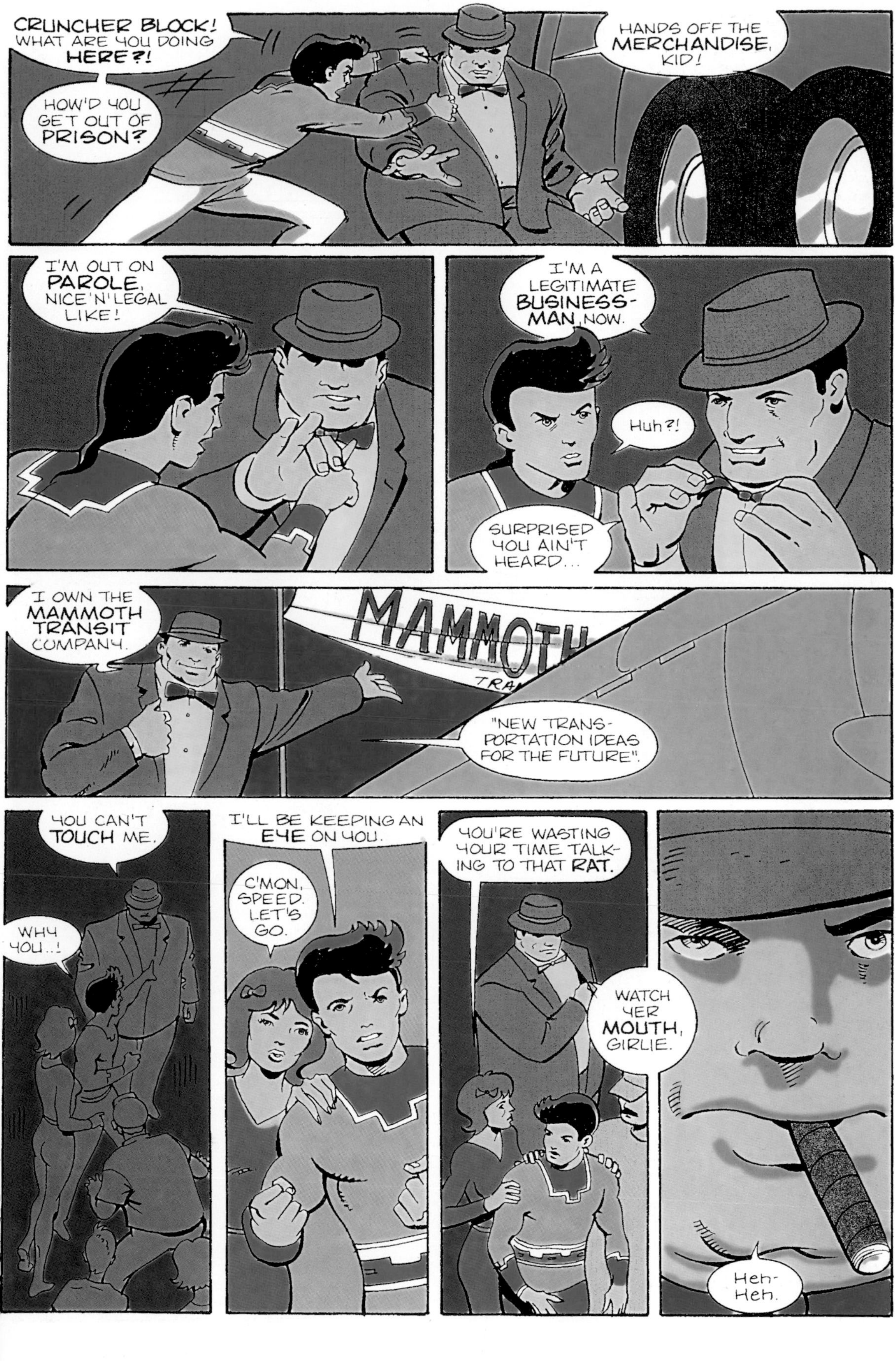
CRUNCHER BLOCK! WHAT ARE YOU DOING HERE?!
HOW'D YOU GET OUT OF PRISON?
HANDS OFF THE MERCHANDISE, KID!
I'M OUT ON PAROLE, NICE'N'LEGAL LIKE!
I'M A LEGITIMATE BUSINESS-MAN, NOW.
Huh?!
SURPRISED YOU AIN'T HEARD...
I OWN THE MAMMOTH TRANSIT COMPANY.
MAMMOTH
"NEW TRANS-PORTATION IDEAS FOR THE FUTURE".
YOU CAN'T TOUCH ME.
WHY YOU...!
I'LL BE KEEPING AN EYE ON YOU.
C'MON, SPEED. LET'S GO.
YOU'RE WASTING YOUR TIME TALK-ING TO THAT RAT.
WATCH YER MOUTH, GIRLIE.
Heh-Heh.

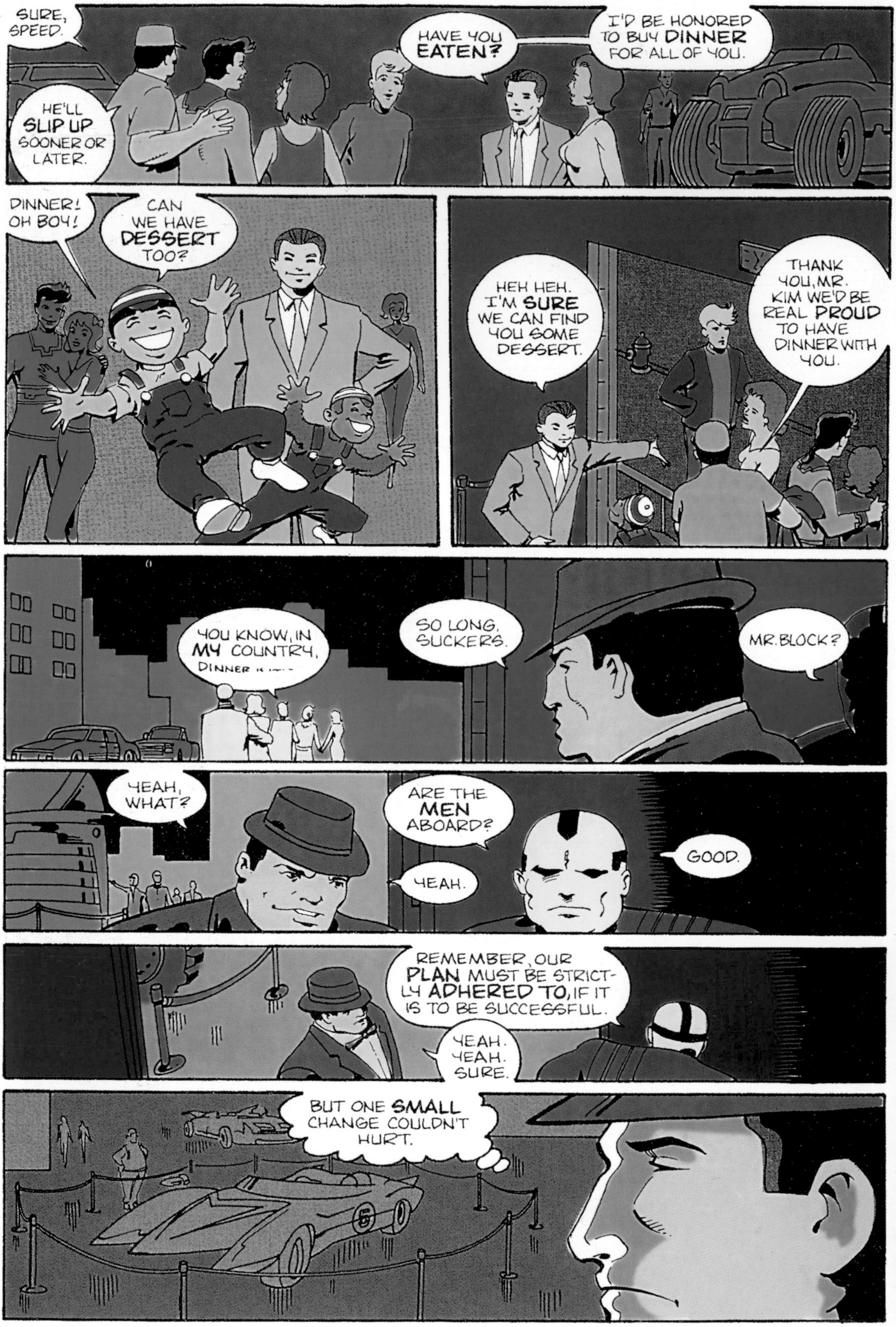
SURE, SPEED.
HE'LL SLIP UP SOONER OR LATER.
HAVE YOU EATEN?
I'D BE HONORED TO BUY DINNER FOR ALL OF YOU.
DINNER! OH BOY!
CAN WE HAVE DESSERT TOO?
HEH HEH. I'M SURE WE CAN FIND YOU SOME DESSERT.
THANK YOU, MR. KIM WE'D BE REAL PROUD TO HAVE DINNER WITH YOU.
YOU KNOW, IN MY COUNTRY,
SO LONG, SUCKERS.
MR. BLOCK?
YEAH, WHAT?
ARE THE MEN ABOARD?
YEAH.
GOOD.
REMEMBER, OUR PLAN MUST BE STRICTLY ADHERED TO, IF IT IS TO BE SUCCESSFUL.
YEAH. YEAH. SURE.
BUT ONE SMALL CHANGE COULDN'T HURT.

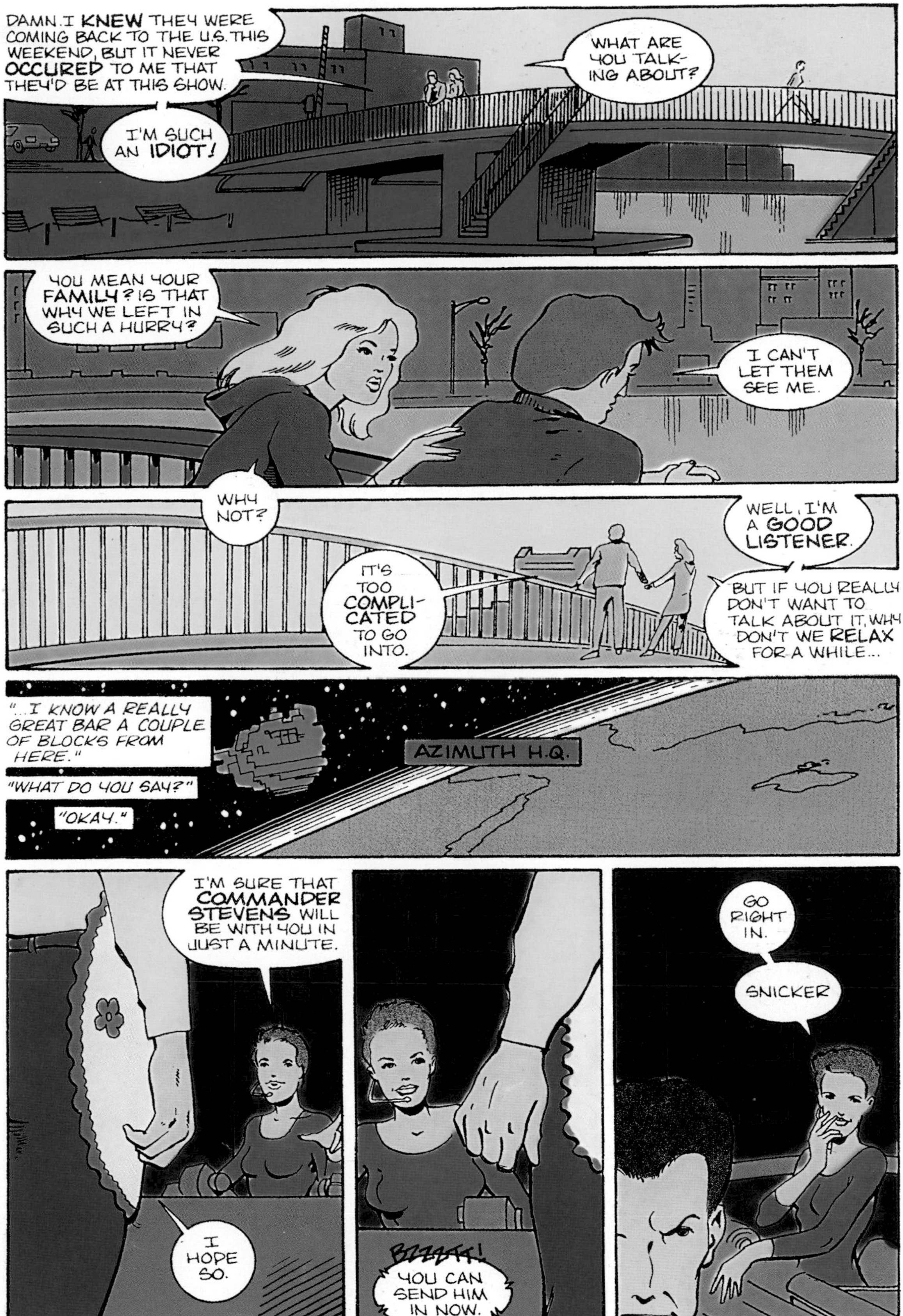
DAMN. I KNEW THEY WERE COMING BACK TO THE U.S. THIS WEEKEND, BUT IT NEVER OCCURED TO ME THAT THEY'D BE AT THIS SHOW.
I'M SUCH AN IDIOT!
WHAT ARE YOU TALKING ABOUT?
YOU MEAN YOUR FAMILY? IS THAT WHY WE LEFT IN SUCH A HURRY?
I CAN'T LET THEM SEE ME.
WHY NOT?
IT'S TOO COMPLICATED TO GO INTO.
WELL, I'M A GOOD LISTENER.
BUT IF YOU REALLY DON'T WANT TO TALK ABOUT IT, WHY DON'T WE RELAX FOR A WHILE...
"...I KNOW A REALLY GREAT BAR A COUPLE OF BLOCKS FROM HERE."
"WHAT DO YOU SAY?"
"OKAY."
AZIMUTH H.Q.
I'M SURE THAT COMMANDER STEVENS WILL BE WITH YOU IN JUST A MINUTE.
I HOPE SO.
BZZZTT!
YOU CAN SEND HIM IN NOW.
GO RIGHT IN.
SNICKER

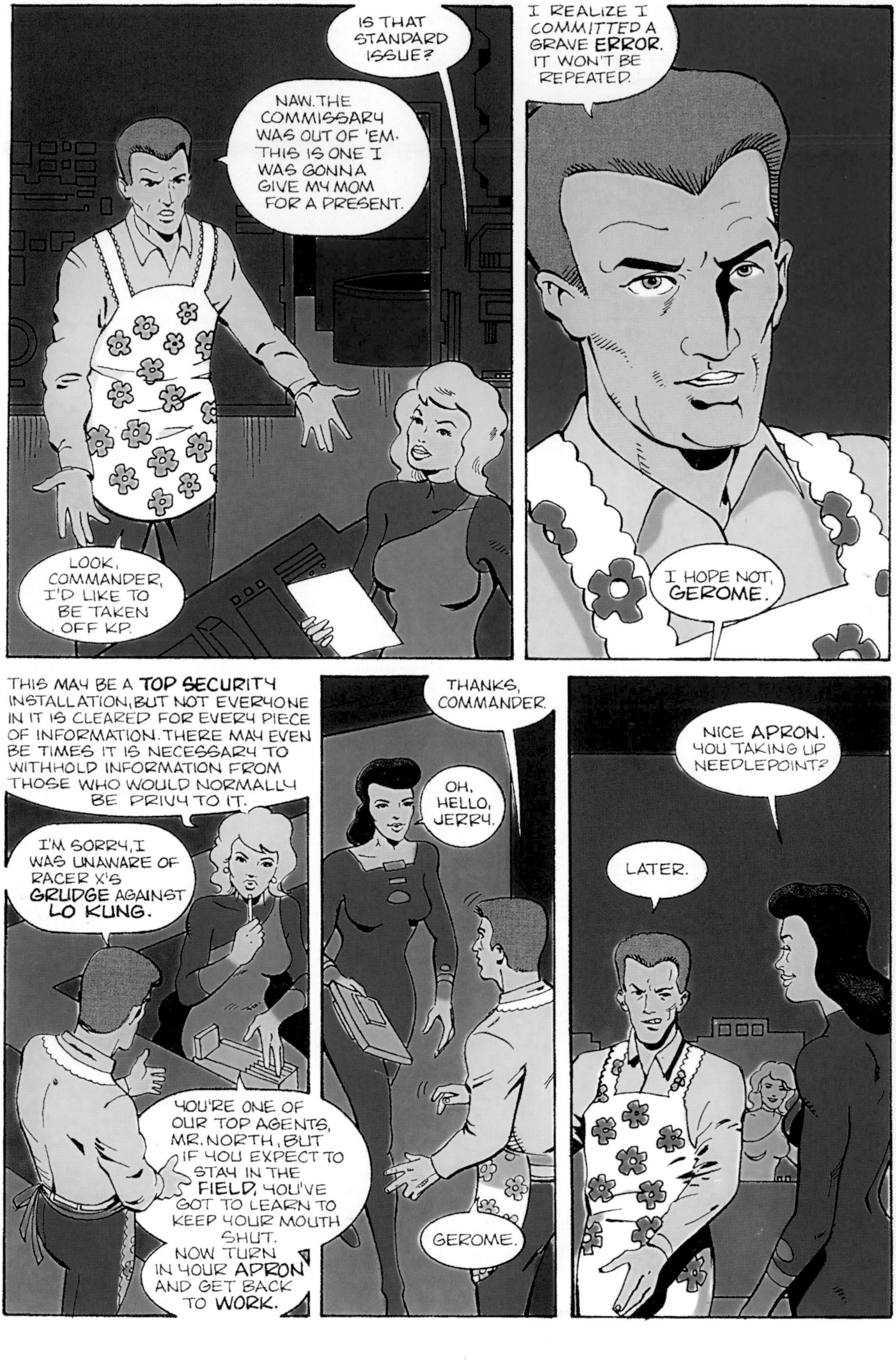
IS THAT STANDARD ISSUE?
NAW. THE COMMISSARY WAS OUT OF 'EM. THIS IS ONE I WAS GONNA GIVE MY MOM FOR A PRESENT.
LOOK, COMMANDER, I'D LIKE TO BE TAKEN OFF KP.
I REALIZE I COMMITTED A GRAVE ERROR. IT WON'T BE REPEATED.
I HOPE NOT, GEROME.
THIS MAY BE A TOP SECURITY INSTALLATION, BUT NOT EVERYONE IN IT IS CLEARED FOR EVERY PIECE OF INFORMATION. THERE MAY EVEN BE TIMES IT IS NECESSARY TO WITHHOLD INFORMATION FROM THOSE WHO WOULD NORMALLY BE PRIVY TO IT.
I'M SORRY, I WAS UNAWARE OF RACER X'S GRUDGE AGAINST LO KUNG.
YOU'RE ONE OF OUR TOP AGENTS, MR. NORTH, BUT IF YOU EXPECT TO STAY IN THE FIELD, YOU'VE GOT TO LEARN TO KEEP YOUR MOUTH SHUT. NOW TURN IN YOUR APRON AND GET BACK TO WORK.
THANKS, COMMANDER.
OH, HELLO, JERRY.
GEROME.
NICE APRON. YOU TAKING UP NEEDLEPOINT?
LATER.

COMMANDER, I'VE GOT THAT REPORT YOU WANTED ON BOPUNAMBIA.

IT DOESN'T LOOK GOOD.

HMM

ALSO, THE **PRELIMINARIES** ON THOSE ARMORED CAR ROBBERIES... TURNS OUT THERE MAY BE A CONNECTION TO THAT TRUCK STOP **EXPLOSION** IN OKLAHOMA.

THANKS, BARNEY. KEEP ME **INFORMED.**

LIZ, I'VE NEVER BEEN REAL **FOND** OF HIM, BUT...

I'M SORRY ABOUT WHAT **HAPPENED** WITH YOU AND **REX.**

WHAT IS THIS, **NATIONAL APOLOGY DAY?**

FIRST, GEROME. NOW YOU.

LOOK, I MADE THE DECISION THAT MUCKED THINGS UP. **ME,** NOBODY ELSE.

MAYBE IT WAS THE **WRONG** THING TO DO, BUT I'M GOING TO HAVE TO LIVE WITH IT.

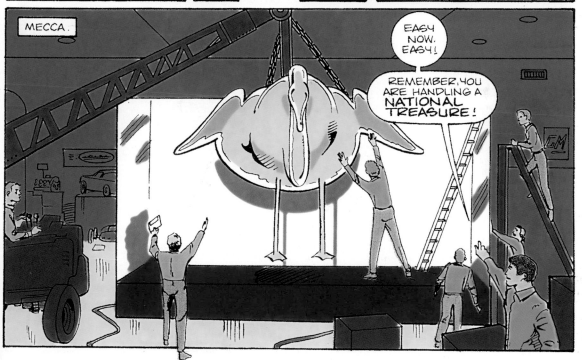

MECCA.

EASY NOW, EASY!

REMEMBER, YOU ARE HANDLING A **NATIONAL TREASURE!**

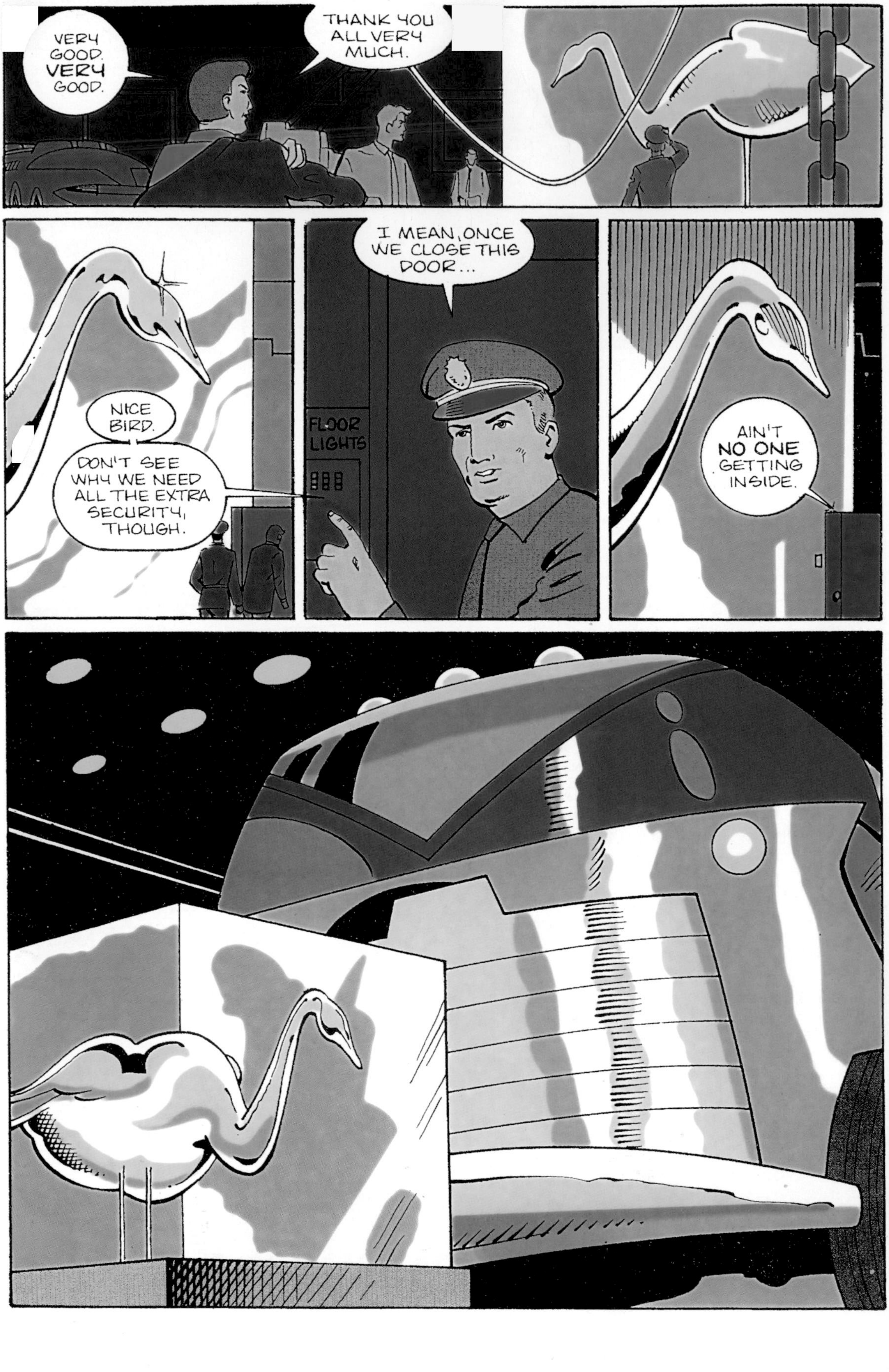
VERY GOOD. VERY GOOD.
THANK YOU ALL VERY MUCH.
NICE BIRD.
DON'T SEE WHY WE NEED ALL THE EXTRA SECURITY, THOUGH.
FLOOR LIGHTS
I MEAN, ONCE WE CLOSE THIS DOOR...
AIN'T NO ONE GETTING INSIDE.

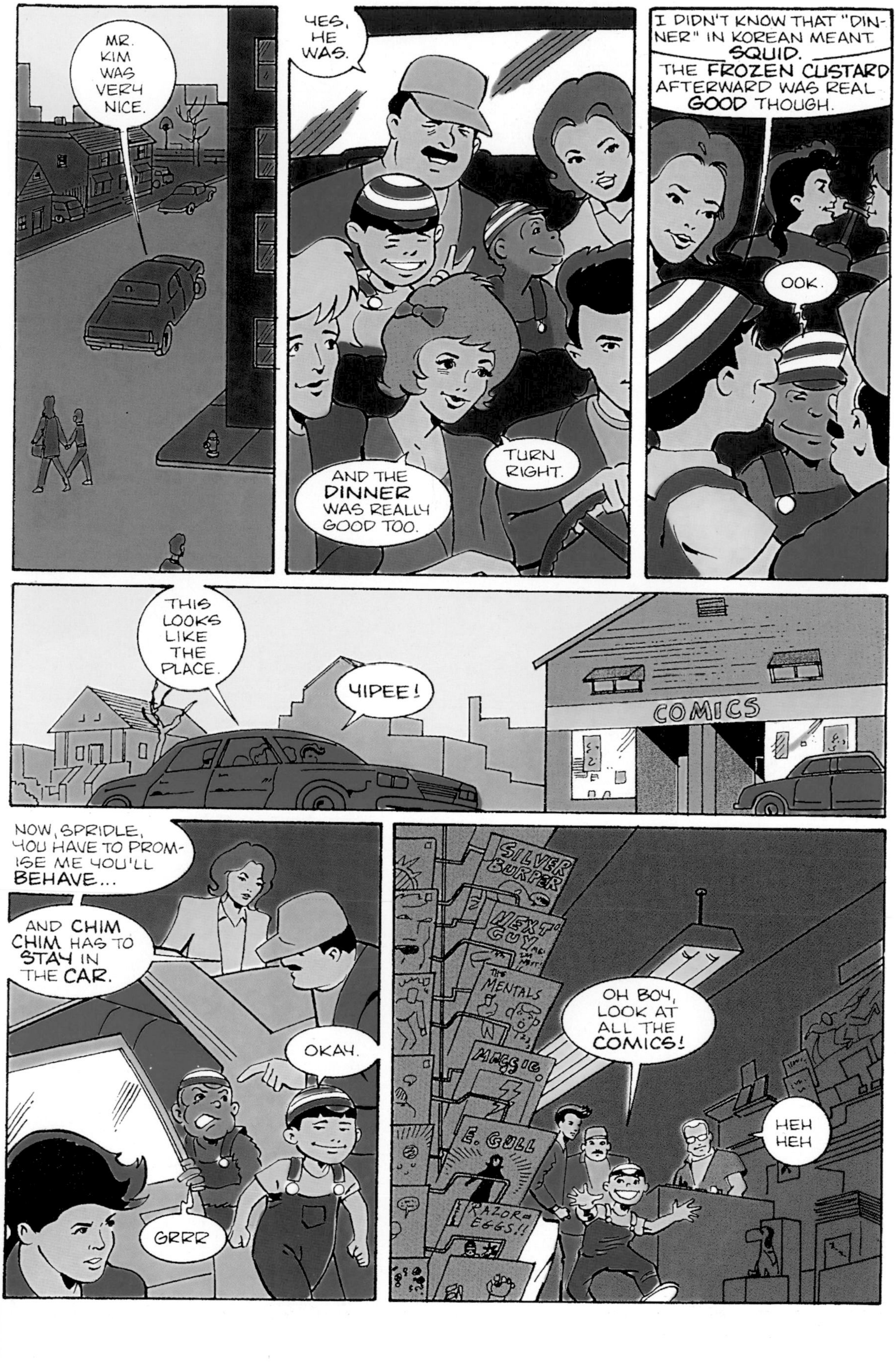
MR. KIM WAS VERY NICE.
YES, HE WAS.
AND THE DINNER WAS REALLY GOOD TOO.
TURN RIGHT.
I DIDN'T KNOW THAT "DINNER" IN KOREAN MEANT SQUID. THE FROZEN CUSTARD AFTERWARD WAS REAL GOOD THOUGH.
OOK.
THIS LOOKS LIKE THE PLACE.
YIPEE!
COMICS
NOW, SPRIDLE, YOU HAVE TO PROMISE ME YOU'LL BEHAVE...
AND CHIM CHIM HAS TO STAY IN THE CAR.
OKAY.
GRRR
SILVER BURPER
NEXT GUY
THE MENTALS
E. GULL
RAZOR EGGS!!
OH BOY, LOOK AT ALL THE COMICS!
HEH HEH

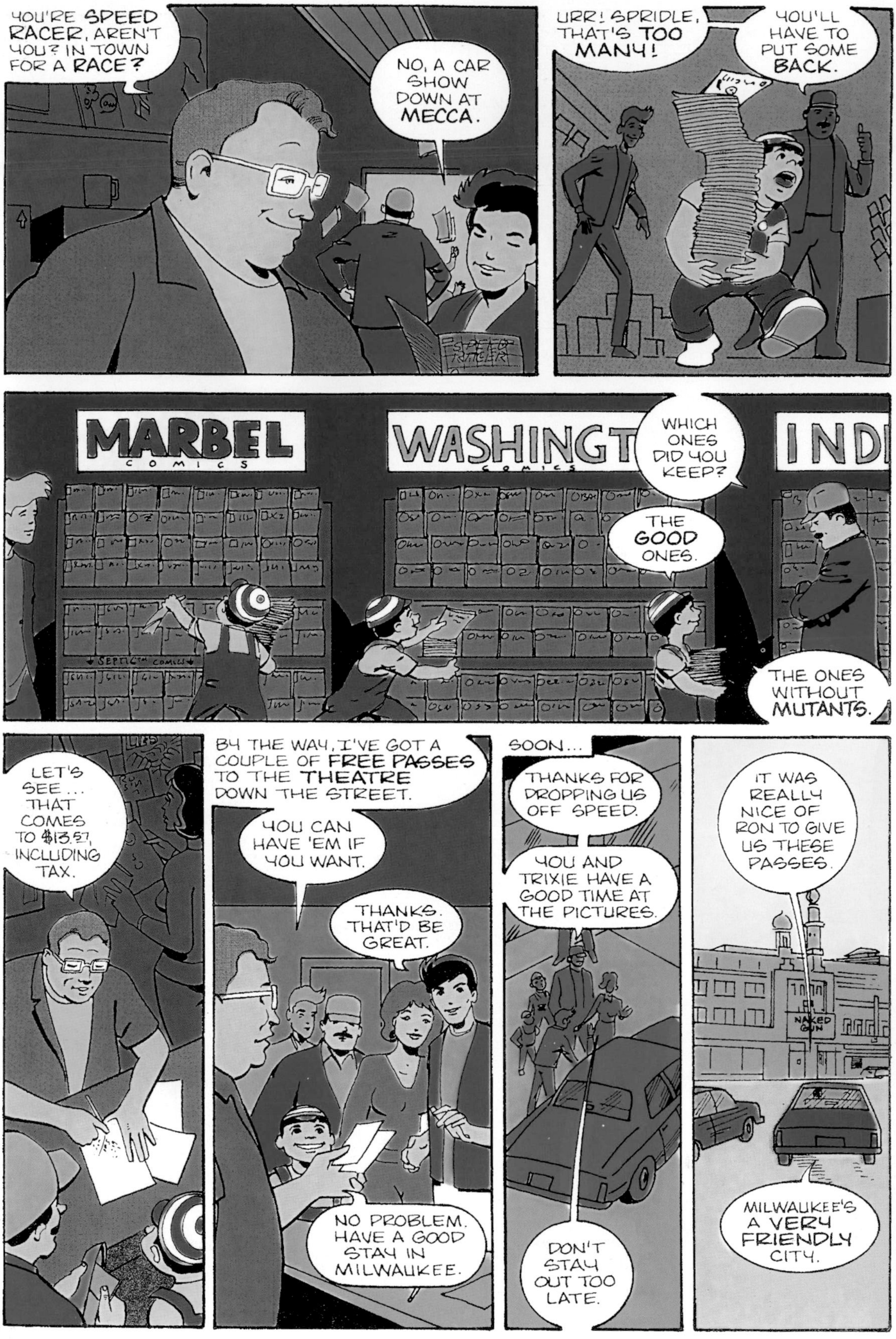
YOU'RE SPEED RACER, AREN'T YOU? IN TOWN FOR A RACE?
NO, A CAR SHOW DOWN AT MECCA.
SPEED RACER
URR! SPRIDLE, THAT'S TOO MANY!
YOU'LL HAVE TO PUT SOME BACK.
MARBEL COMICS
WASHINGT
COMICS
INDI
SEPTIC COMICS
WHICH ONES DID YOU KEEP?
THE GOOD ONES.
THE ONES WITHOUT MUTANTS.
LET'S SEE... THAT COMES TO $13.57, INCLUDING TAX.
BY THE WAY, I'VE GOT A COUPLE OF FREE PASSES TO THE THEATRE DOWN THE STREET.
YOU CAN HAVE 'EM IF YOU WANT.
THANKS. THAT'D BE GREAT.
NO PROBLEM. HAVE A GOOD STAY IN MILWAUKEE.
SOON...
THANKS FOR DROPPING US OFF SPEED.
YOU AND TRIXIE HAVE A GOOD TIME AT THE PICTURES.
DON'T STAY OUT TOO LATE.
IT WAS REALLY NICE OF RON TO GIVE US THESE PASSES.
NAKED GUN
MILWAUKEE'S A VERY FRIENDLY CITY.

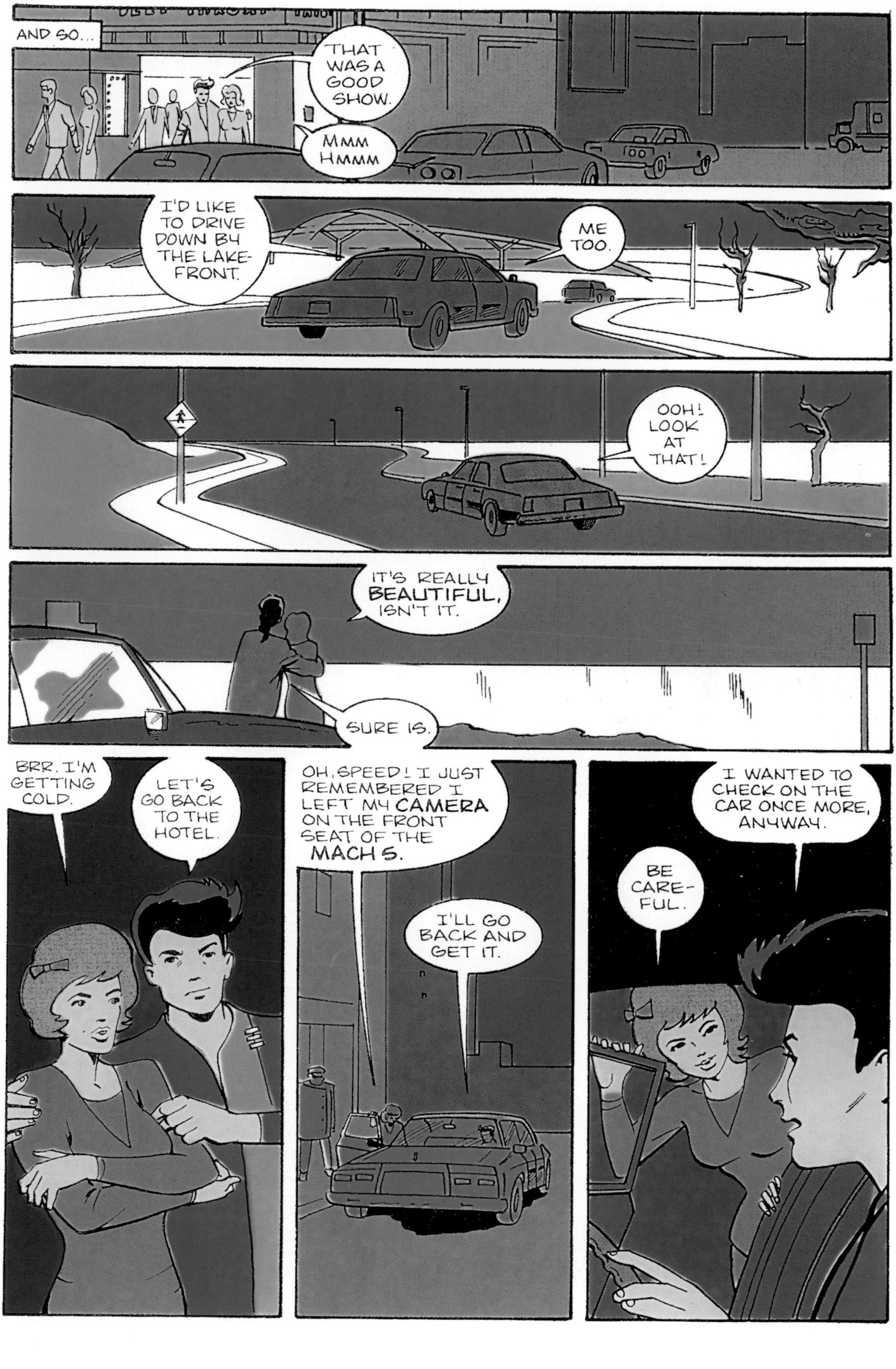
AND SO...
THAT WAS A GOOD SHOW.
MMM HMMM
I'D LIKE TO DRIVE DOWN BY THE LAKE-FRONT.
ME TOO.
OOH! LOOK AT THAT!
IT'S REALLY BEAUTIFUL, ISN'T IT.
SURE IS.
BRR. I'M GETTING COLD.
LET'S GO BACK TO THE HOTEL.
OH, SPEED! I JUST REMEMBERED I LEFT MY CAMERA ON THE FRONT SEAT OF THE MACH 5.
I'LL GO BACK AND GET IT.
I WANTED TO CHECK ON THE CAR ONCE MORE, ANYWAY.
BE CARE-FUL.

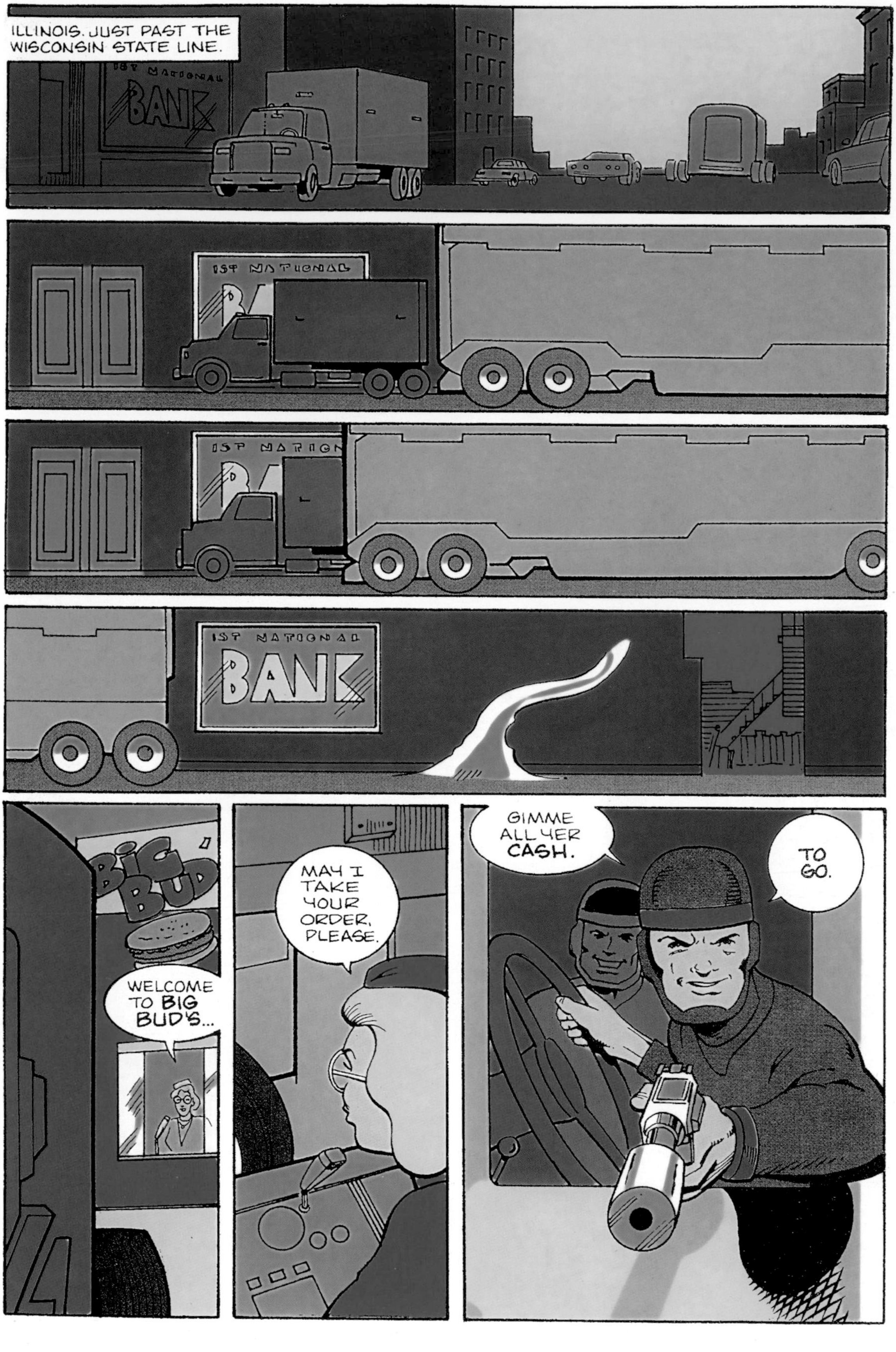
ILLINOIS. JUST PAST THE WISCONSIN STATE LINE.
1ST NATIONAL BANK
BIG BUD
WELCOME TO BIG BUD'S...
MAY I TAKE YOUR ORDER, PLEASE.
GIMME ALL YER CASH.
TO GO.

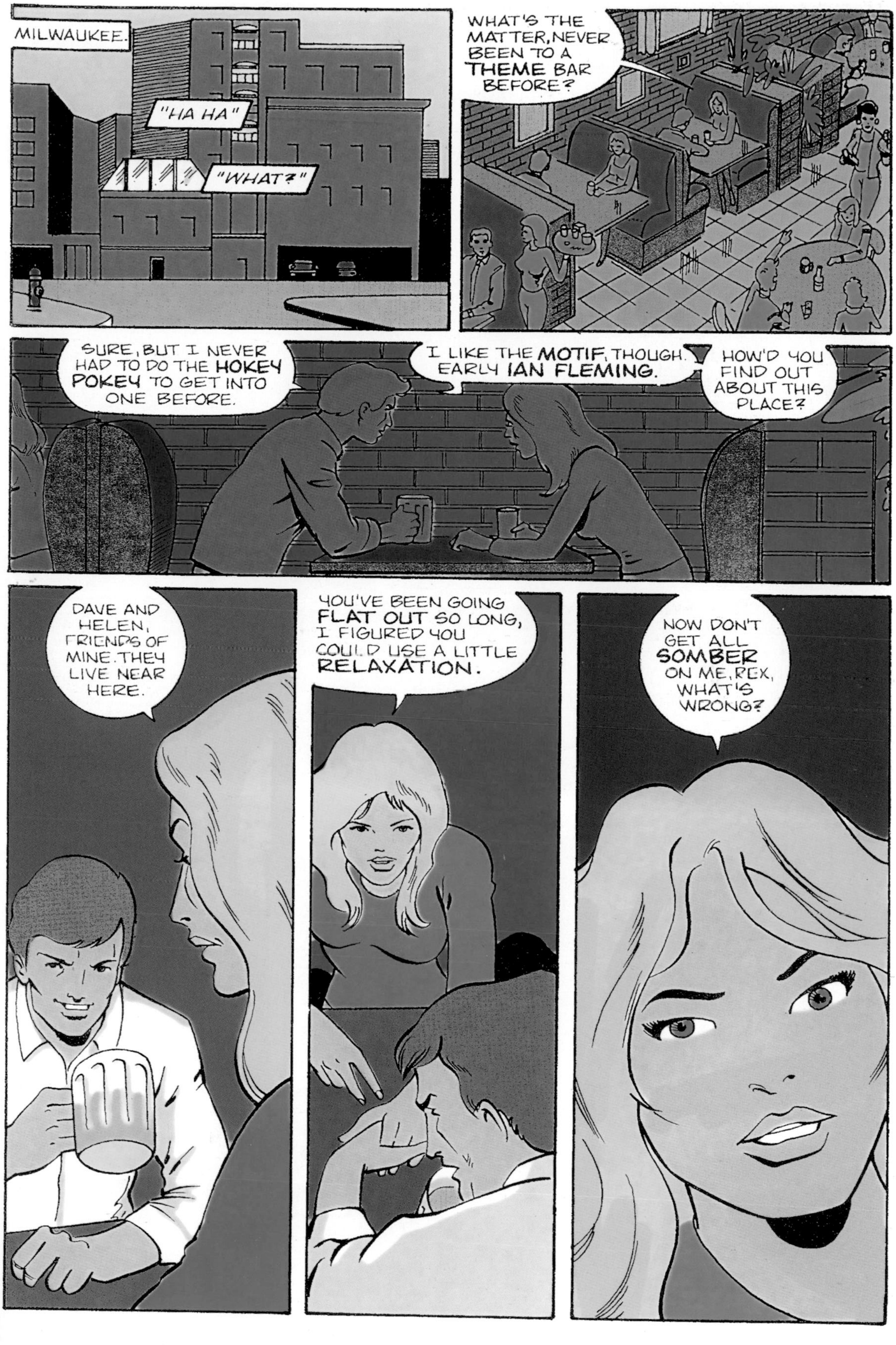
MILWAUKEE.
"HA HA"
"WHAT?"
WHAT'S THE MATTER, NEVER BEEN TO A THEME BAR BEFORE?
SURE, BUT I NEVER HAD TO DO THE HOKEY POKEY TO GET INTO ONE BEFORE.
I LIKE THE MOTIF, THOUGH. EARLY IAN FLEMING.
HOW'D YOU FIND OUT ABOUT THIS PLACE?
DAVE AND HELEN, FRIENDS OF MINE. THEY LIVE NEAR HERE.
YOU'VE BEEN GOING FLAT OUT SO LONG, I FIGURED YOU COULD USE A LITTLE RELAXATION.
NOW DON'T GET ALL SOMBER ON ME, REX, WHAT'S WRONG?

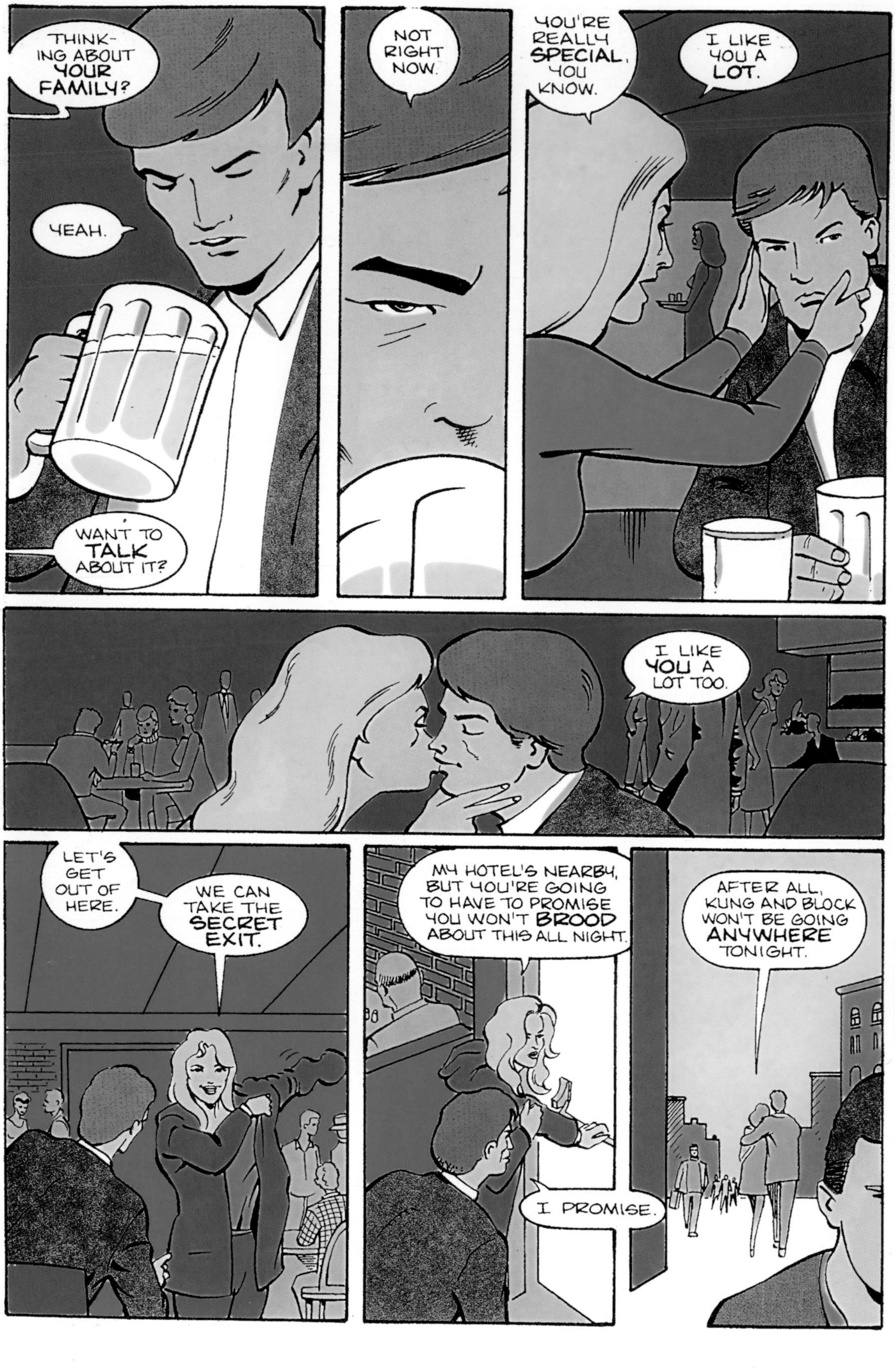
THINKING ABOUT YOUR FAMILY?
YEAH.
WANT TO TALK ABOUT IT?
NOT RIGHT NOW.
YOU'RE REALLY SPECIAL, YOU KNOW.
I LIKE YOU A LOT.
I LIKE YOU A LOT TOO.
LET'S GET OUT OF HERE.
WE CAN TAKE THE SECRET EXIT.
MY HOTEL'S NEARBY, BUT YOU'RE GOING TO HAVE TO PROMISE YOU WON'T BROOD ABOUT THIS ALL NIGHT.
I PROMISE.
AFTER ALL, KUNG AND BLOCK WON'T BE GOING ANYWHERE TONIGHT.

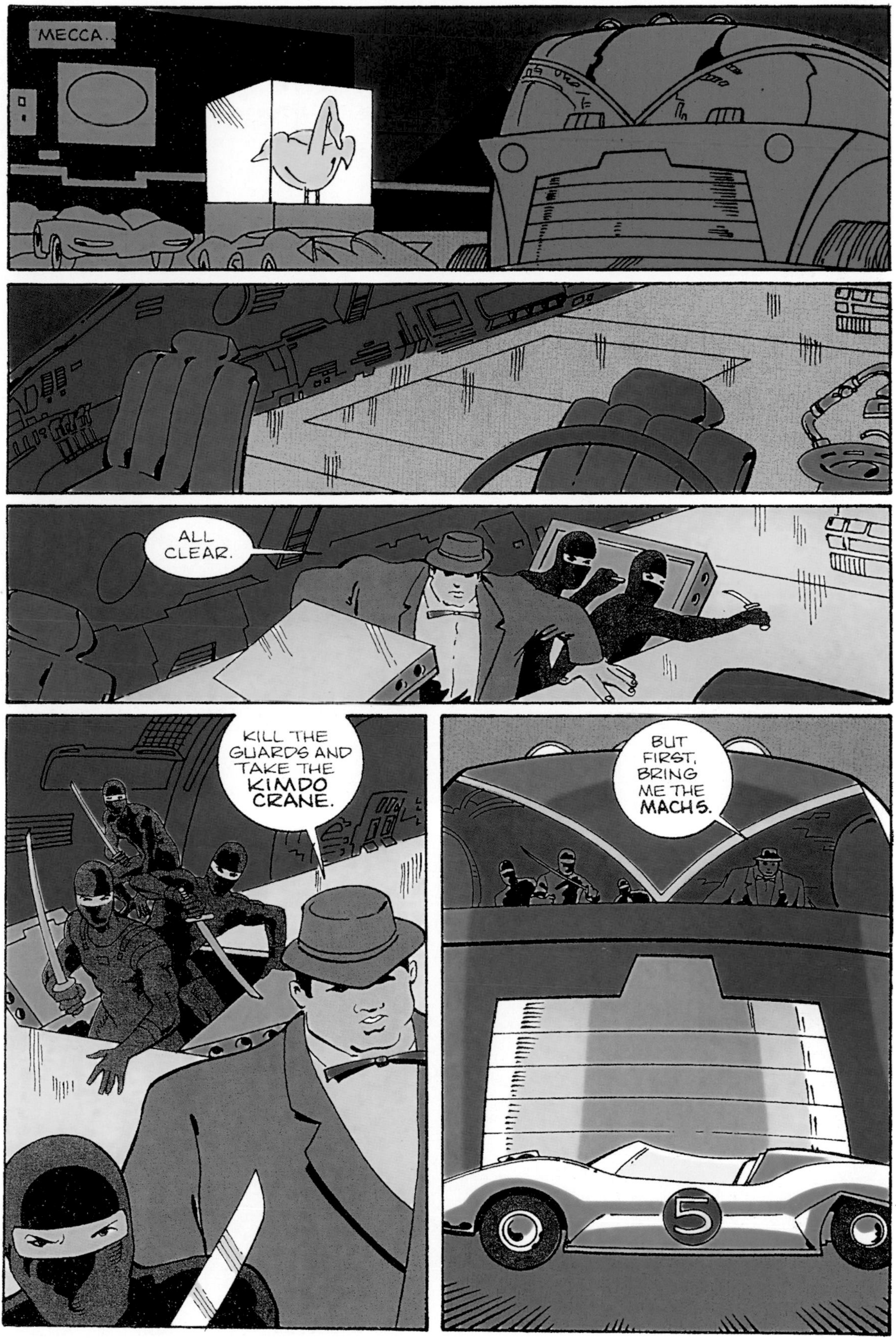
MECCA...
ALL CLEAR.
KILL THE GUARDS AND TAKE THE KIMDO CRANE.
BUT FIRST, BRING ME THE MACH 5.

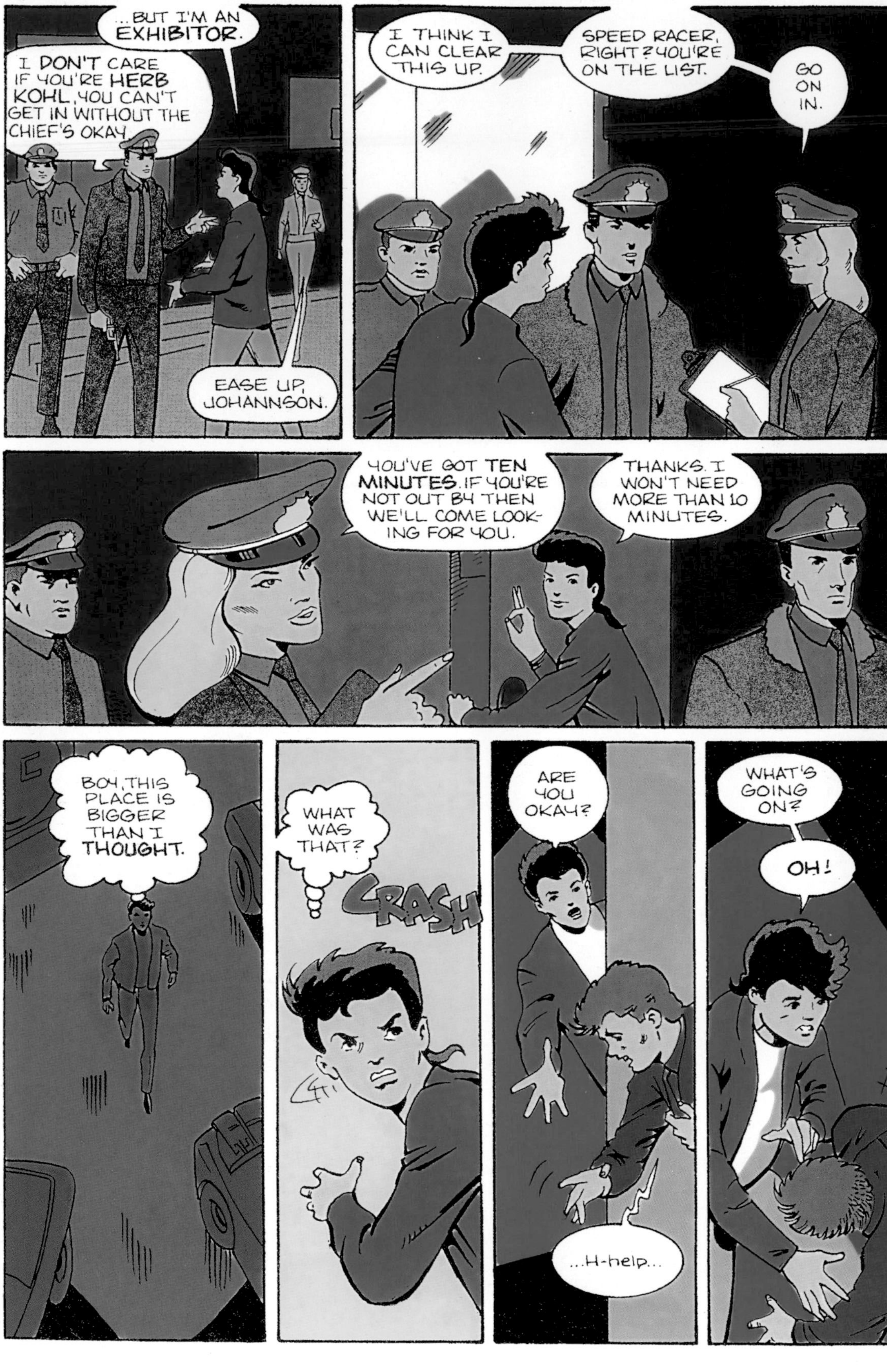
...BUT I'M AN EXHIBITOR.
I DON'T CARE IF YOU'RE HERB KOHL, YOU CAN'T GET IN WITHOUT THE CHIEF'S OKAY.
EASE UP, JOHANNSON.
I THINK I CAN CLEAR THIS UP.
SPEED RACER, RIGHT? YOU'RE ON THE LIST.
GO ON IN.
YOU'VE GOT TEN MINUTES. IF YOU'RE NOT OUT BY THEN WE'LL COME LOOKING FOR YOU.
THANKS. I WON'T NEED MORE THAN 10 MINUTES.
BOY, THIS PLACE IS BIGGER THAN I THOUGHT.
WHAT WAS THAT?
CRASH
ARE YOU OKAY?
...H-help...
WHAT'S GOING ON?
OH!

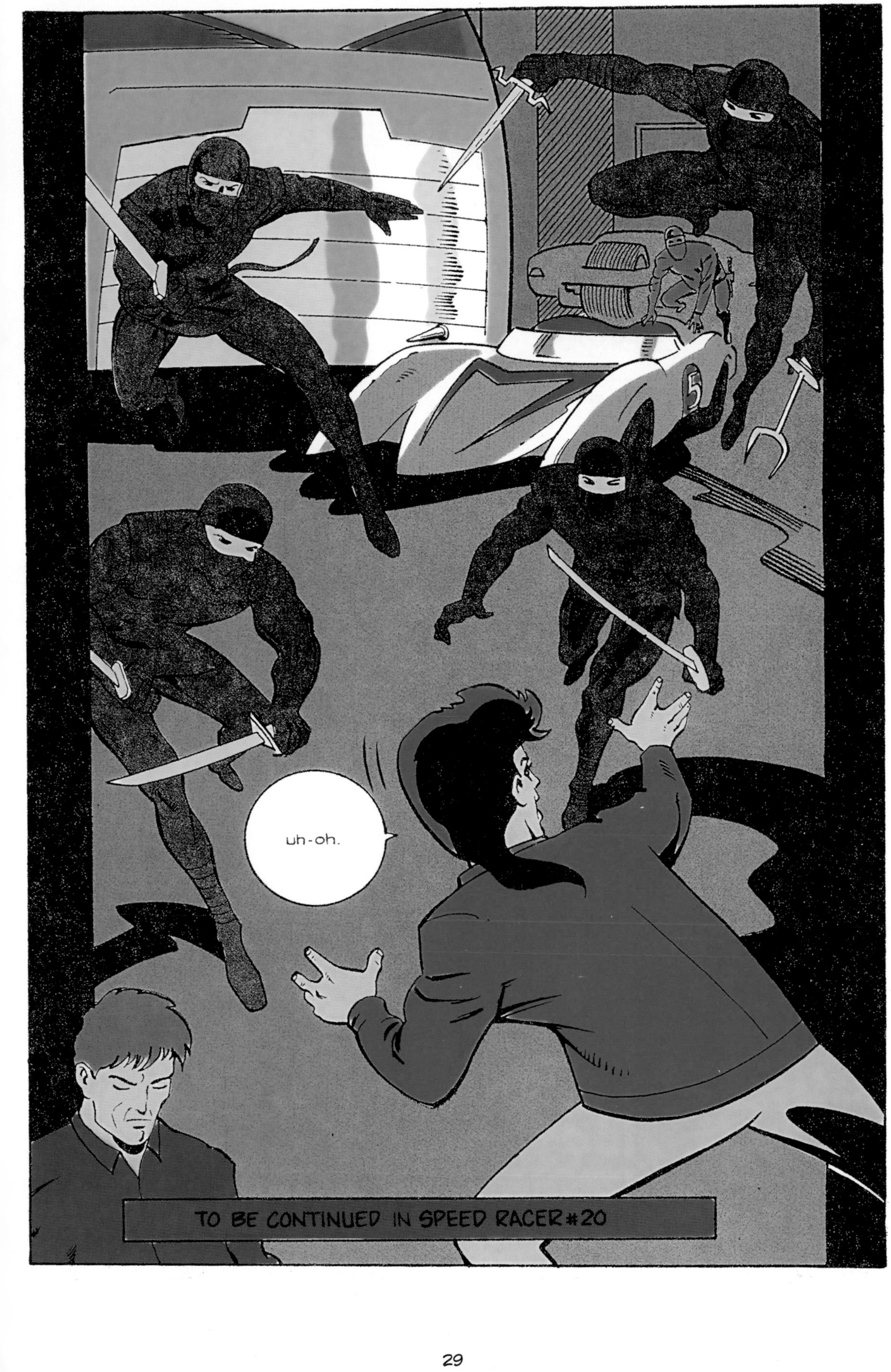
uh-oh.
TO BE CONTINUED IN SPEED RACER #20

Speed Racer #20

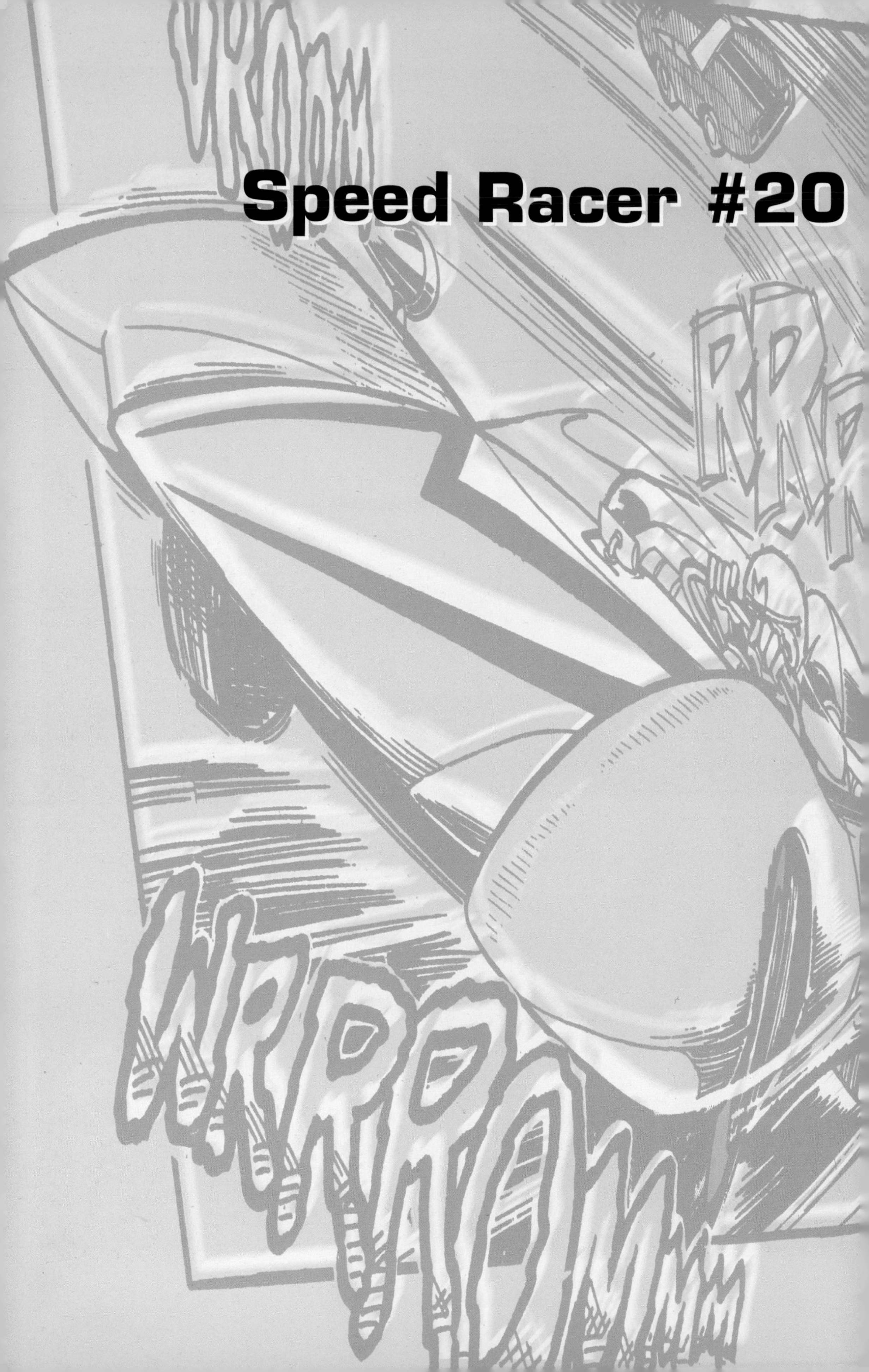

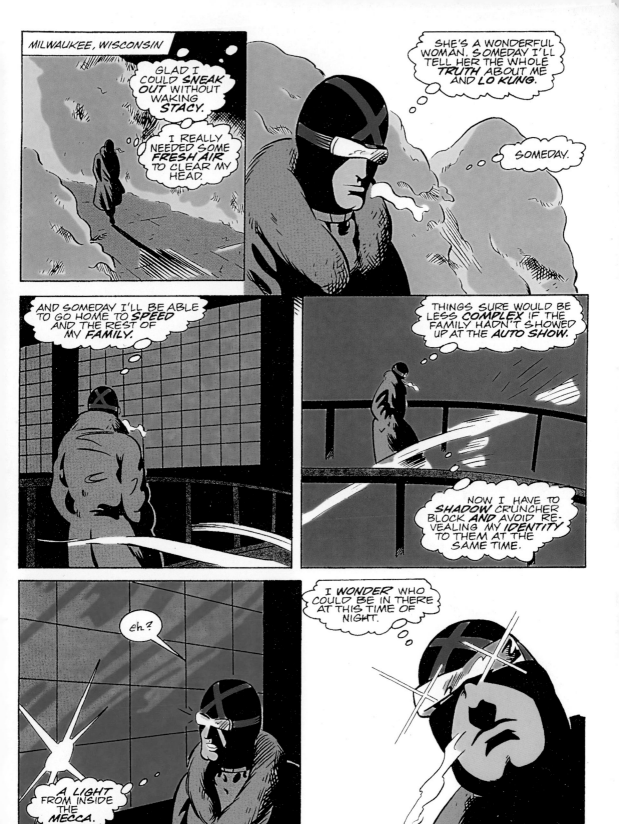

MILWAUKEE, WISCONSIN

GLAD I COULD *SNEAK OUT* WITHOUT WAKING *STACY.*

I REALLY NEEDED SOME *FRESH AIR* TO CLEAR MY HEAD.

SHE'S A WONDERFUL WOMAN. SOMEDAY I'LL TELL HER THE WHOLE *TRUTH* ABOUT ME AND *LO KUNG.*

SOMEDAY.

AND SOMEDAY I'LL BE ABLE TO GO HOME TO *SPEED* AND THE REST OF MY *FAMILY.*

THINGS SURE WOULD BE LESS *COMPLEX* IF THE FAMILY HADN'T SHOWED UP AT THE *AUTO SHOW.*

NOW I HAVE TO *SHADOW* CRUNCHER BLOCK *AND* AVOID RE-VEALING MY *IDENTITY* TO THEM AT THE SAME TIME.

eh?

A *LIGHT* FROM INSIDE THE *MECCA.*

I *WONDER* WHO COULD BE IN THERE AT THIS TIME OF NIGHT.

31

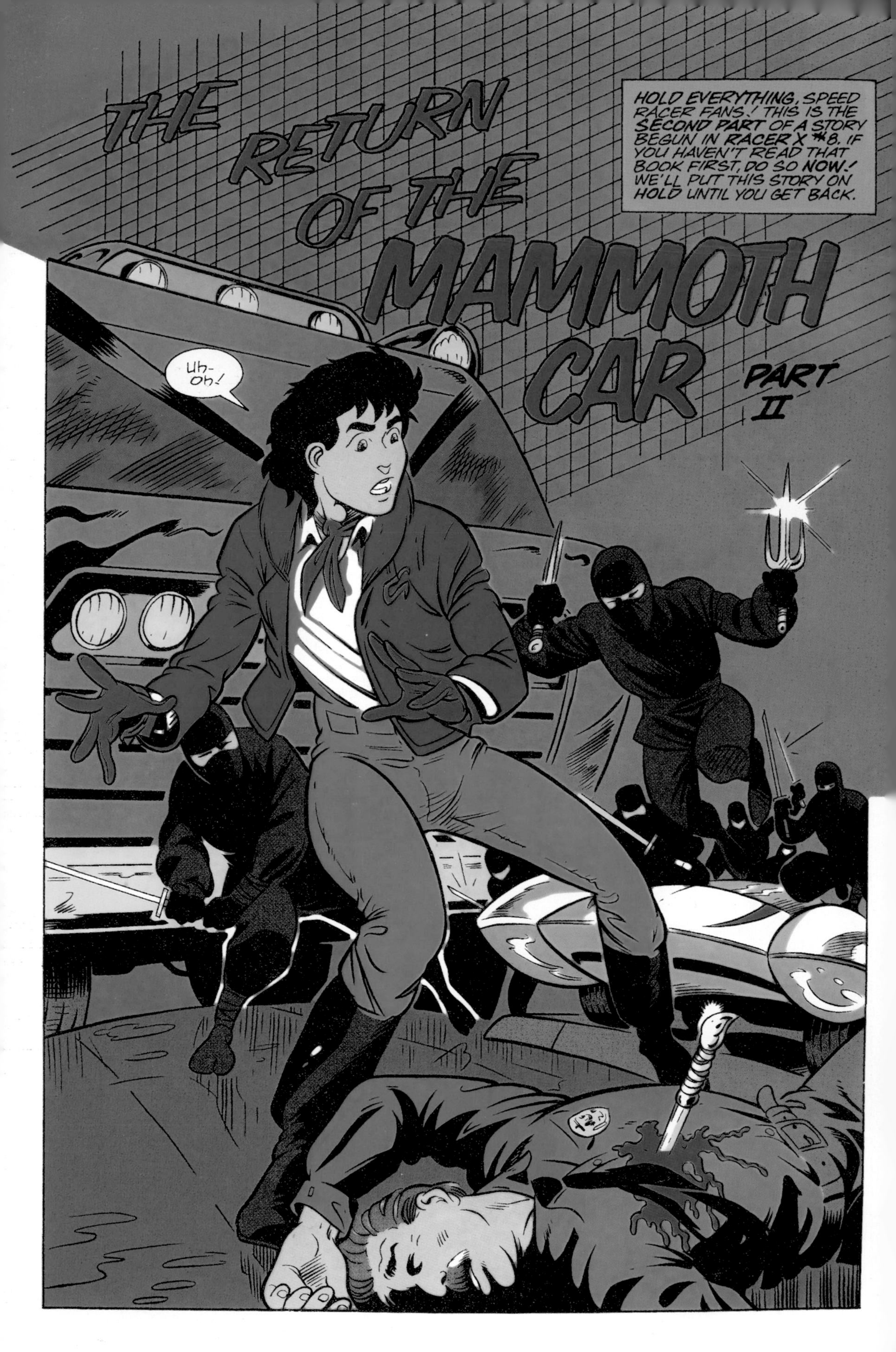
THE RETURN OF THE MAMMOTH CAR PART II
HOLD EVERYTHING, SPEED RACER FANS! THIS IS THE SECOND PART OF A STORY BEGUN IN RACER X #8. IF YOU HAVEN'T READ THAT BOOK FIRST, DO SO NOW! WE'LL PUT THIS STORY ON HOLD UNTIL YOU GET BACK.
UH-OH!

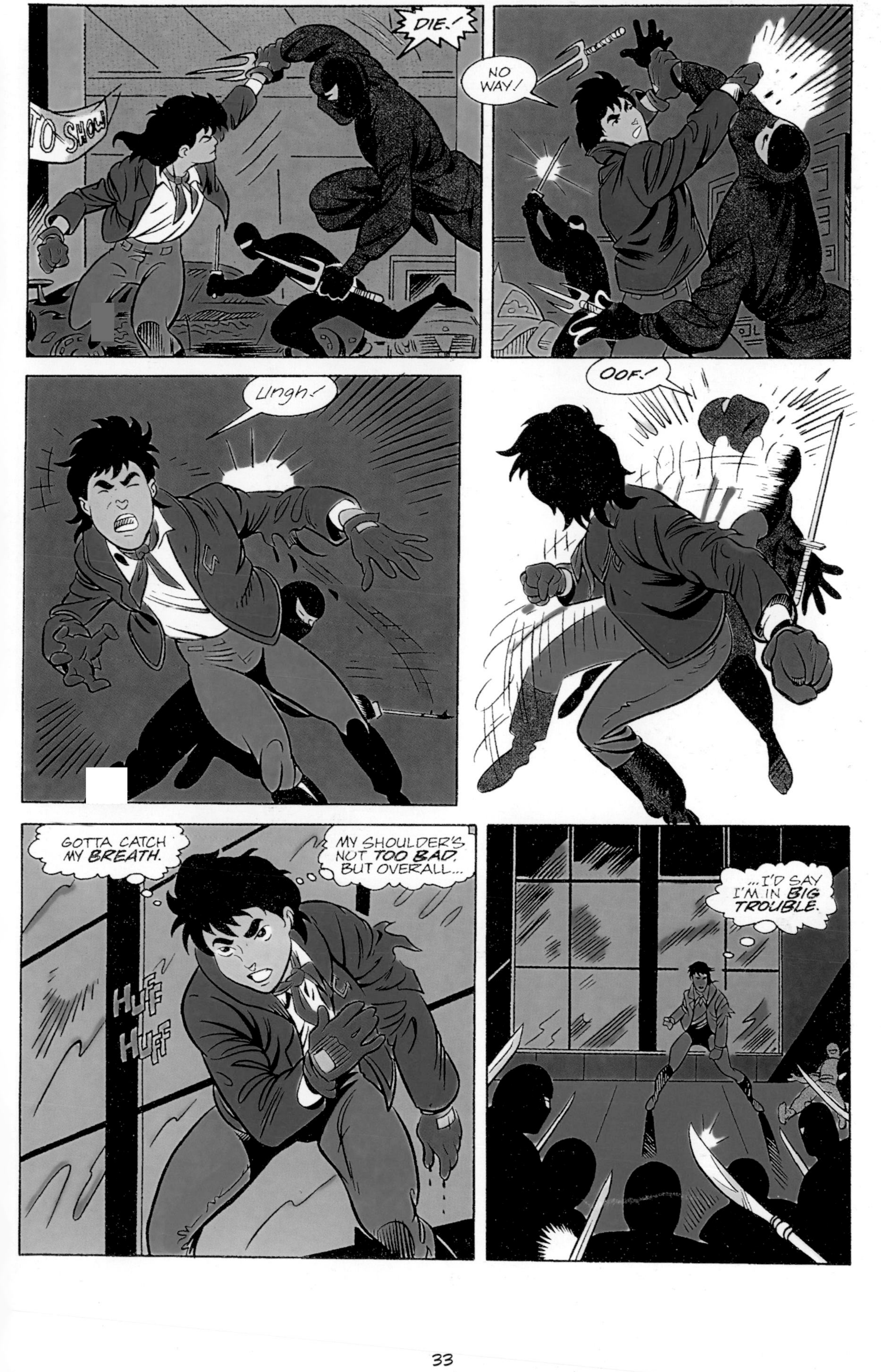
DIE!
TO SHOW
NO WAY!
Ungh!
OOF!
GOTTA CATCH MY BREATH.
MY SHOULDER'S NOT TOO BAD, BUT OVERALL...
HUFF HUFF
...I'D SAY I'M IN BIG TROUBLE.

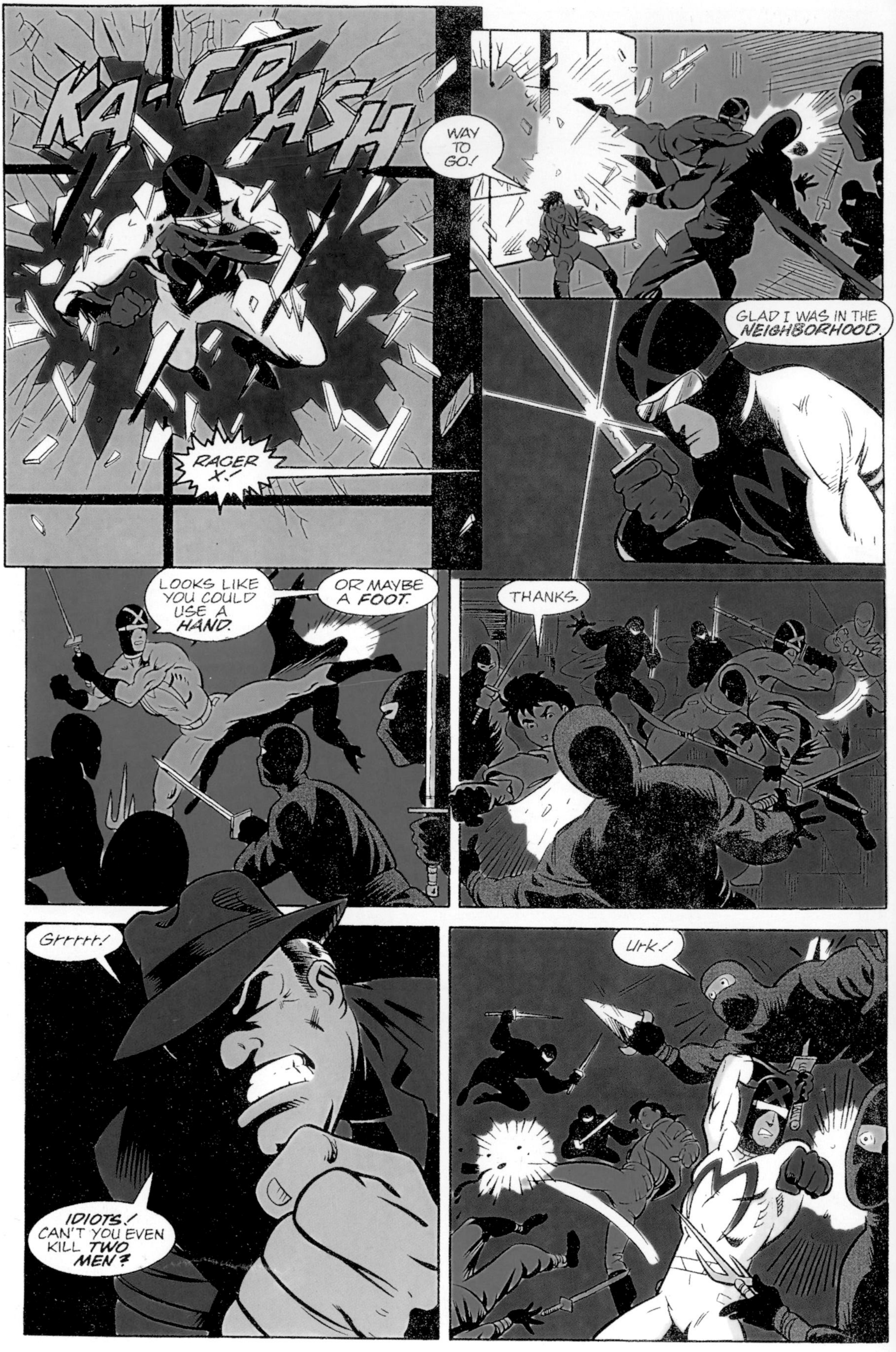
KA-CRASH
RACER X!
WAY TO GO!
GLAD I WAS IN THE NEIGHBORHOOD.
LOOKS LIKE YOU COULD USE A HAND.
OR MAYBE A FOOT.
THANKS.
Grrrrr!
IDIOTS! CAN'T YOU EVEN KILL TWO MEN?
Urk!

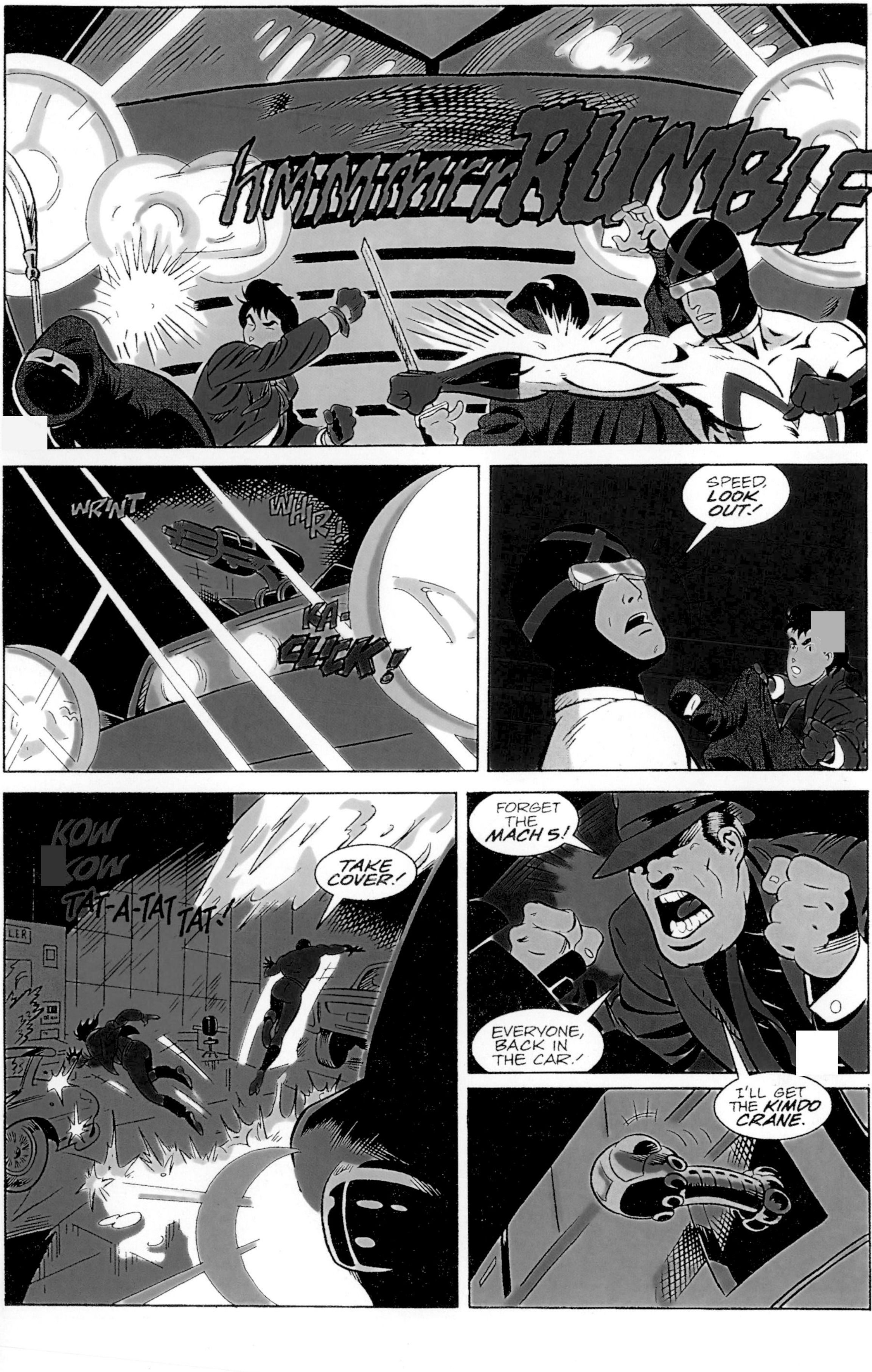
RUMBLE
WRINT
WHIR!
KA-CLICK!
SPEED, LOOK OUT!
KOW
[redacted]OW
TAT-A-TAT TAT!
TAKE COVER!
FORGET THE MACH 5!
EVERYONE, BACK IN THE CAR!
I'LL GET THE KIMDO CRANE.

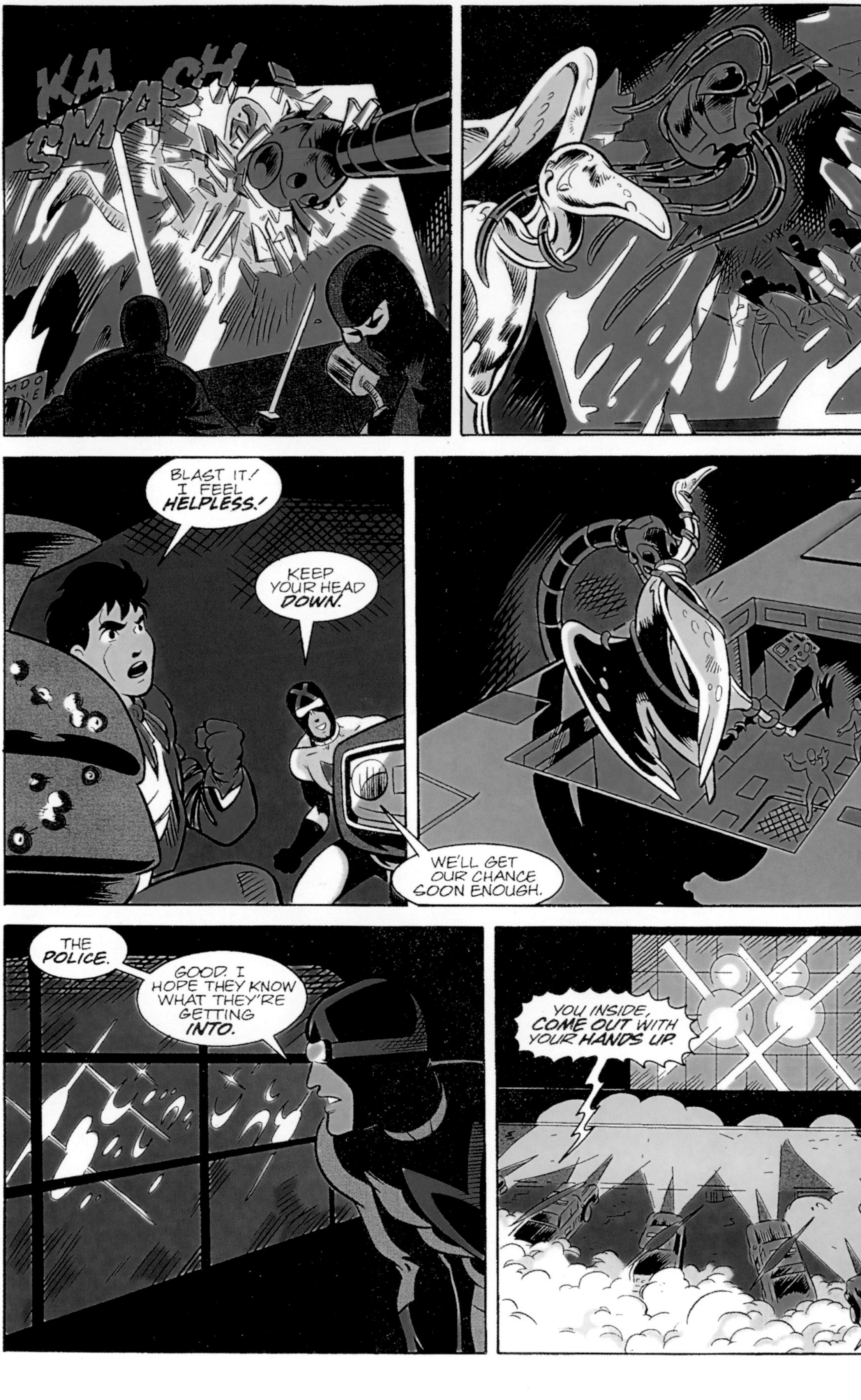
KA SMASH
BLAST IT! I FEEL HELPLESS!
KEEP YOUR HEAD DOWN.
WE'LL GET OUR CHANCE SOON ENOUGH.
THE POLICE.
GOOD. I HOPE THEY KNOW WHAT THEY'RE GETTING INTO.
YOU INSIDE, COME OUT WITH YOUR HANDS UP.

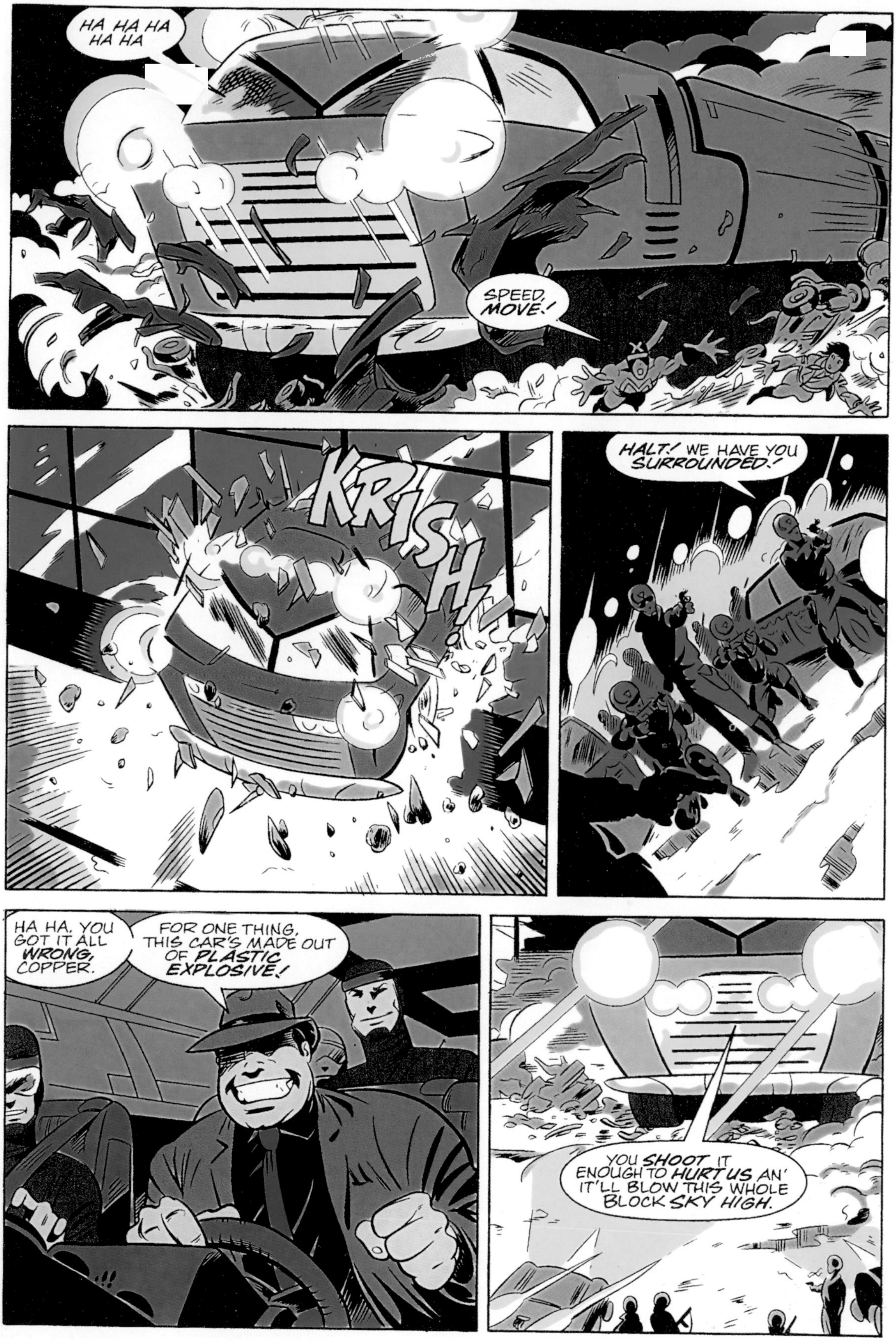
HA HA HA HA HA
SPEED, MOVE!
KRISH!
HALT! WE HAVE YOU SURROUNDED!
HA HA. YOU GOT IT ALL WRONG, COPPER.
FOR ONE THING, THIS CAR'S MADE OUT OF PLASTIC EXPLOSIVE!
YOU SHOOT IT ENOUGH TO HURT US AN' IT'LL BLOW THIS WHOLE BLOCK SKY HIGH.

ASK YOUR *CAPTAIN* WHAT HAPPENED IN *OKLAHOMA* LAST MONTH.

HE MUST MEAN THAT *TRUCK STOP* EXPLOSION.

Heh, Heh.!

BESIDES, YOU AIN'T GOT *ME* SURROUNDED...

RRRUUMMMBBLLE

WHAT THE--?

GOOD LORD.!

HOLY....!

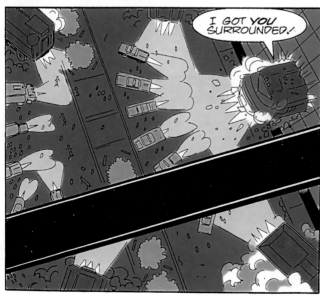

I GOT *YOU* SURROUNDED.!

NOW WHAT ?

DAMN.!

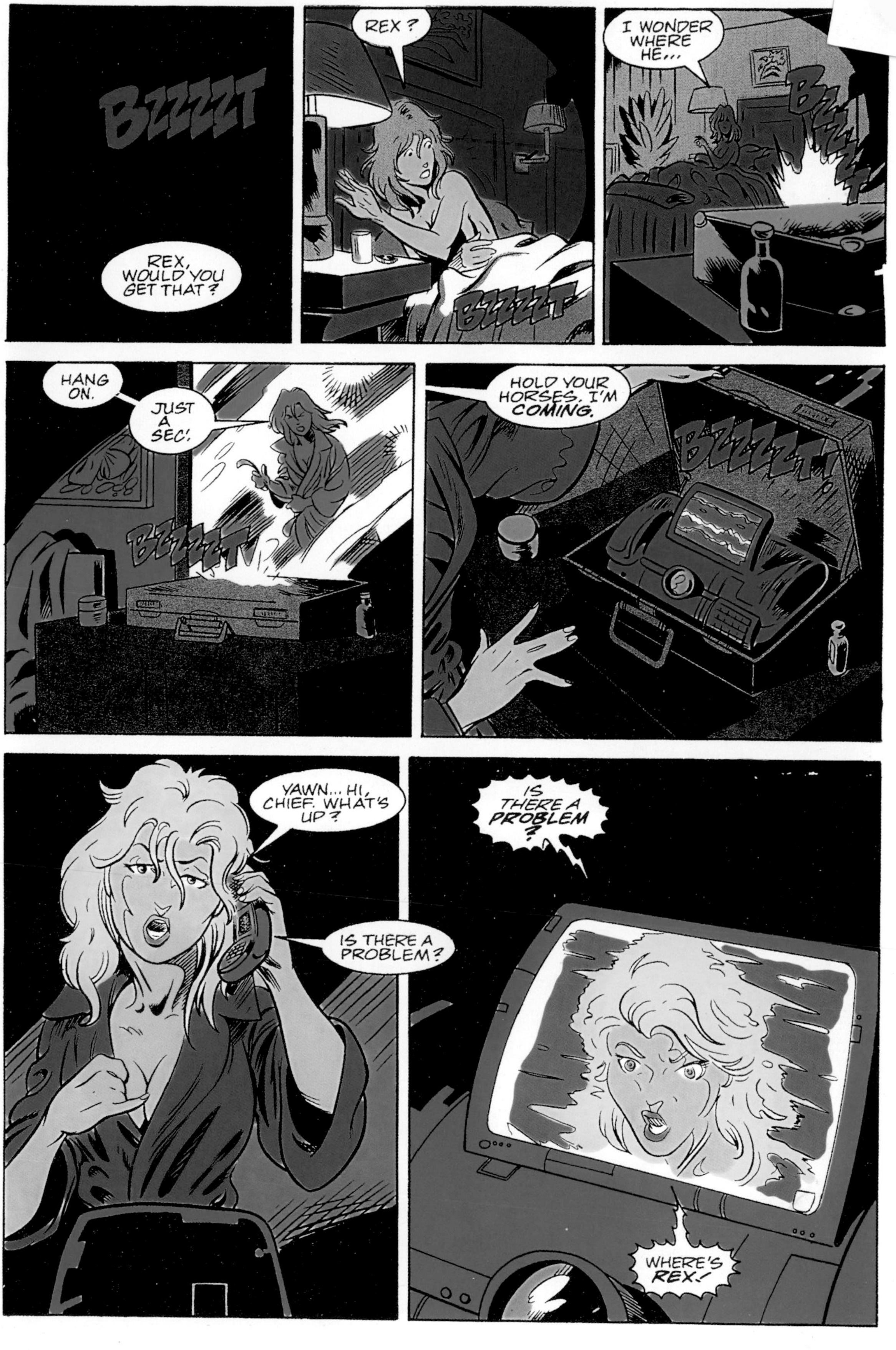
BZZZZZT
REX, WOULD YOU GET THAT?
REX?
BZZZZT
I WONDER WHERE HE...
BZZZZT
HANG ON.
JUST A SEC!
BZZZZT
HOLD YOUR HORSES. I'M COMING.
BZZZZT!
YAWN... HI, CHIEF. WHAT'S UP?
IS THERE A PROBLEM?
IS THERE A PROBLEM?
WHERE'S REX!

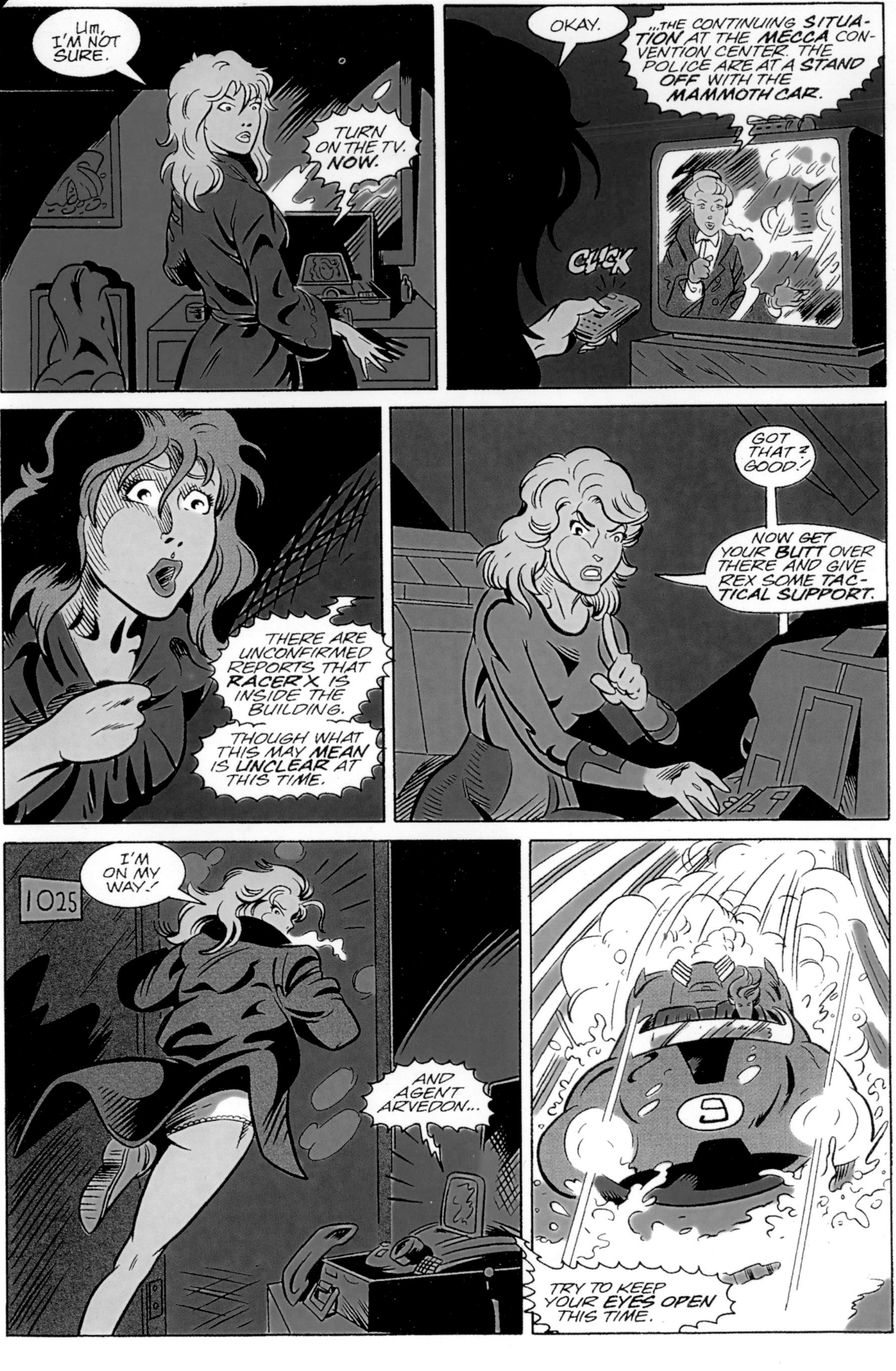
UM, I'M NOT SURE.
TURN ON THE TV. NOW.
OKAY.
...THE CONTINUING SITUATION AT THE MECCA CONVENTION CENTER. THE POLICE ARE AT A STAND OFF WITH THE MAMMOTH CAR.
CLICK
THERE ARE UNCONFIRMED REPORTS THAT RACER X IS INSIDE THE BUILDING.
THOUGH WHAT THIS MAY MEAN IS UNCLEAR AT THIS TIME.
GOT THAT? GOOD!
NOW GET YOUR BUTT OVER THERE AND GIVE REX SOME TACTICAL SUPPORT.
I'M ON MY WAY!
1025
AND AGENT ARVEDON...
TRY TO KEEP YOUR EYES OPEN THIS TIME.

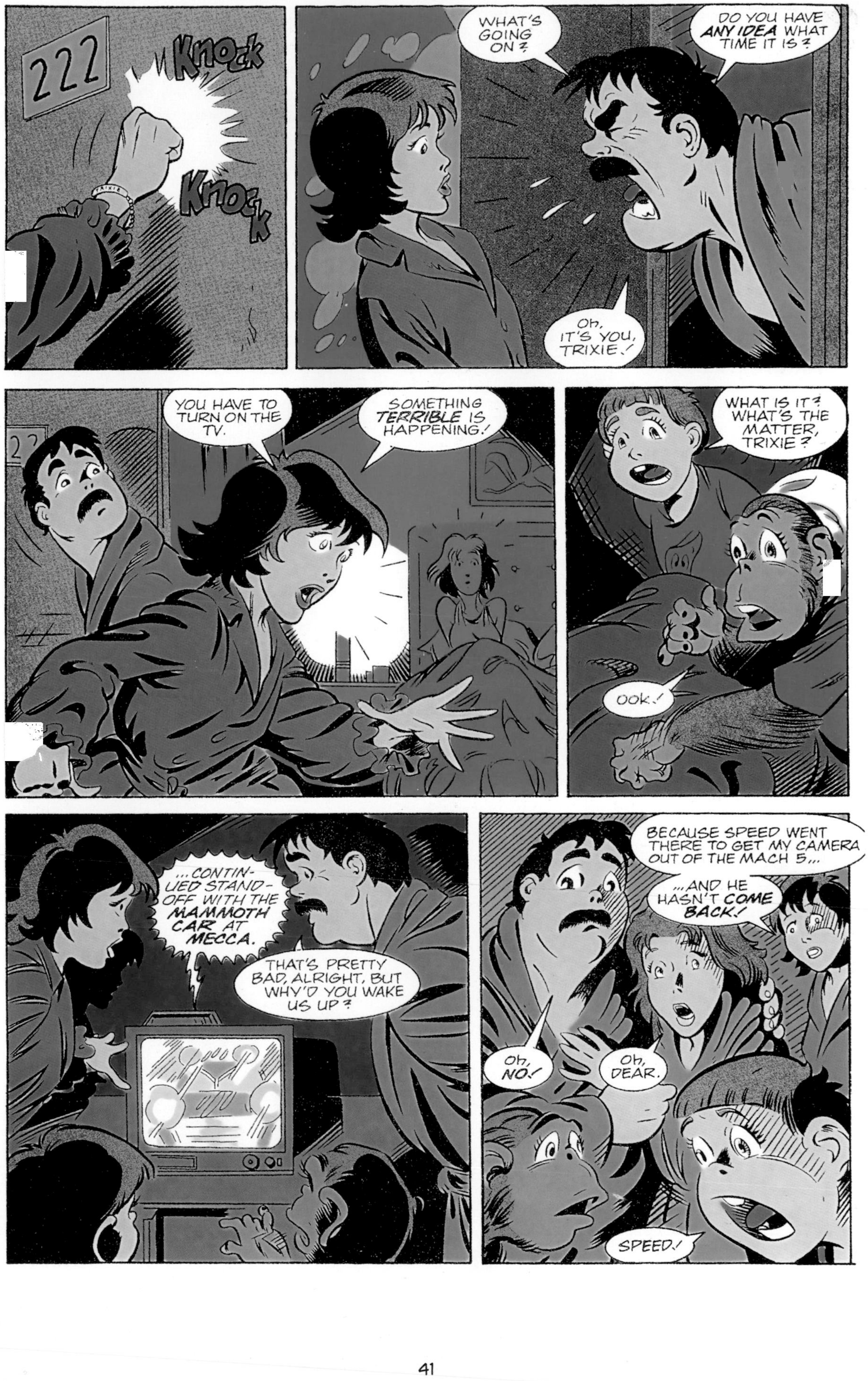
222
KNOCK
KNOCK
WHAT'S GOING ON?
DO YOU HAVE ANY IDEA WHAT TIME IT IS?
OH, IT'S YOU, TRIXIE!
YOU HAVE TO TURN ON THE TV.
SOMETHING TERRIBLE IS HAPPENING!
WHAT IS IT? WHAT'S THE MATTER, TRIXIE?
OOK!
...CONTINUED STAND-OFF WITH THE MAMMOTH CAR AT MECCA.
THAT'S PRETTY BAD, ALRIGHT, BUT WHY'D YOU WAKE US UP?
BECAUSE SPEED WENT THERE TO GET MY CAMERA OUT OF THE MACH 5...
...AND HE HASN'T COME BACK!
OH, NO!
OH, DEAR.
SPEED!

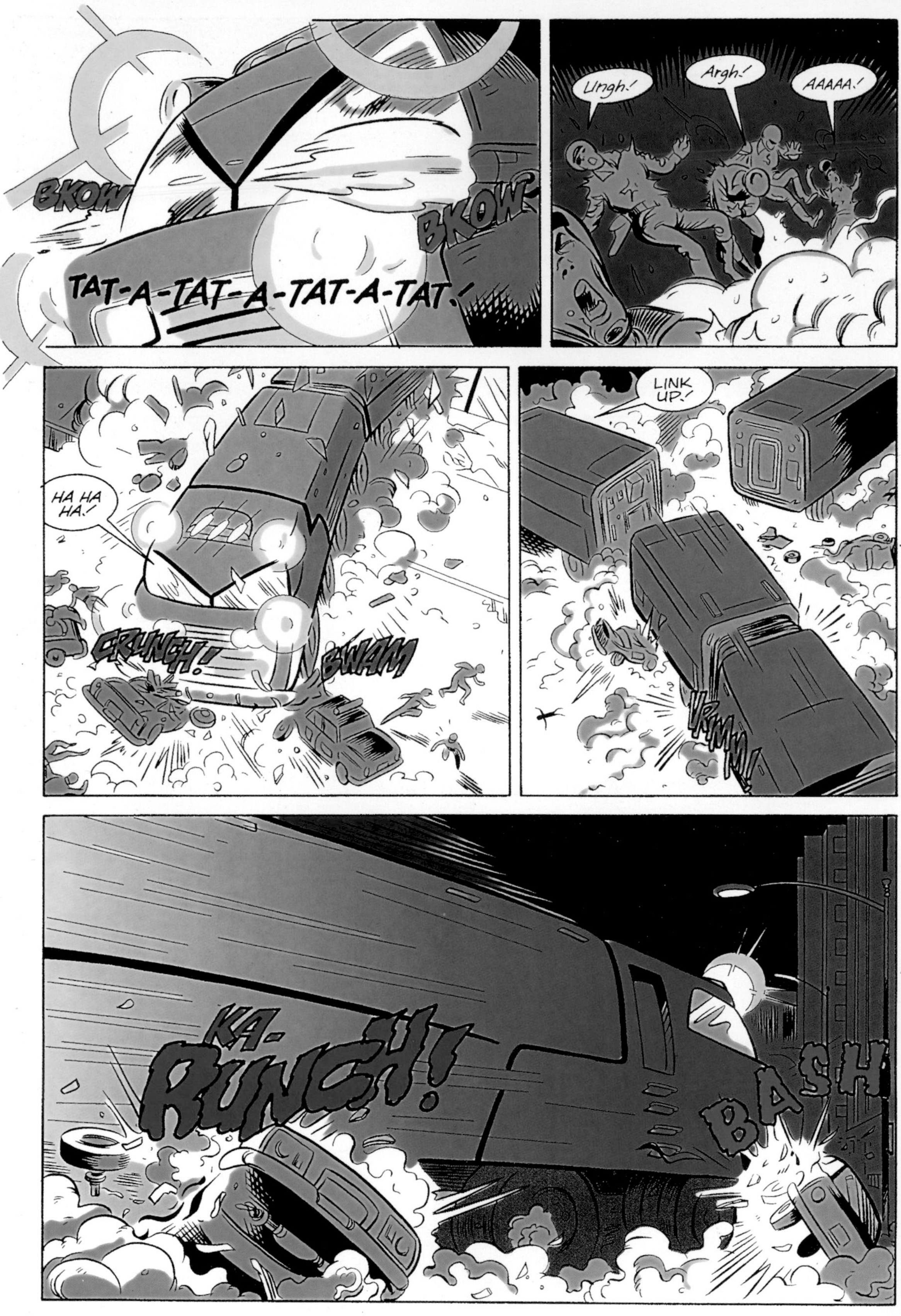
BKOW
BKOW
TAT-A-TAT-A-TAT-A-TAT!
Ungh!
Argh!
AAAAA!
HA HA HA!
CRUNCH!
BWAM
LINK UP!
VRMM!
KA-RUNCH!
BASH

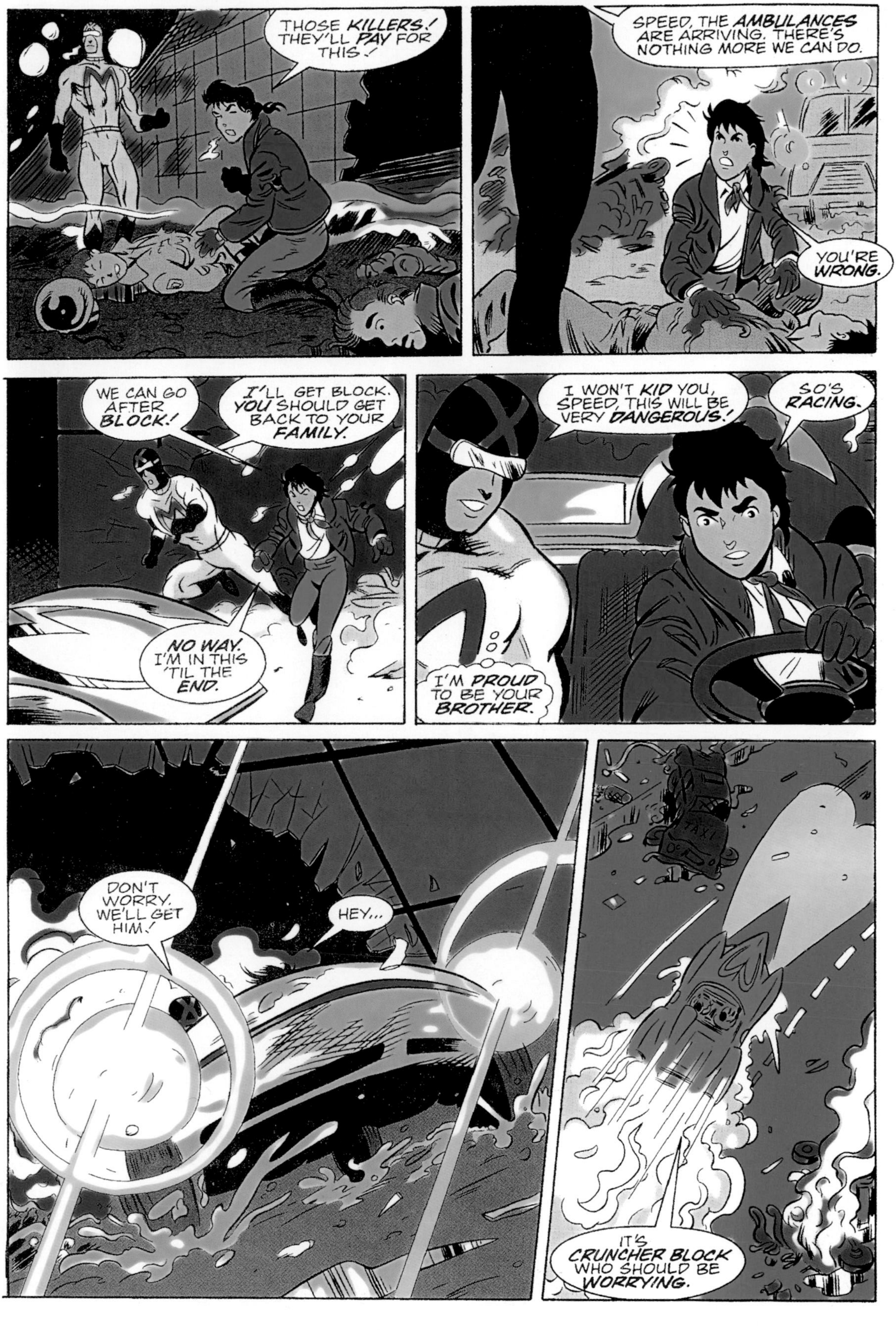
THOSE KILLERS! THEY'LL PAY FOR THIS!
SPEED, THE AMBULANCES ARE ARRIVING. THERE'S NOTHING MORE WE CAN DO.
YOU'RE WRONG.
WE CAN GO AFTER BLOCK!
I'LL GET BLOCK. YOU SHOULD GET BACK TO YOUR FAMILY.
NO WAY. I'M IN THIS 'TIL THE END.
I WON'T KID YOU, SPEED, THIS WILL BE VERY DANGEROUS!
SO'S RACING.
I'M PROUD TO BE YOUR BROTHER.
DON'T WORRY. WE'LL GET HIM!
HEY...
IT'S CRUNCHER BLOCK WHO SHOULD BE WORRYING.

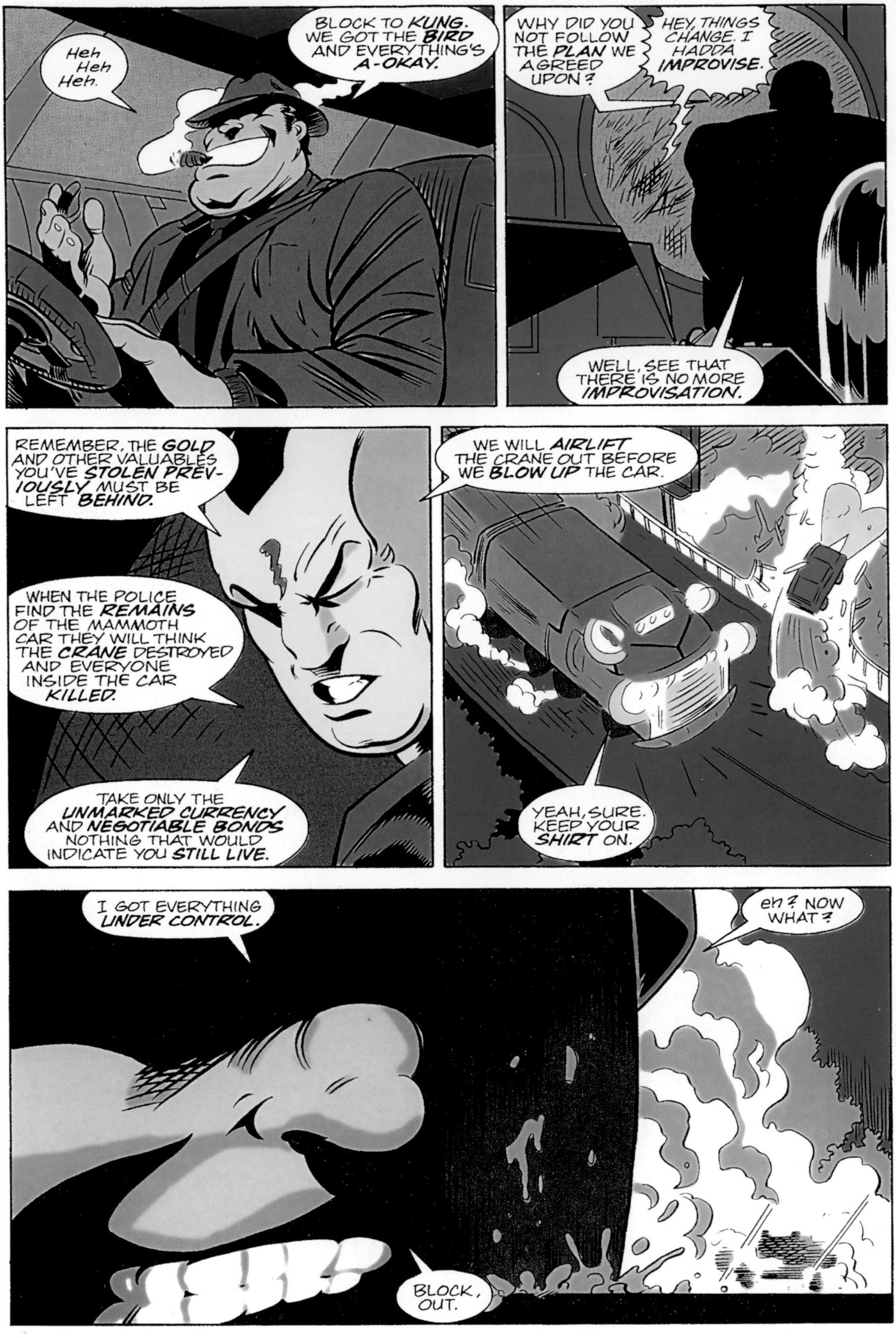
Heh Heh Heh.
BLOCK TO KUNG. WE GOT THE BIRD AND EVERYTHING'S A-OKAY.
WHY DID YOU NOT FOLLOW THE PLAN WE AGREED UPON?
HEY, THINGS CHANGE. I HADDA IMPROVISE.
WELL, SEE THAT THERE IS NO MORE IMPROVISATION.
REMEMBER, THE GOLD AND OTHER VALUABLES YOU'VE STOLEN PREVIOUSLY MUST BE LEFT BEHIND.
WHEN THE POLICE FIND THE REMAINS OF THE MAMMOTH CAR THEY WILL THINK THE CRANE DESTROYED AND EVERYONE INSIDE THE CAR KILLED.
TAKE ONLY THE UNMARKED CURRENCY AND NEGOTIABLE BONDS NOTHING THAT WOULD INDICATE YOU STILL LIVE.
WE WILL AIRLIFT THE CRANE OUT BEFORE WE BLOW UP THE CAR.
YEAH, SURE. KEEP YOUR SHIRT ON.
I GOT EVERYTHING UNDER CONTROL.
eh? NOW WHAT?
BLOCK, OUT.

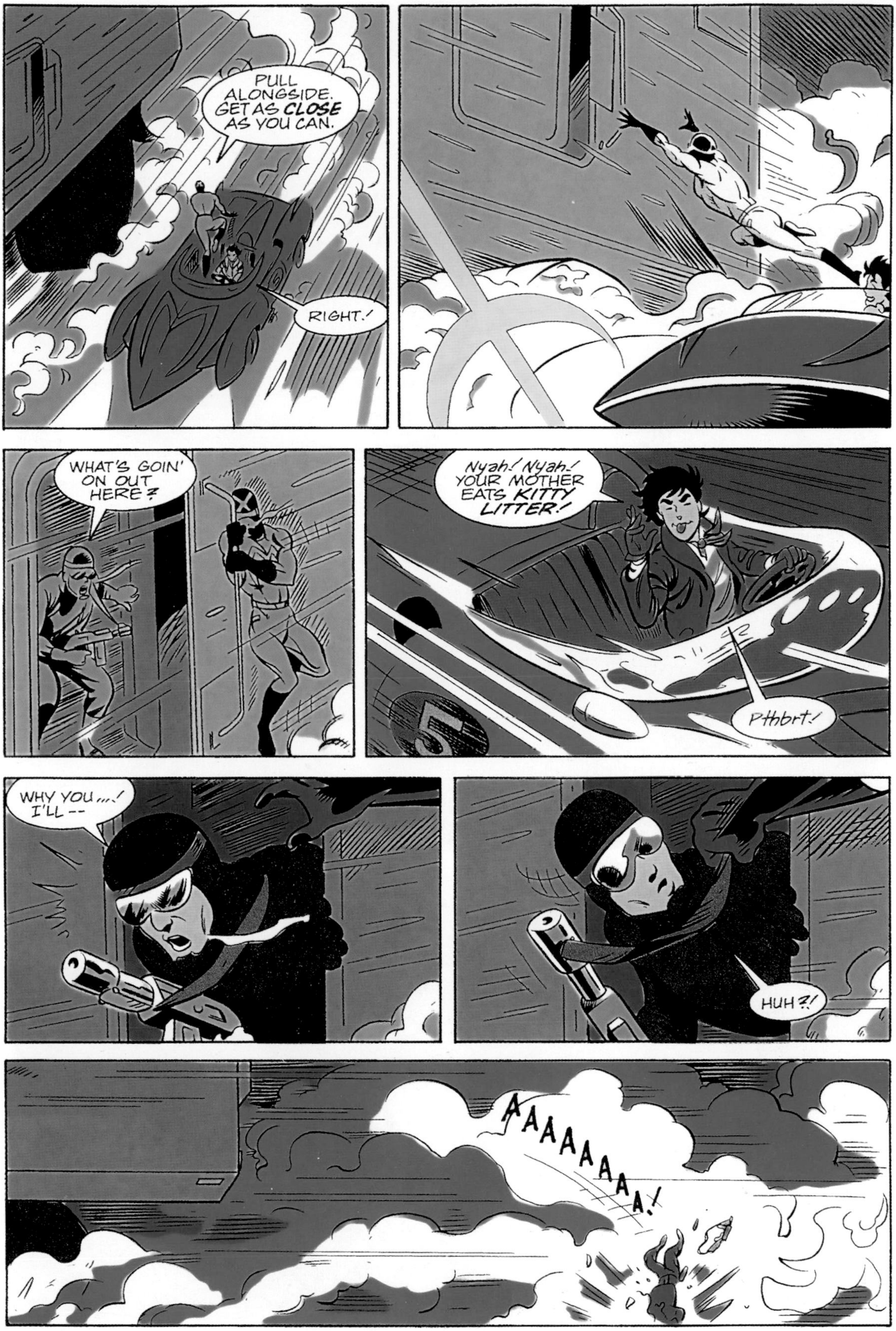
PULL ALONGSIDE. GET AS CLOSE AS YOU CAN.
RIGHT!
WHAT'S GOIN' ON OUT HERE?
Nyah! Nyah! YOUR MOTHER EATS KITTY LITTER!
Pthbrt!
WHY YOU...! I'LL --
HUH?!
AAAAAAAAA!

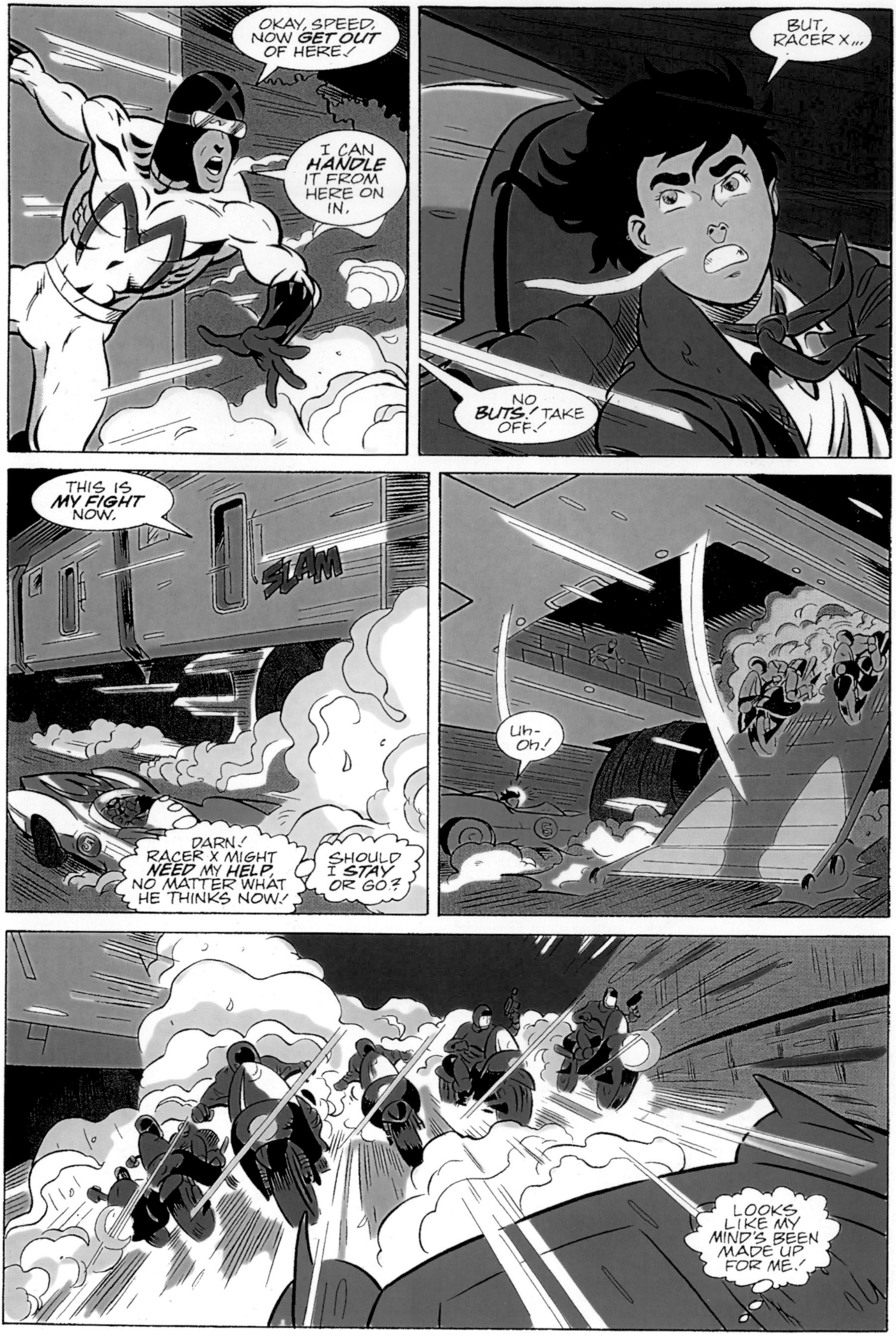
OKAY, SPEED, NOW GET OUT OF HERE!
I CAN HANDLE IT FROM HERE ON IN.
BUT, RACER X...
NO BUTS! TAKE OFF!
THIS IS MY FIGHT NOW.
SLAM
DARN! RACER X MIGHT NEED MY HELP, NO MATTER WHAT HE THINKS NOW!
SHOULD I STAY OR GO?
Uh-Oh!
LOOKS LIKE MY MIND'S BEEN MADE UP FOR ME!

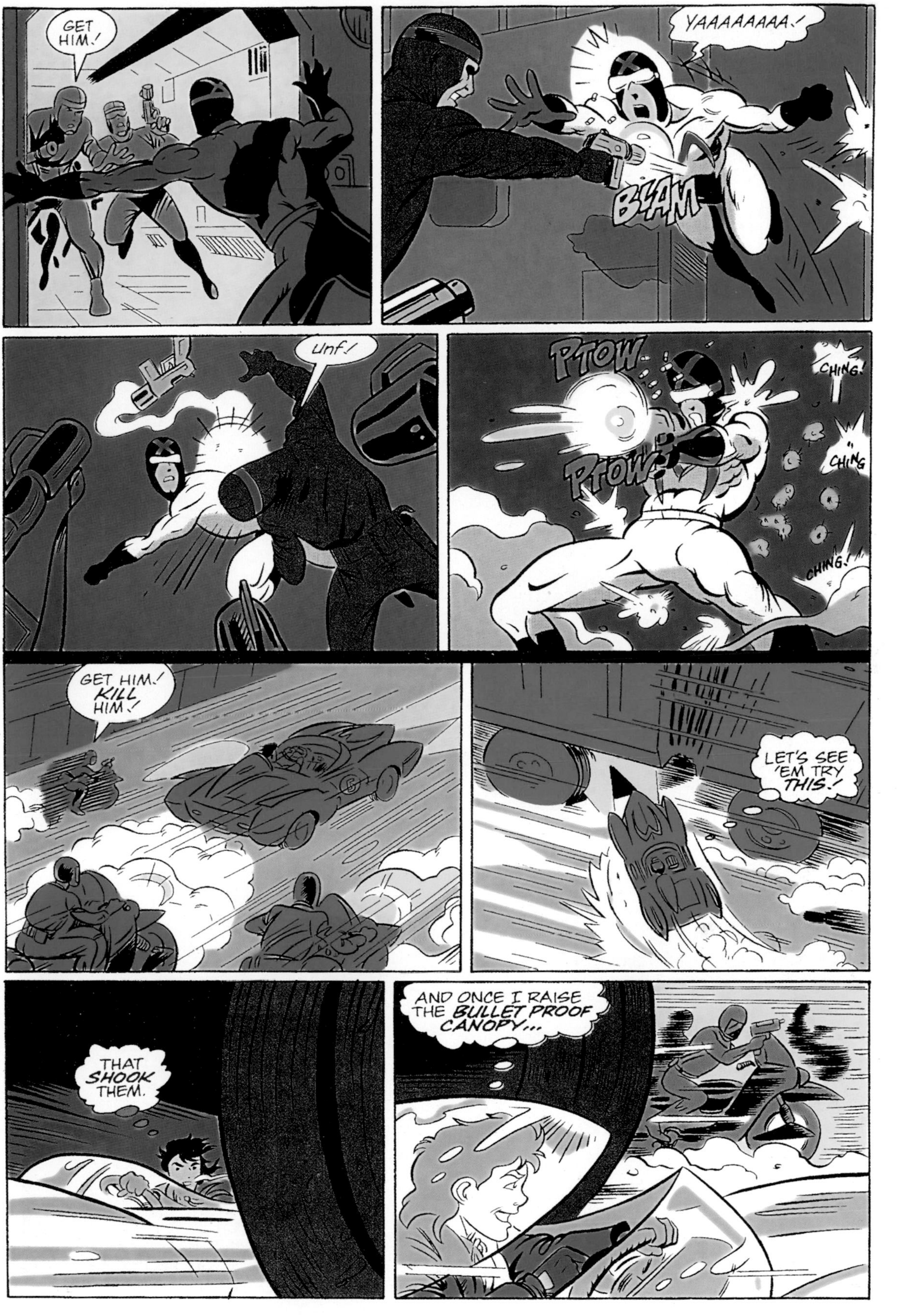
GET HIM!
YAAAAAAAA!
BLAM
Unf!
PTOW
PTOW!
CHING!
CHING
CHING!
GET HIM! KILL HIM!
LET'S SEE 'EM TRY THIS!
THAT SHOOK THEM.
AND ONCE I RAISE THE BULLET PROOF CANOPY...

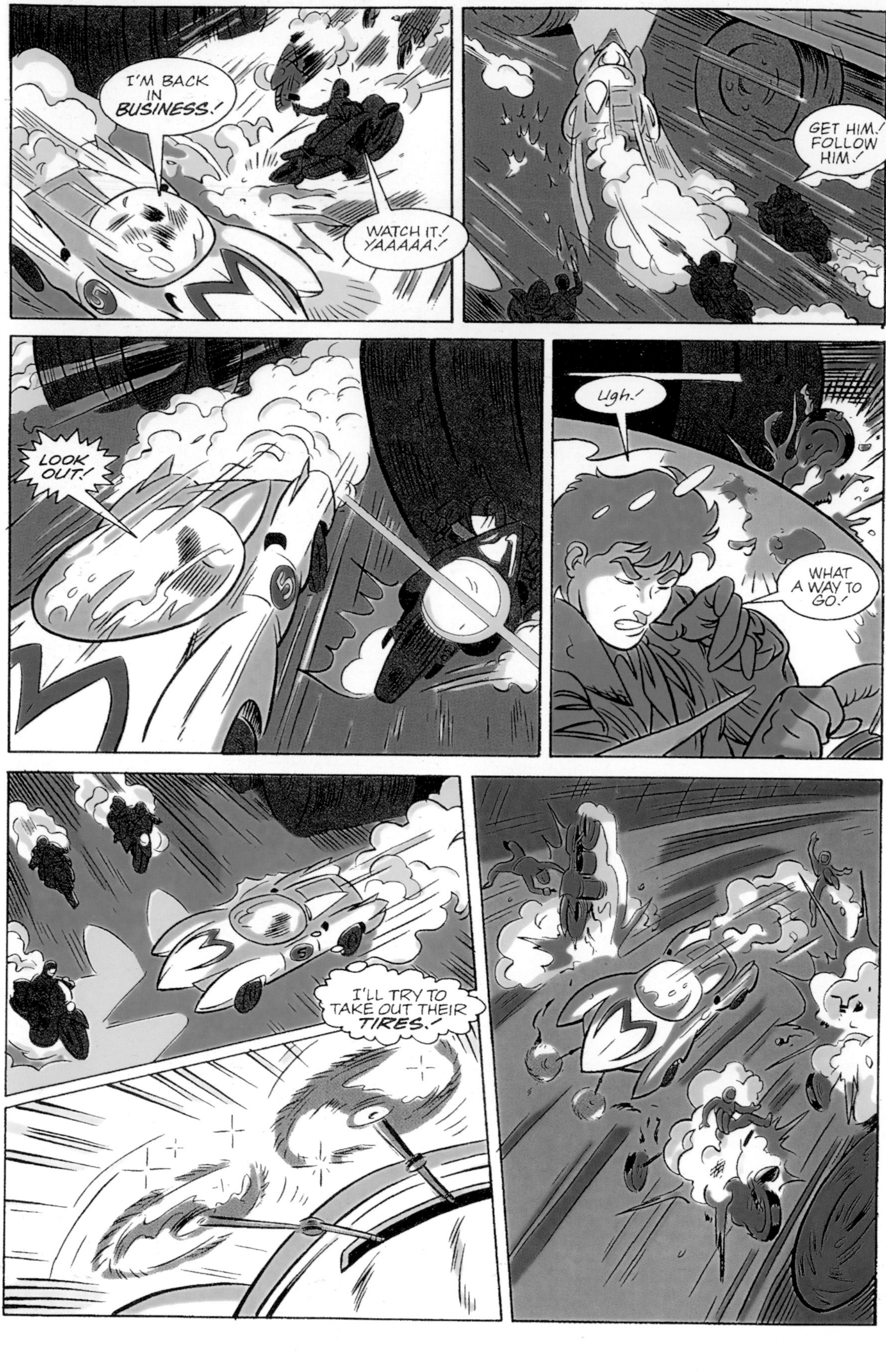
I'M BACK IN BUSINESS.!
WATCH IT.! YAAAAA.!
GET HIM.! FOLLOW HIM.!
LOOK OUT.!
Ugh.!
WHAT A WAY TO GO.!
I'LL TRY TO TAKE OUT THEIR TIRES.!

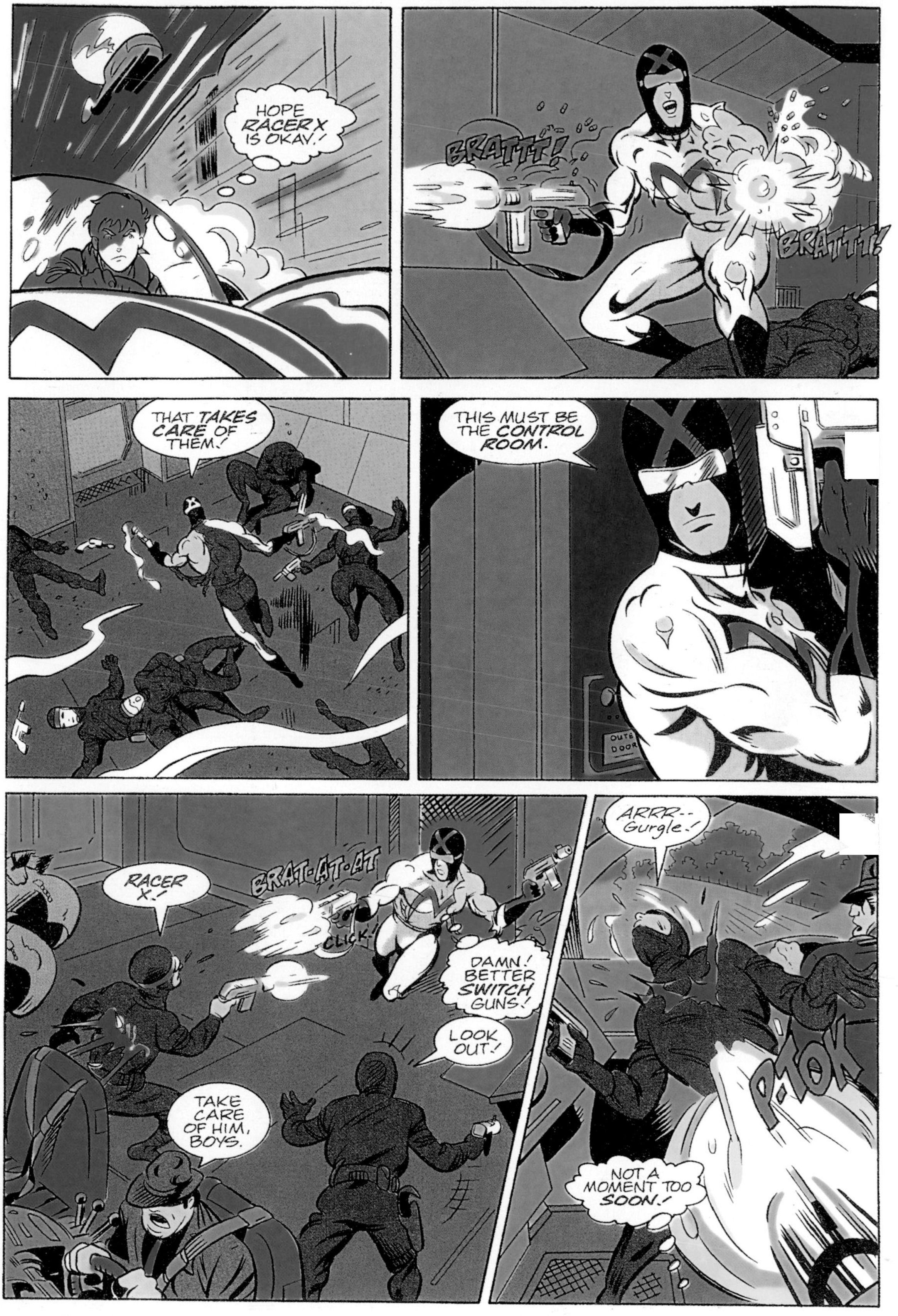

HOPE RACER X IS OKAY.!
BRATTT!
BRATTT!
THAT TAKES CARE OF THEM.!
THIS MUST BE THE CONTROL ROOM.
OUTER DOOR
RACER X.!
BRAT-AT-AT
CLICK!
DAMN! BETTER SWITCH GUNS!
LOOK OUT!
TAKE CARE OF HIM, BOYS.
ARRR-- Gurgle.!
P-TOK
NOT A MOMENT TOO SOON.!

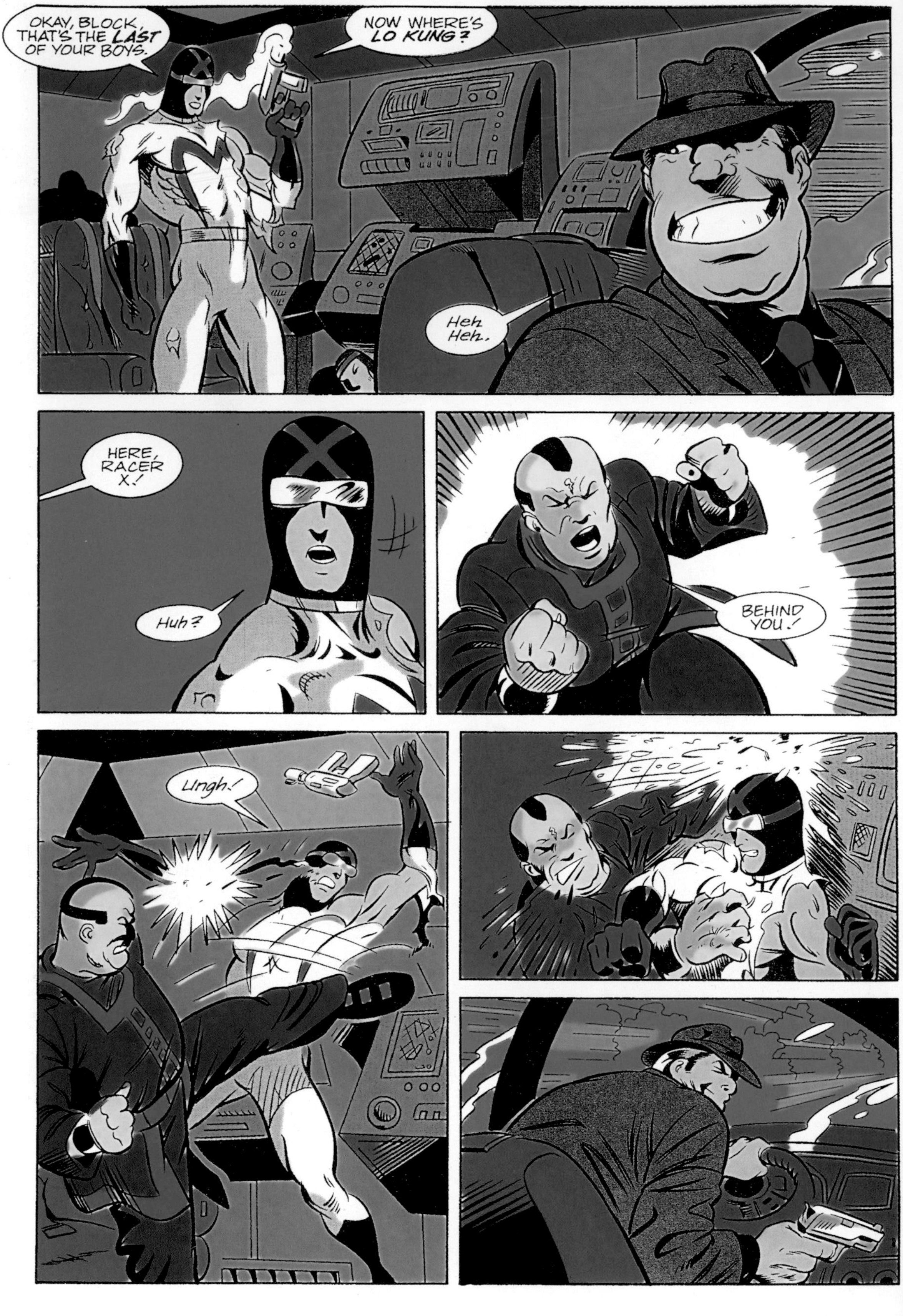

OKAY, BLOCK, THAT'S THE LAST OF YOUR BOYS.
NOW WHERE'S LO KUNG?
Heh Heh.
HERE, RACER X!
Huh?
BEHIND YOU!
Ungh!

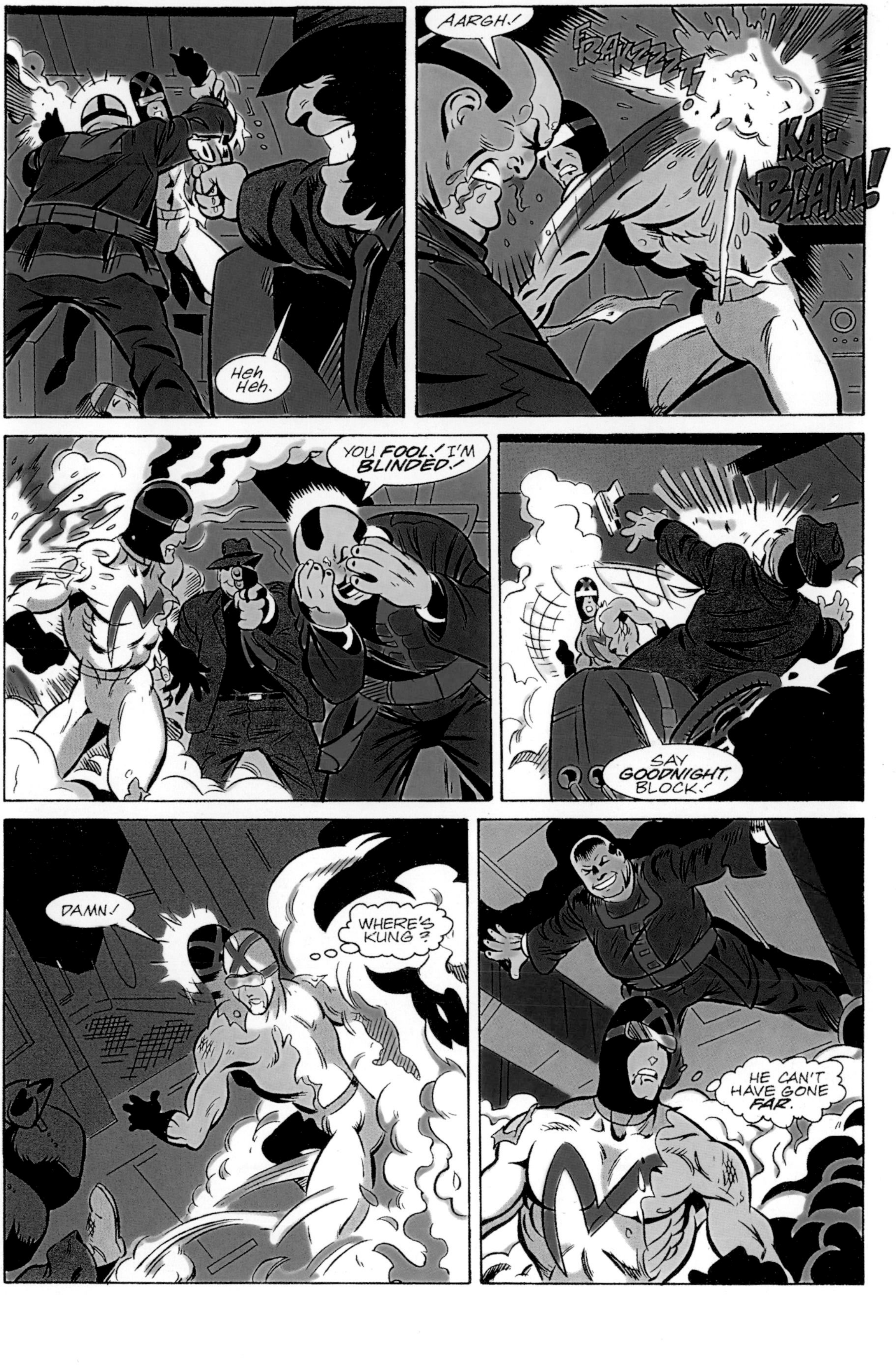
Heh Heh.
AARGH!
FRAZZZT
KA-BLAM!
YOU FOOL! I'M BLINDED!
SAY GOODNIGHT, BLOCK!
DAMN!
WHERE'S KUNG?
HE CAN'T HAVE GONE FAR.

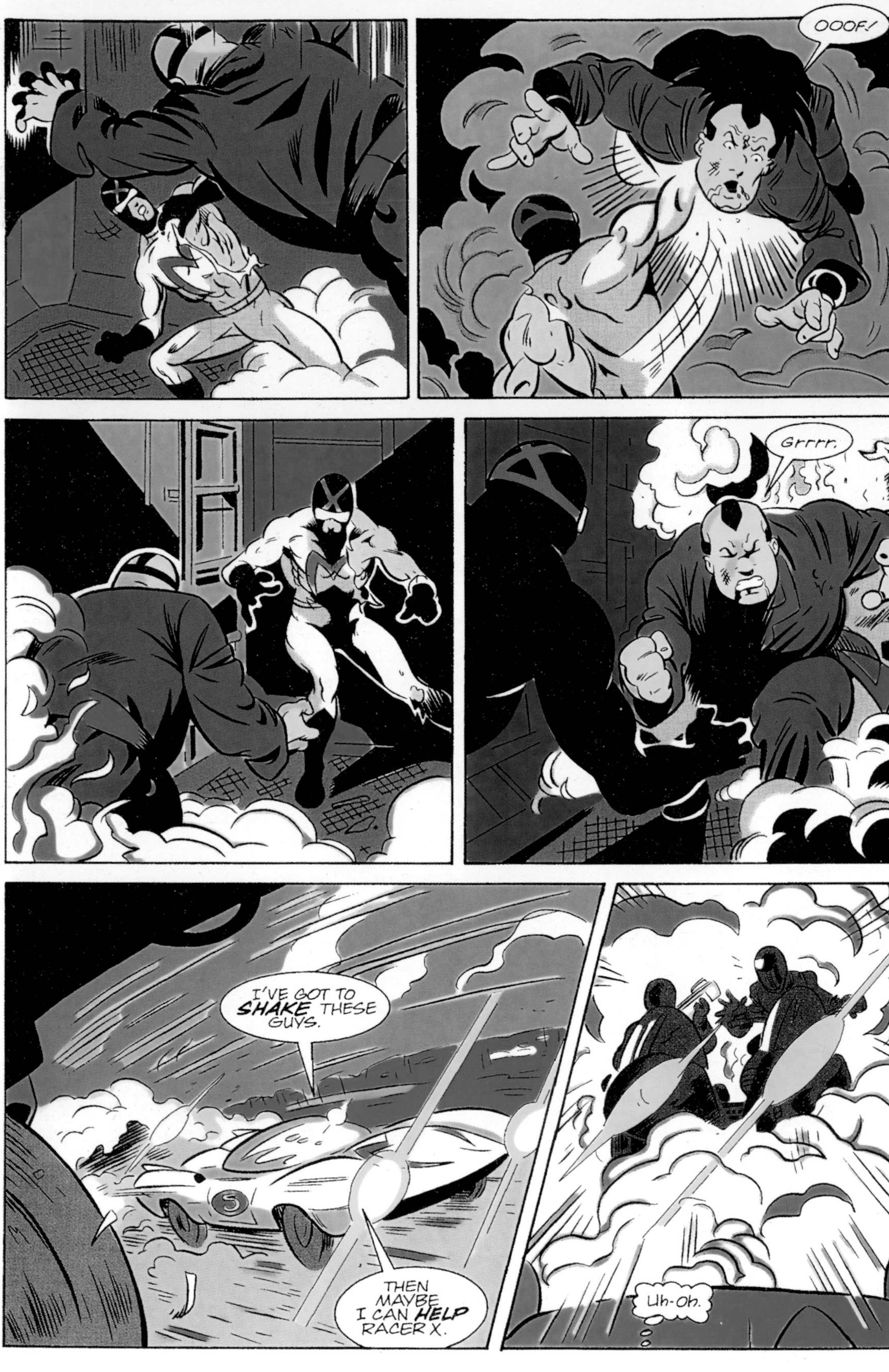
OOOF!
Grrrr.
I'VE GOT TO SHAKE THESE GUYS.
THEN MAYBE I CAN HELP RACER X.
Uh-Oh.

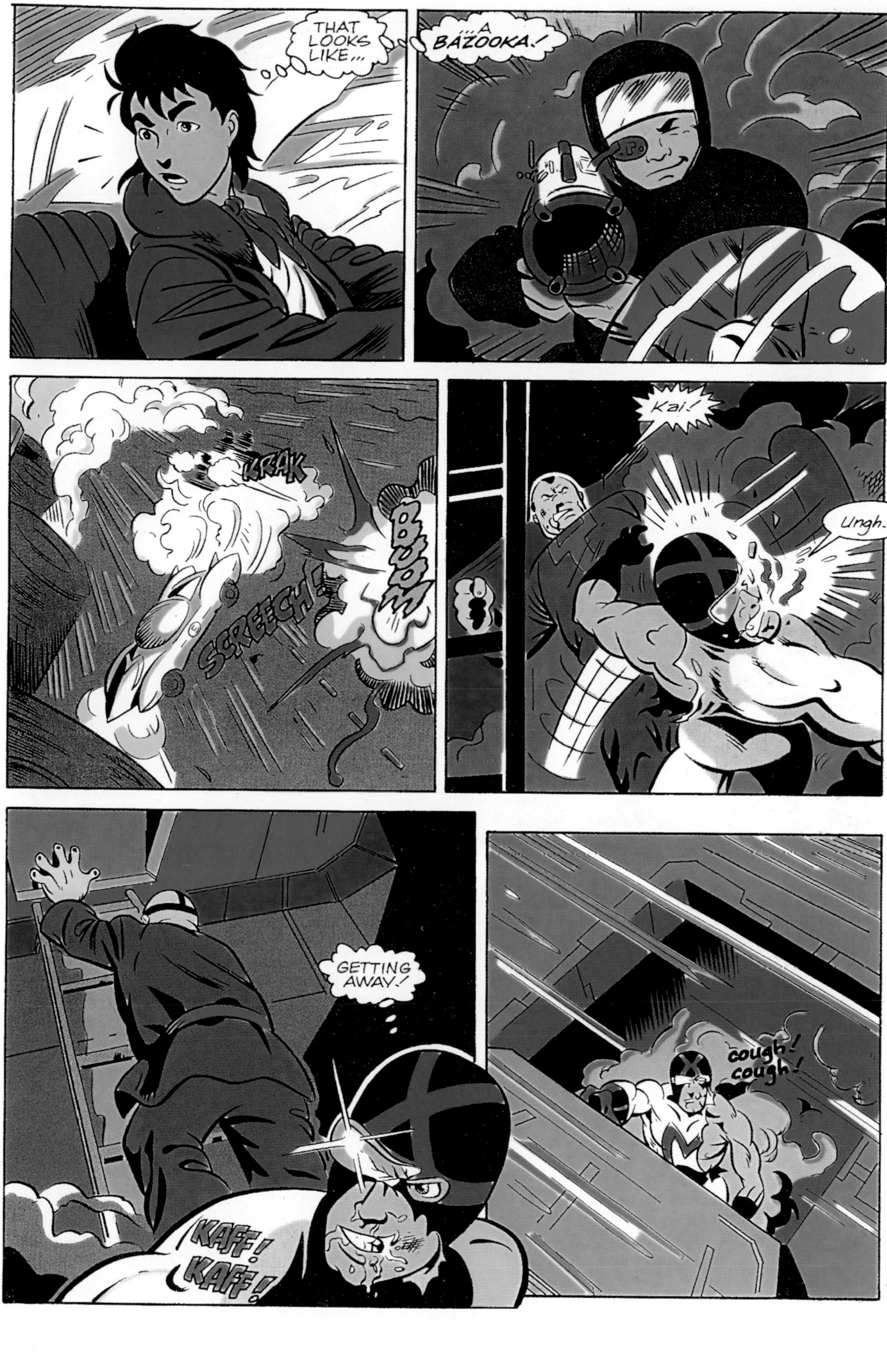
THAT LOOKS LIKE...
...A BAZOOKA!
KRAK
BOOM
SCREECH!
Kai!
Ungh!
GETTING AWAY!
KAFF! KAFF!
cough! cough!

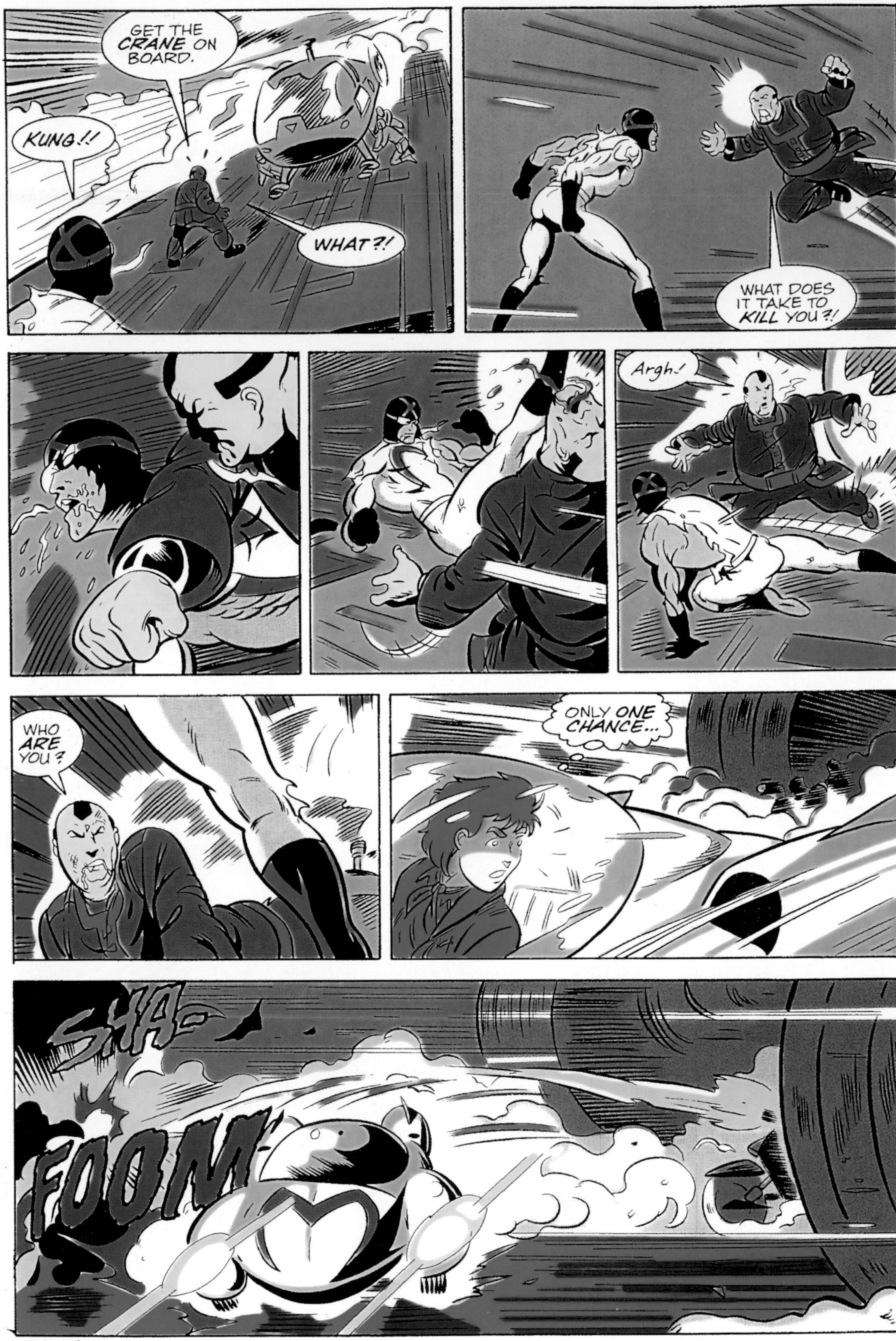
GET THE CRANE ON BOARD.
KUNG!!
WHAT?!
WHAT DOES IT TAKE TO KILL YOU?!
Argh!
WHO ARE YOU?
ONLY ONE CHANCE...
SHA-
FOOM

SPRANG
HISSS!
FLAM!
AAAAAAAAA!
WHAT THE-?
HA HA HA.
FAREWELL, RACER X!
Oh, NO!
PLANG!
LIFT OFF, HURRY!
WE'LL DETONATE THE CAR ONCE WE'RE CLEAR.
KA-WHACK!
Ungh!
DAMN!

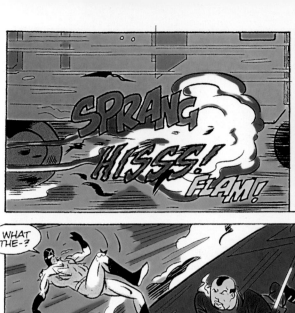

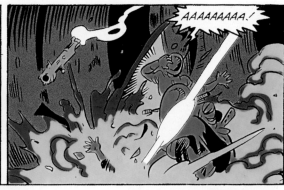

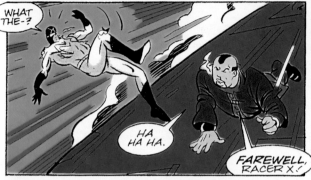

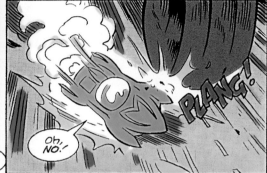

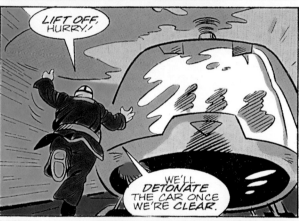

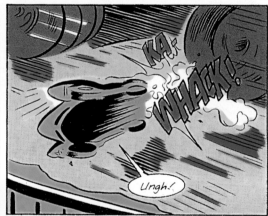

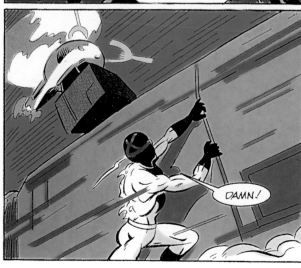

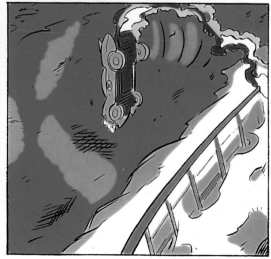

CRASH!!

BLOCK MAY HAVE *SURVIVED* THE FIGHT. WE MUST LEAVE *NO WITNESSES!*

HAND ME THE *REMOTE DETONATOR.*

Ungh!

BEEP BEEP

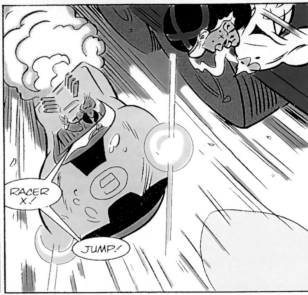

RACER X!

JUMP!

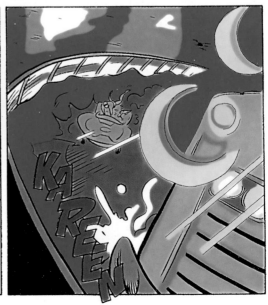

KA REEM

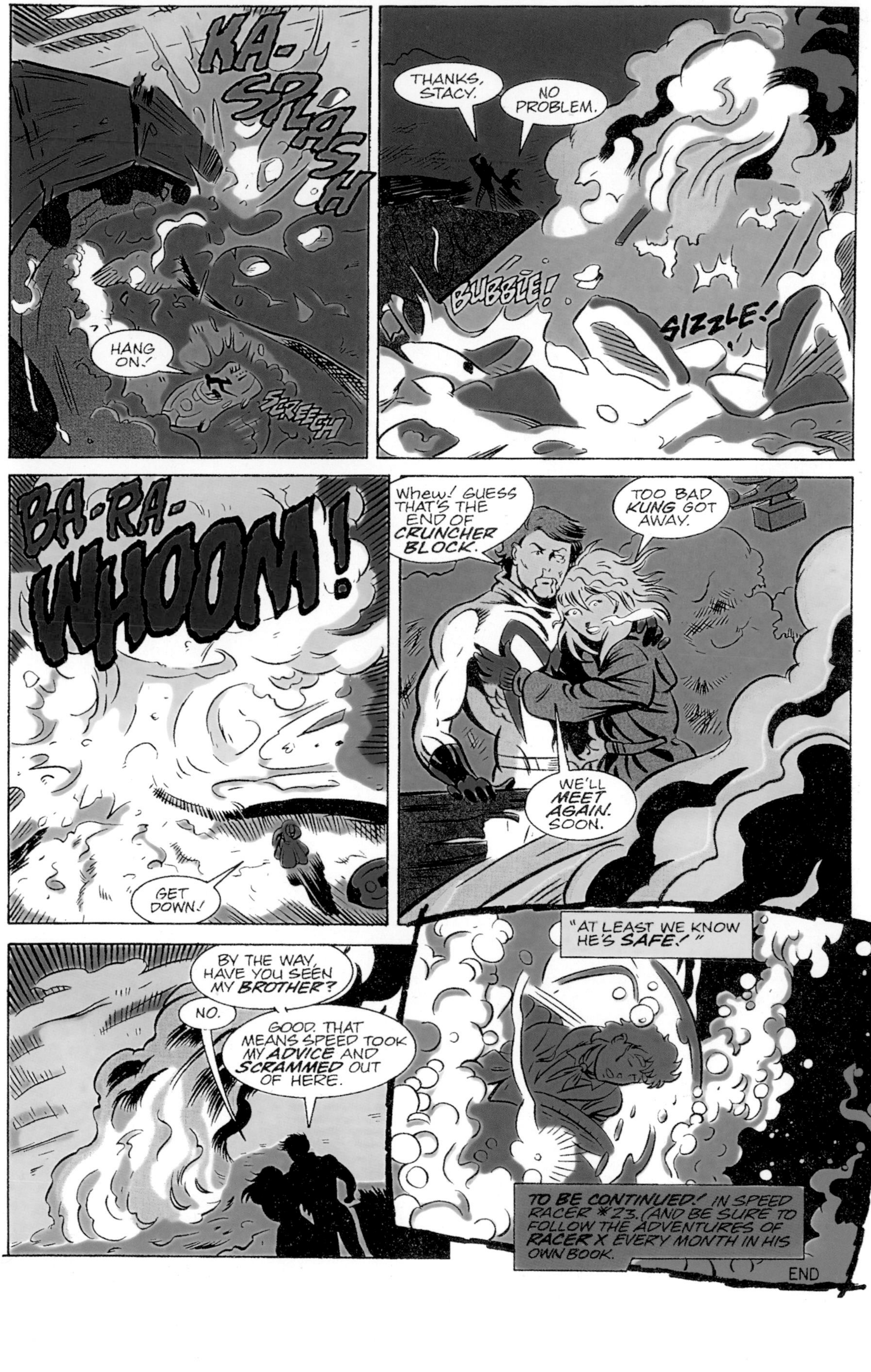
KA-SPLASH
HANG ON!
SCREEECH
THANKS, STACY.
NO PROBLEM.
BUBBLE!
SIZZLE!
BA-RA-WHOOM!
GET DOWN!
Whew! GUESS THAT'S THE END OF CRUNCHER BLOCK.
TOO BAD KUNG GOT AWAY.
WE'LL MEET AGAIN. SOON.
BY THE WAY, HAVE YOU SEEN MY BROTHER?
NO.
GOOD. THAT MEANS SPEED TOOK MY ADVICE AND SCRAMMED OUT OF HERE.
"AT LEAST WE KNOW HE'S SAFE!"
TO BE CONTINUED! IN SPEED RACER #23. (AND BE SURE TO FOLLOW THE ADVENTURES OF RACER X EVERY MONTH IN HIS OWN BOOK.
END

Speed Racer #21

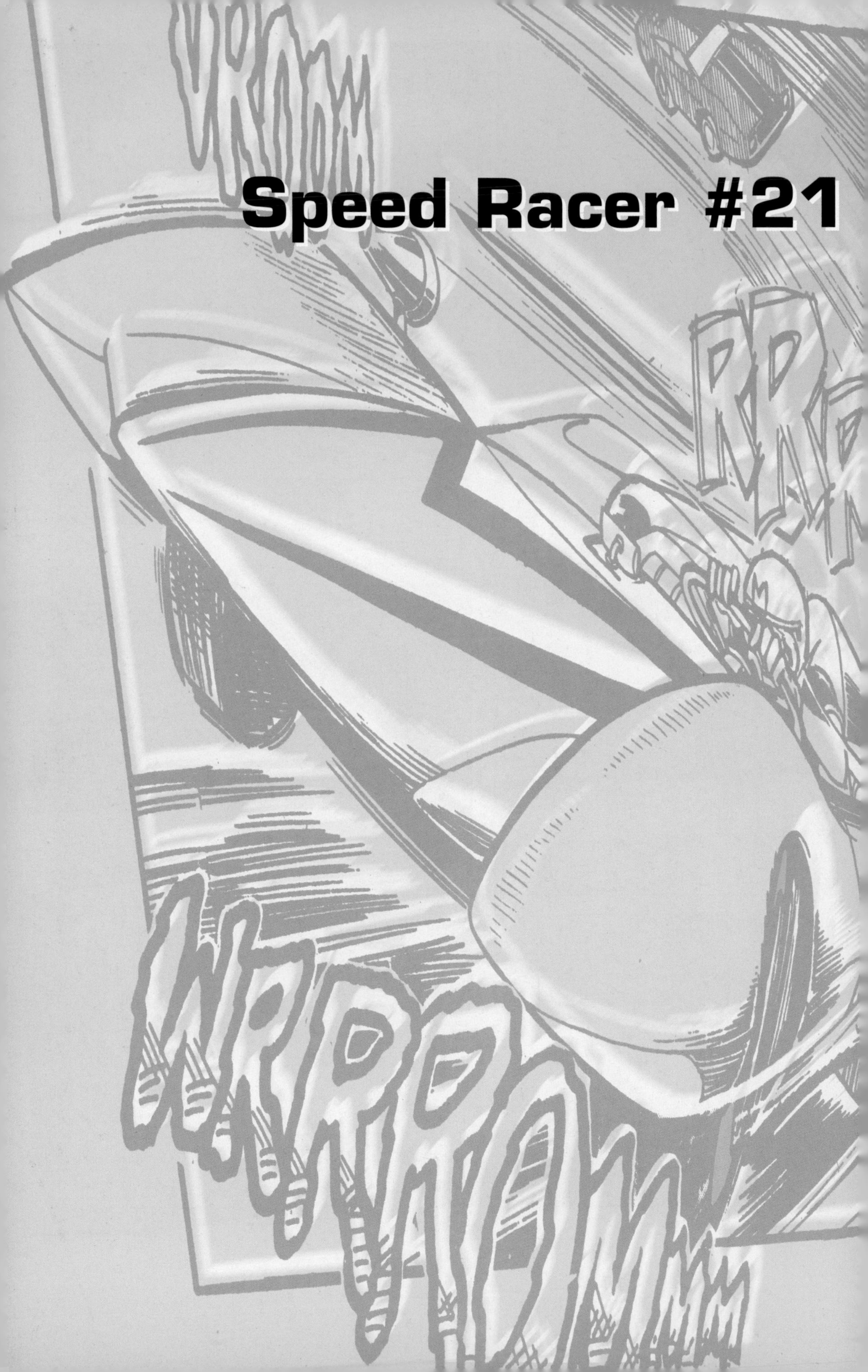

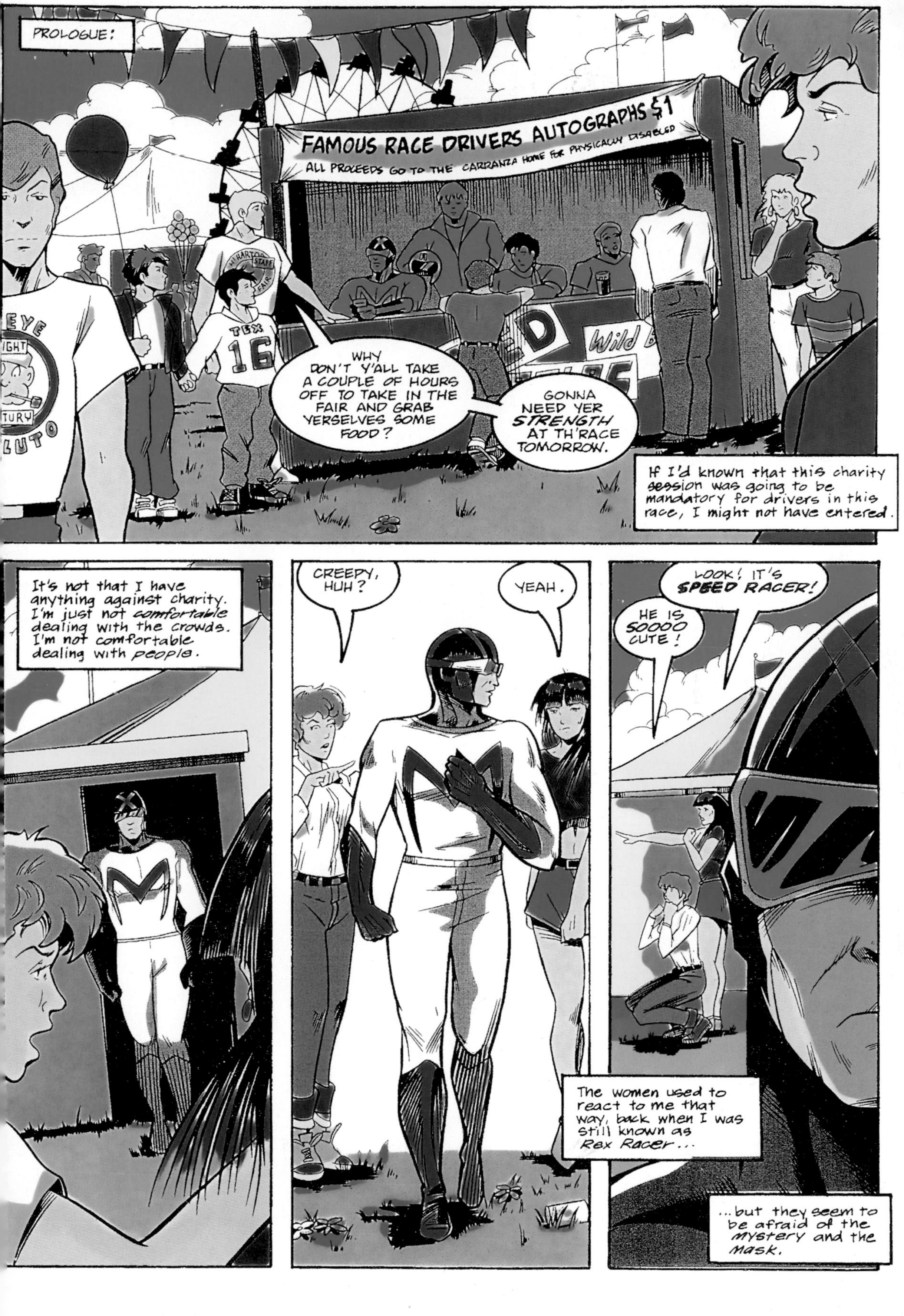
PROLOGUE:
FAMOUS RACE DRIVERS AUTOGRAPHS $1
ALL PROCEEDS GO TO THE CARRANZA HOME FOR PHYSICALLY DISABLED
WHY DON'T Y'ALL TAKE A COUPLE OF HOURS OFF TO TAKE IN THE FAIR AND GRAB YERSELVES SOME FOOD?
GONNA NEED YER STRENGTH AT TH'RACE TOMORROW.
If I'd known that this charity session was going to be mandatory for drivers in this race, I might not have entered.
It's not that I have anything against charity. I'm just not comfortable dealing with the crowds. I'm not comfortable dealing with people.
CREEPY, HUH?
YEAH.
LOOK! IT'S SPEED RACER!
HE IS SOOOO CUTE!
The women used to react to me that way, back when I was still known as Rex Racer...
...but they seem to be afraid of the mystery and the mask.

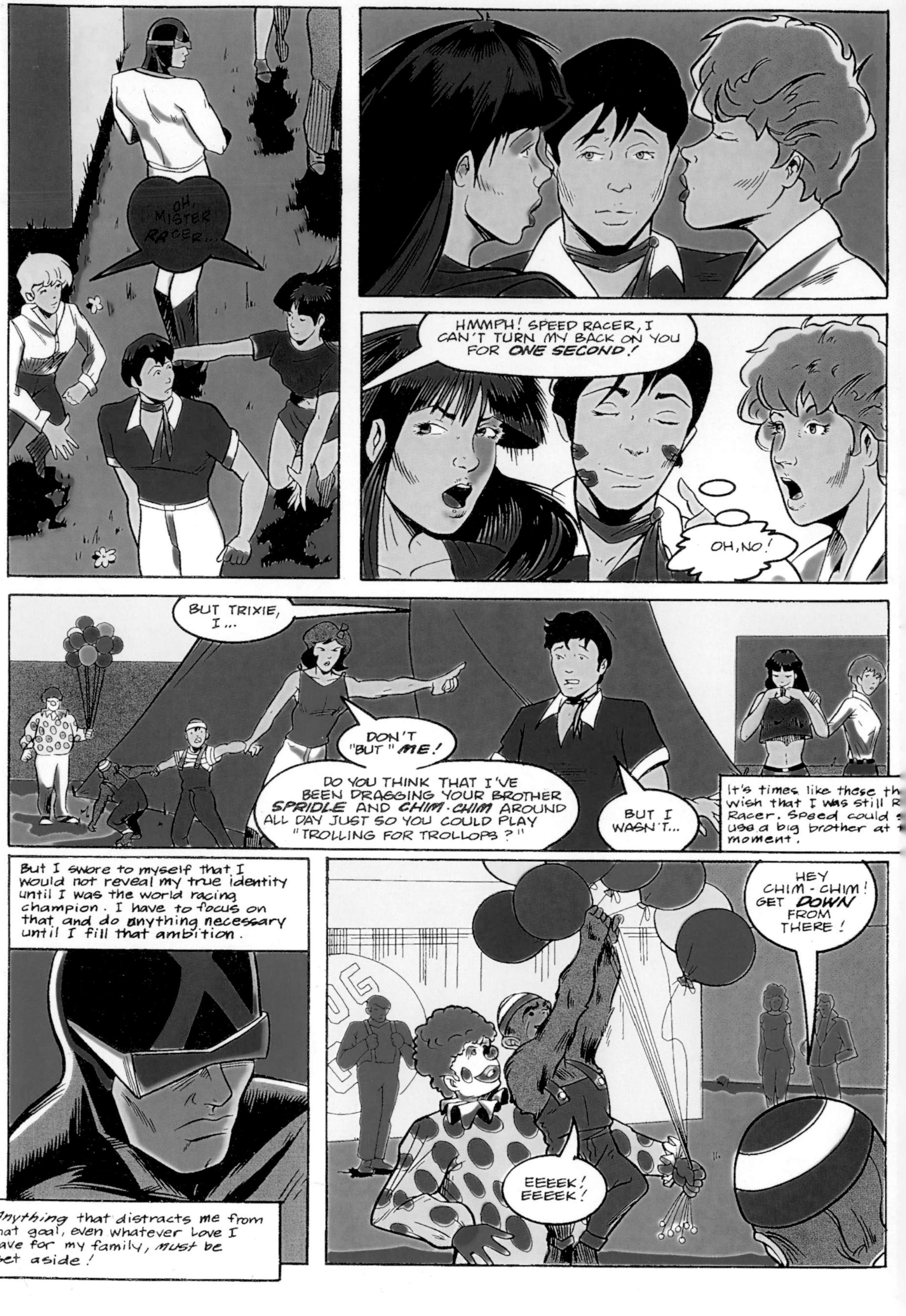
OH, MISTER RACER...
HMMPH! SPEED RACER, I CAN'T TURN MY BACK ON YOU FOR ONE SECOND!
OH, NO!
BUT TRIXIE, I...
DON'T "BUT" ME!
DO YOU THINK THAT I'VE BEEN DRAGGING YOUR BROTHER SPRIDLE AND CHIM-CHIM AROUND ALL DAY JUST SO YOU COULD PLAY "TROLLING FOR TROLLOPS?"
BUT I WASN'T...
But I swore to myself that I would not reveal my true identity until I was the world racing champion. I have to focus on that and do anything necessary until I fill that ambition.
Anything that distracts me from that goal, even whatever love I have for my family, must be set aside!
HEY CHIM-CHIM! GET DOWN FROM THERE!
EEEEK! EEEEK!

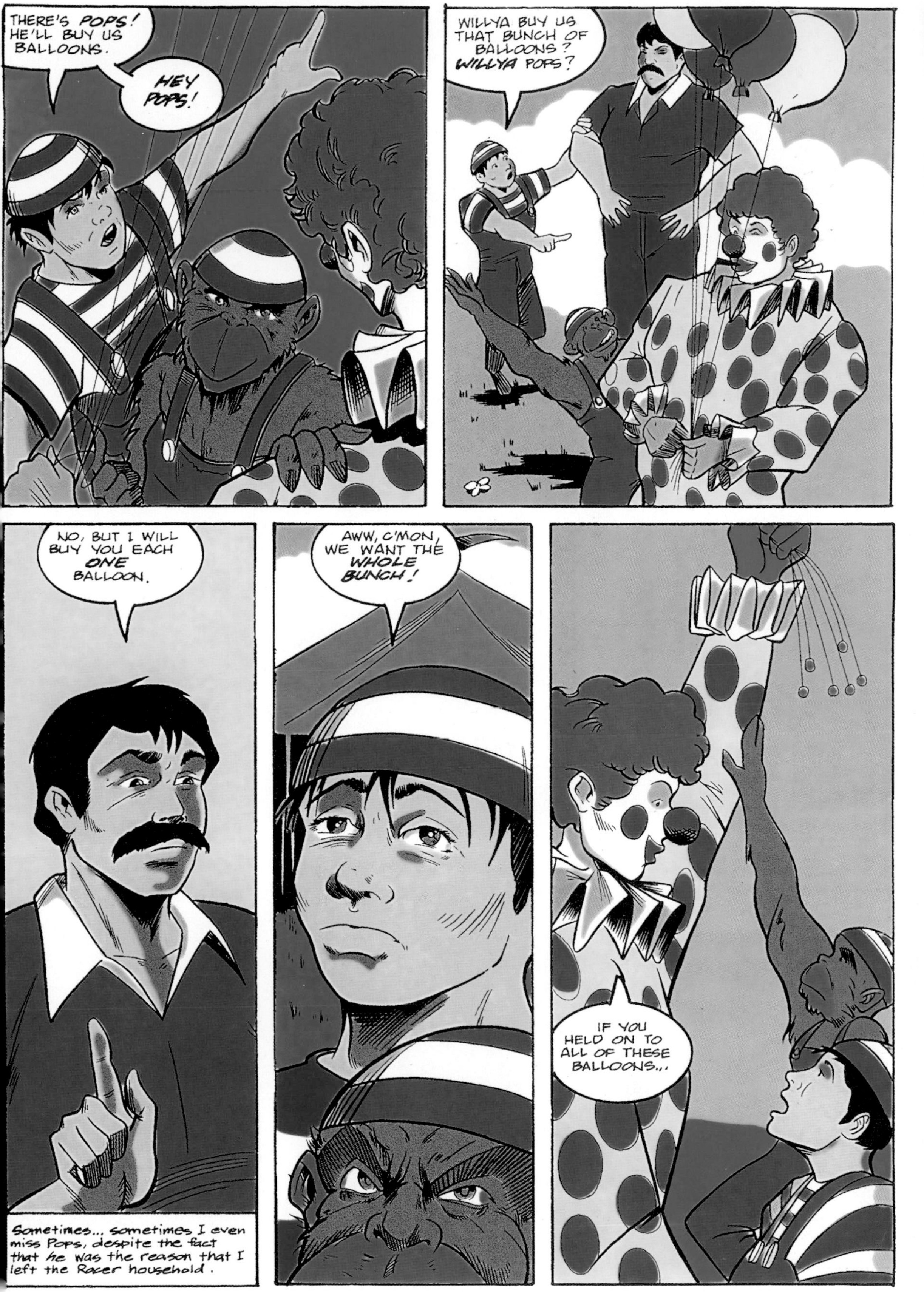

THERE'S POPS! HE'LL BUY US BALLOONS.
HEY POPS!
WILLYA BUY US THAT BUNCH OF BALLOONS? WILLYA POPS?
NO, BUT I WILL BUY YOU EACH ONE BALLOON.
Sometimes... sometimes I even miss Pops, despite the fact that he was the reason that I left the Racer household.
AWW, C'MON, WE WANT THE WHOLE BUNCH!
IF YOU HELD ON TO ALL OF THESE BALLOONS...

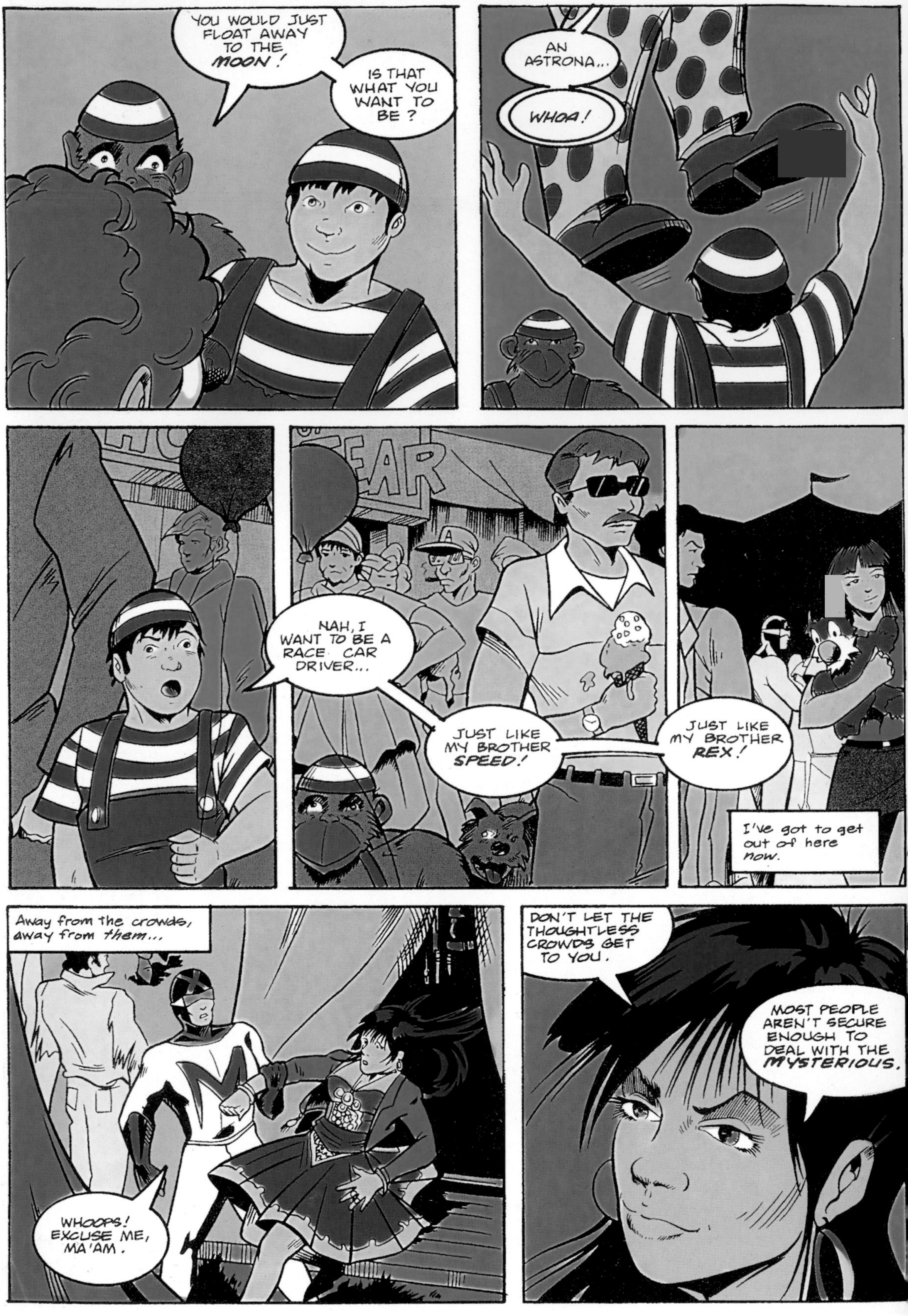
YOU WOULD JUST FLOAT AWAY TO THE MOON!
IS THAT WHAT YOU WANT TO BE?
AN ASTRONA...
WHOA!
NAH, I WANT TO BE A RACE CAR DRIVER...
JUST LIKE MY BROTHER SPEED!
JUST LIKE MY BROTHER REX!
I've got to get out of here now.
Away from the crowds, away from them...
WHOOPS! EXCUSE ME, MA'AM.
DON'T LET THE THOUGHTLESS CROWDS GET TO YOU.
MOST PEOPLE AREN'T SECURE ENOUGH TO DEAL WITH THE MYSTERIOUS.

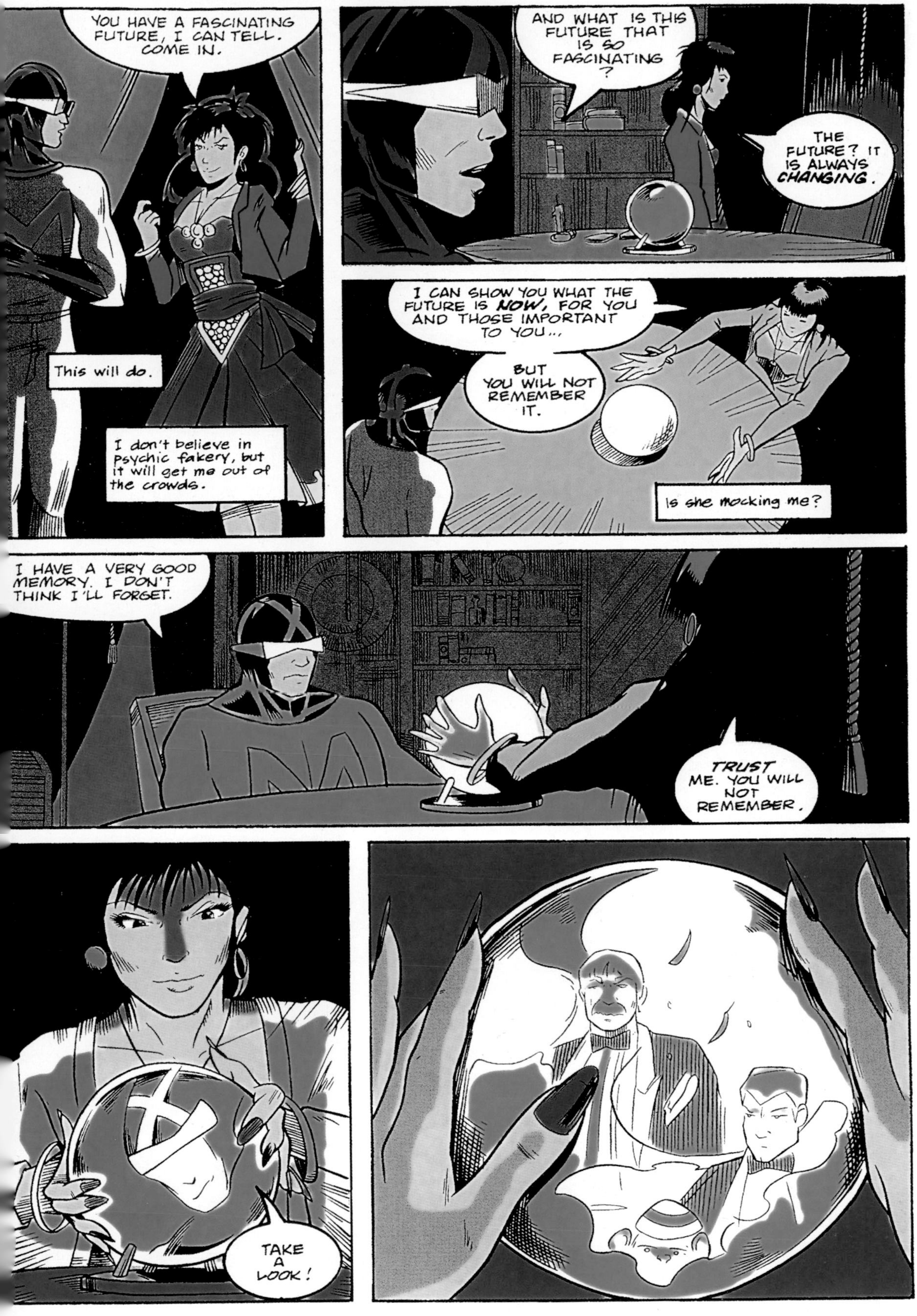
YOU HAVE A FASCINATING FUTURE, I CAN TELL. COME IN.
This will do.
I don't believe in psychic fakery, but it will get me out of the crowds.
AND WHAT IS THIS FUTURE THAT IS SO FASCINATING?
THE FUTURE? IT IS ALWAYS CHANGING.
I CAN SHOW YOU WHAT THE FUTURE IS NOW, FOR YOU AND THOSE IMPORTANT TO YOU...
BUT YOU WILL NOT REMEMBER IT.
Is she mocking me?
I HAVE A VERY GOOD MEMORY. I DON'T THINK I'LL FORGET.
TRUST ME. YOU WILL NOT REMEMBER.
TAKE A LOOK!

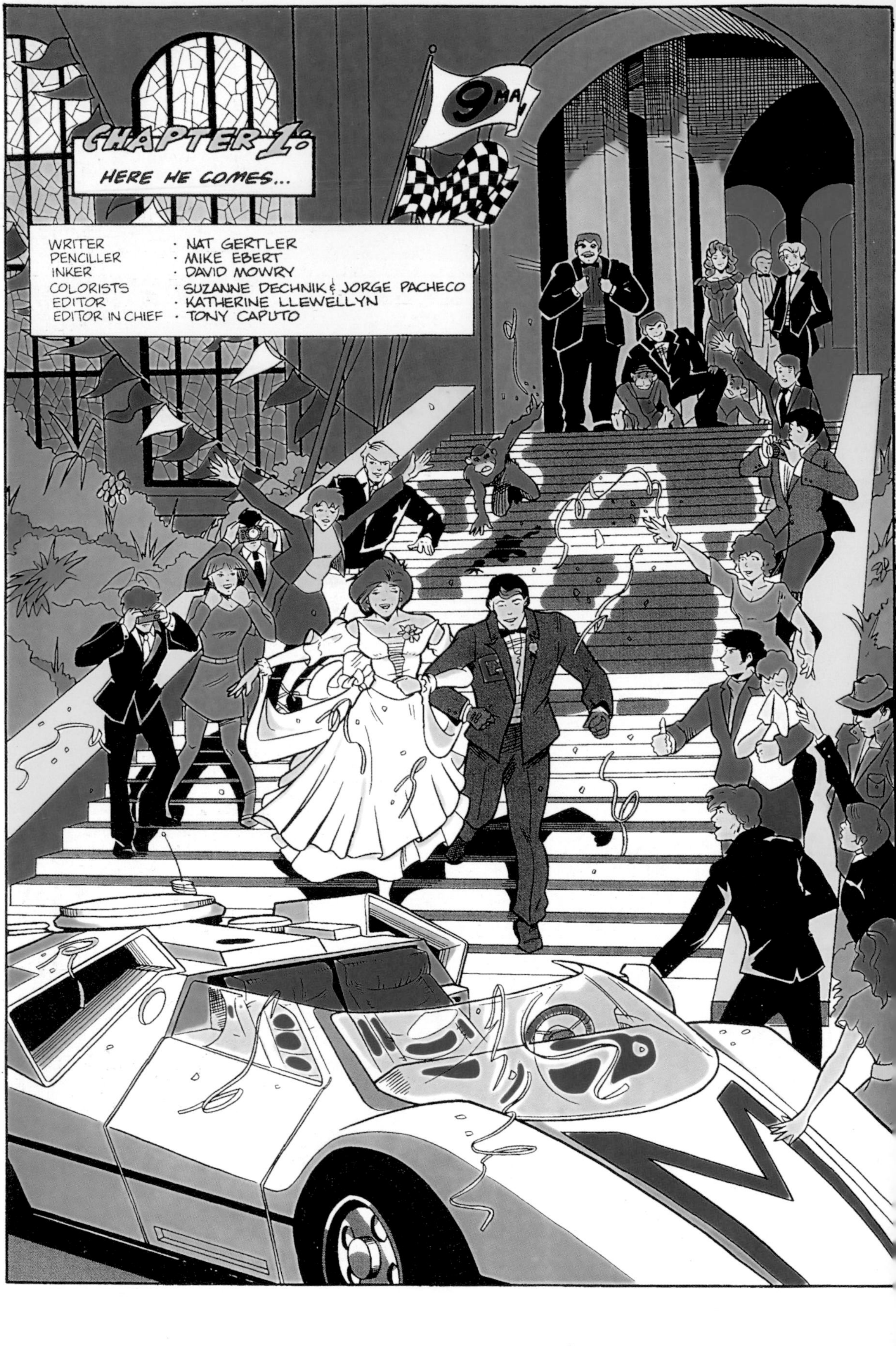
CHAPTER 1:
HERE HE COMES...
WRITER · NAT GERTLER
PENCILLER · MIKE EBERT
INKER · DAVID MOWRY
COLORISTS · SUZANNE DECHNIK & JORGE PACHECO
EDITOR · KATHERINE LLEWELLYN
EDITOR IN CHIEF · TONY CAPUTO

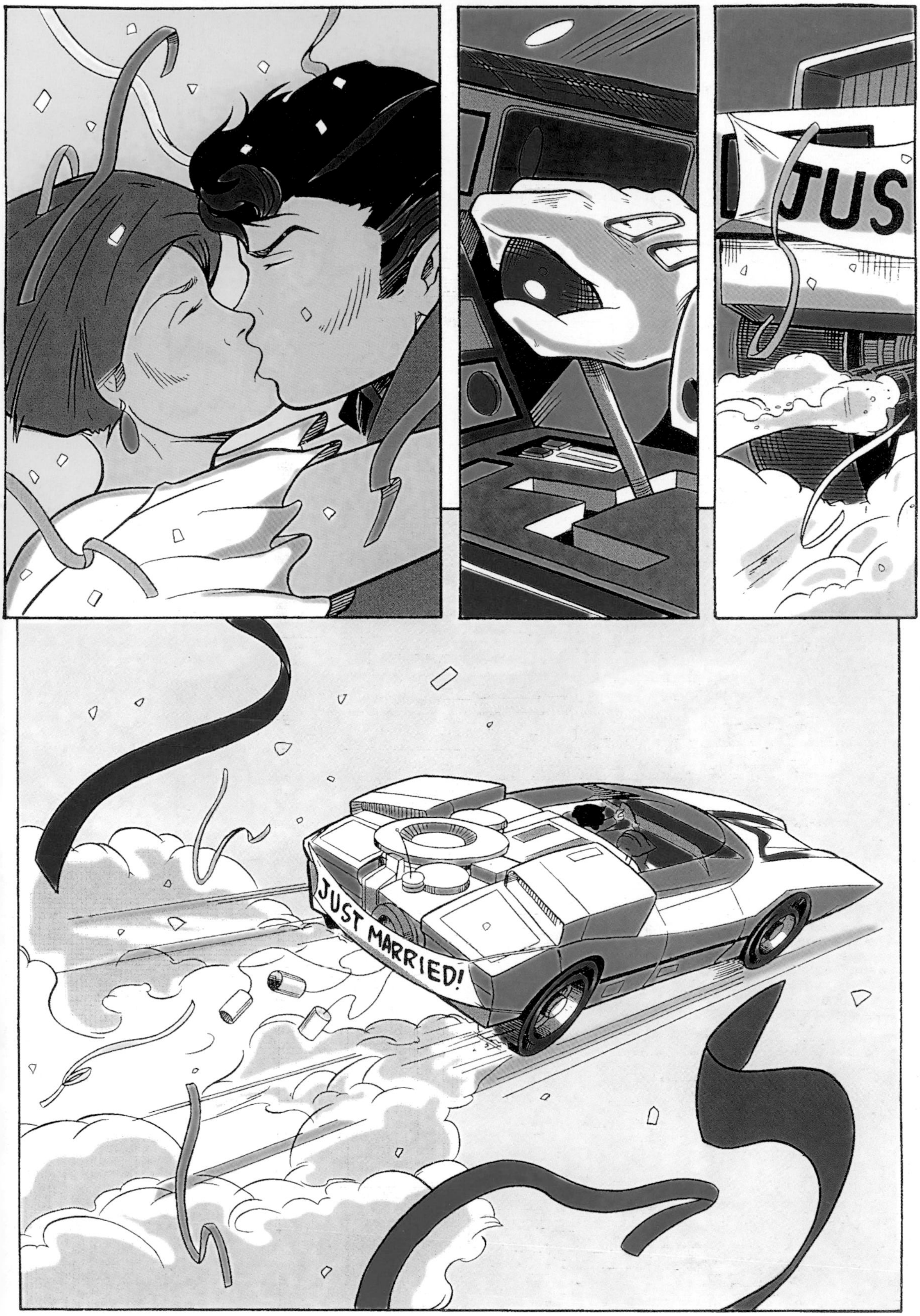
JUS
JUST MARRIED!

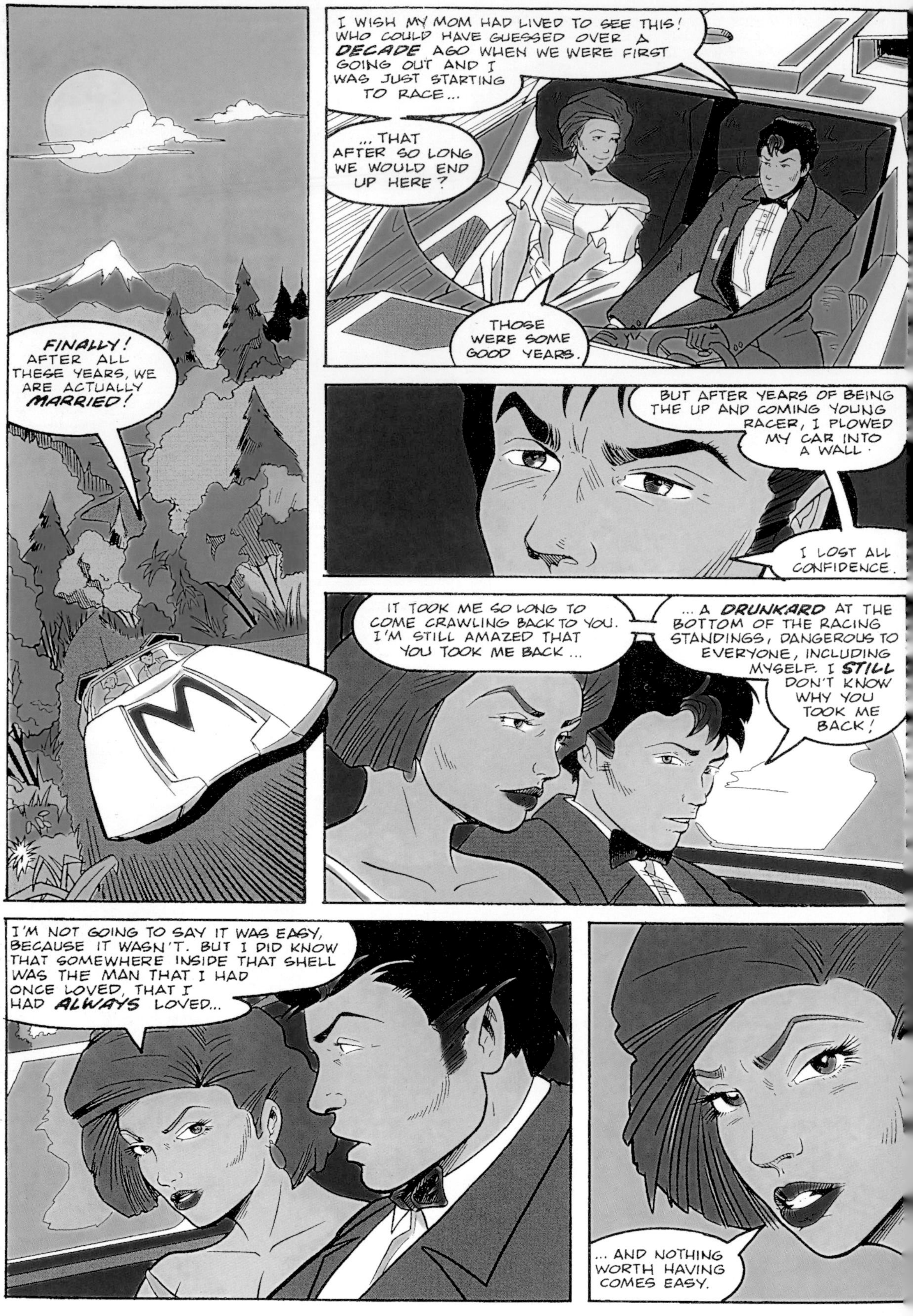
FINALLY! AFTER ALL THESE YEARS, WE ARE ACTUALLY MARRIED!
I WISH MY MOM HAD LIVED TO SEE THIS! WHO COULD HAVE GUESSED OVER A DECADE AGO WHEN WE WERE FIRST GOING OUT AND I WAS JUST STARTING TO RACE...
... THAT AFTER SO LONG WE WOULD END UP HERE?
THOSE WERE SOME GOOD YEARS.
BUT AFTER YEARS OF BEING THE UP AND COMING YOUNG RACER, I PLOWED MY CAR INTO A WALL.
I LOST ALL CONFIDENCE.
... A DRUNKARD AT THE BOTTOM OF THE RACING STANDINGS, DANGEROUS TO EVERYONE, INCLUDING MYSELF. I STILL DON'T KNOW WHY YOU TOOK ME BACK!
IT TOOK ME SO LONG TO COME CRAWLING BACK TO YOU. I'M STILL AMAZED THAT YOU TOOK ME BACK...
I'M NOT GOING TO SAY IT WAS EASY, BECAUSE IT WASN'T. BUT I DID KNOW THAT SOMEWHERE INSIDE THAT SHELL WAS THE MAN THAT I HAD ONCE LOVED, THAT I HAD ALWAYS LOVED...
... AND NOTHING WORTH HAVING COMES EASY.

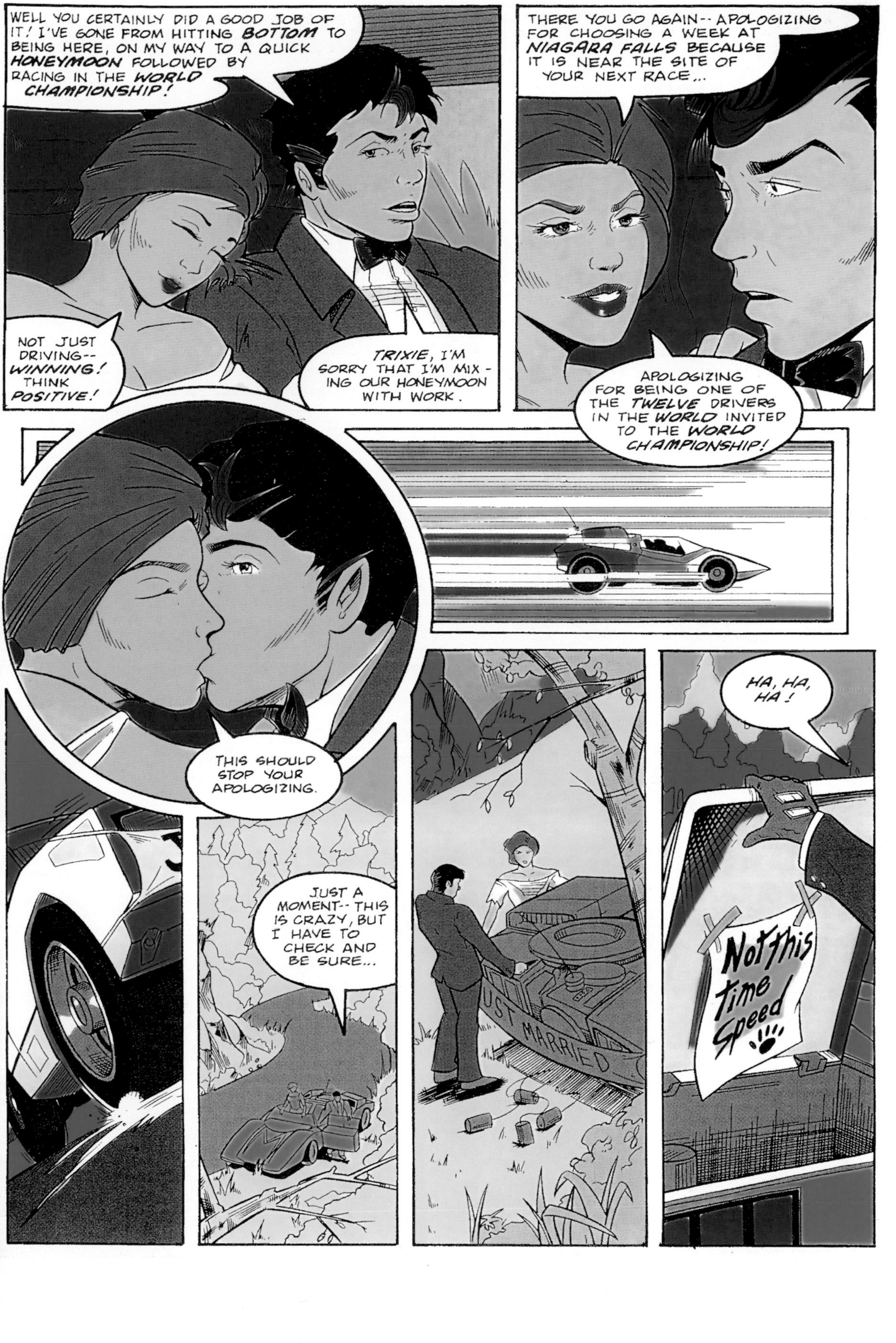

WELL YOU CERTAINLY DID A GOOD JOB OF IT! I'VE GONE FROM HITTING BOTTOM TO BEING HERE, ON MY WAY TO A QUICK HONEYMOON FOLLOWED BY RACING IN THE WORLD CHAMPIONSHIP!
NOT JUST DRIVING-- WINNING! THINK POSITIVE!
TRIXIE, I'M SORRY THAT I'M MIXING OUR HONEYMOON WITH WORK.
THERE YOU GO AGAIN-- APOLOGIZING FOR CHOOSING A WEEK AT NIAGARA FALLS BECAUSE IT IS NEAR THE SITE OF YOUR NEXT RACE...
APOLOGIZING FOR BEING ONE OF THE TWELVE DRIVERS IN THE WORLD INVITED TO THE WORLD CHAMPIONSHIP!
THIS SHOULD STOP YOUR APOLOGIZING.
JUST A MOMENT-- THIS IS CRAZY, BUT I HAVE TO CHECK AND BE SURE...
UST MARRIED
HA, HA, HA!
Not this time Speed

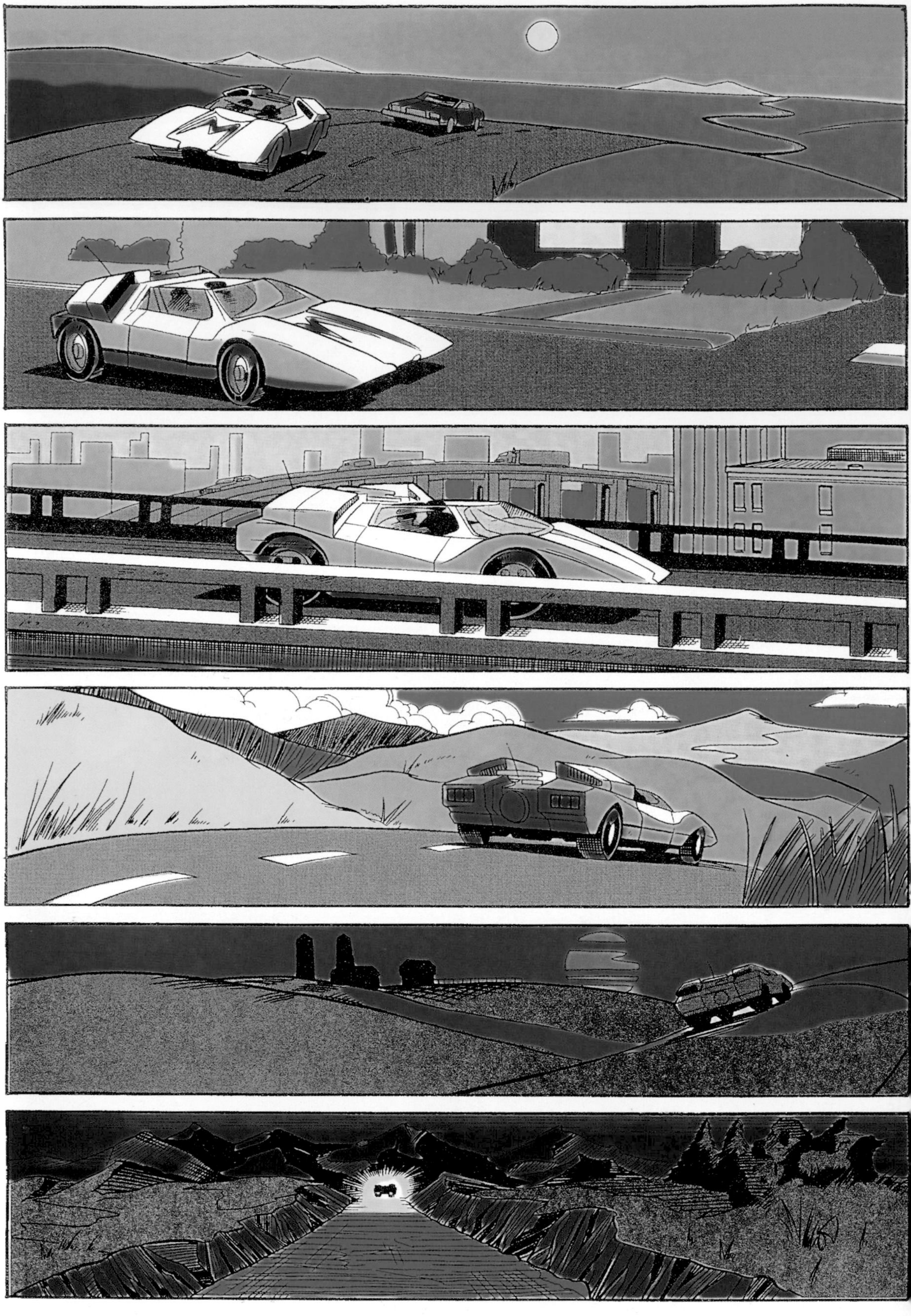

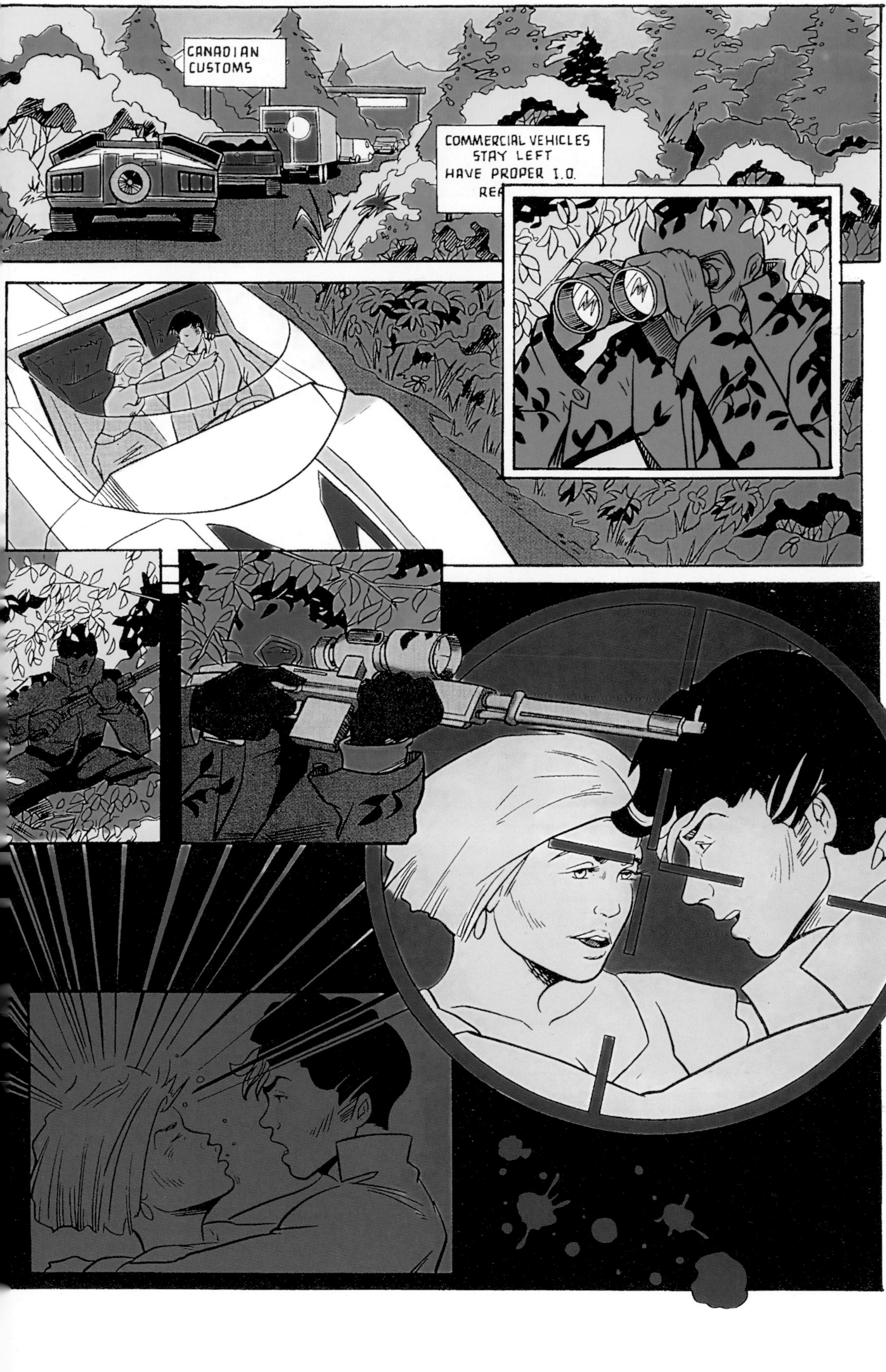
CANADIAN
CUSTOMS
TRUCK
COMMERCIAL VEHICLES
STAY LEFT
HAVE PROPER I.D.
REA

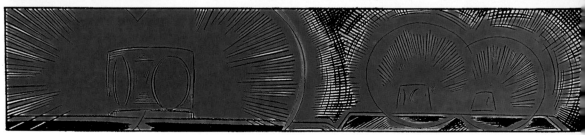

CHAPTER 2:
A DEMON ON WHEELS

MAHOOCH MEMORIAL HOSPITAL

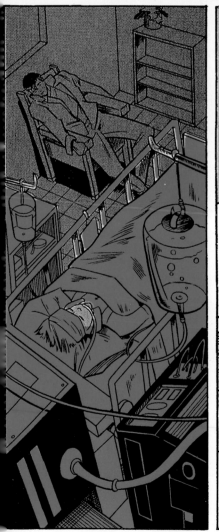

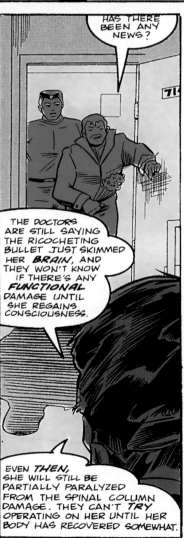

HAS THERE BEEN ANY NEWS?

THE DOCTORS ARE STILL SAYING THE RICOCHETING BULLET JUST SKIMMED HER *BRAIN*, AND THEY WON'T KNOW IF THERE'S ANY *FUNCTIONAL* DAMAGE UNTIL SHE REGAINS CONSCIOUSNESS.

EVEN *THEN*, SHE WILL STILL BE PARTIALLY PARALYZED FROM THE SPINAL COLUMN DAMAGE. THEY CAN'T *TRY* OPERATING ON HER UNTIL HER BODY HAS RECOVERED SOMEWHAT.

AND IT'S ALL *MY* FAULT! THAT BULLET *MUST* HAVE MEANT FOR ME! IF I HADN'T...

...IF I HADN'T...

71

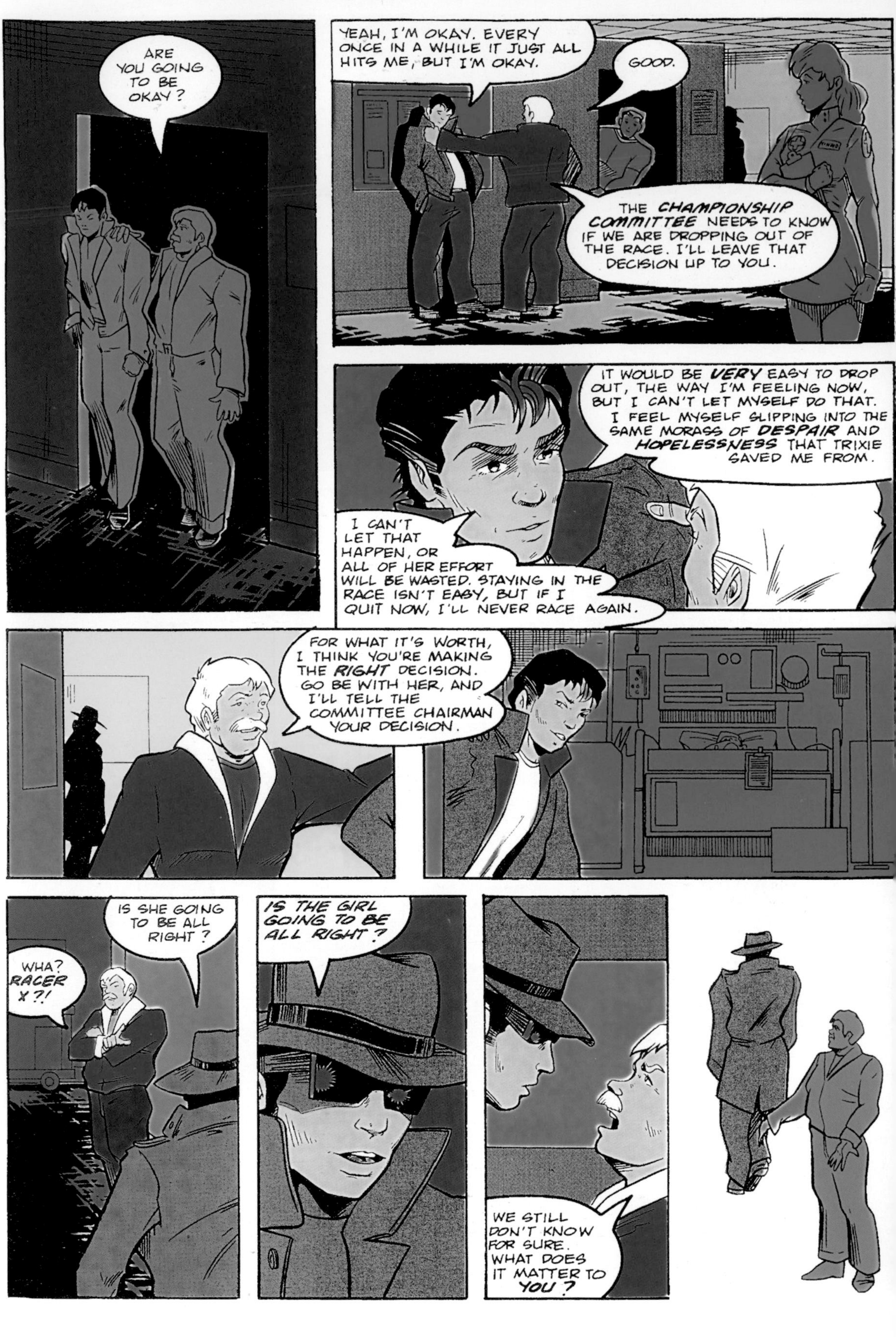

ARE YOU GOING TO BE OKAY?
YEAH, I'M OKAY. EVERY ONCE IN A WHILE IT JUST ALL HITS ME, BUT I'M OKAY.
GOOD.
THE CHAMPIONSHIP COMMITTEE NEEDS TO KNOW IF WE ARE DROPPING OUT OF THE RACE. I'LL LEAVE THAT DECISION UP TO YOU.
IT WOULD BE VERY EASY TO DROP OUT, THE WAY I'M FEELING NOW, BUT I CAN'T LET MYSELF DO THAT. I FEEL MYSELF SLIPPING INTO THE SAME MORASS OF DESPAIR AND HOPELESSNESS THAT TRIXIE SAVED ME FROM.
I CAN'T LET THAT HAPPEN, OR ALL OF HER EFFORT WILL BE WASTED. STAYING IN THE RACE ISN'T EASY, BUT IF I QUIT NOW, I'LL NEVER RACE AGAIN.
FOR WHAT IT'S WORTH, I THINK YOU'RE MAKING THE RIGHT DECISION. GO BE WITH HER, AND I'LL TELL THE COMMITTEE CHAIRMAN YOUR DECISION.
IS SHE GOING TO BE ALL RIGHT?
WHA? RACER X?!
IS THE GIRL GOING TO BE ALL RIGHT?
WE STILL DON'T KNOW FOR SURE. WHAT DOES IT MATTER TO YOU?

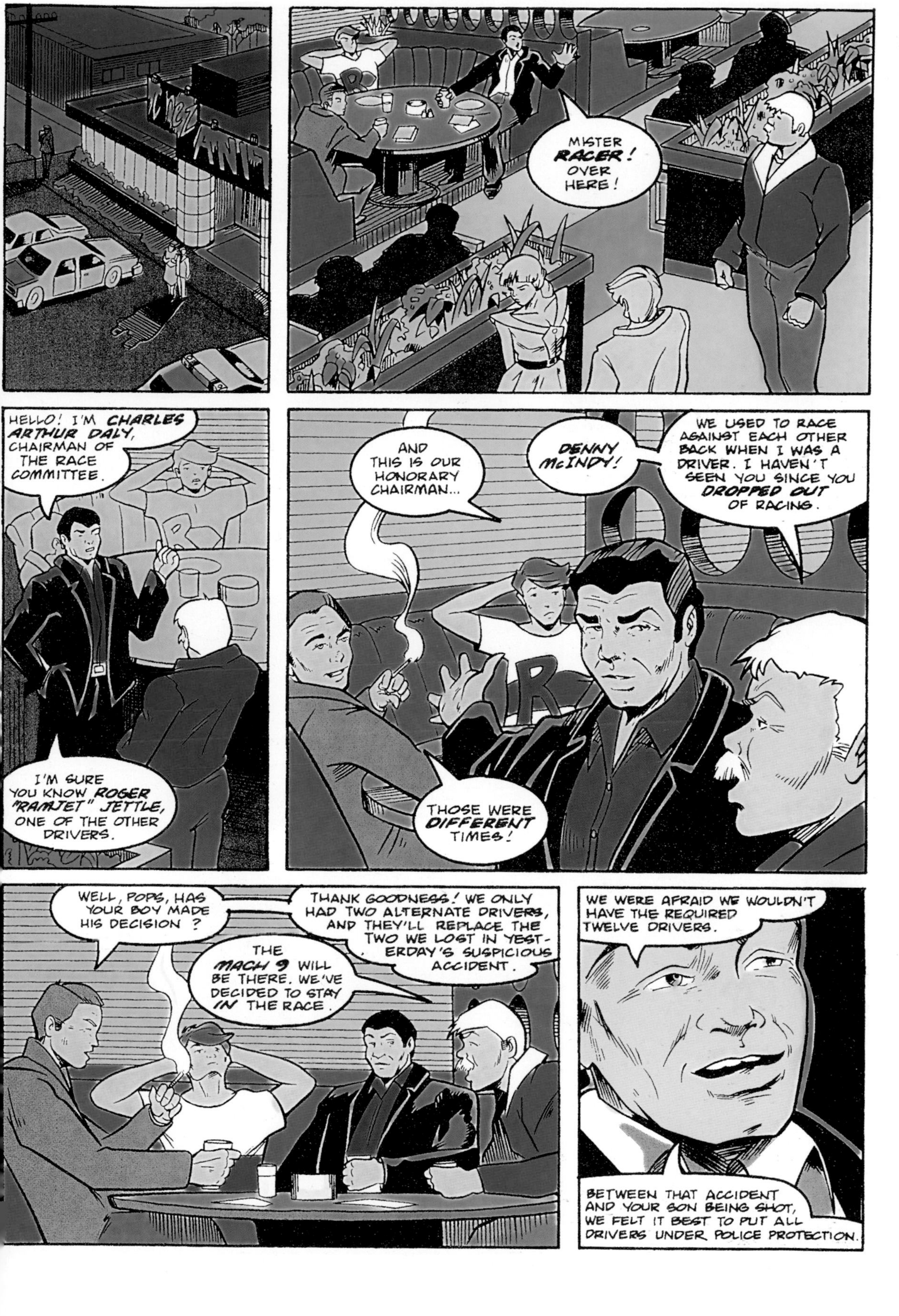
MISTER RACER! OVER HERE!
HELLO! I'M CHARLES ARTHUR DALY, CHAIRMAN OF THE RACE COMMITTEE.
I'M SURE YOU KNOW ROGER "RAMJET" JETTLE, ONE OF THE OTHER DRIVERS.
AND THIS IS OUR HONORARY CHAIRMAN...
DENNY McINDY!
WE USED TO RACE AGAINST EACH OTHER BACK WHEN I WAS A DRIVER. I HAVEN'T SEEN YOU SINCE YOU DROPPED OUT OF RACING.
THOSE WERE DIFFERENT TIMES!
WELL, POPS, HAS YOUR BOY MADE HIS DECISION ?
THE MACH 9 WILL BE THERE. WE'VE DECIDED TO STAY IN THE RACE.
THANK GOODNESS! WE ONLY HAD TWO ALTERNATE DRIVERS, AND THEY'LL REPLACE THE TWO WE LOST IN YESTERDAY'S SUSPICIOUS ACCIDENT.
WE WERE AFRAID WE WOULDN'T HAVE THE REQUIRED TWELVE DRIVERS.
BETWEEN THAT ACCIDENT AND YOUR SON BEING SHOT, WE FELT IT BEST TO PUT ALL DRIVERS UNDER POLICE PROTECTION.

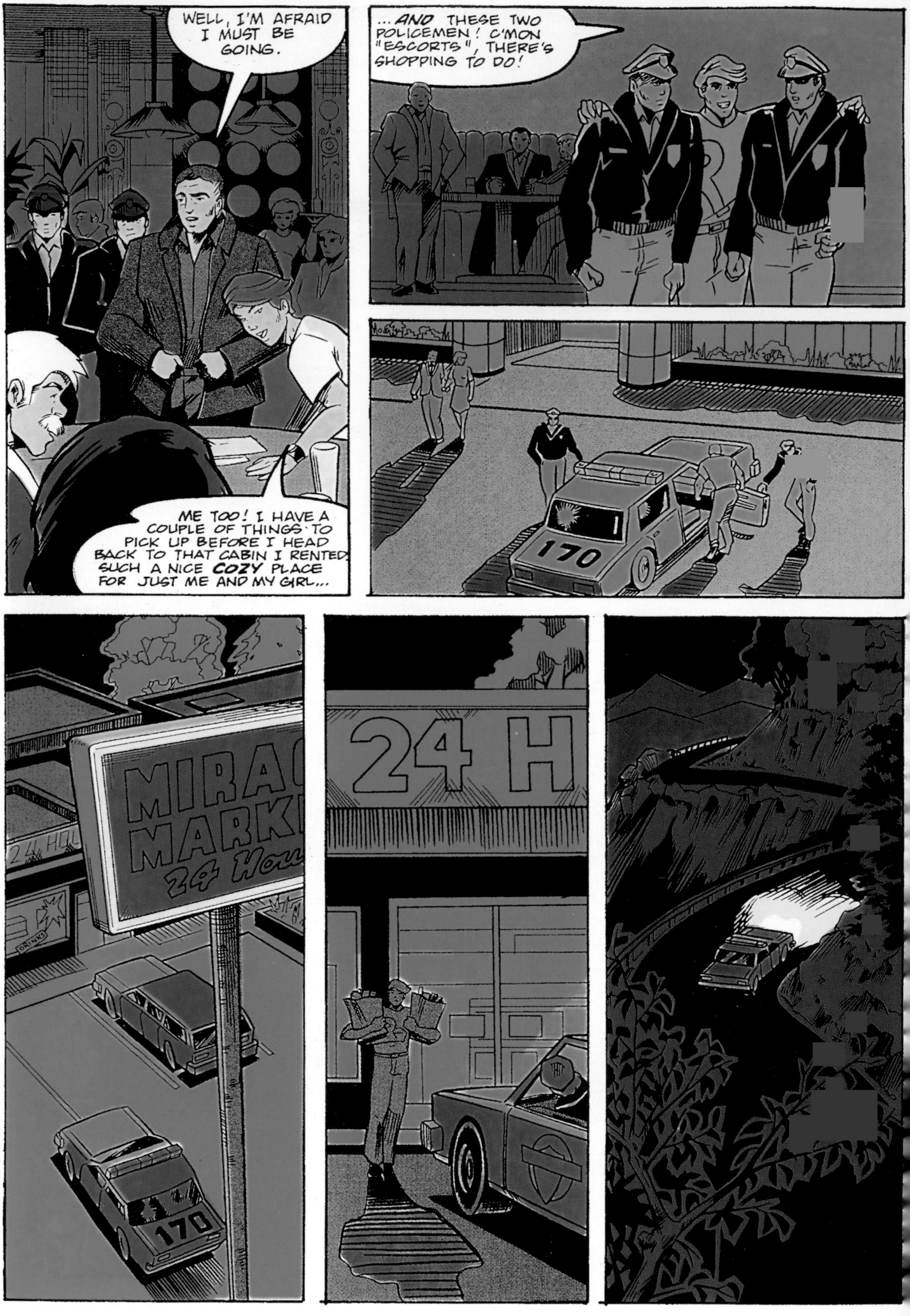
WELL, I'M AFRAID I MUST BE GOING.
ME TOO! I HAVE A COUPLE OF THINGS TO PICK UP BEFORE I HEAD BACK TO THAT CABIN I RENTED. SUCH A NICE COZY PLACE FOR JUST ME AND MY GIRL...
...AND THESE TWO POLICEMEN! C'MON "ESCORTS", THERE'S SHOPPING TO DO!
170
170

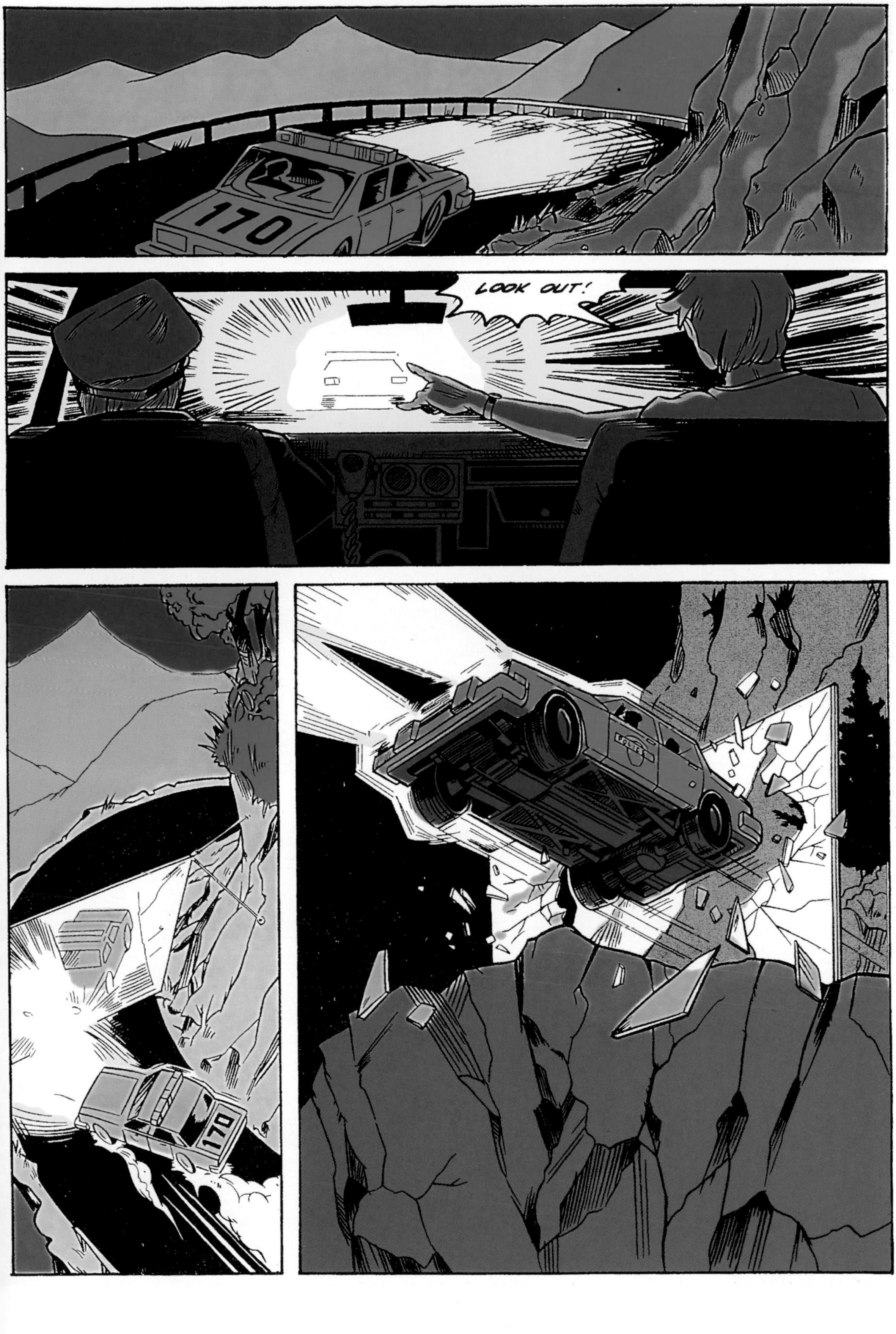
170
LOOK OUT!
170
POLICE

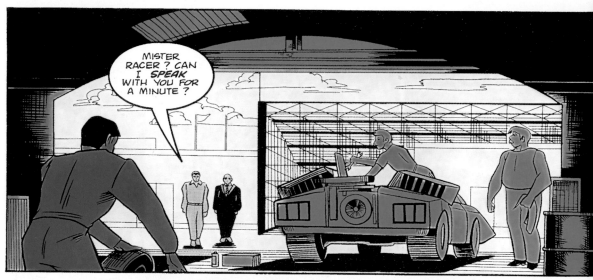

MISTER RACER? CAN I *SPEAK* WITH YOU FOR A MINUTE?

THIS IS *BRENDON PISTON*, MAIN BACKER OF THE *RAMJET RACING TEAM*. I SUPPOSE YOU HEARD ABOUT WHAT HAPPENED TO RAMJET JETTLE?

YES, FRANKLY, THIS ALL HAS ME *VERY* WORRIED.

IT HAS *EVERYONE* WORRIED. THE POLICE HAVE *DOUBLED* THE MANPOWER ON THE INVESTIGATION. WE HOPE TO CATCH THE CULPRIT BEFORE THE RACE.

WE WERE WORRIED THAT WE WOULDN'T HAVE THE FULL FIELD OF *TWELVE* THAT THE REGULATIONS REQUIRE, BUT THE RAMJET TEAM FOUND A REPLACEMENT DRIVER.

OH, REALLY? WHERE DID THEY FIND A SUITABLE DRIVER? MOST OF THE BETTER DRIVERS ARE IN *BRAZIL* FOR THE CONSOLATION RACE.

LET ME SHOW YOU.

THERE'S THE "NEW" DRIVER.

McINDY? YOU'RE COMING OUT OF RETIREMENT?

ABSOLUTELY. I WAS TIRED OF RUNNING A SERVICE STATION, WATCHING *KIDS* WIN RACES. I WANTED ONE MORE CHANCE TO SHOW WHAT *I* CAN DO!

ARE YOU READY FOR THIS? RACING HAS *CHANGED* AN AWFUL LOT SINCE WHEN *WE* USED TO RACE.

YOU BET IT'S CHANGED! NOW A DRIVER HAS SO MANY INCREDIBLE TOOLS TO HELP HIM DO HIS JOB BETTER!

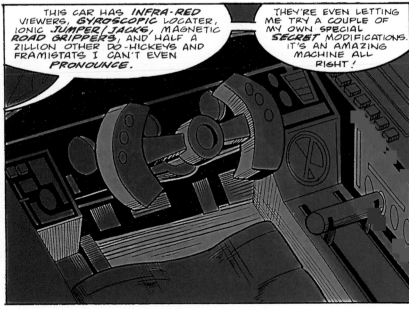

THIS CAR HAS *INFRA-RED* VIEWERS, *GYROSCOPIC* LOCATER, IONIC *JUMPER/JACKS*, MAGNETIC *ROAD GRIPPERS*, AND HALF A ZILLION OTHER DO-HICKEYS AND FRAMISTATS I CAN'T EVEN *PRONOUNCE*.

THEY'RE EVEN LETTING ME TRY A COUPLE OF MY OWN SPECIAL *SECRET* MODIFICATIONS. IT'S AN AMAZING MACHINE ALL RIGHT!

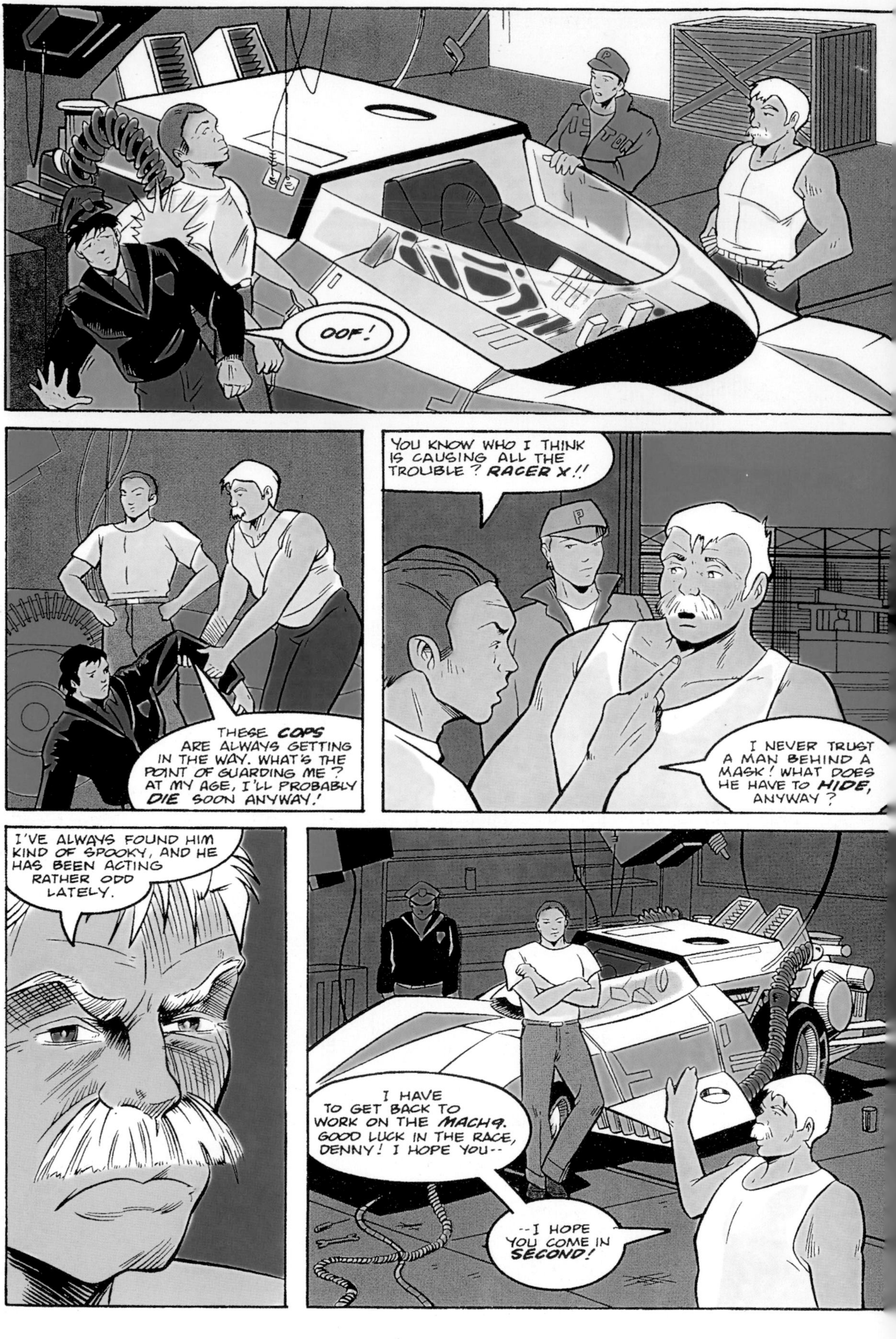
OOF!
THESE COPS ARE ALWAYS GETTING IN THE WAY. WHAT'S THE POINT OF GUARDING ME? AT MY AGE, I'LL PROBABLY DIE SOON ANYWAY!
YOU KNOW WHO I THINK IS CAUSING ALL THE TROUBLE? RACER X!!
I NEVER TRUST A MAN BEHIND A MASK! WHAT DOES HE HAVE TO HIDE, ANYWAY?
I'VE ALWAYS FOUND HIM KIND OF SPOOKY, AND HE HAS BEEN ACTING RATHER ODD LATELY.
I HAVE TO GET BACK TO WORK ON THE MACH9. GOOD LUCK IN THE RACE, DENNY! I HOPE YOU--
--I HOPE YOU COME IN SECOND!

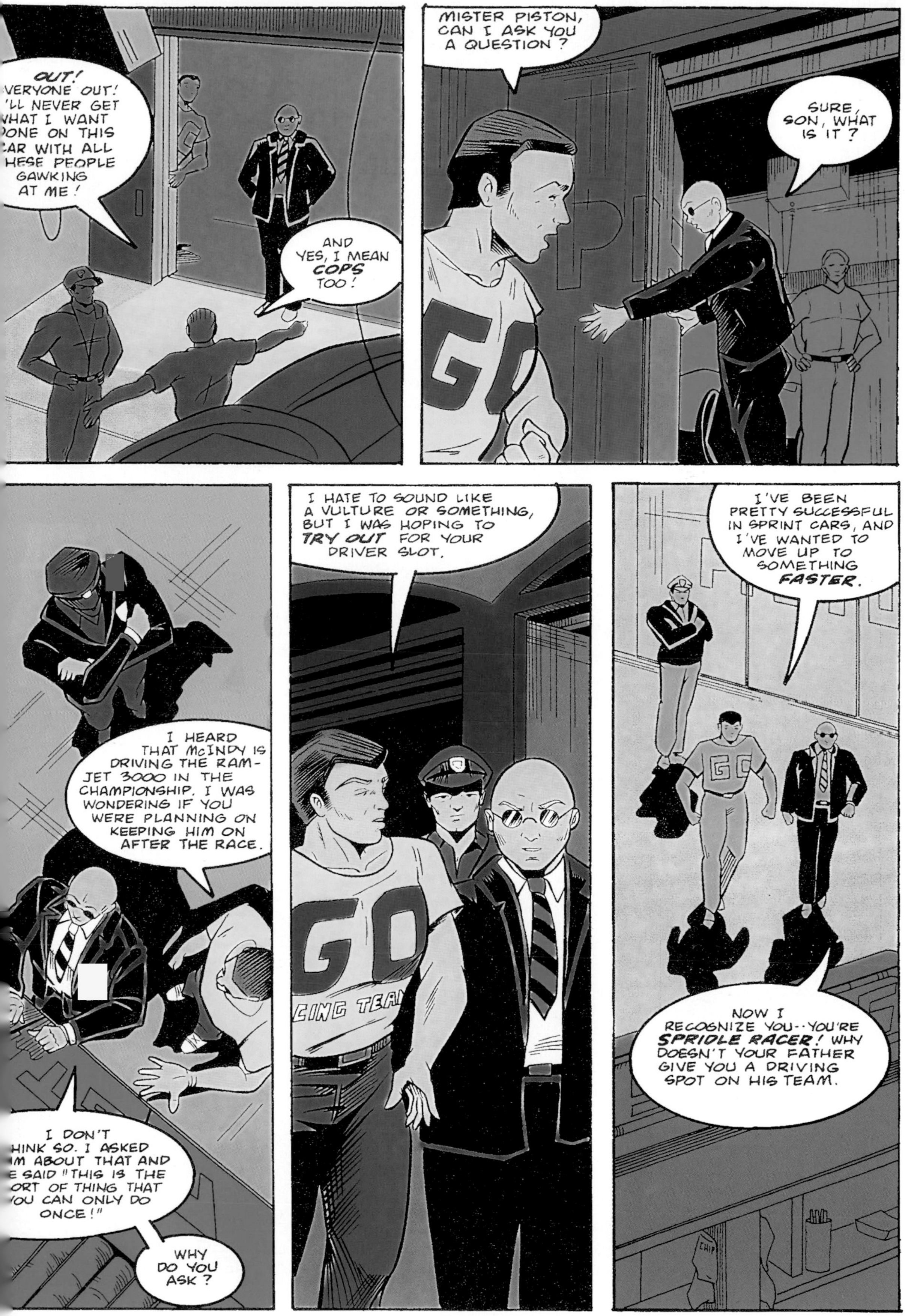
OUT! VERYONE OUT! 'LL NEVER GET VHAT I WANT ONE ON THIS AR WITH ALL HESE PEOPLE GAWKING AT ME!
AND YES, I MEAN COPS TOO!
MISTER PISTON, CAN I ASK YOU A QUESTION?
SURE, SON, WHAT IS IT?
I HEARD THAT McINDY IS DRIVING THE RAM-JET 3000 IN THE CHAMPIONSHIP. I WAS WONDERING IF YOU WERE PLANNING ON KEEPING HIM ON AFTER THE RACE.
I DON'T HINK SO. I ASKED M ABOUT THAT AND E SAID "THIS IS THE ORT OF THING THAT OU CAN ONLY DO ONCE!"
WHY DO YOU ASK?
I HATE TO SOUND LIKE A VULTURE OR SOMETHING, BUT I WAS HOPING TO TRY OUT FOR YOUR DRIVER SLOT.
I'VE BEEN PRETTY SUCCESSFUL IN SPRINT CARS, AND I'VE WANTED TO MOVE UP TO SOMETHING FASTER.
NOW I RECOGNIZE YOU--YOU'RE SPRIDLE RACER! WHY DOESN'T YOUR FATHER GIVE YOU A DRIVING SPOT ON HIS TEAM.

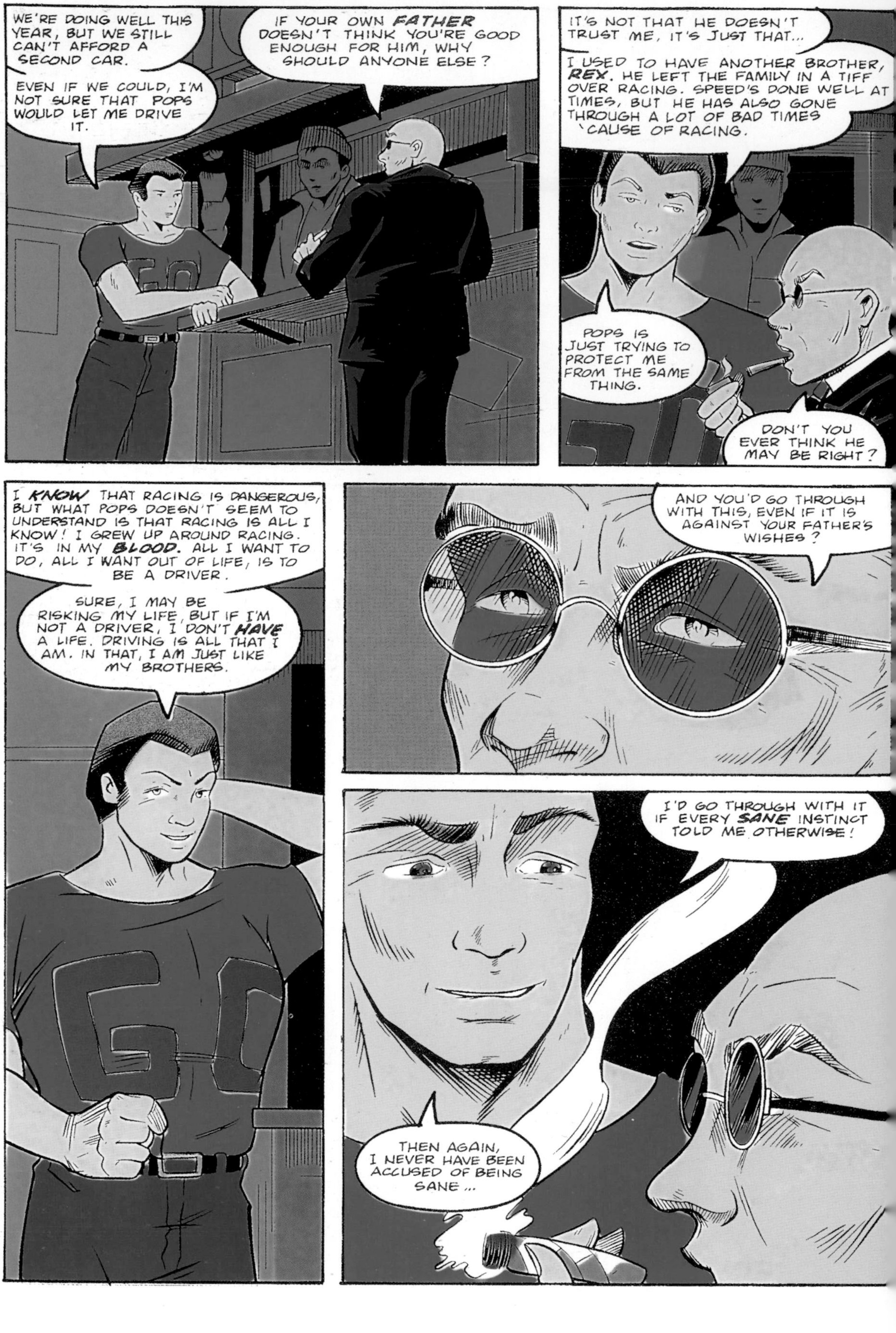
WE'RE DOING WELL THIS YEAR, BUT WE STILL CAN'T AFFORD A SECOND CAR.
EVEN IF WE COULD, I'M NOT SURE THAT POPS WOULD LET ME DRIVE IT.
IF YOUR OWN FATHER DOESN'T THINK YOU'RE GOOD ENOUGH FOR HIM, WHY SHOULD ANYONE ELSE?
IT'S NOT THAT HE DOESN'T TRUST ME, IT'S JUST THAT...
I USED TO HAVE ANOTHER BROTHER, REX. HE LEFT THE FAMILY IN A TIFF OVER RACING. SPEED'S DONE WELL AT TIMES, BUT HE HAS ALSO GONE THROUGH A LOT OF BAD TIMES 'CAUSE OF RACING.
POPS IS JUST TRYING TO PROTECT ME FROM THE SAME THING.
DON'T YOU EVER THINK HE MAY BE RIGHT?
I KNOW THAT RACING IS DANGEROUS, BUT WHAT POPS DOESN'T SEEM TO UNDERSTAND IS THAT RACING IS ALL I KNOW! I GREW UP AROUND RACING. IT'S IN MY BLOOD. ALL I WANT TO DO, ALL I WANT OUT OF LIFE, IS TO BE A DRIVER.
SURE, I MAY BE RISKING MY LIFE, BUT IF I'M NOT A DRIVER, I DON'T HAVE A LIFE. DRIVING IS ALL THAT I AM. IN THAT, I AM JUST LIKE MY BROTHERS.
AND YOU'D GO THROUGH WITH THIS, EVEN IF IT IS AGAINST YOUR FATHER'S WISHES?
I'D GO THROUGH WITH IT IF EVERY SANE INSTINCT TOLD ME OTHERWISE!
THEN AGAIN, I NEVER HAVE BEEN ACCUSED OF BEING SANE...

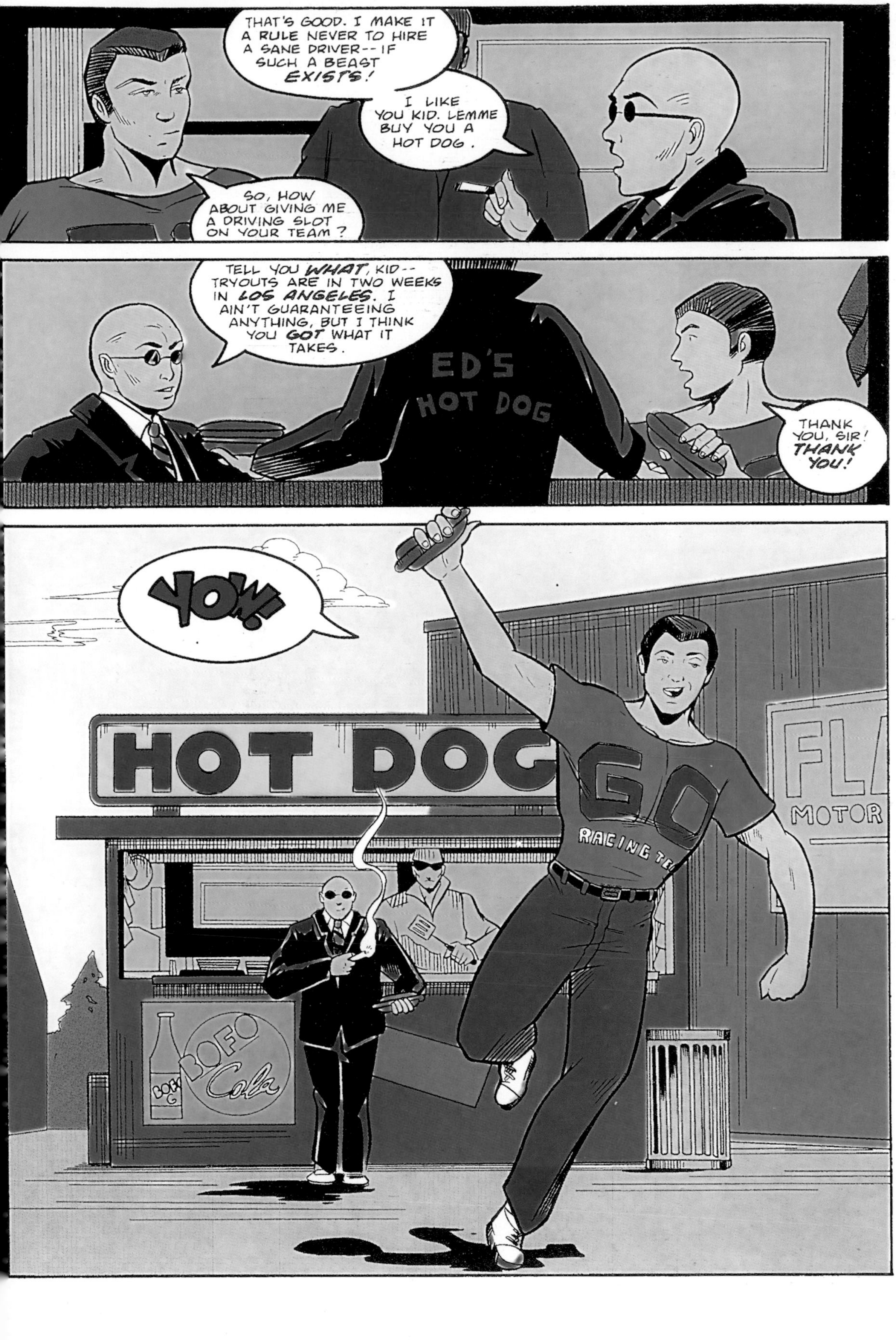
THAT'S GOOD. I MAKE IT A RULE NEVER TO HIRE A SANE DRIVER-- IF SUCH A BEAST EXISTS!
I LIKE YOU KID. LEMME BUY YOU A HOT DOG.
SO, HOW ABOUT GIVING ME A DRIVING SLOT ON YOUR TEAM?
TELL YOU WHAT, KID-- TRYOUTS ARE IN TWO WEEKS IN LOS ANGELES. I AIN'T GUARANTEEING ANYTHING, BUT I THINK YOU GOT WHAT IT TAKES.
ED'S HOT DOG
THANK YOU, SIR! THANK YOU!
YOW!
HOT DOG
GO
RACING TE
FL
MOTOR
BOFO Cola

Speed Racer #22

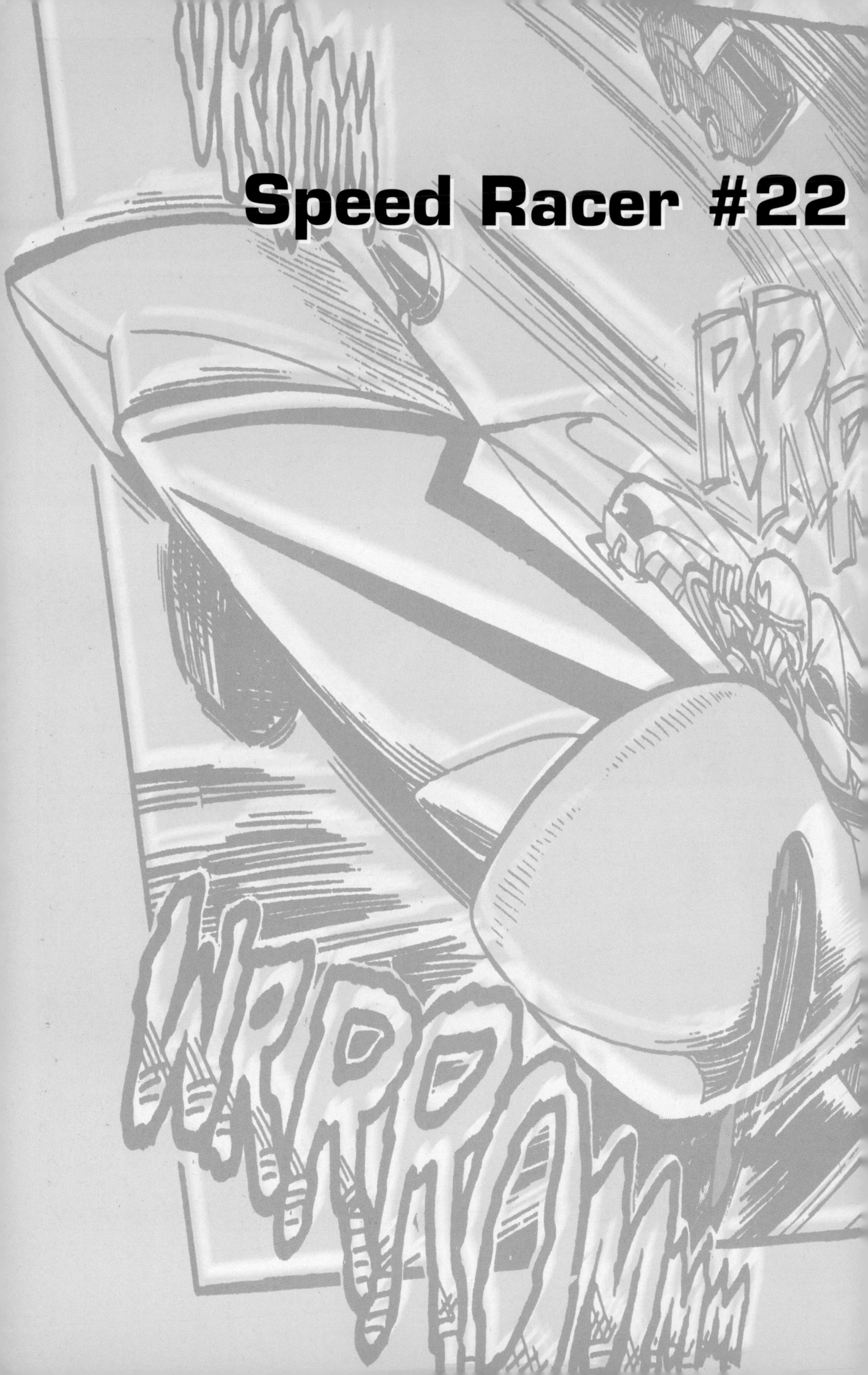

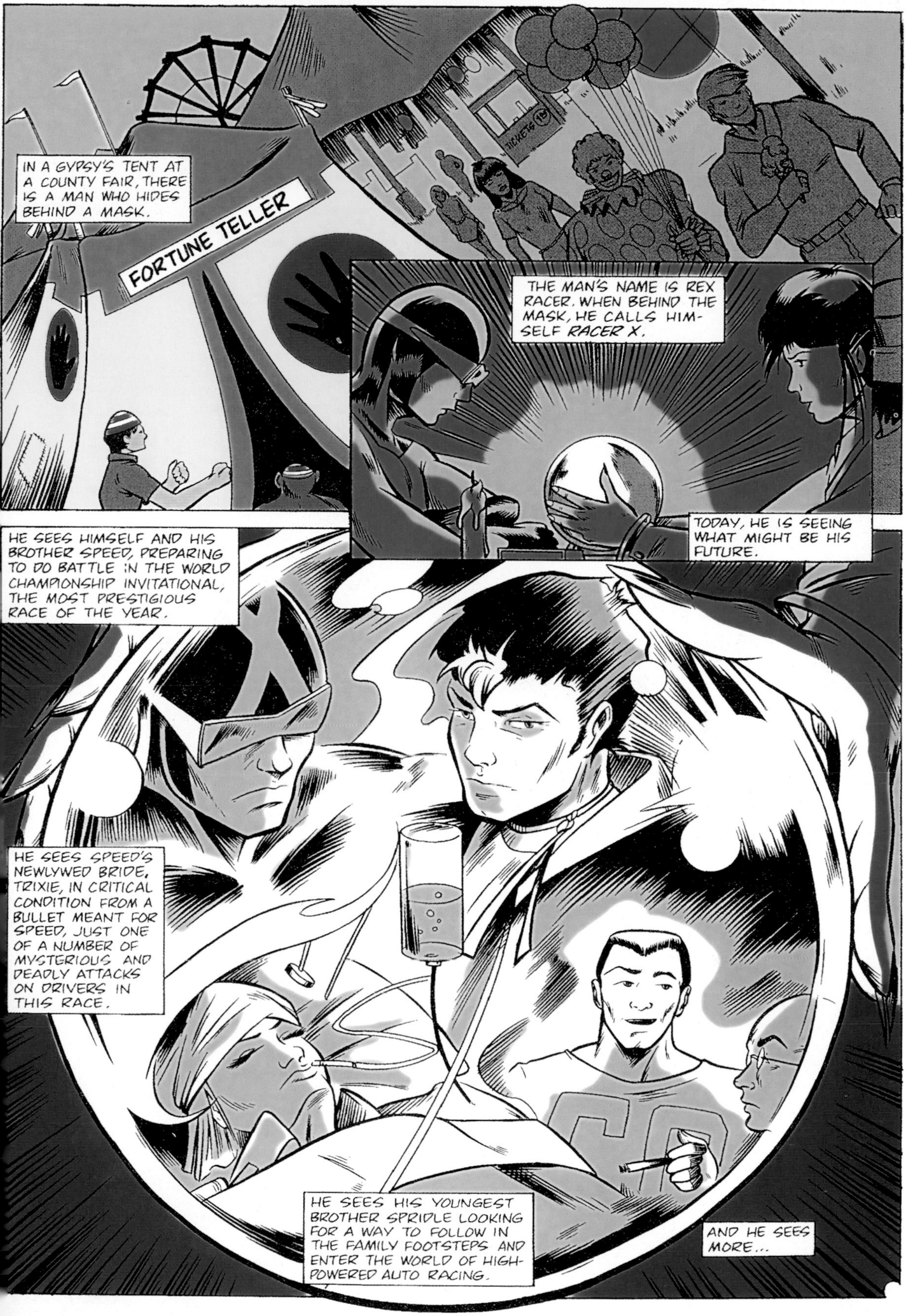
IN A GYPSY'S TENT AT A COUNTY FAIR, THERE IS A MAN WHO HIDES BEHIND A MASK.
FORTUNE TELLER
TICKETS
THE MAN'S NAME IS REX RACER. WHEN BEHIND THE MASK, HE CALLS HIMSELF *RACER X*.
TODAY, HE IS SEEING WHAT MIGHT BE HIS FUTURE.
HE SEES HIMSELF AND HIS BROTHER SPEED, PREPARING TO DO BATTLE IN THE WORLD CHAMPIONSHIP INVITATIONAL, THE MOST PRESTIGIOUS RACE OF THE YEAR.
HE SEES SPEED'S NEWLYWED BRIDE, TRIXIE, IN CRITICAL CONDITION FROM A BULLET MEANT FOR SPEED, JUST ONE OF A NUMBER OF MYSTERIOUS AND DEADLY ATTACKS ON DRIVERS IN THIS RACE.
HE SEES HIS YOUNGEST BROTHER SPRIDLE LOOKING FOR A WAY TO FOLLOW IN THE FAMILY FOOTSTEPS AND ENTER THE WORLD OF HIGH-POWERED AUTO RACING.
AND HE SEES MORE...

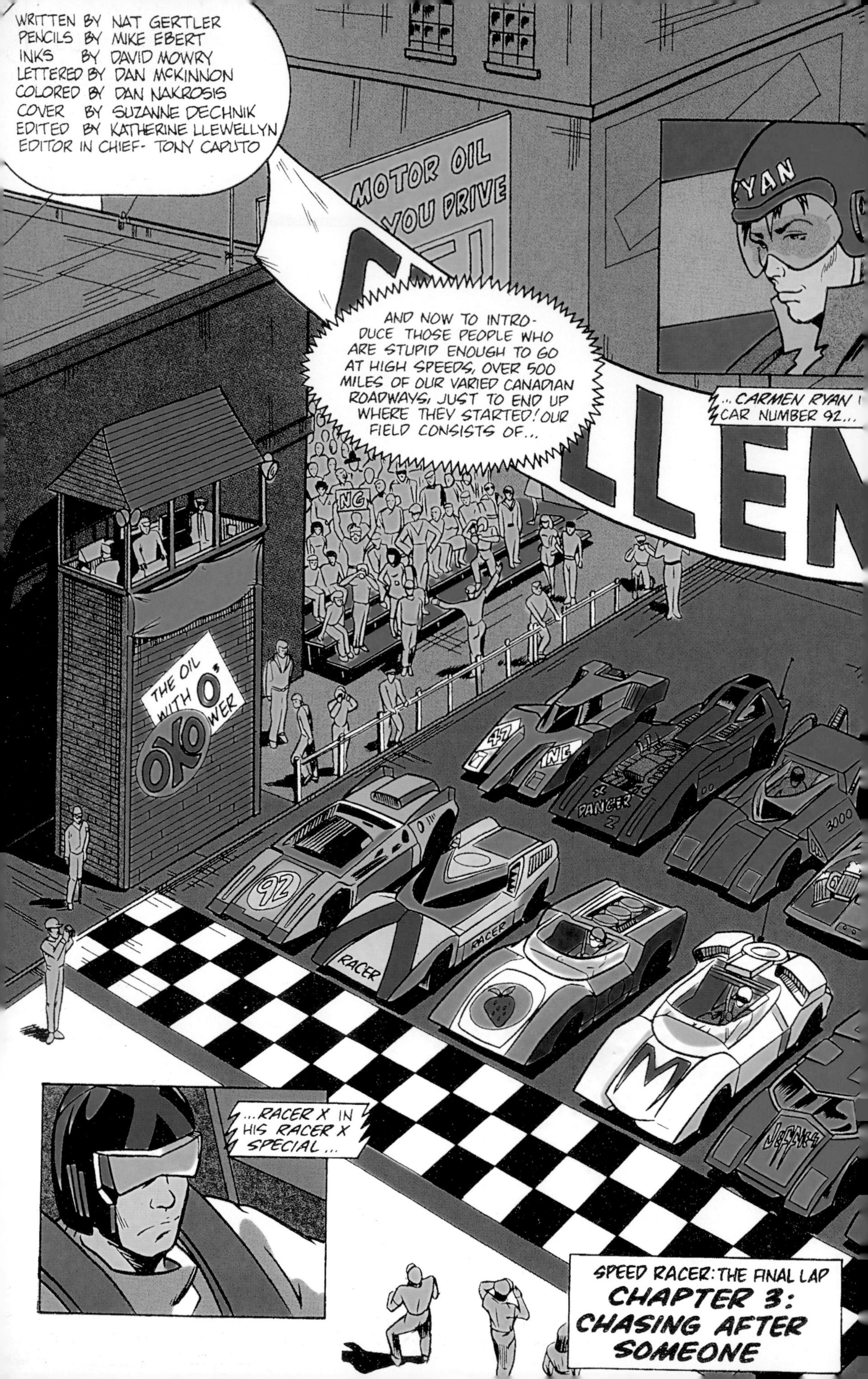

WRITTEN BY NAT GERTLER
PENCILS BY MIKE EBERT
INKS BY DAVID MOWRY
LETTERED BY DAN McKINNON
COLORED BY DAN NAKROSIS
COVER BY SUZANNE DECHNIK
EDITED BY KATHERINE LLEWELLYN
EDITOR IN CHIEF- TONY CAPUTO
MOTOR OIL
YOU DRIVE
RYAN
AND NOW TO INTRO-DUCE THOSE PEOPLE WHO ARE STUPID ENOUGH TO GO AT HIGH SPEEDS, OVER 500 MILES OF OUR VARIED CANADIAN ROADWAYS, JUST TO END UP WHERE THEY STARTED! OUR FIELD CONSISTS OF...
...CARMEN RYAN! CAR NUMBER 92...
THE OIL WITH O3 POWER
OXO
NG
DANGER 2
3000
92
RACER
RACER
M
...RACER X IN HIS RACER X SPECIAL...
SPEED RACER: THE FINAL LAP
CHAPTER 3: CHASING AFTER SOMEONE

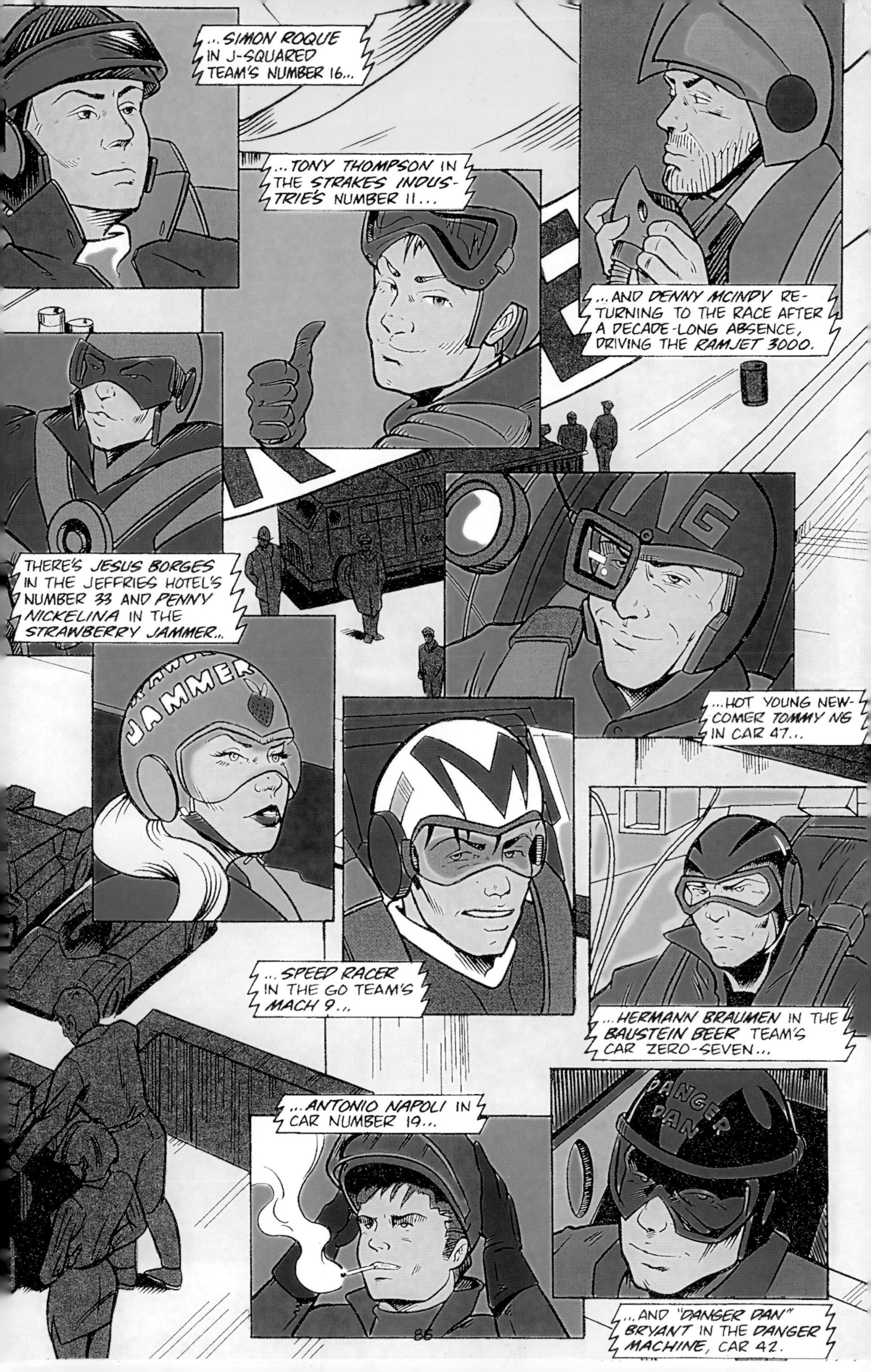
...SIMON ROQUE IN J-SQUARED TEAM'S NUMBER 16...
...TONY THOMPSON IN THE STRAKES INDUSTRIE'S NUMBER 11...
...AND DENNY MCINDY RETURNING TO THE RACE AFTER A DECADE-LONG ABSENCE, DRIVING THE RAMJET 3000.
THERE'S JESUS BORGES IN THE JEFFRIES HOTEL'S NUMBER 33 AND PENNY NICKELINA IN THE STRAWBERRY JAMMER...
JAMMER
...HOT YOUNG NEWCOMER TOMMY NG IN CAR 47...
...SPEED RACER IN THE GO TEAM'S MACH 9...
...HERMANN BRAUMEN IN THE BAUSTEIN BEER TEAM'S CAR ZERO-SEVEN...
...ANTONIO NAPOLI IN CAR NUMBER 19...
DANGER DAN
...AND "DANGER DAN" BRYANT IN THE DANGER MACHINE, CAR 42.

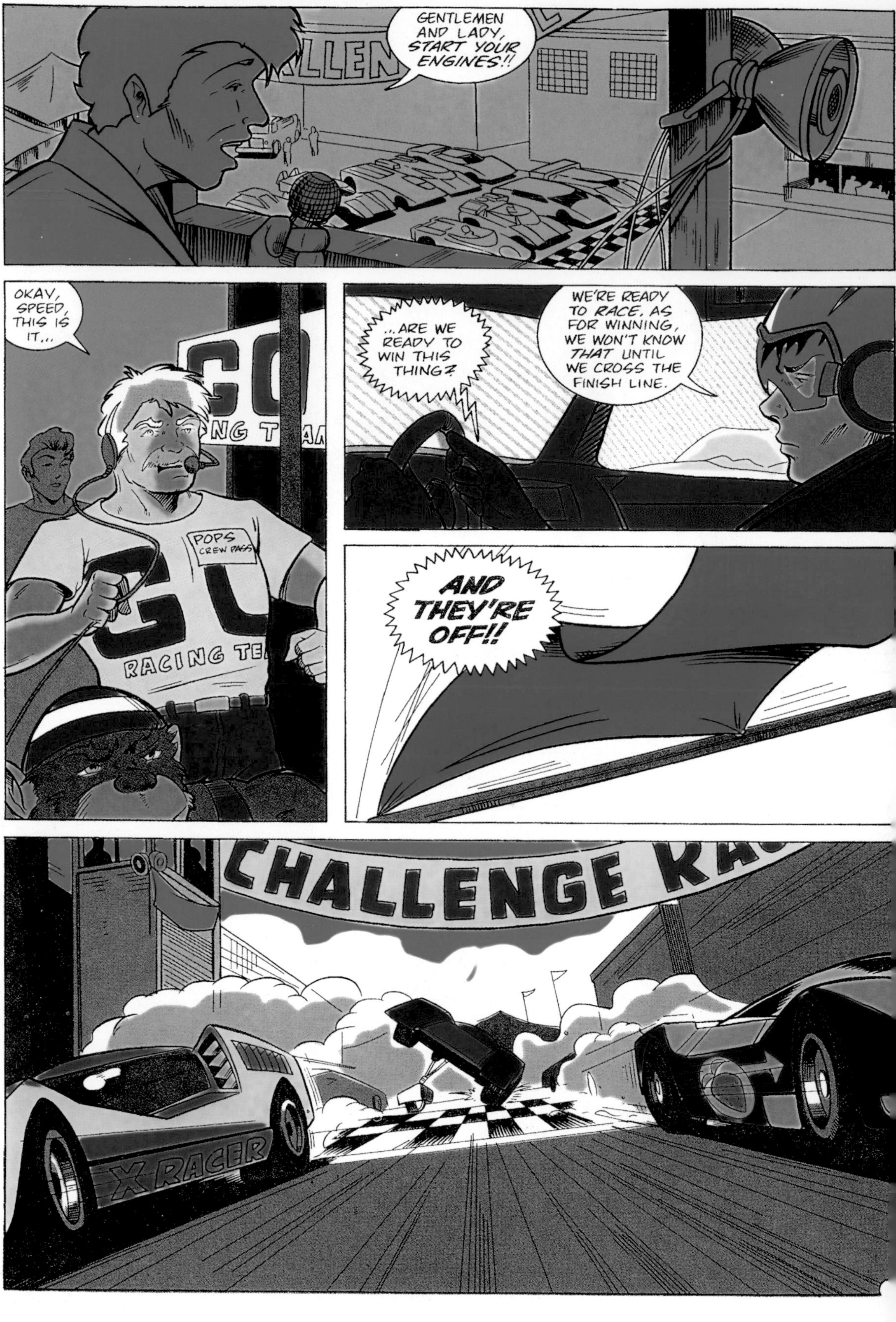
GENTLEMEN AND LADY, START YOUR ENGINES!!
OKAY, SPEED, THIS IS IT...
...ARE WE READY TO WIN THIS THING?
WE'RE READY TO RACE. AS FOR WINNING, WE WON'T KNOW THAT UNTIL WE CROSS THE FINISH LINE.
POPS
CREW PASS
RACING TE
AND THEY'RE OFF!!
CHALLENGE RA
X RACER

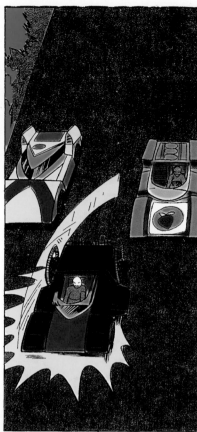

THAT WAS A DANGEROUS STUNT DENNY JUST PULLED. I HOPE THAT BEING OUT OF PRACTICE HASN'T MADE HIM RECKLESS!

DON'T WORRY ABOUT HIM NOW. JUST WORRY ABOUT *YOURSELF!* THERE ARE STILL 500 MILES TO GO!

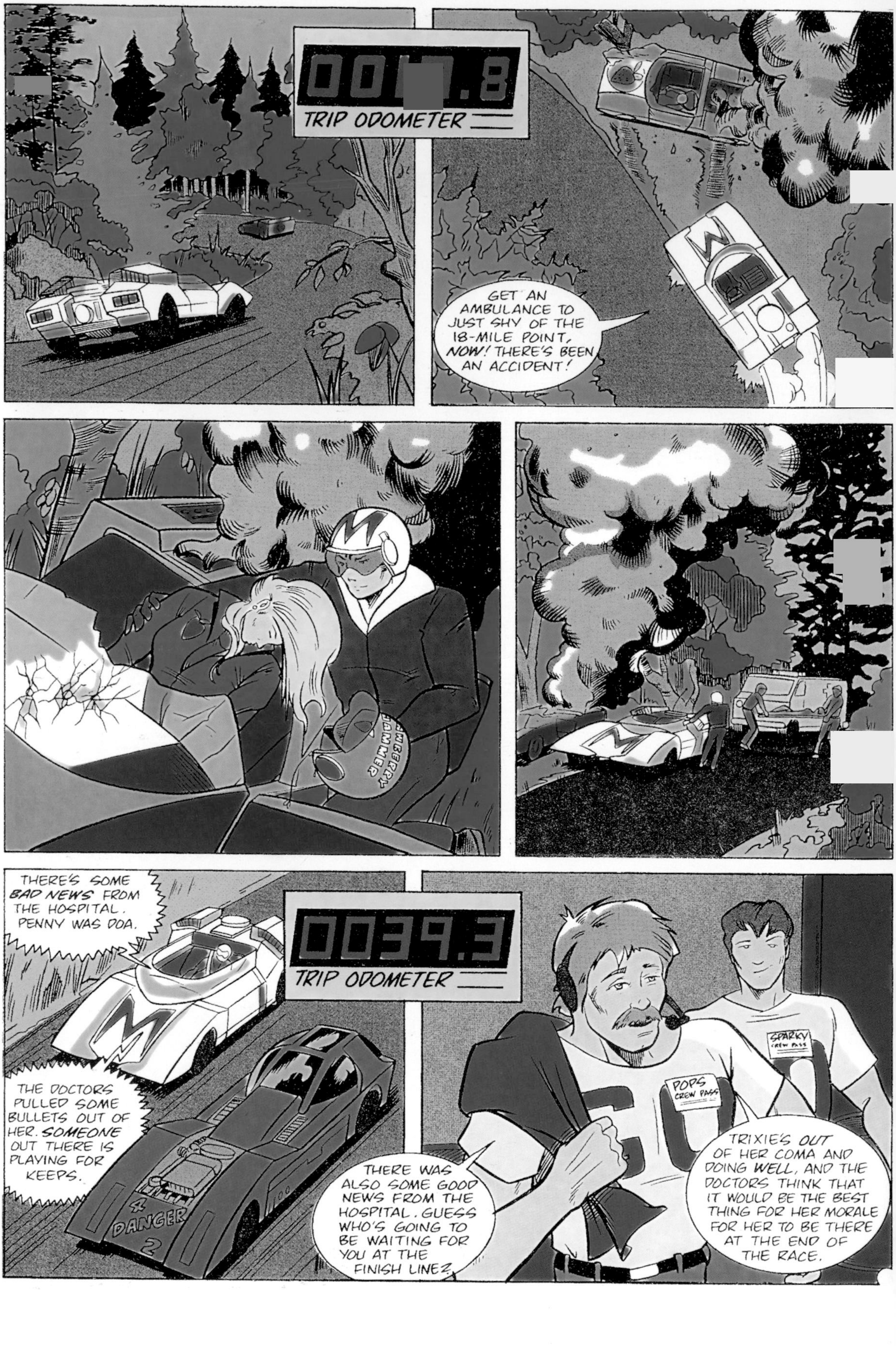
TRIP ODOMETER
GET AN AMBULANCE TO JUST SHY OF THE 18-MILE POINT, NOW! THERE'S BEEN AN ACCIDENT!
THERE'S SOME BAD NEWS FROM THE HOSPITAL. PENNY WAS DOA.
0039.3
TRIP ODOMETER
THE DOCTORS PULLED SOME BULLETS OUT OF HER. SOMEONE OUT THERE IS PLAYING FOR KEEPS.
4 DANGER 2
POPS CREW PASS
SPARKY CREW PASS
THERE WAS ALSO SOME GOOD NEWS FROM THE HOSPITAL. GUESS WHO'S GOING TO BE WAITING FOR YOU AT THE FINISH LINE?
TRIXIE'S OUT OF HER COMA AND DOING WELL, AND THE DOCTORS THINK THAT IT WOULD BE THE BEST THING FOR HER MORALE FOR HER TO BE THERE AT THE END OF THE RACE.

I MAY HAVE FALLEN INTO LAST PLACE TRYING TO SAVE PENNY, BUT IF *TRIXIE* IS GOING TO BE THERE, I'LL GIVE IT MY BEST TO BE FIRST ACROSS THAT FINISH LINE!

YAHOO!

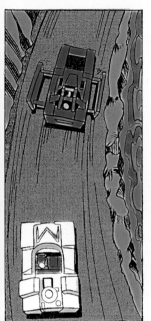

CAR-- SWITCH TO SPEEDBOAT MODE.

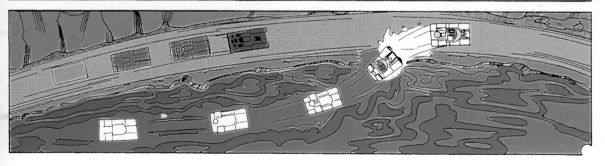

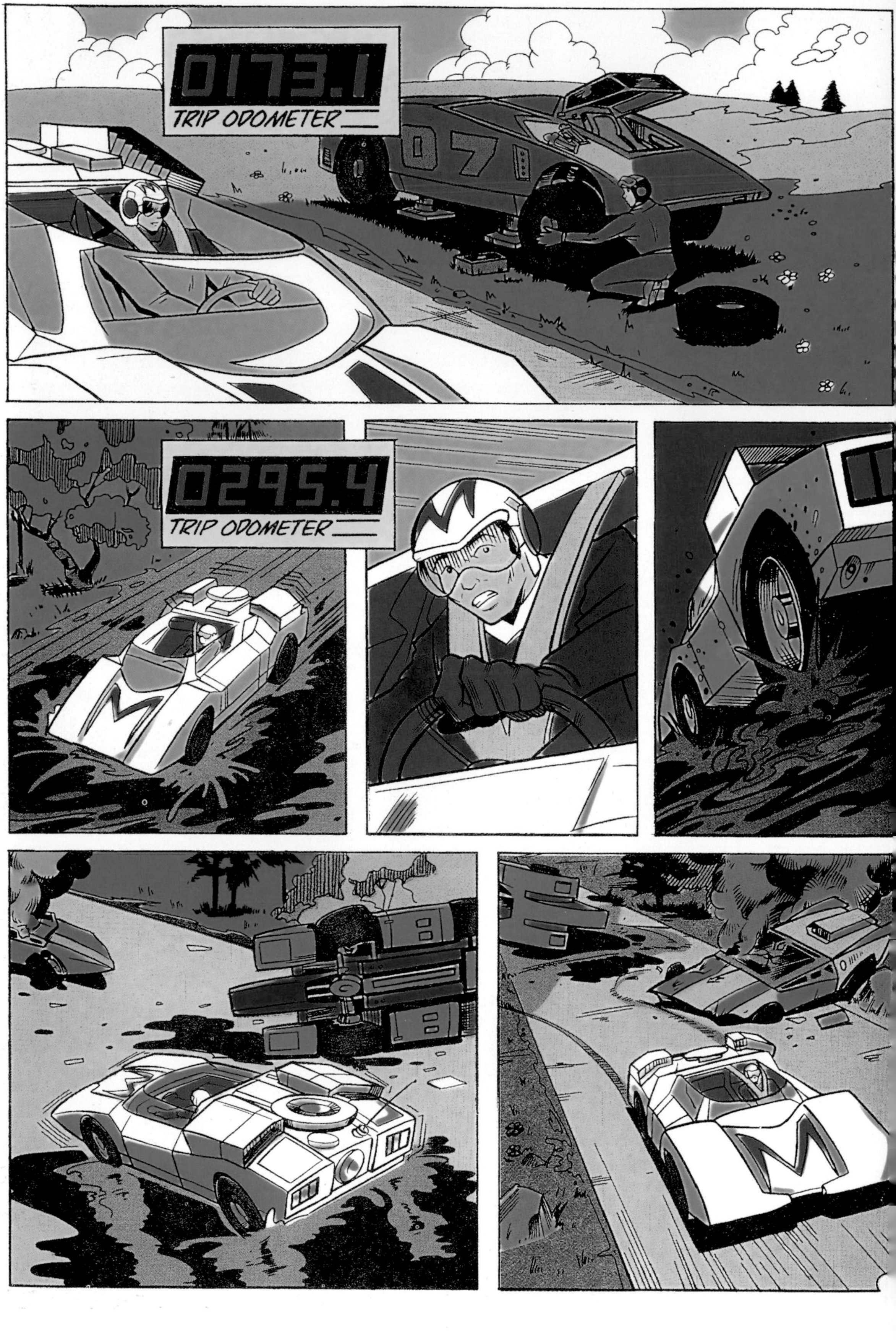
0173.1
TRIP ODOMETER
071
0295.4
TRIP ODOMETER

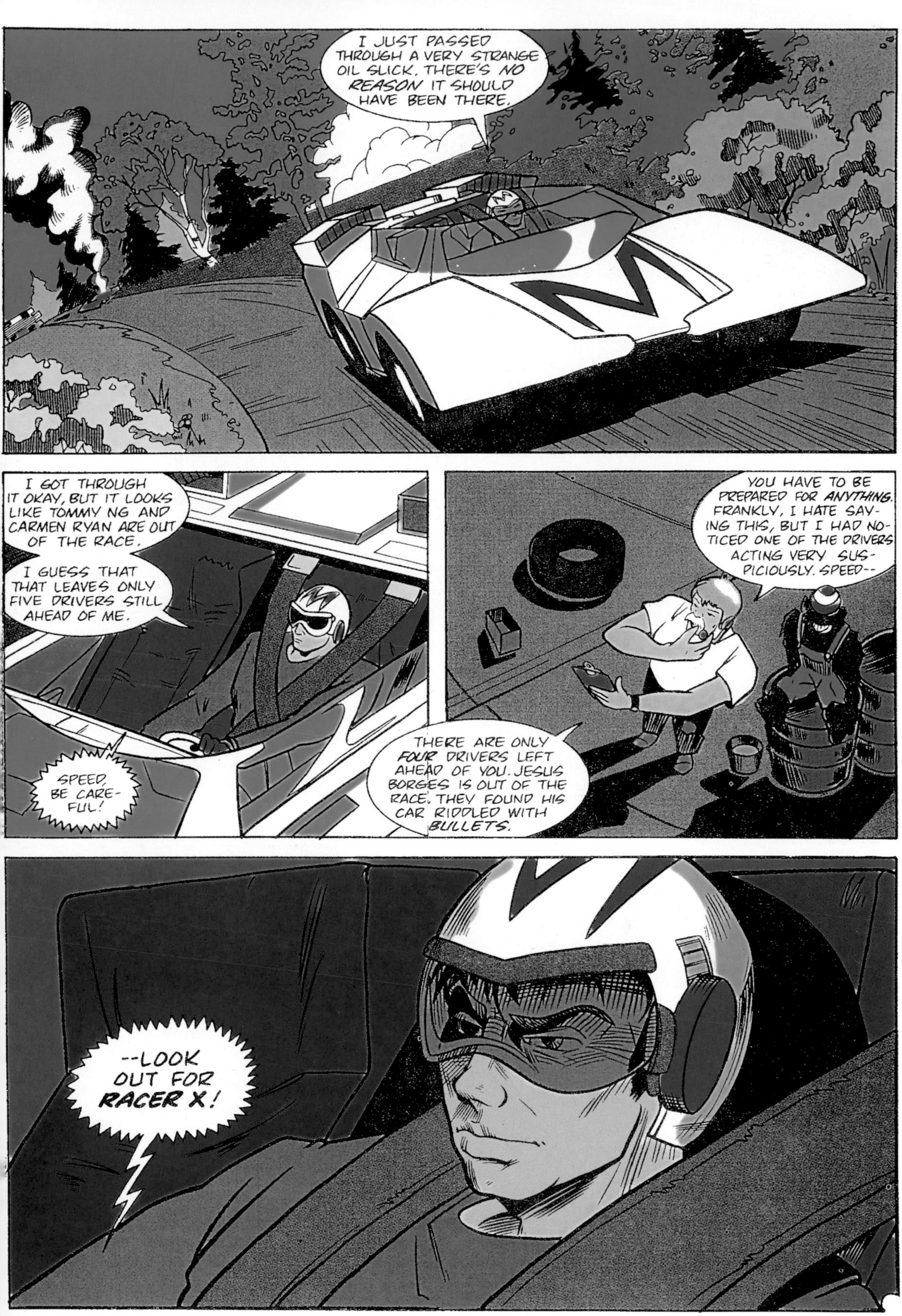
I JUST PASSED THROUGH A VERY STRANGE OIL SLICK. THERE'S NO REASON IT SHOULD HAVE BEEN THERE.
I GOT THROUGH IT OKAY, BUT IT LOOKS LIKE TOMMY NG AND CARMEN RYAN ARE OUT OF THE RACE.
I GUESS THAT THAT LEAVES ONLY FIVE DRIVERS STILL AHEAD OF ME.
SPEED, BE CARE-FUL!
THERE ARE ONLY FOUR DRIVERS LEFT AHEAD OF YOU. JESUS BORGES IS OUT OF THE RACE. THEY FOUND HIS CAR RIDDLED WITH BULLETS.
YOU HAVE TO BE PREPARED FOR ANYTHING. FRANKLY, I HATE SAY-ING THIS, BUT I HAD NO-TICED ONE OF THE DRIVERS ACTING VERY SUS-PICIOUSLY. SPEED--
--LOOK OUT FOR RACER X!

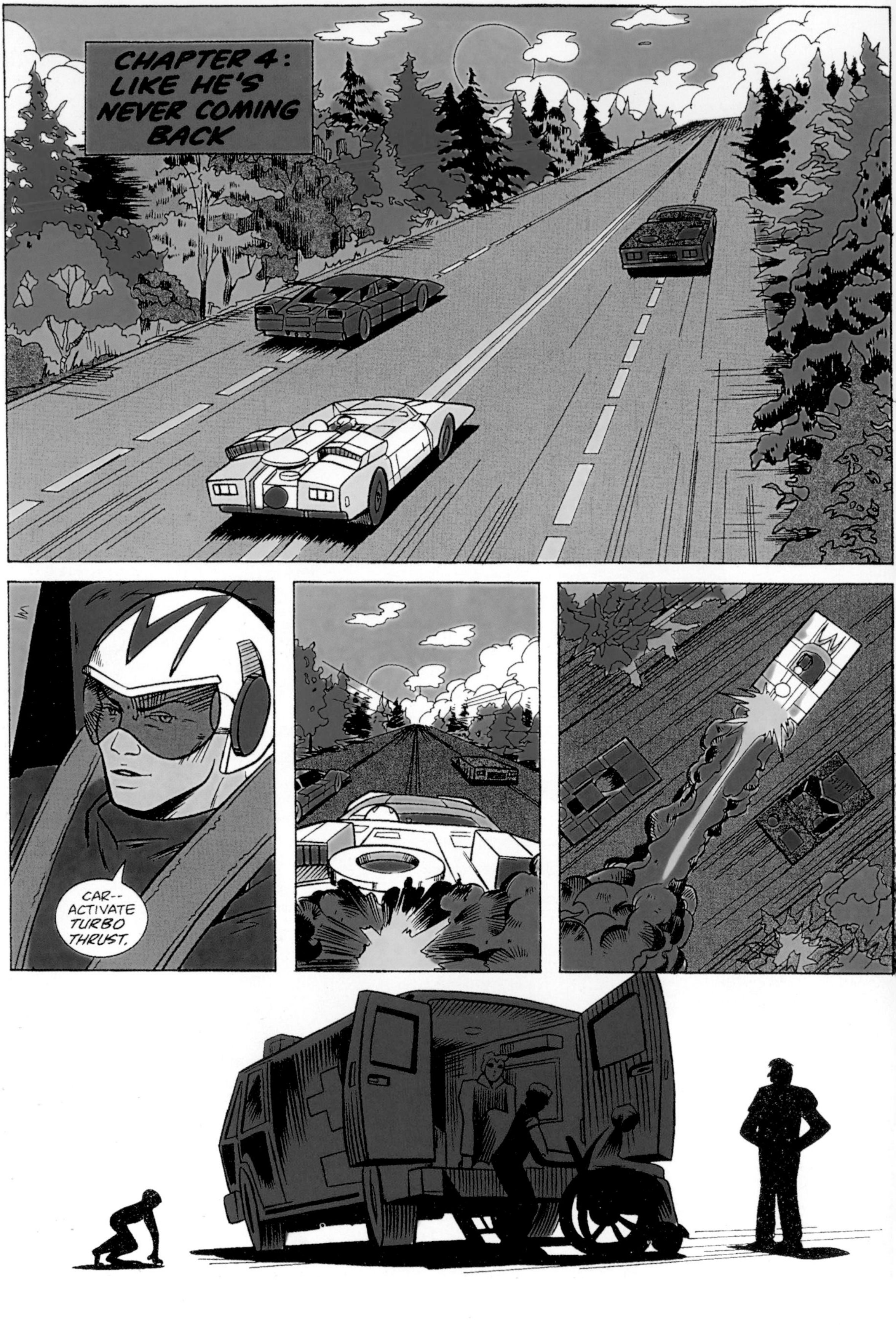
CHAPTER 4: LIKE HE'S NEVER COMING BACK
CAR-- ACTIVATE TURBO THRUST.

THIS WILL BE A GOOD SPOT FOR WATCHING THE END OF THE RACE. THE LAST COUPLE OF MILES ARE A LONG STRAIGHTAWAY, SO WE'LL BE ABLE TO SEE THEM COMING.

THEY SHOULD BE HERE IN A FEW MINUTES.

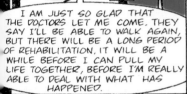

I AM JUST SO GLAD THAT THE DOCTORS LET ME COME. THEY SAY I'LL BE ABLE TO WALK AGAIN, BUT THERE WILL BE A LONG PERIOD OF REHABILITATION, IT WILL BE A WHILE BEFORE I CAN PULL MY LIFE TOGETHER, BEFORE I'M REALLY ABLE TO DEAL WITH WHAT HAS HAPPENED.

SUDDENLY, I NEED HIM TO BE STRONG FOR ME, JUST LIKE I ONCE HAD TO BE FOR HIM.

MAYBE *THIS* IS WHAT LOVE IS TRULY ABOUT... THE TOUGH TIMES.

I SHOULD WARN YOU NOW THAT SPEED MAY BE IN SOME DANGER. THE PERSON WHO SHOT AT YOU HAS KILLED SOME OTHER PEOPLE. WE STILL AREN'T *SURE* WHO HE IS, BUT WE THINK THAT HE'S IN THE RACE.

OH NO! I HOPE THAT SPEED CAN...

I *KNOW* HE CAN HANDLE IT. HE'S BEEN DEALING WITH DANGER EVER SINCE HE GOT INTO RACING.

0496.2
TRIP ODOMETER

93

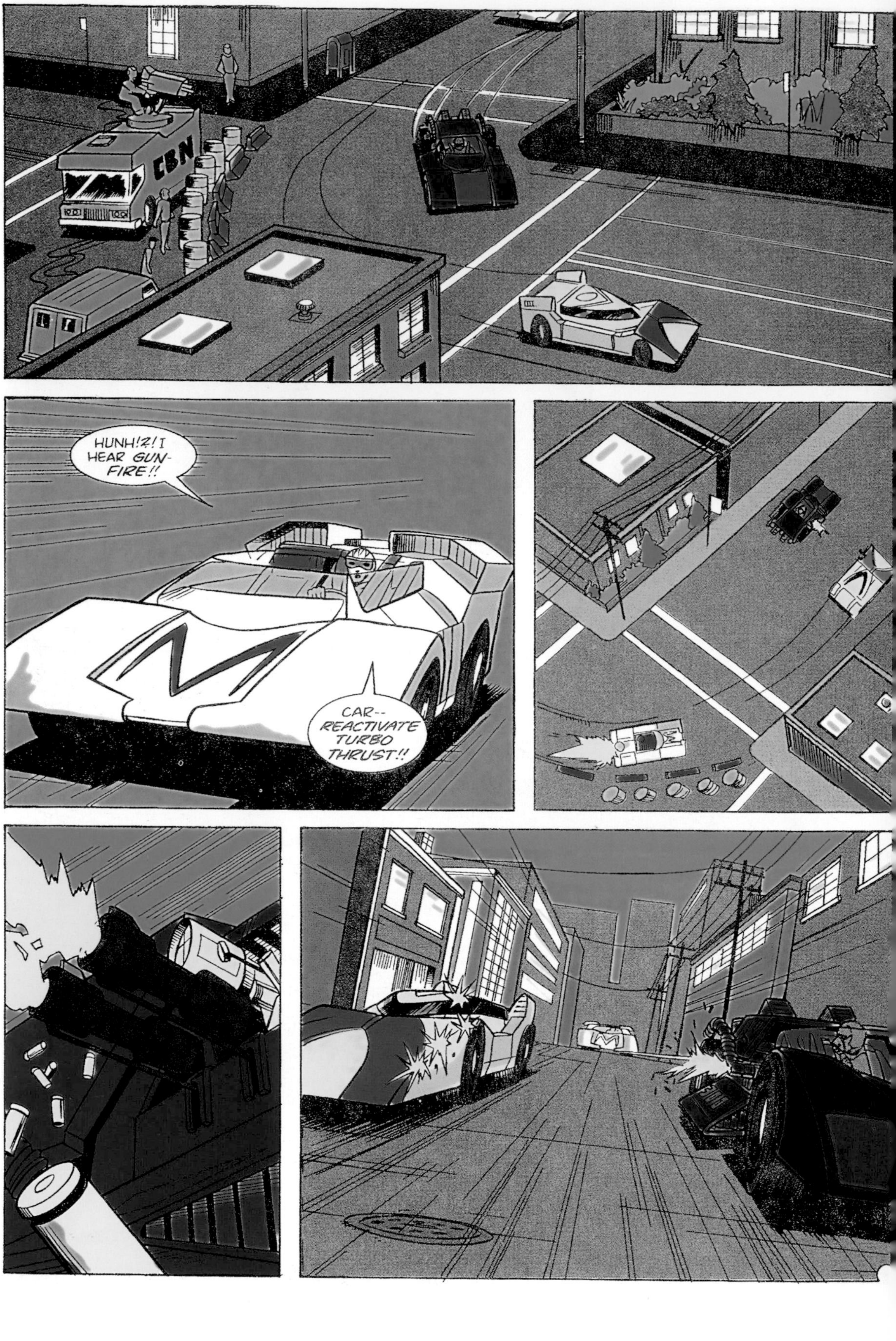
CBN
HUNH!?! I HEAR GUN-FIRE!!
CAR-- REACTIVATE TURBO THRUST!!

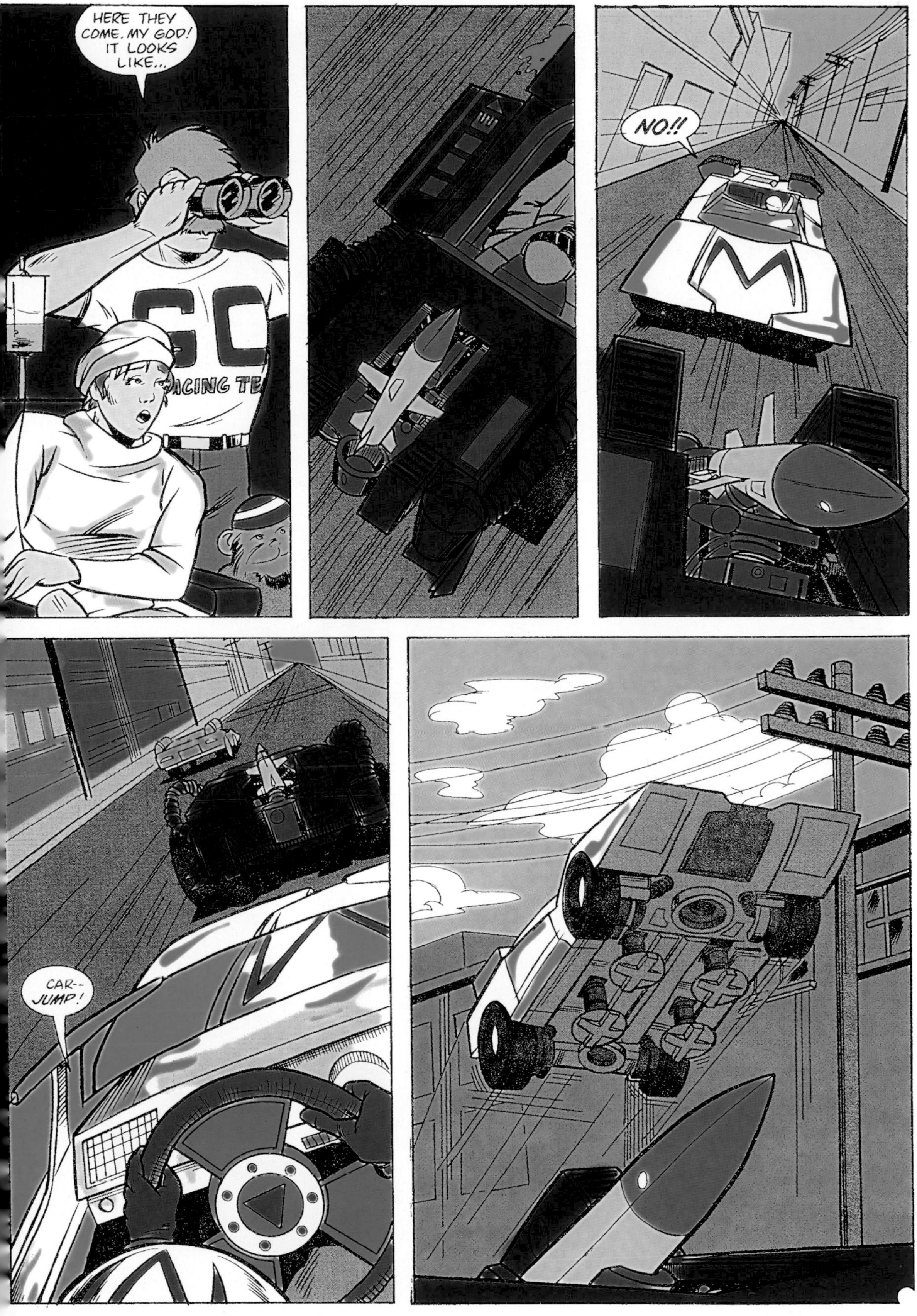
HERE THEY COME. MY GOD! IT LOOKS LIKE...
GO
RACING TE
NO!!
M
CAR-- JUMP!

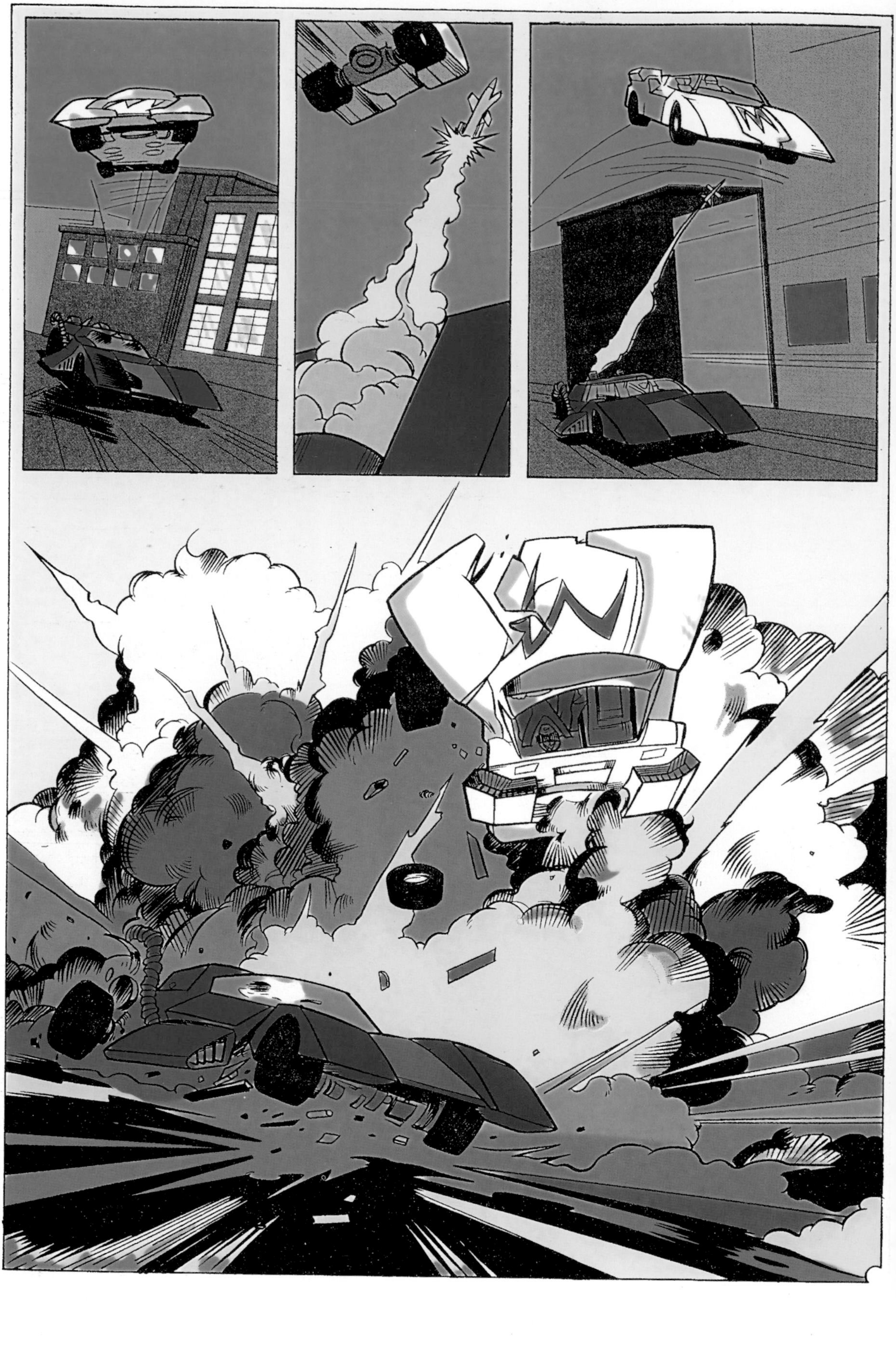

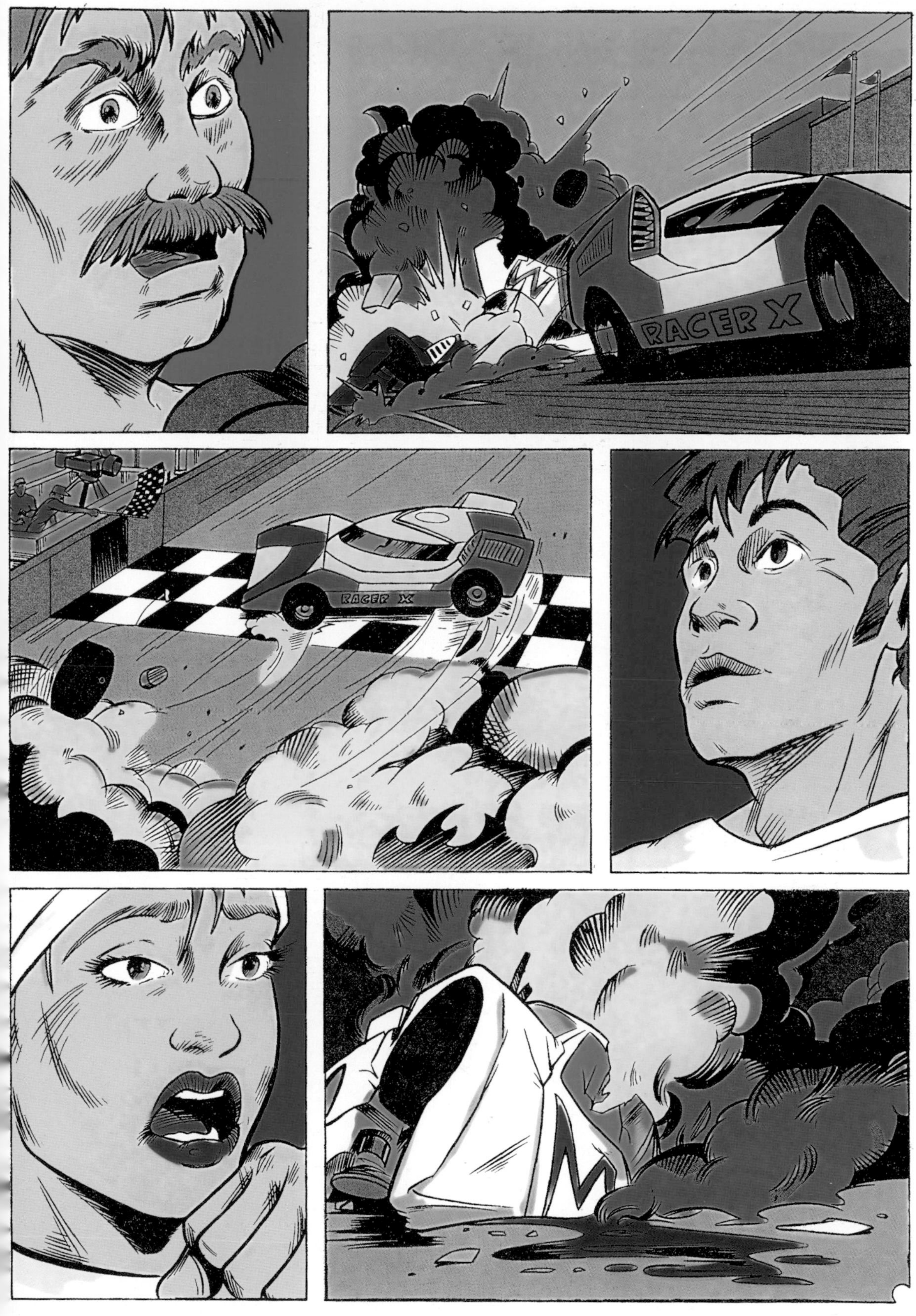
RACER X
RACER X

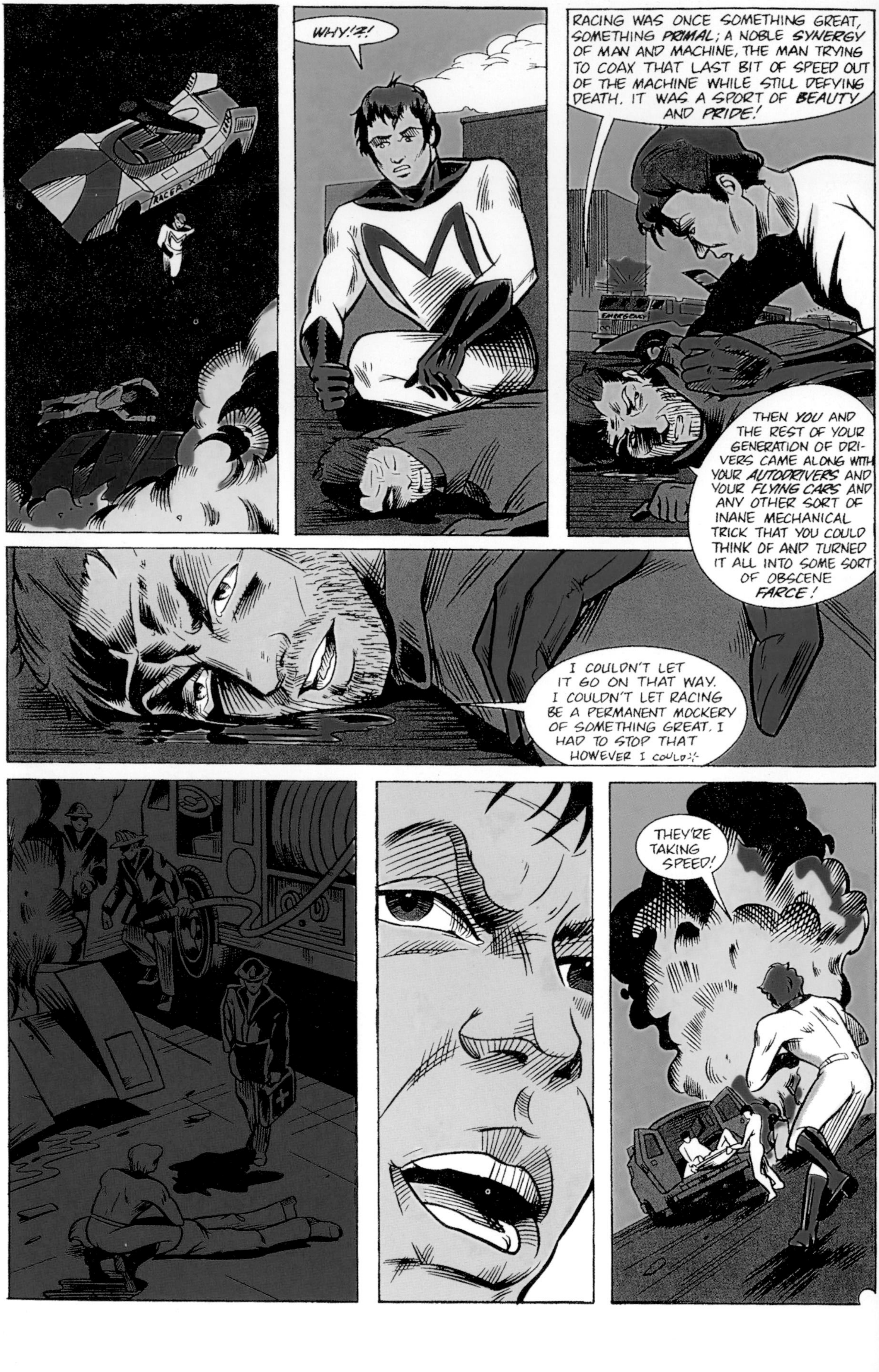
WHY!?!
RACING WAS ONCE SOMETHING GREAT, SOMETHING PRIMAL; A NOBLE SYNERGY OF MAN AND MACHINE, THE MAN TRYING TO COAX THAT LAST BIT OF SPEED OUT OF THE MACHINE WHILE STILL DEFYING DEATH. IT WAS A SPORT OF BEAUTY AND PRIDE!
THEN YOU AND THE REST OF YOUR GENERATION OF DRIVERS CAME ALONG WITH YOUR AUTODRIVERS AND YOUR FLYING CARS AND ANY OTHER SORT OF INANE MECHANICAL TRICK THAT YOU COULD THINK OF AND TURNED IT ALL INTO SOME SORT OF OBSCENE FARCE!
I COULDN'T LET IT GO ON THAT WAY. I COULDN'T LET RACING BE A PERMANENT MOCKERY OF SOMETHING GREAT. I HAD TO STOP THAT HOWEVER I COULD
THEY'RE TAKING SPEED!

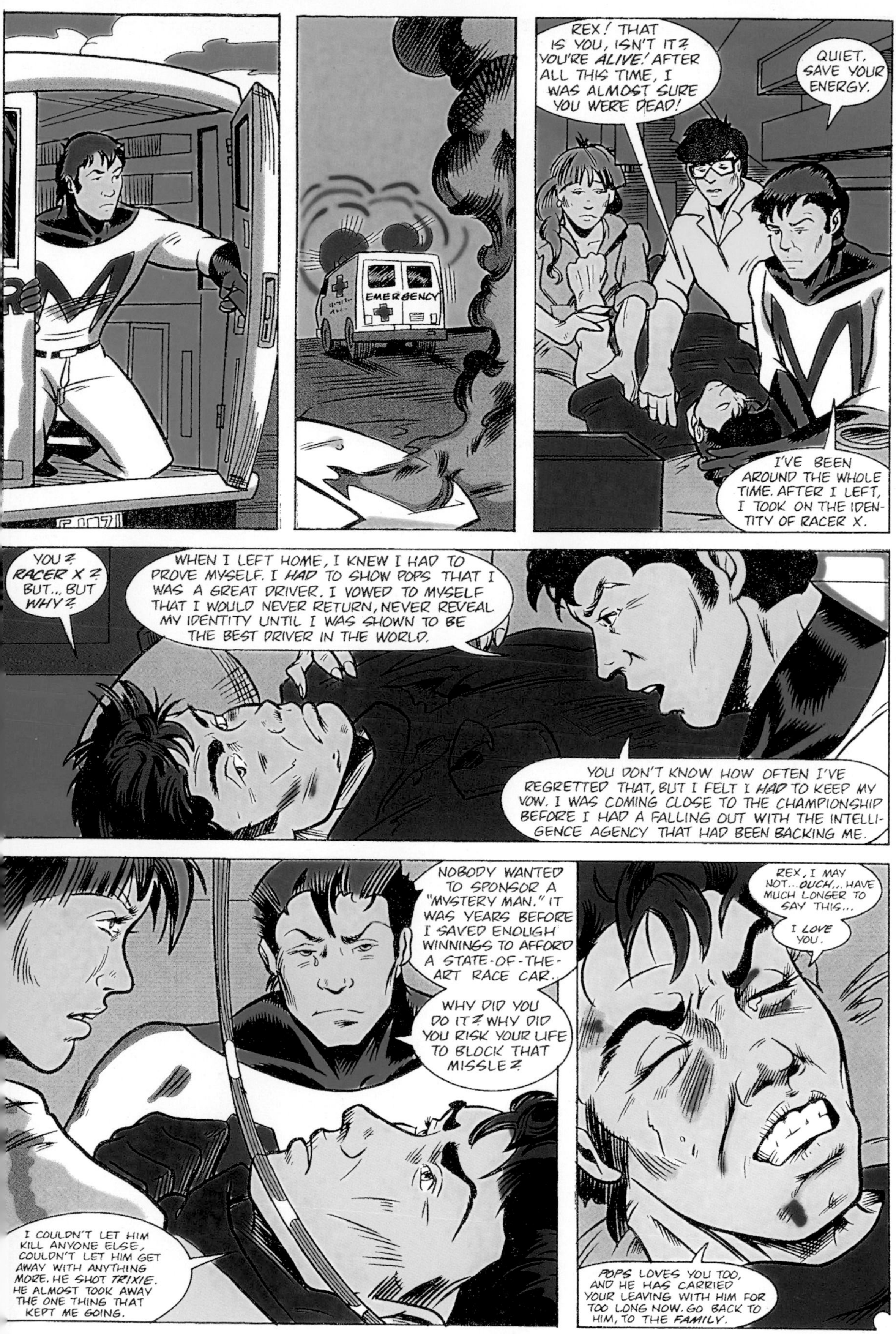
EMERGENCY
REX! THAT IS YOU, ISN'T IT? YOU'RE ALIVE! AFTER ALL THIS TIME, I WAS ALMOST SURE YOU WERE DEAD!
QUIET. SAVE YOUR ENERGY.
I'VE BEEN AROUND THE WHOLE TIME. AFTER I LEFT, I TOOK ON THE IDENTITY OF RACER X.
YOU? RACER X? BUT... BUT WHY?
WHEN I LEFT HOME, I KNEW I HAD TO PROVE MYSELF. I HAD TO SHOW POPS THAT I WAS A GREAT DRIVER. I VOWED TO MYSELF THAT I WOULD NEVER RETURN, NEVER REVEAL MY IDENTITY UNTIL I WAS SHOWN TO BE THE BEST DRIVER IN THE WORLD.
YOU DON'T KNOW HOW OFTEN I'VE REGRETTED THAT, BUT I FELT I HAD TO KEEP MY VOW. I WAS COMING CLOSE TO THE CHAMPIONSHIP BEFORE I HAD A FALLING OUT WITH THE INTELLIGENCE AGENCY THAT HAD BEEN BACKING ME.
NOBODY WANTED TO SPONSOR A "MYSTERY MAN." IT WAS YEARS BEFORE I SAVED ENOUGH WINNINGS TO AFFORD A STATE-OF-THE-ART RACE CAR.
WHY DID YOU DO IT? WHY DID YOU RISK YOUR LIFE TO BLOCK THAT MISSLE?
I COULDN'T LET HIM KILL ANYONE ELSE, COULDN'T LET HIM GET AWAY WITH ANYTHING MORE. HE SHOT TRIXIE. HE ALMOST TOOK AWAY THE ONE THING THAT KEPT ME GOING.
REX, I MAY NOT... OUCH... HAVE MUCH LONGER TO SAY THIS...
I LOVE YOU.
POPS LOVES YOU TOO, AND HE HAS CARRIED YOUR LEAVING WITH HIM FOR TOO LONG NOW. GO BACK TO HIM, TO THE FAMILY.

I CAN'T GO, IT'S MY FAULT THIS HAPPENED TO YOU. I COULDN'T FACE THEM KNOWING THAT.

REX, I...I CAN'T ARGUE NOW. *PROMISE* ME YOU'LL GO BACK. IF IT IS THE *LAST* THING I DO, I WANT TO BRING YOU BACK INTO THE FAMILY.

I PROMISE.

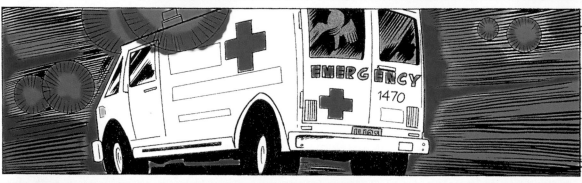

WE ARE NOT HERE TODAY TO BURY SPEED RACER. WE ARE HERE MERELY TO BURY HIS BODY. HIS SPIRIT, THAT WHICH MADE HIM WHAT HE TRULY IS, IS FAR TOO POWERFUL AND LARGE FOR ANY WOODEN BOX TO HOLD.

BUT THAT DOESN'T MEAN THAT HIS SPIRIT ISN'T HERE NOW. HIS SPIRIT IS VERY MUCH HERE. IT IS A SPIRIT THAT IS FELT BY ALL THOSE WHO REMEMBER HIM, ALL THOSE THAT LOOKED UP TO HIM, ALL THOSE WHO LOVED HIM.

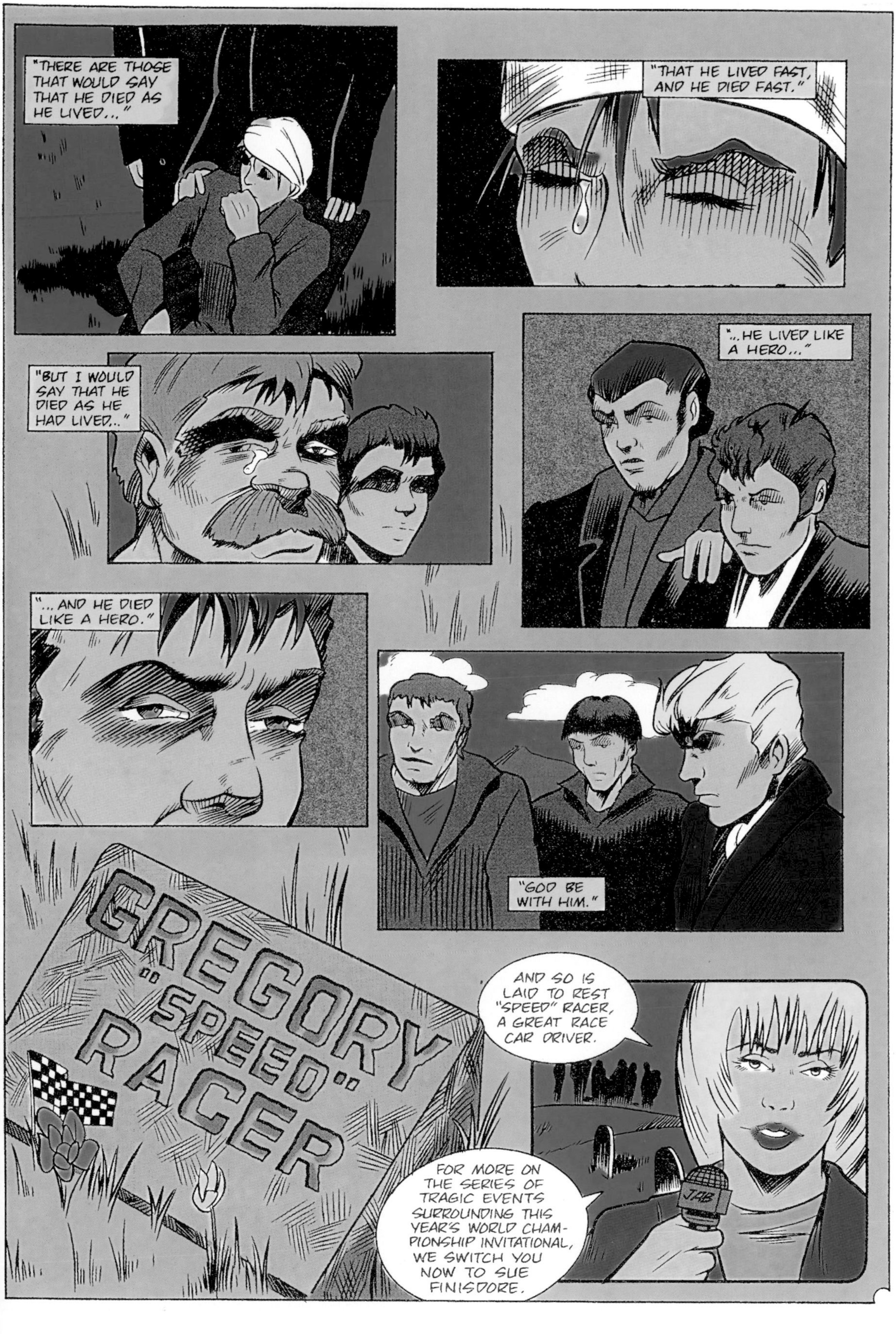

"THERE ARE THOSE THAT WOULD SAY THAT HE DIED AS HE LIVED..."
"THAT HE LIVED FAST, AND HE DIED FAST."
"BUT I WOULD SAY THAT HE DIED AS HE HAD LIVED..."
"...HE LIVED LIKE A HERO..."
"... AND HE DIED LIKE A HERO."
"GOD BE WITH HIM."
GREGORY "SPEED" RACER
AND SO IS LAID TO REST "SPEED" RACER, A GREAT RACE CAR DRIVER.
FOR MORE ON THE SERIES OF TRAGIC EVENTS SURROUNDING THIS YEAR'S WORLD CHAMPIONSHIP INVITATIONAL, WE SWITCH YOU NOW TO SUE FINISDORE.
JAB

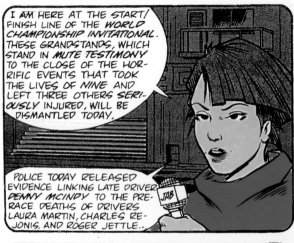

I AM HERE AT THE START/ FINISH LINE OF THE WORLD CHAMPIONSHIP INVITATIONAL. THESE GRANDSTANDS, WHICH STAND IN MUTE TESTIMONY TO THE CLOSE OF THE HORRIFIC EVENTS THAT TOOK THE LIVES OF NINE AND LEFT THREE OTHERS SERIOUSLY INJURED, WILL BE DISMANTLED TODAY.
POLICE TODAY RELEASED EVIDENCE LINKING LATE DRIVER DENNY MCINDY TO THE PRE-RACE DEATHS OF DRIVERS LAURA MARTIN, CHARLES REJONIS, AND ROGER JETTLE...
JAB
...AND TO AN ATTEMPTED SHOOTING OF "SPEED" RACER IN THE WEEKS BEFORE THE RACE.
AS MORE CLUES ARE REVEALED, IT IS BECOMING CLEARER WHAT HAPPENED, BUT NOT WHY. IT MAY NEVER BE CLEAR WHY MCINDY CREATED SUCH A CAREFULLY PLANNED PLOT OF DESTRUCTION.
WHEN THE GRANDSTANDS ARE DOWN, THIS CAR ABANDONED HERE AFTER THE RACE WILL PERHAPS BE THE LAST REMAINING REMINDER OF THE TRAGEDY. THIS CAR CARRIES WITH IT THE MYSTERY OF ITS DRIVER.
RACER X HAS NOT BEEN SEEN SINCE THE RACE. HE MAY NEVER BE SEEN AGAIN, AND THE LONG-HELD SECRET OF HIS TRUE IDENTITY MAY REMAIN HIDDEN FOREVER.
RACER X
"THE RACER'S CHOICE
RACER X
HOURS LATER...
RACER X
A FIGURE APPEARS...
RACER X
ALTHOUGH HE LOOKS FAMILIAR...
HE'S NOT THE TRUE OWNER OF THIS CAR...

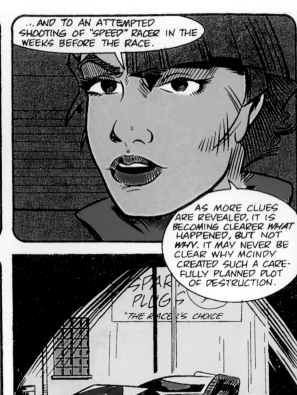

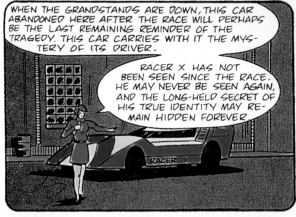

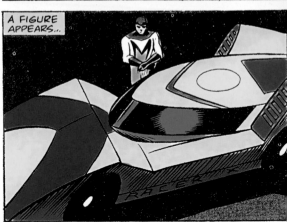

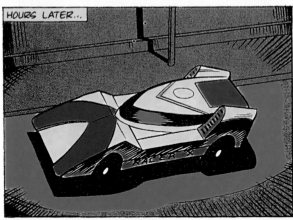

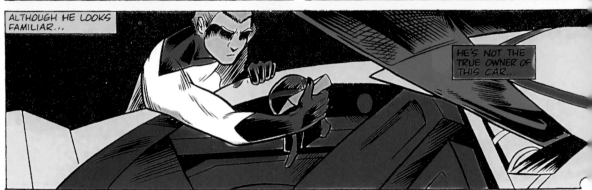

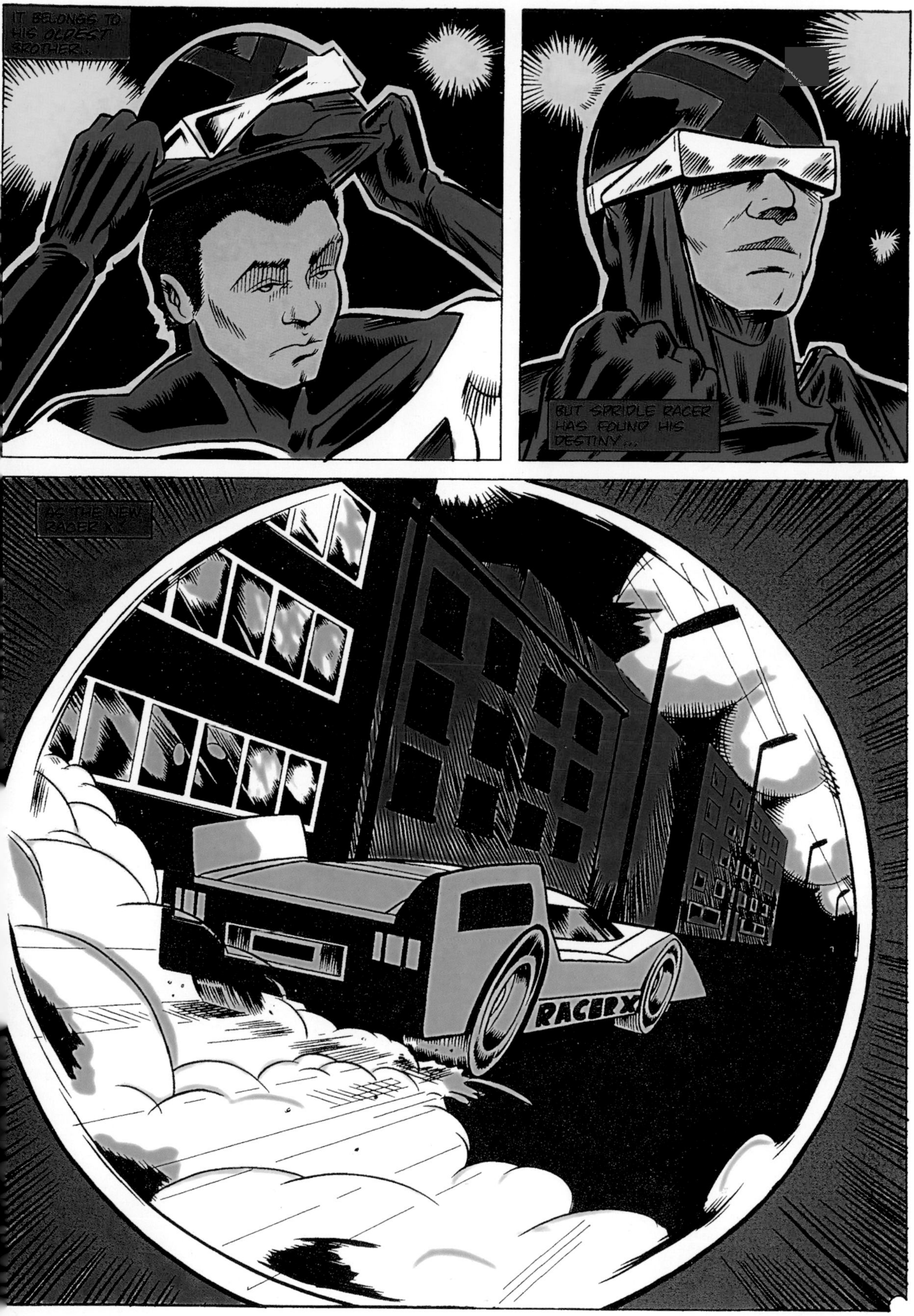
IT BELONGS TO HIS OLDEST BROTHER...
BUT SPRIDLE RACER HAS FOUND HIS DESTINY...
AS THE NEW RACER X.
RACER X

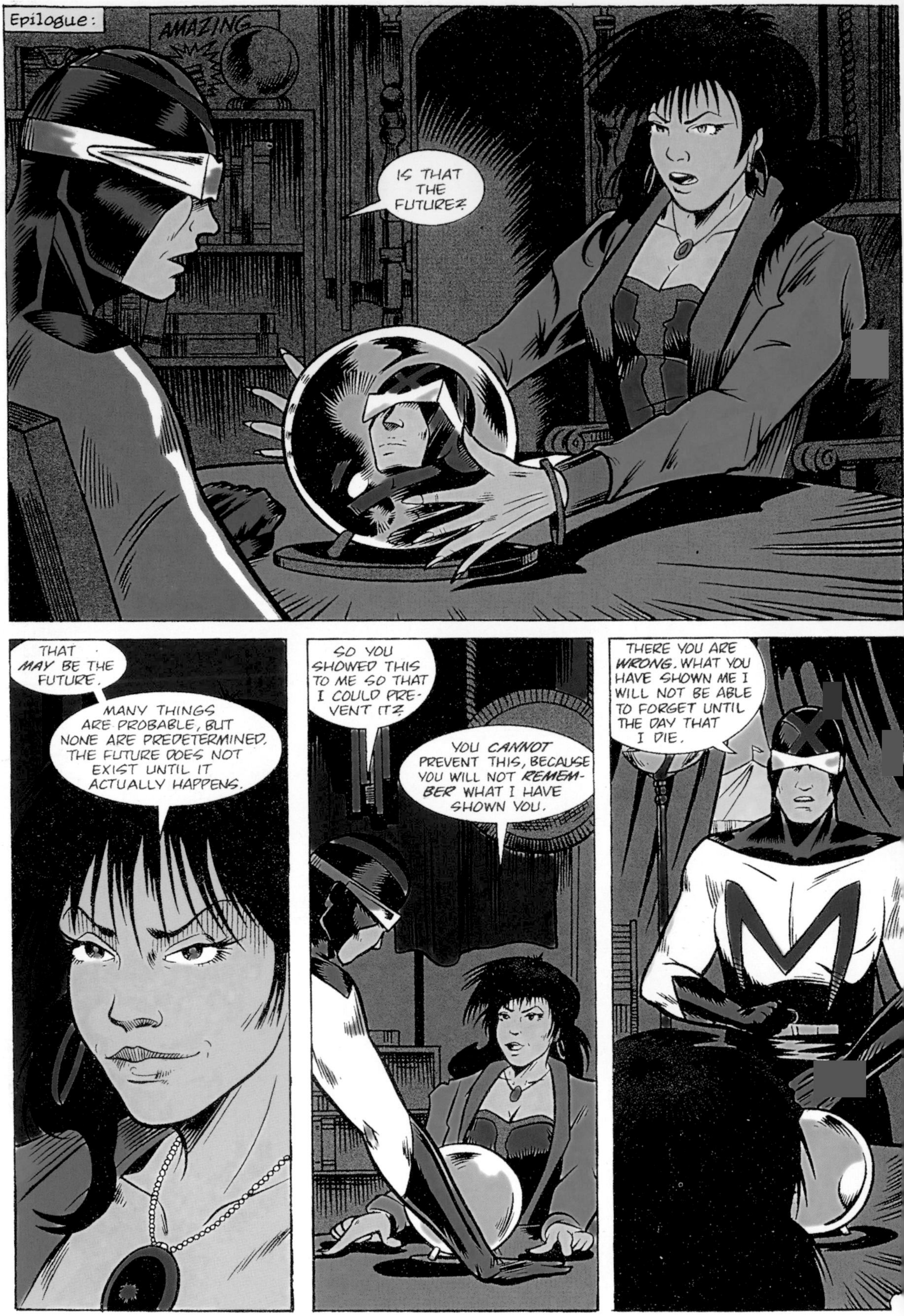
Epilogue:
AMAZING
IS THAT THE FUTURE?
THAT MAY BE THE FUTURE.
MANY THINGS ARE PROBABLE, BUT NONE ARE PREDETERMINED. THE FUTURE DOES NOT EXIST UNTIL IT ACTUALLY HAPPENS.
SO YOU SHOWED THIS TO ME SO THAT I COULD PREVENT IT?
YOU CANNOT PREVENT THIS, BECAUSE YOU WILL NOT REMEMBER WHAT I HAVE SHOWN YOU.
THERE YOU ARE WRONG. WHAT YOU HAVE SHOWN ME I WILL NOT BE ABLE TO FORGET UNTIL THE DAY THAT I DIE.

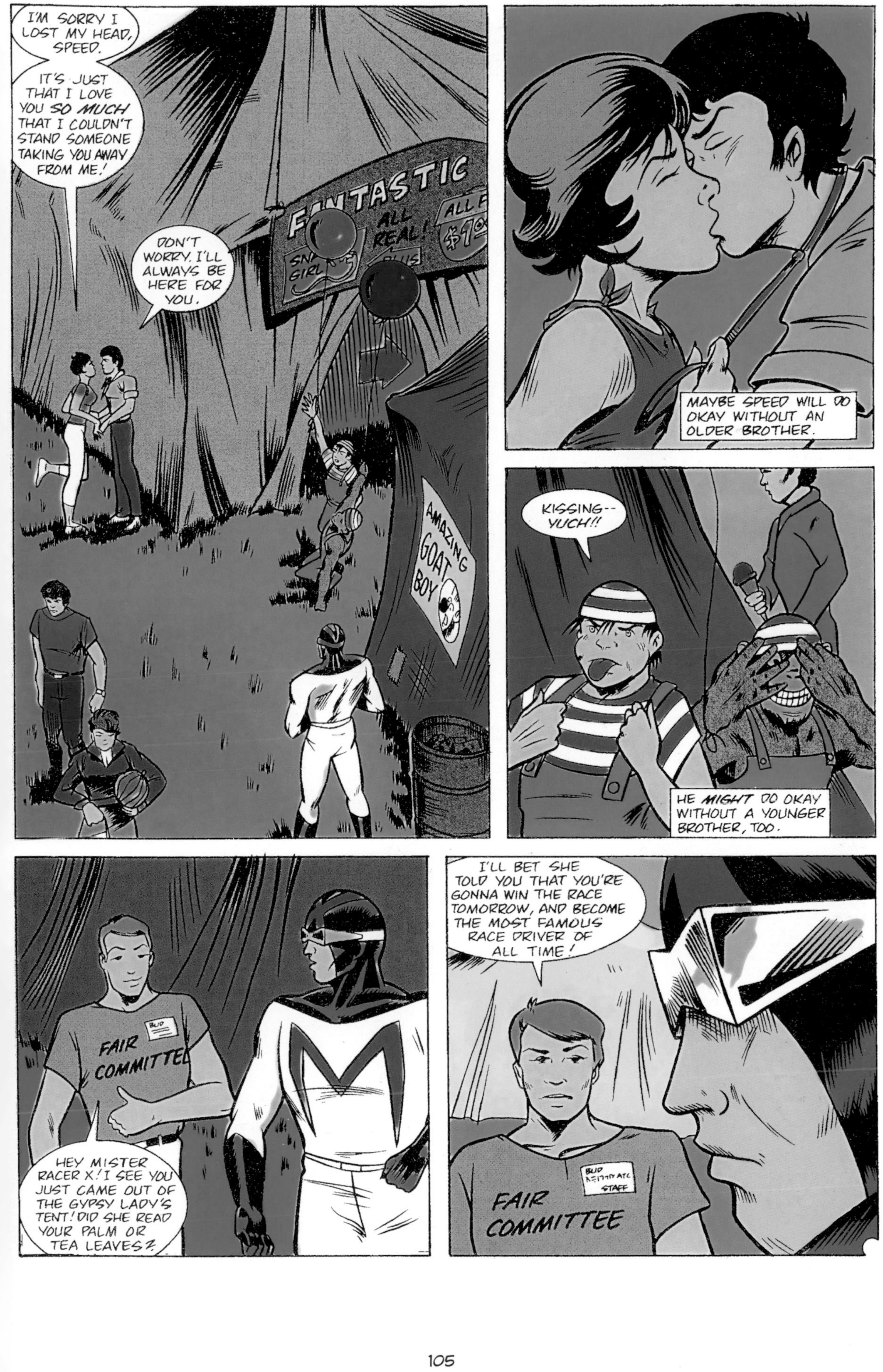
I'M SORRY I LOST MY HEAD, SPEED.
IT'S JUST THAT I LOVE YOU SO MUCH THAT I COULDN'T STAND SOMEONE TAKING YOU AWAY FROM ME!
FANTASTIC
ALL REAL!
DON'T WORRY. I'LL ALWAYS BE HERE FOR YOU.
AMAZING GOAT BOY
MAYBE SPEED WILL DO OKAY WITHOUT AN OLDER BROTHER.
KISSING-- YUCH!!
HE MIGHT DO OKAY WITHOUT A YOUNGER BROTHER, TOO.
FAIR COMMITTEE
HEY MISTER RACER X! I SEE YOU JUST CAME OUT OF THE GYPSY LADY'S TENT! DID SHE READ YOUR PALM OR TEA LEAVES?
I'LL BET SHE TOLD YOU THAT YOU'RE GONNA WIN THE RACE TOMORROW, AND BECOME THE MOST FAMOUS RACE DRIVER OF ALL TIME!
FAIR COMMITTEE

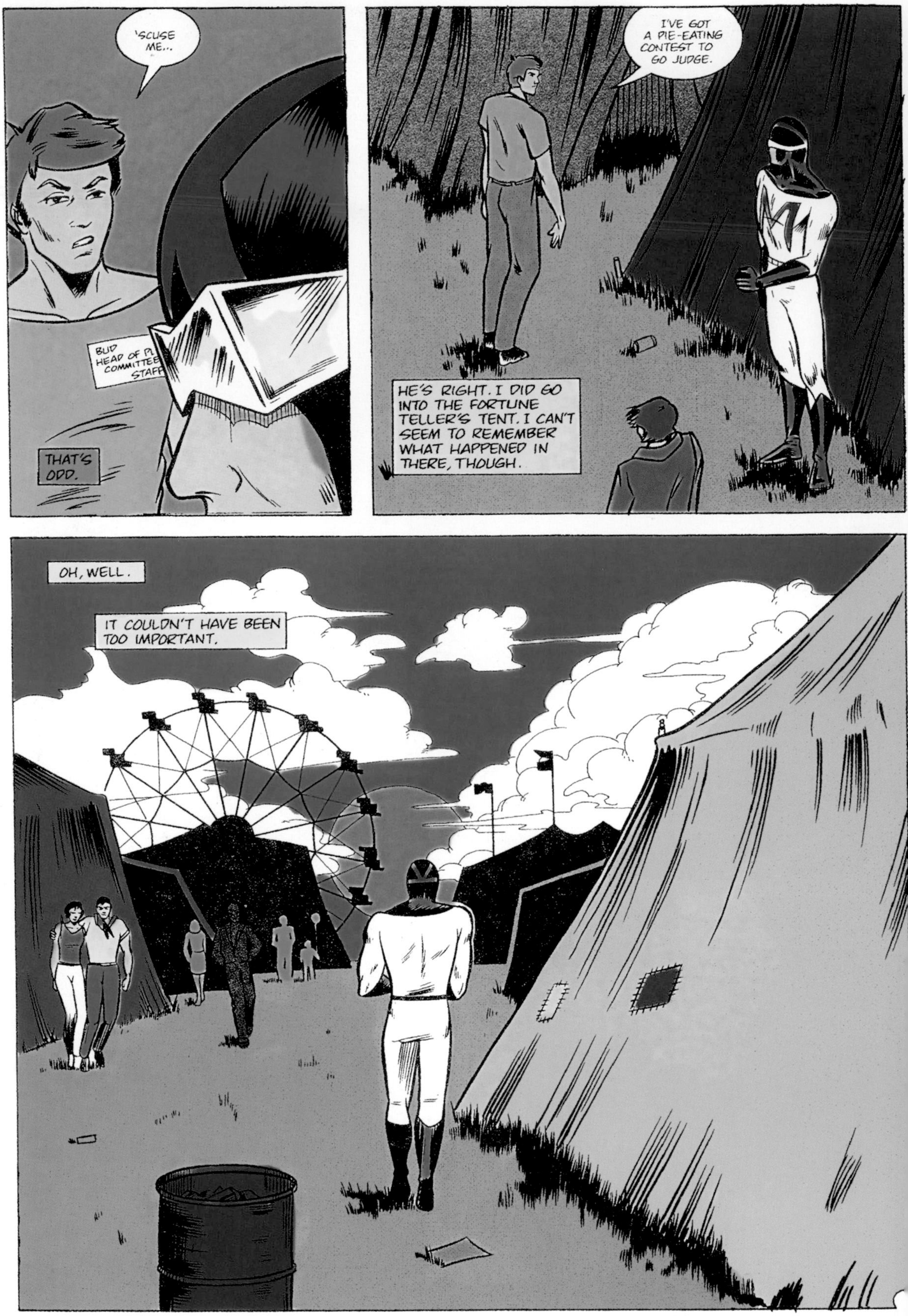
'SCUSE ME...
BUD HEAD OF PL COMMITTEE STAFF
THAT'S ODD.
I'VE GOT A PIE-EATING CONTEST TO GO JUDGE.
HE'S RIGHT. I DID GO INTO THE FORTUNE TELLER'S TENT. I CAN'T SEEM TO REMEMBER WHAT HAPPENED IN THERE, THOUGH.
OH, WELL.
IT COULDN'T HAVE BEEN TOO IMPORTANT.

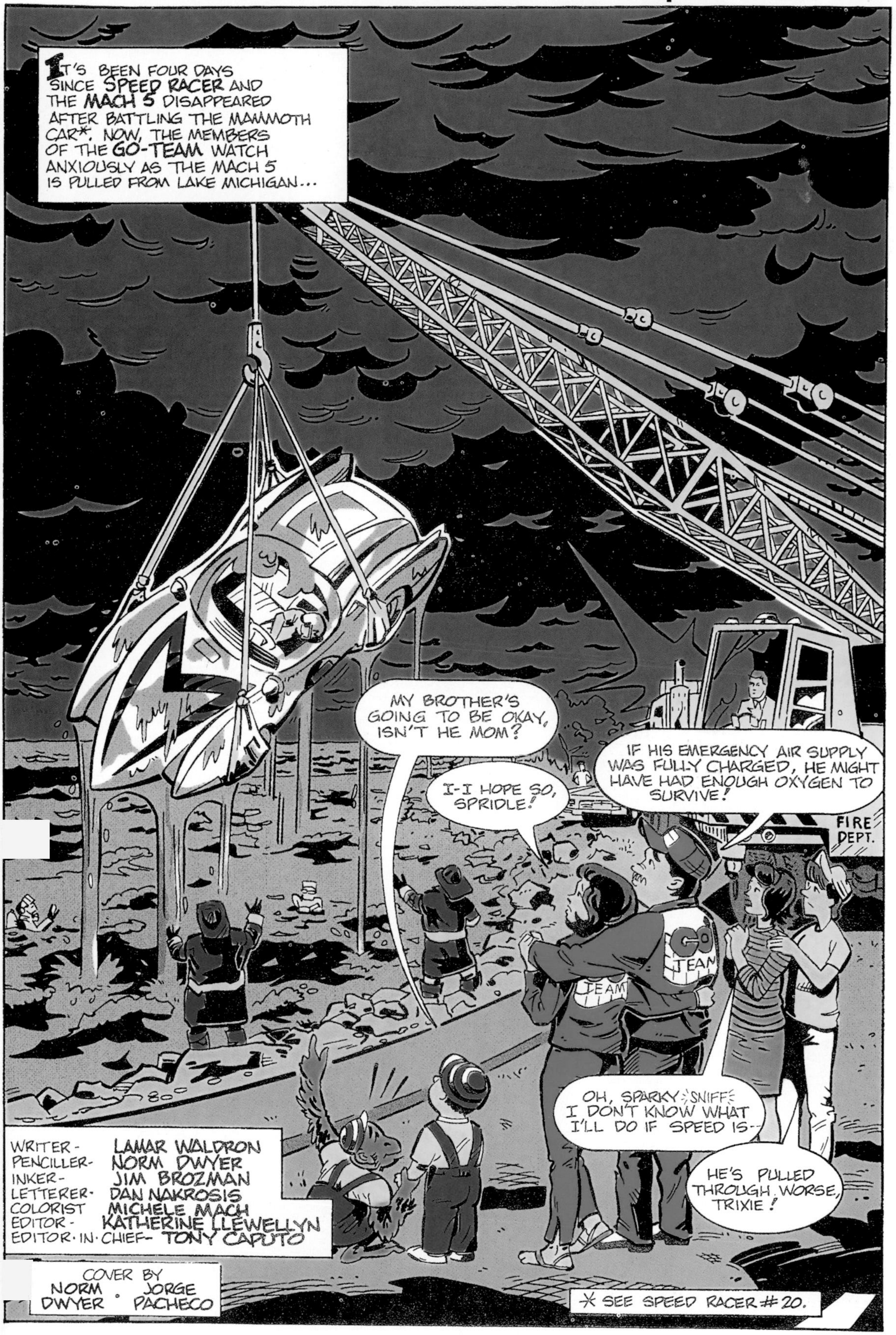
IT'S BEEN FOUR DAYS SINCE SPEED RACER AND THE MACH 5 DISAPPEARED AFTER BATTLING THE MAMMOTH CAR*. NOW, THE MEMBERS OF THE GO-TEAM WATCH ANXIOUSLY AS THE MACH 5 IS PULLED FROM LAKE MICHIGAN...
MY BROTHER'S GOING TO BE OKAY, ISN'T HE MOM?
I-I HOPE SO, SPRIDLE!
IF HIS EMERGENCY AIR SUPPLY WAS FULLY CHARGED, HE MIGHT HAVE HAD ENOUGH OXYGEN TO SURVIVE!
FIRE DEPT.
GO TEAM
TEAM
OH, SPARKY SNIFF I DON'T KNOW WHAT I'LL DO IF SPEED IS--
HE'S PULLED THROUGH WORSE, TRIXIE!
WRITER - LAMAR WALDRON
PENCILLER - NORM DWYER
INKER - JIM BROZMAN
LETTERER - DAN NAKROSIS
COLORIST MICHELE MACH
EDITOR - KATHERINE LLEWELLYN
EDITOR-IN-CHIEF - TONY CAPUTO
COVER BY NORM DWYER · JORGE PACHECO
* SEE SPEED RACER #20.

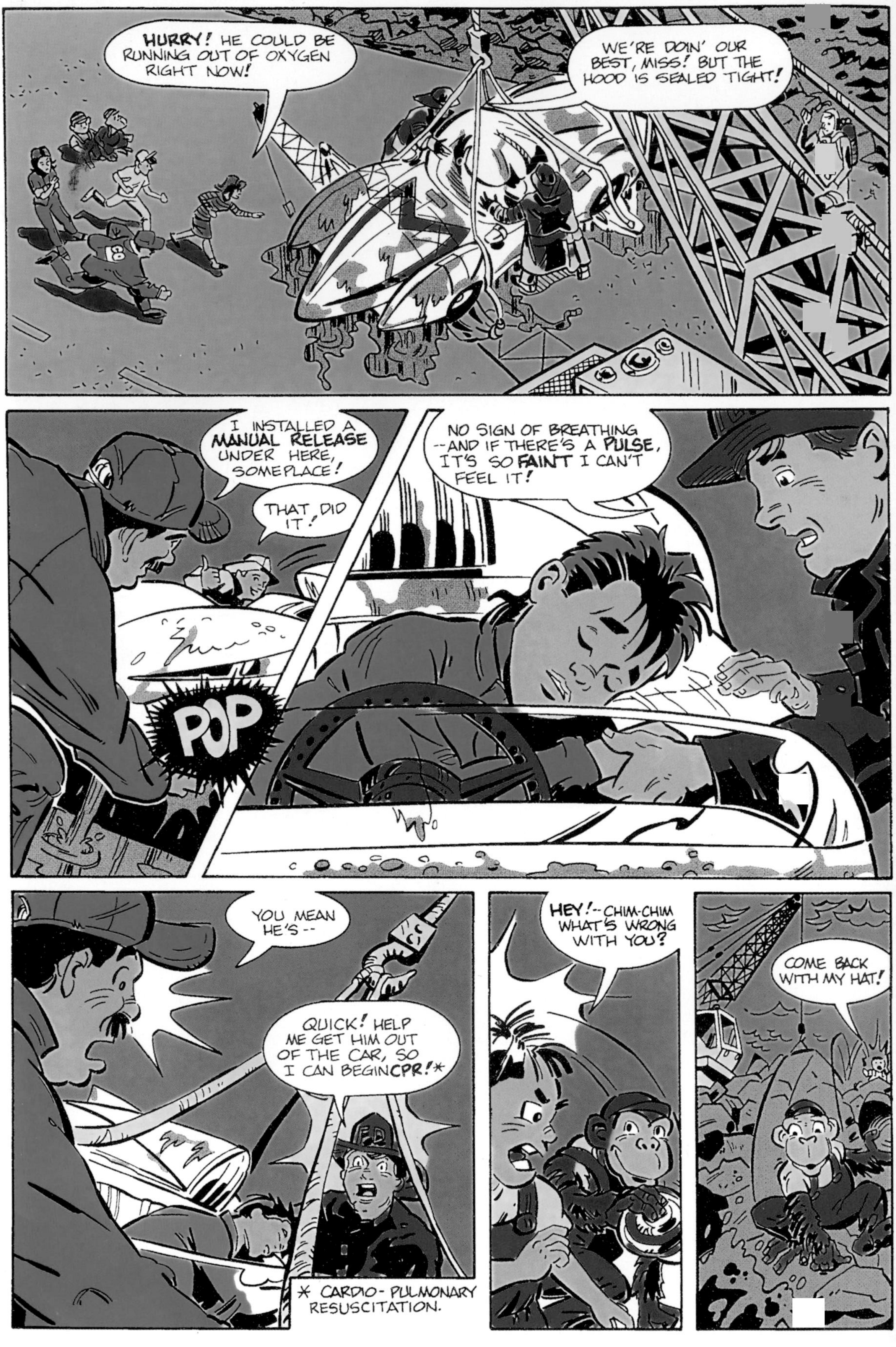
HURRY! HE COULD BE RUNNING OUT OF OXYGEN RIGHT NOW!
WE'RE DOIN' OUR BEST, MISS! BUT THE HOOD IS SEALED TIGHT!
I INSTALLED A MANUAL RELEASE UNDER HERE, SOMEPLACE!
THAT DID IT!
POP
NO SIGN OF BREATHING --AND IF THERE'S A PULSE, IT'S SO FAINT I CAN'T FEEL IT!
YOU MEAN HE'S --
QUICK! HELP ME GET HIM OUT OF THE CAR, SO I CAN BEGIN CPR!*
* CARDIO-PULMONARY RESUSCITATION.
FD
HEY!--CHIM-CHIM WHAT'S WRONG WITH YOU?
COME BACK WITH MY HAT!

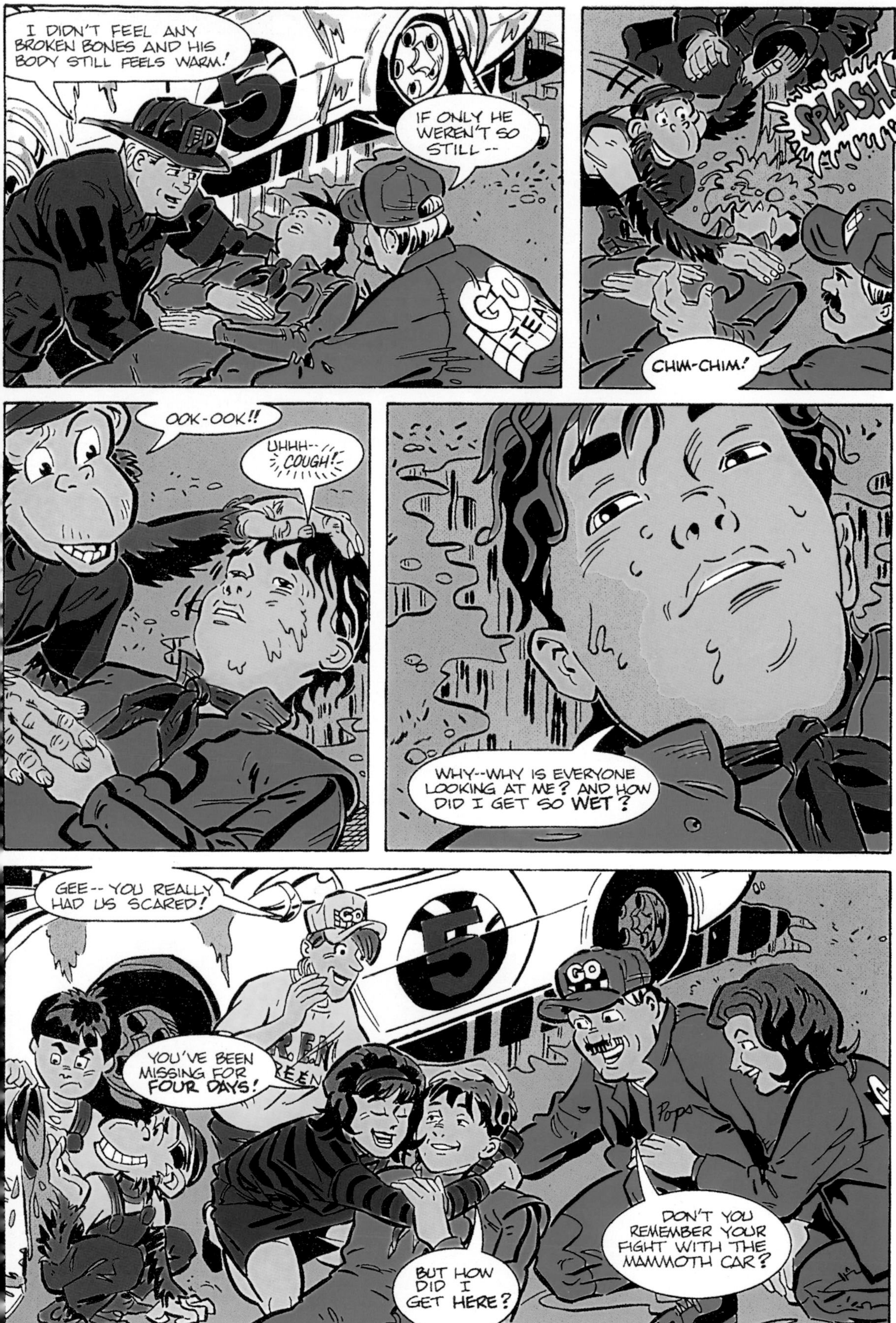
I DIDN'T FEEL ANY BROKEN BONES AND HIS BODY STILL FEELS WARM!
IF ONLY HE WEREN'T SO STILL --
SPLASH!
CHIM-CHIM!
OOK-OOK!!
UHHH-- COUGH!
WHY--WHY IS EVERYONE LOOKING AT ME? AND HOW DID I GET SO **WET**?
GEE-- YOU REALLY HAD US SCARED!
YOU'VE BEEN MISSING FOR **FOUR DAYS**!
Pops
DON'T YOU REMEMBER YOUR FIGHT WITH THE MAMMOTH CAR?
BUT HOW DID I GET **HERE**?

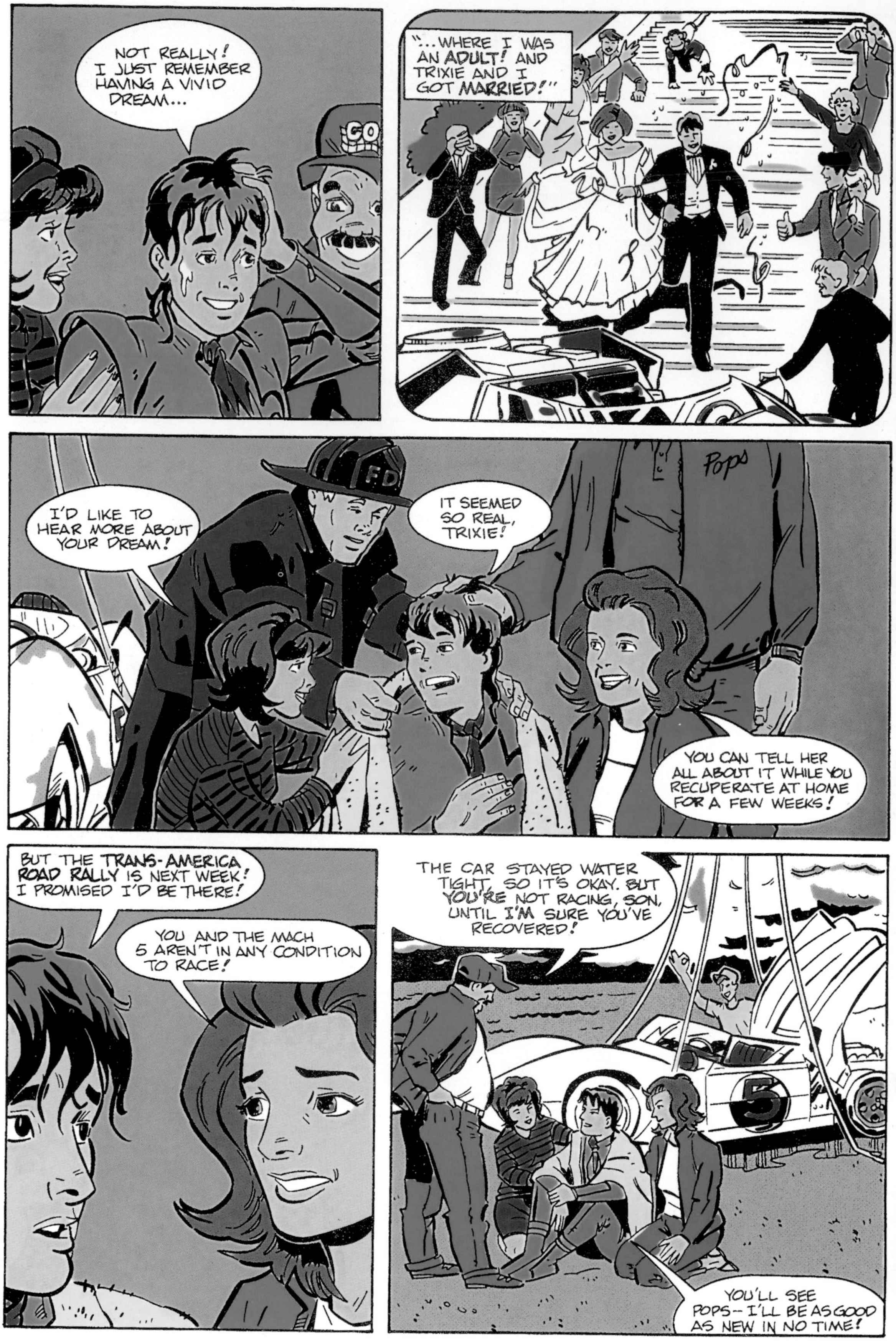
NOT REALLY! I JUST REMEMBER HAVING A VIVID DREAM...
"...WHERE I WAS AN ADULT! AND TRIXIE AND I GOT MARRIED!"
I'D LIKE TO HEAR MORE ABOUT YOUR DREAM!
IT SEEMED SO REAL, TRIXIE!
FD
Pops
YOU CAN TELL HER ALL ABOUT IT WHILE YOU RECUPERATE AT HOME FOR A FEW WEEKS!
BUT THE TRANS-AMERICA ROAD RALLY IS NEXT WEEK! I PROMISED I'D BE THERE!
YOU AND THE MACH 5 AREN'T IN ANY CONDITION TO RACE!
THE CAR STAYED WATER TIGHT, SO IT'S OKAY. BUT YOU'RE NOT RACING, SON, UNTIL I'M SURE YOU'VE RECOVERED!
YOU'LL SEE POPS-- I'LL BE AS GOOD AS NEW IN NO TIME!

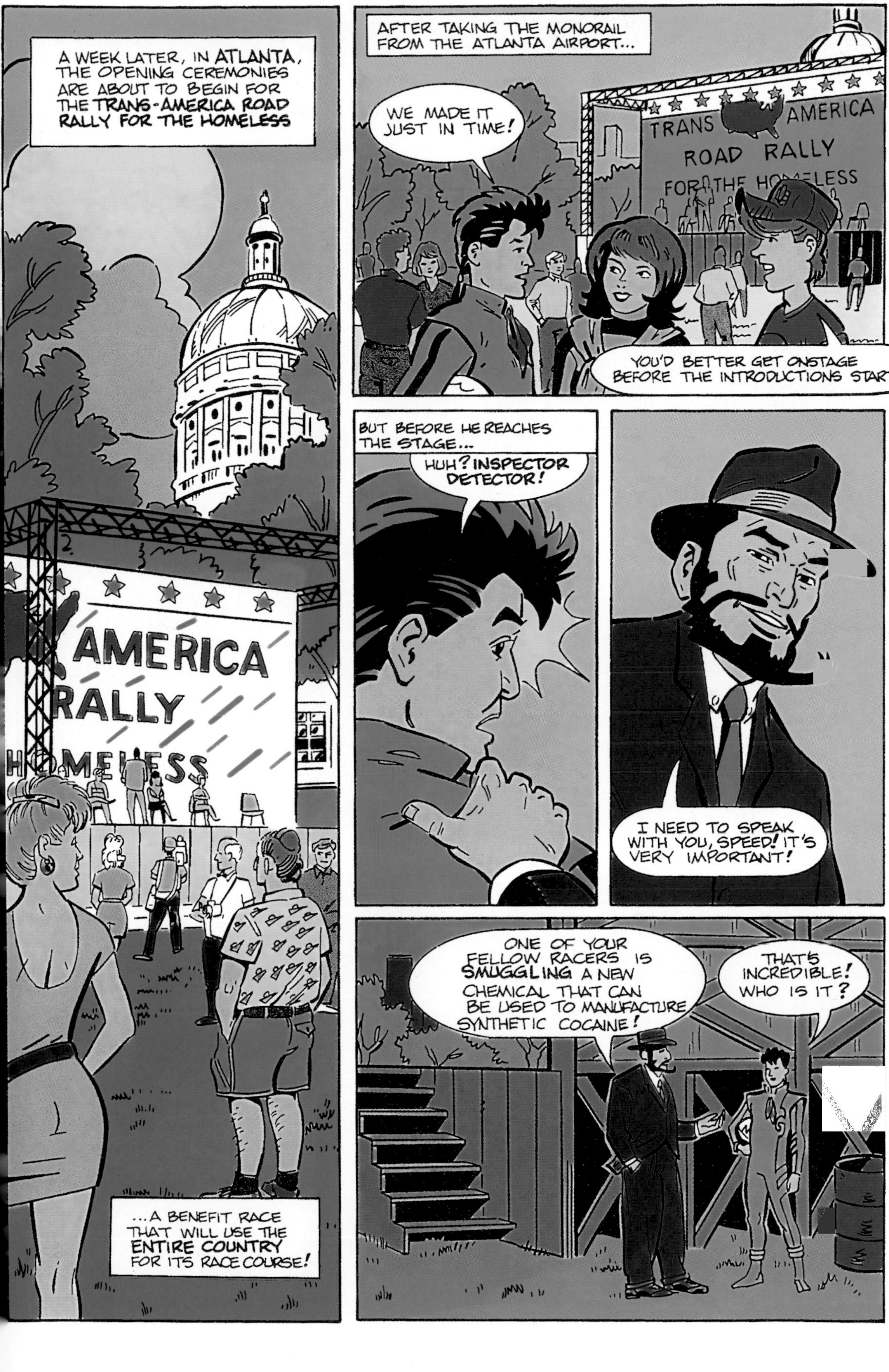
A WEEK LATER, IN ATLANTA, THE OPENING CEREMONIES ARE ABOUT TO BEGIN FOR THE TRANS-AMERICA ROAD RALLY FOR THE HOMELESS
AMERICA
RALLY
...A BENEFIT RACE THAT WILL USE THE ENTIRE COUNTRY FOR ITS RACE COURSE!
AFTER TAKING THE MONORAIL FROM THE ATLANTA AIRPORT...
WE MADE IT JUST IN TIME!
TRANS AMERICA ROAD RALLY FOR THE HOMELESS
YOU'D BETTER GET ONSTAGE BEFORE THE INTRODUCTIONS START!
BUT BEFORE HE REACHES THE STAGE...
HUH? INSPECTOR DETECTOR!
I NEED TO SPEAK WITH YOU, SPEED! IT'S VERY IMPORTANT!
ONE OF YOUR FELLOW RACERS IS SMUGGLING A NEW CHEMICAL THAT CAN BE USED TO MANUFACTURE SYNTHETIC COCAINE!
THAT'S INCREDIBLE! WHO IS IT?

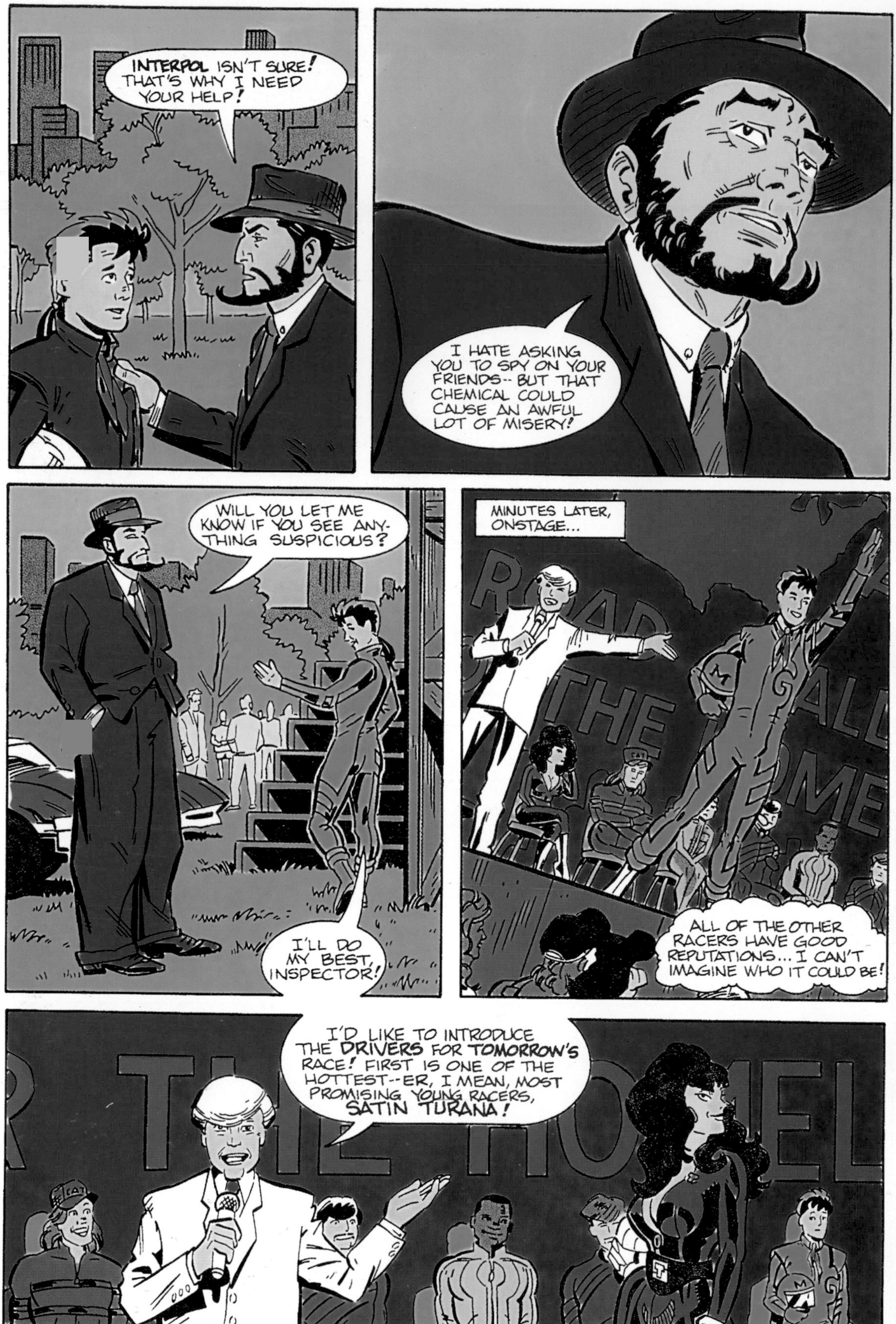
INTERPOL ISN'T SURE! THAT'S WHY I NEED YOUR HELP!
I HATE ASKING YOU TO SPY ON YOUR FRIENDS-- BUT THAT CHEMICAL COULD CAUSE AN AWFUL LOT OF MISERY!
WILL YOU LET ME KNOW IF YOU SEE ANY-THING SUSPICIOUS?
I'LL DO MY BEST, INSPECTOR!
MINUTES LATER, ONSTAGE...
ALL OF THE OTHER RACERS HAVE GOOD REPUTATIONS... I CAN'T IMAGINE WHO IT COULD BE!
I'D LIKE TO INTRODUCE THE DRIVERS FOR TOMORROW'S RACE! FIRST IS ONE OF THE HOTTEST--ER, I MEAN, MOST PROMISING YOUNG RACERS, SATIN TURANA!

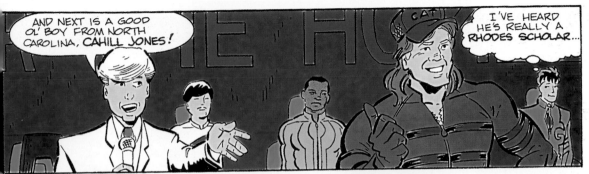

AND NEXT IS A GOOD OL' BOY FROM NORTH CAROLINA, CAHILL JONES!

I'VE HEARD HE'S REALLY A RHODES SCHOLAR...

JOINING US ALL THE WAY FROM LONDON IS LADY ELAINE DUNHILL!

SHE'S PROBABLY THE ONLY RACER WHO TRAVELS AROUND THE WORLD MORE THAN I DO...

WE'RE HONORED TO WELCOME THE SOUTH AMERICAN GRAND PRIX CHAMPION SPITFIRE MORELLO!

HE'S ALWAYS BEEN A REAL GENTLEMAN... BUT IS THAT JUST A FACADE?

I DON'T KNOW TOO MUCH ABOUT HIM...

AND WE'RE HAPPY TO WELCOME A NATIVE ATLANTAN, CARL JACKSON!

LAST--BUT CERTAINLY NOT LEAST--IS A YOUNG MAN WHO DIVIDES HIS TIME BETWEEN HOLLYWOOD AND RACING-- PAUL TRUMAN!

I'M GLAD PAUL AND I BECAME FRIENDS, INSTEAD OF RIVALS!

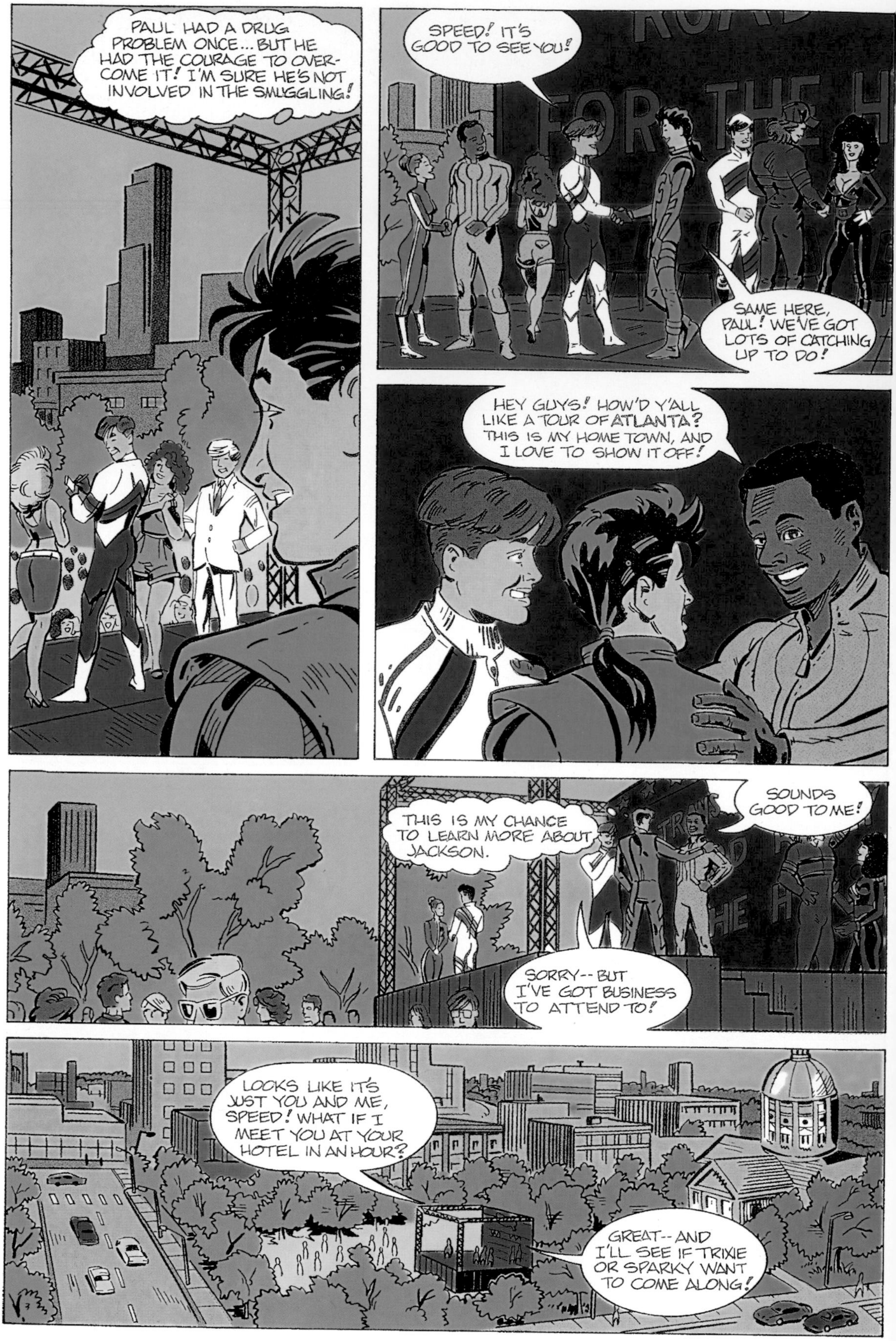
PAUL HAD A DRUG PROBLEM ONCE... BUT HE HAD THE COURAGE TO OVERCOME IT! I'M SURE HE'S NOT INVOLVED IN THE SMUGGLING!
SPEED! IT'S GOOD TO SEE YOU!
SAME HERE, PAUL! WE'VE GOT LOTS OF CATCHING UP TO DO!
HEY GUYS! HOW'D Y'ALL LIKE A TOUR OF ATLANTA? THIS IS MY HOME TOWN, AND I LOVE TO SHOW IT OFF!
THIS IS MY CHANCE TO LEARN MORE ABOUT JACKSON.
SOUNDS GOOD TO ME!
SORRY-- BUT I'VE GOT BUSINESS TO ATTEND TO!
LOOKS LIKE IT'S JUST YOU AND ME, SPEED! WHAT IF I MEET YOU AT YOUR HOTEL IN AN HOUR?
GREAT-- AND I'LL SEE IF TRIXIE OR SPARKY WANT TO COME ALONG!

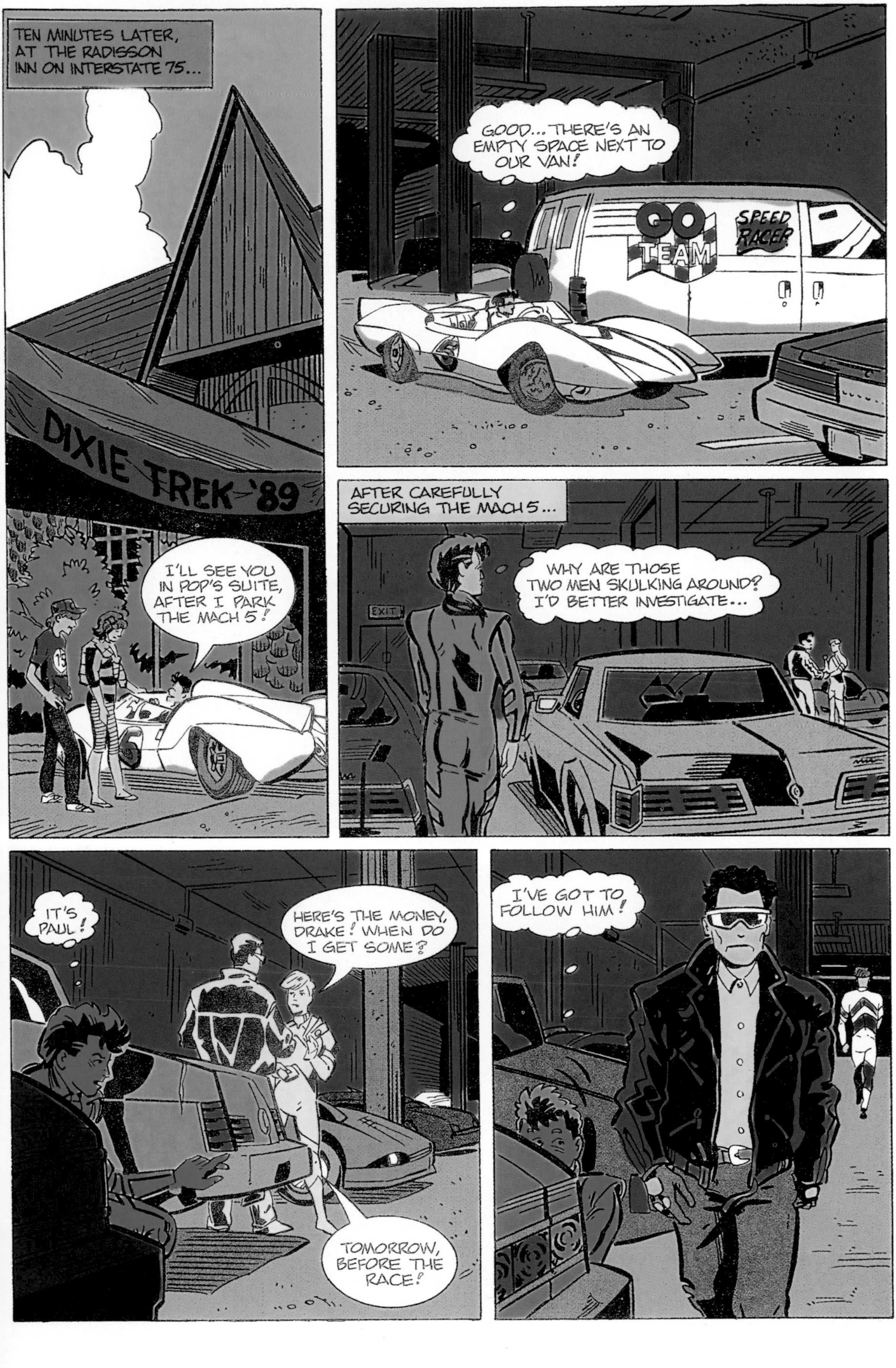
TEN MINUTES LATER, AT THE RADISSON INN ON INTERSTATE 75...
DIXIE TREK '89
I'LL SEE YOU IN POP'S SUITE, AFTER I PARK THE MACH 5!
GOOD... THERE'S AN EMPTY SPACE NEXT TO OUR VAN!
GO TEAM
SPEED RACER
AFTER CAREFULLY SECURING THE MACH 5...
WHY ARE THOSE TWO MEN SKULKING AROUND? I'D BETTER INVESTIGATE...
EXIT
IT'S PAUL!
HERE'S THE MONEY, DRAKE! WHEN DO I GET SOME?
TOMORROW, BEFORE THE RACE!
I'VE GOT TO FOLLOW HIM!

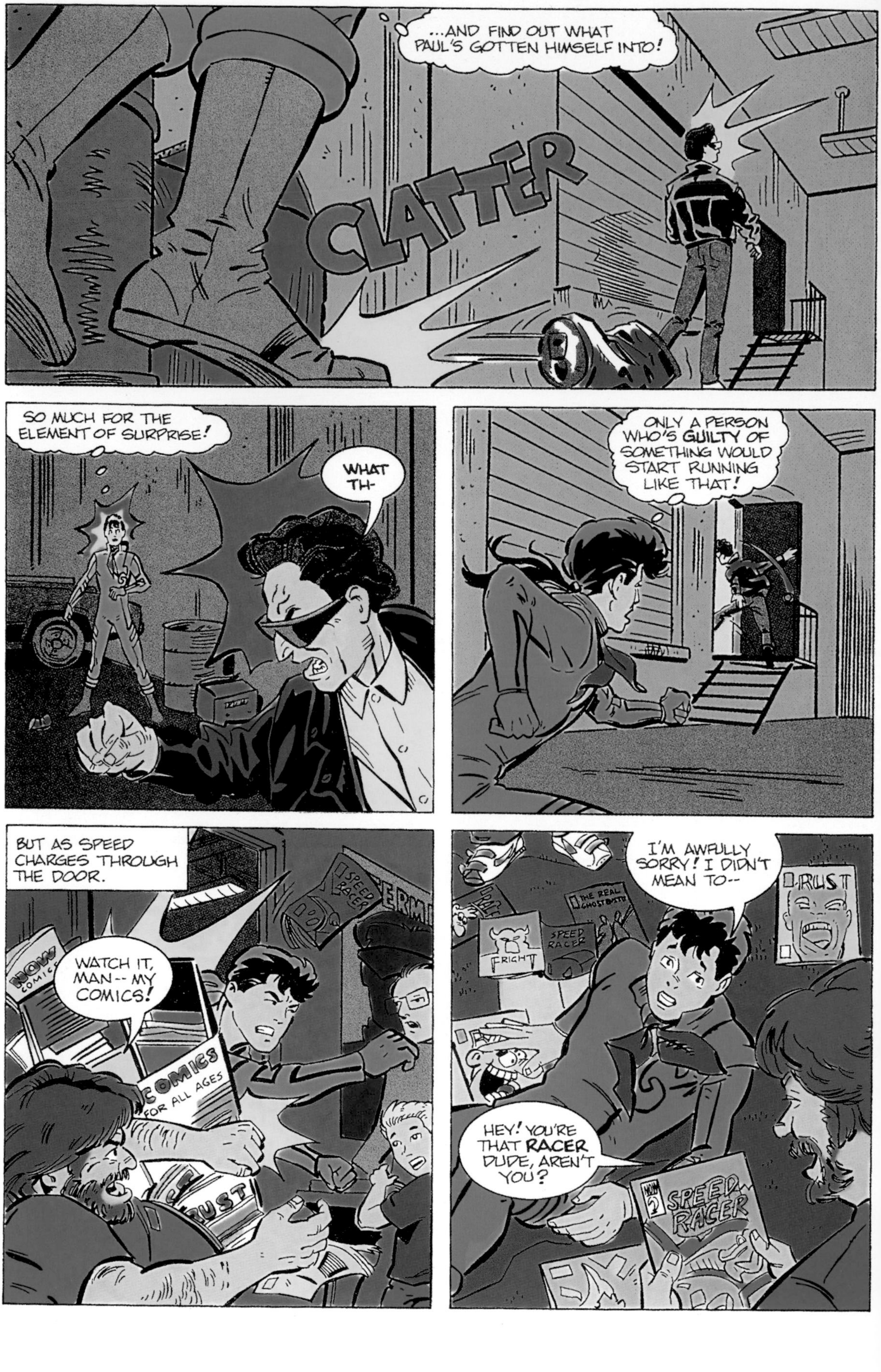
...AND FIND OUT WHAT PAUL'S GOTTEN HIMSELF INTO!
CLATTER
SO MUCH FOR THE ELEMENT OF SURPRISE!
WHAT TH-
ONLY A PERSON WHO'S **GUILTY** OF SOMETHING WOULD START RUNNING LIKE THAT!
BUT AS SPEED CHARGES THROUGH THE DOOR.
WATCH IT, MAN-- MY COMICS!
COMICS FOR ALL AGES
RUST
I'M AWFULLY SORRY! I DIDN'T MEAN TO--
HEY! YOU'RE THAT **RACER** DUDE, AREN'T YOU?
SPEED RACER

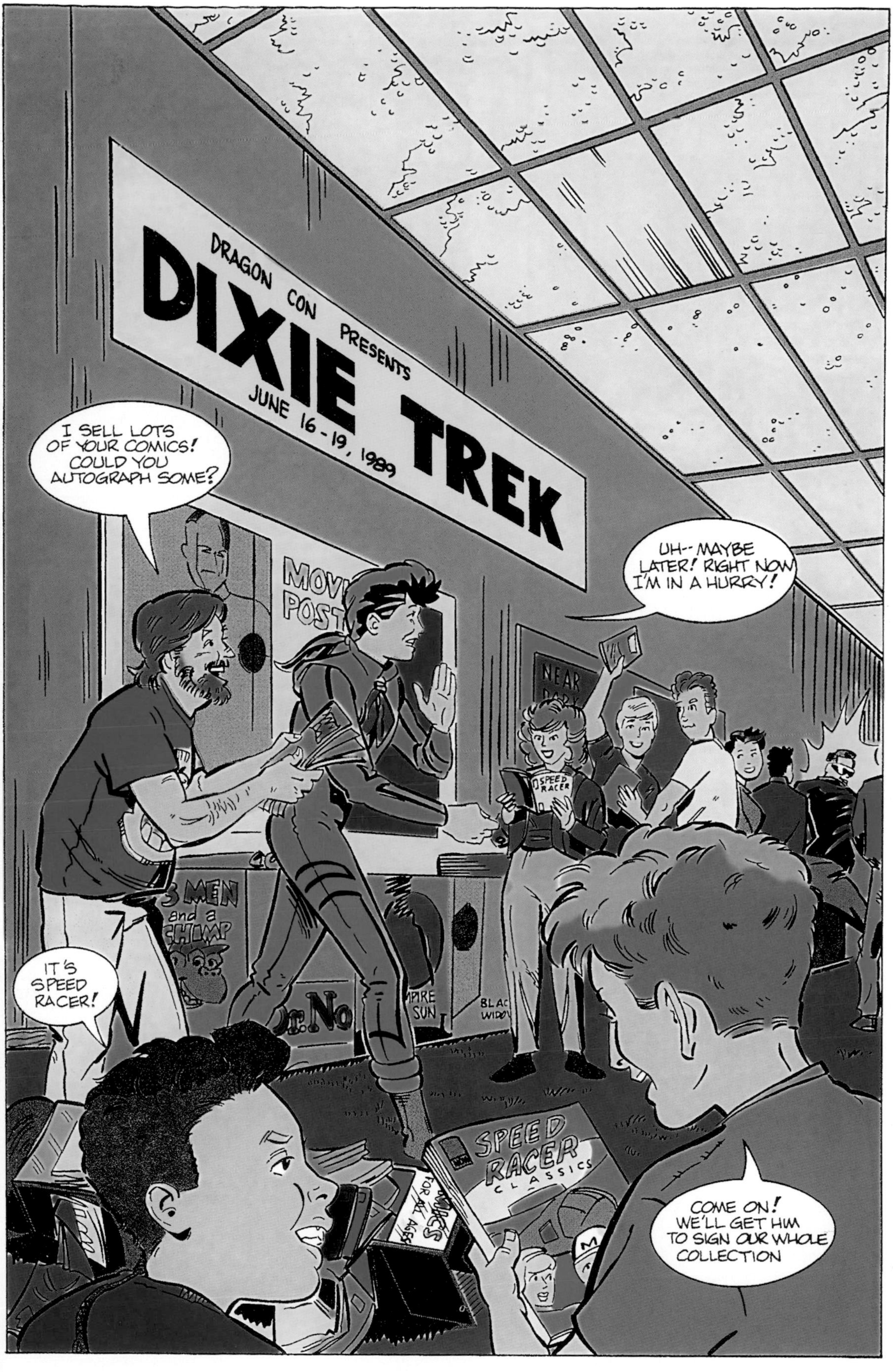

DRAGON CON PRESENTS
DIXIE TREK
JUNE 16-19, 1989
I SELL LOTS OF YOUR COMICS! COULD YOU AUTOGRAPH SOME?
UH-- MAYBE LATER! RIGHT NOW I'M IN A HURRY!
IT'S SPEED RACER!
COME ON! WE'LL GET HIM TO SIGN OUR WHOLE COLLECTION
SPEED RACER CLASSICS
SPEED RACER
3 MEN and a CHIMP
Dr. No
BLACK WIDOW

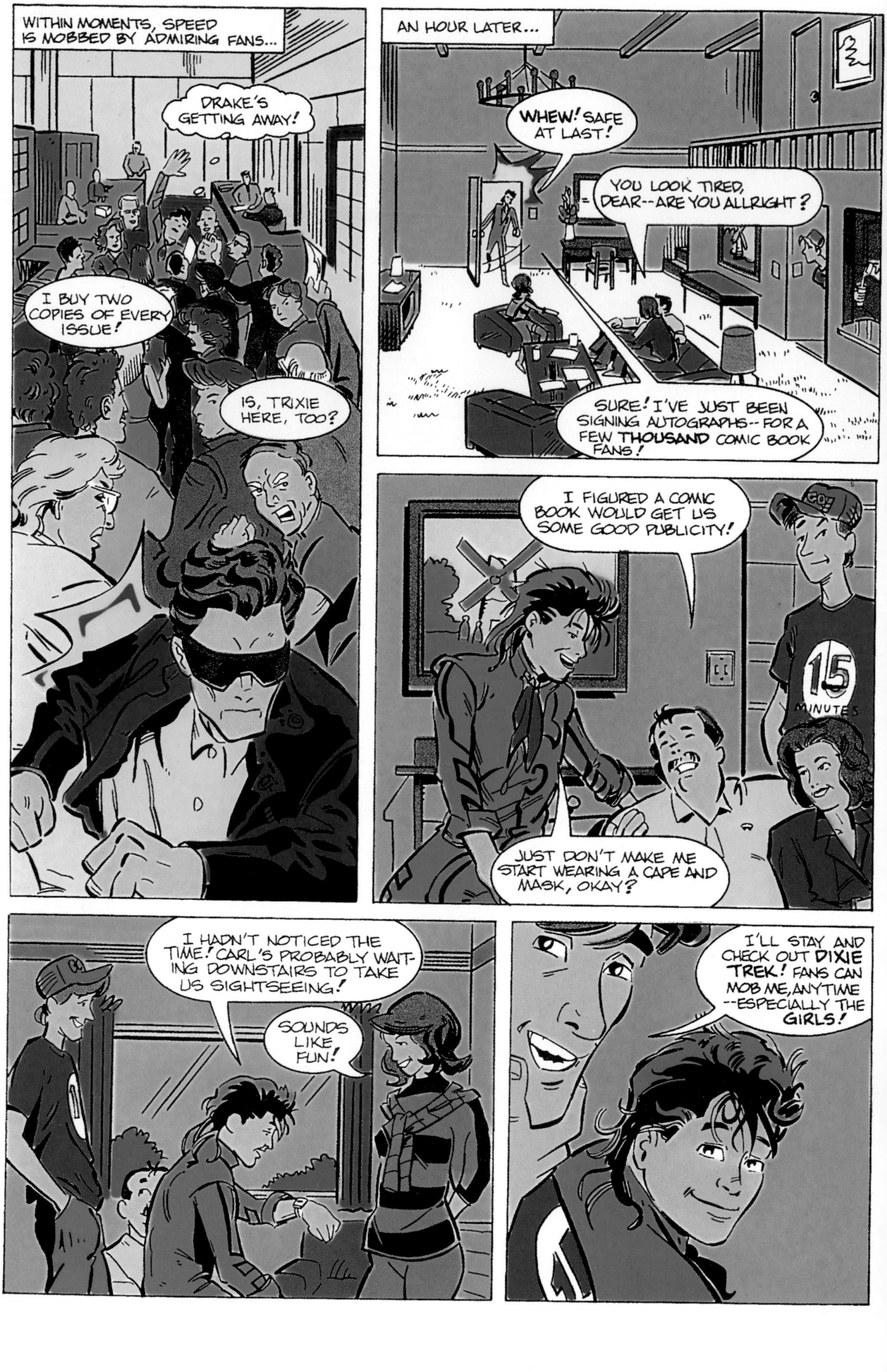

WITHIN MOMENTS, SPEED IS MOBBED BY ADMIRING FANS...
DRAKE'S GETTING AWAY!
I BUY TWO COPIES OF EVERY ISSUE!
IS, TRIXIE HERE, TOO?
AN HOUR LATER...
WHEW! SAFE AT LAST!
YOU LOOK TIRED, DEAR--ARE YOU ALLRIGHT?
SURE! I'VE JUST BEEN SIGNING AUTOGRAPHS--FOR A FEW THOUSAND COMIC BOOK FANS!
I FIGURED A COMIC BOOK WOULD GET US SOME GOOD PUBLICITY!
15 MINUTES
JUST DON'T MAKE ME START WEARING A CAPE AND MASK, OKAY?
I HADN'T NOTICED THE TIME! CARL'S PROBABLY WAITING DOWNSTAIRS TO TAKE US SIGHTSEEING!
SOUNDS LIKE FUN!
I'LL STAY AND CHECK OUT DIXIE TREK! FANS CAN MOB ME, ANYTIME --ESPECIALLY THE GIRLS!

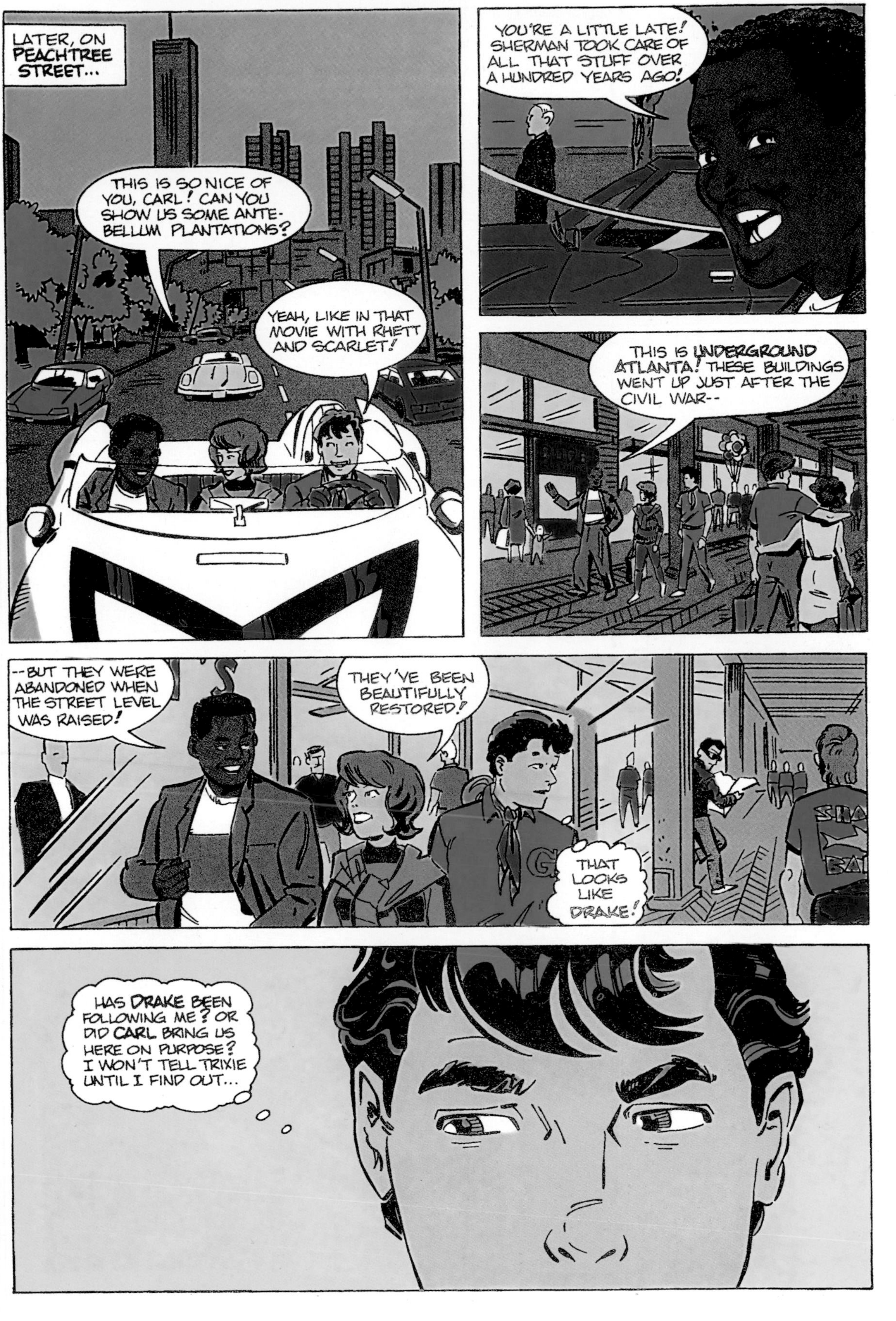
LATER, ON PEACHTREE STREET...
THIS IS SO NICE OF YOU, CARL! CAN YOU SHOW US SOME ANTE-BELLUM PLANTATIONS?
YEAH, LIKE IN THAT MOVIE WITH RHETT AND SCARLET!
YOU'RE A LITTLE LATE! SHERMAN TOOK CARE OF ALL THAT STUFF OVER A HUNDRED YEARS AGO!
THIS IS UNDERGROUND ATLANTA! THESE BUILDINGS WENT UP JUST AFTER THE CIVIL WAR--
--BUT THEY WERE ABANDONED WHEN THE STREET LEVEL WAS RAISED!
THEY'VE BEEN BEAUTIFULLY RESTORED!
THAT LOOKS LIKE DRAKE!
HAS DRAKE BEEN FOLLOWING ME? OR DID CARL BRING US HERE ON PURPOSE? I WON'T TELL TRIXIE UNTIL I FIND OUT...

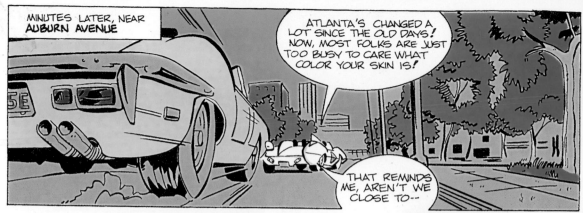

MINUTES LATER, NEAR **AUBURN AVENUE**

ATLANTA'S CHANGED A LOT SINCE THE OLD DAYS! NOW, MOST FOLKS ARE JUST TOO BUSY TO CARE WHAT COLOR YOUR SKIN IS!

THAT REMINDS ME, AREN'T WE CLOSE TO--

EXCUSE ME TRIXIE- BUT DO Y'ALL KNOW ANYONE WHO DRIVES A JAGUAR? THEY'VE BEEN FOLLOWING US ALL DAY!

CARL WOULDN'T HAVE SAID ANYTHING IF HE WERE INVOLVED...

WHO COULD IT BE?

I'LL EXPLAIN LATER!

BUT FIRST, I'M GOING TO TEACH THAT GUY A LESSON!

WE'LL DUCK IN HERE TILL HE PASSES!

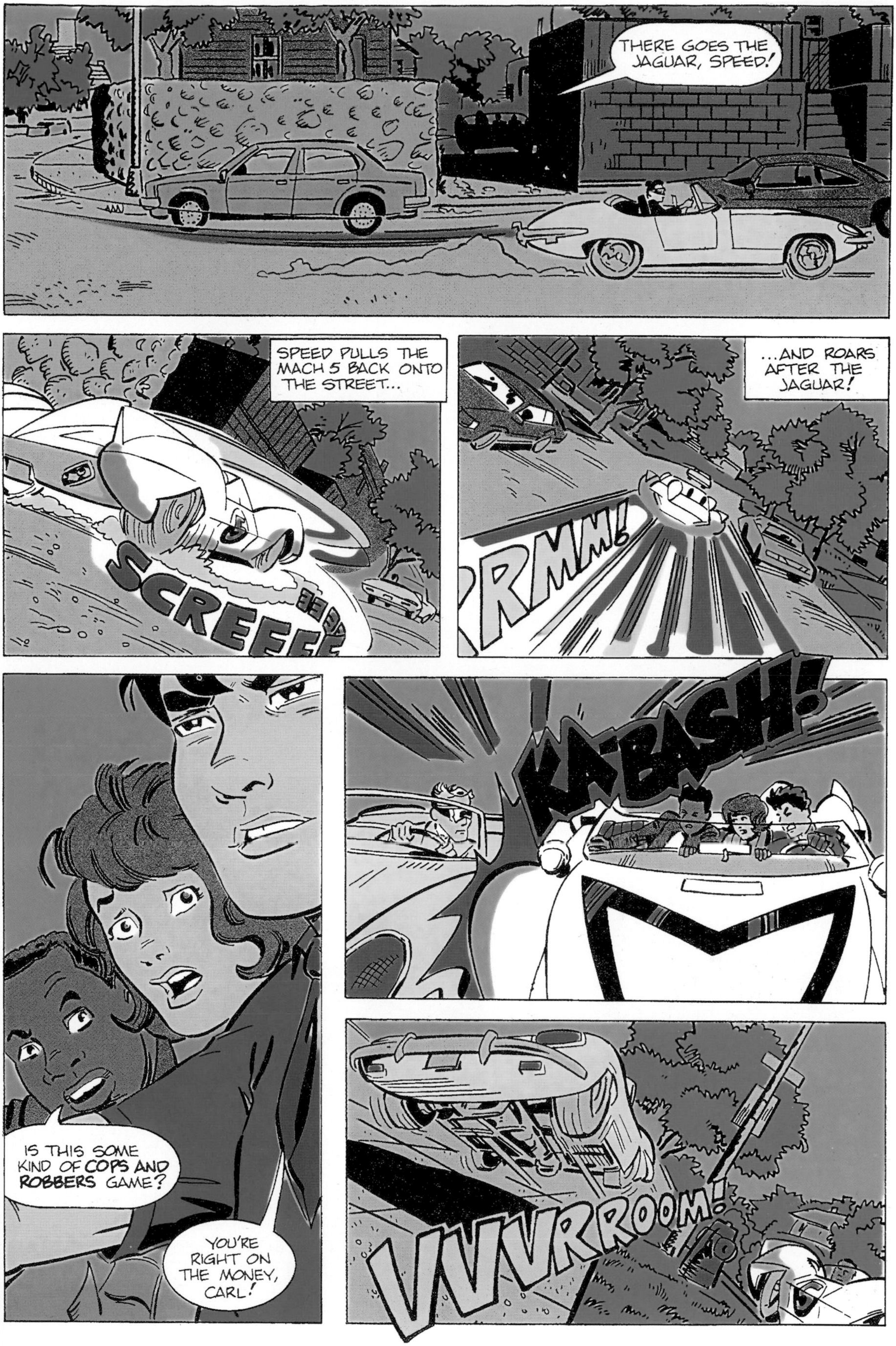
THERE GOES THE JAGUAR, SPEED!
SPEED PULLS THE MACH 5 BACK ONTO THE STREET...
SCREEEEEEE
...AND ROARS AFTER THE JAGUAR!
RMMM!
IS THIS SOME KIND OF COPS AND ROBBERS GAME?
YOU'RE RIGHT ON THE MONEY, CARL!
KA-BASH!
VVVVRROOM!

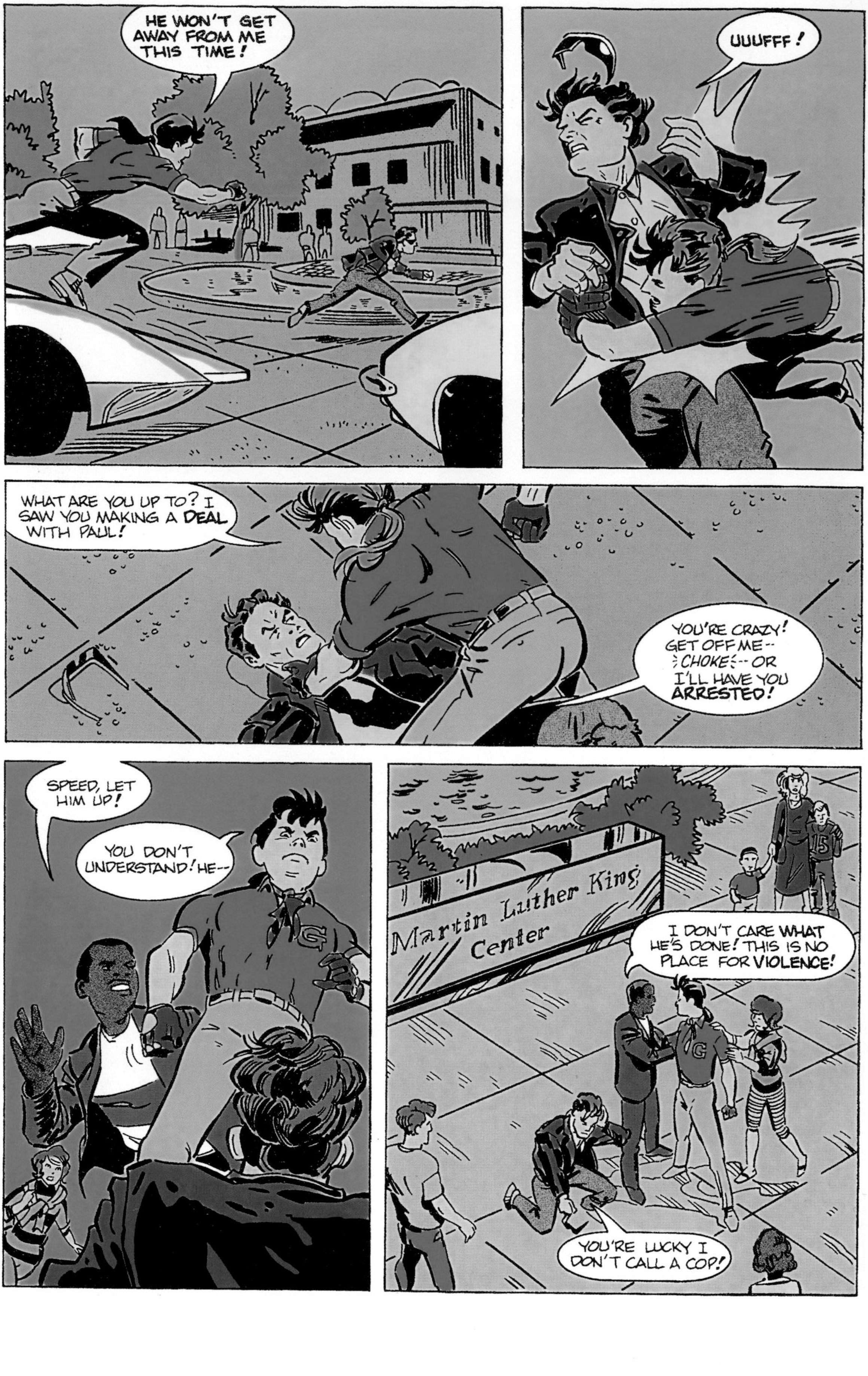
HE WON'T GET AWAY FROM ME THIS TIME!
UUUFFF!
WHAT ARE YOU UP TO? I SAW YOU MAKING A **DEAL** WITH PAUL!
YOU'RE CRAZY! GET OFF ME-- *CHOKE*-- OR I'LL HAVE YOU **ARRESTED**!
SPEED, LET HIM UP!
YOU DON'T UNDERSTAND! HE--
Martin Luther King Center
I DON'T CARE **WHAT** HE'S DONE! THIS IS NO PLACE FOR **VIOLENCE**!
YOU'RE LUCKY I DON'T CALL A COP!

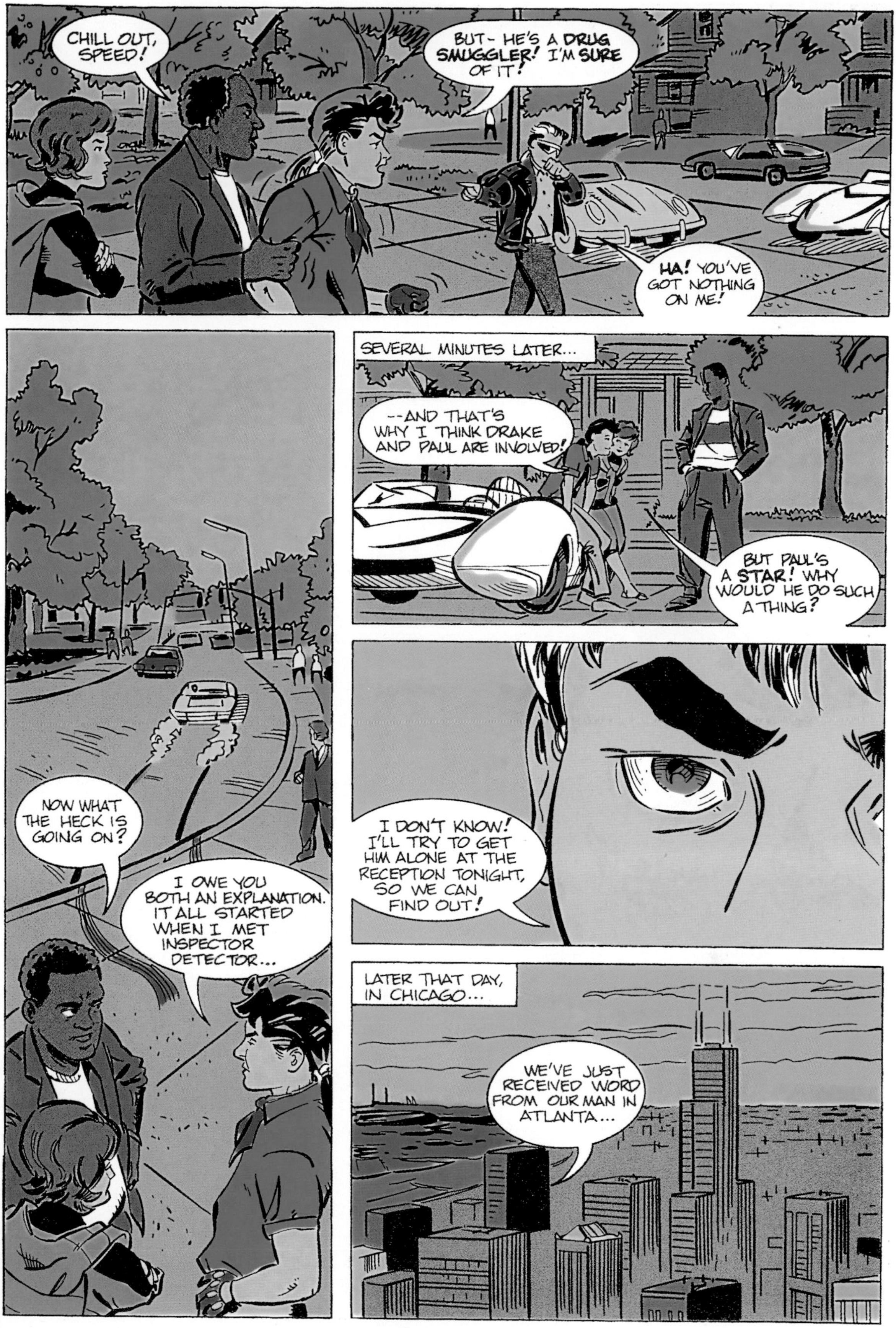

CHILL OUT, SPEED!
BUT- HE'S A DRUG SMUGGLER! I'M SURE OF IT!
HA! YOU'VE GOT NOTHING ON ME!
NOW WHAT THE HECK IS GOING ON?
I OWE YOU BOTH AN EXPLANATION. IT ALL STARTED WHEN I MET INSPECTOR DETECTOR...
SEVERAL MINUTES LATER...
--AND THAT'S WHY I THINK DRAKE AND PAUL ARE INVOLVED!
BUT PAUL'S A STAR! WHY WOULD HE DO SUCH A THING?
I DON'T KNOW! I'LL TRY TO GET HIM ALONE AT THE RECEPTION TONIGHT, SO WE CAN FIND OUT!
LATER THAT DAY, IN CHICAGO...
WE'VE JUST RECEIVED WORD FROM OUR MAN IN ATLANTA...

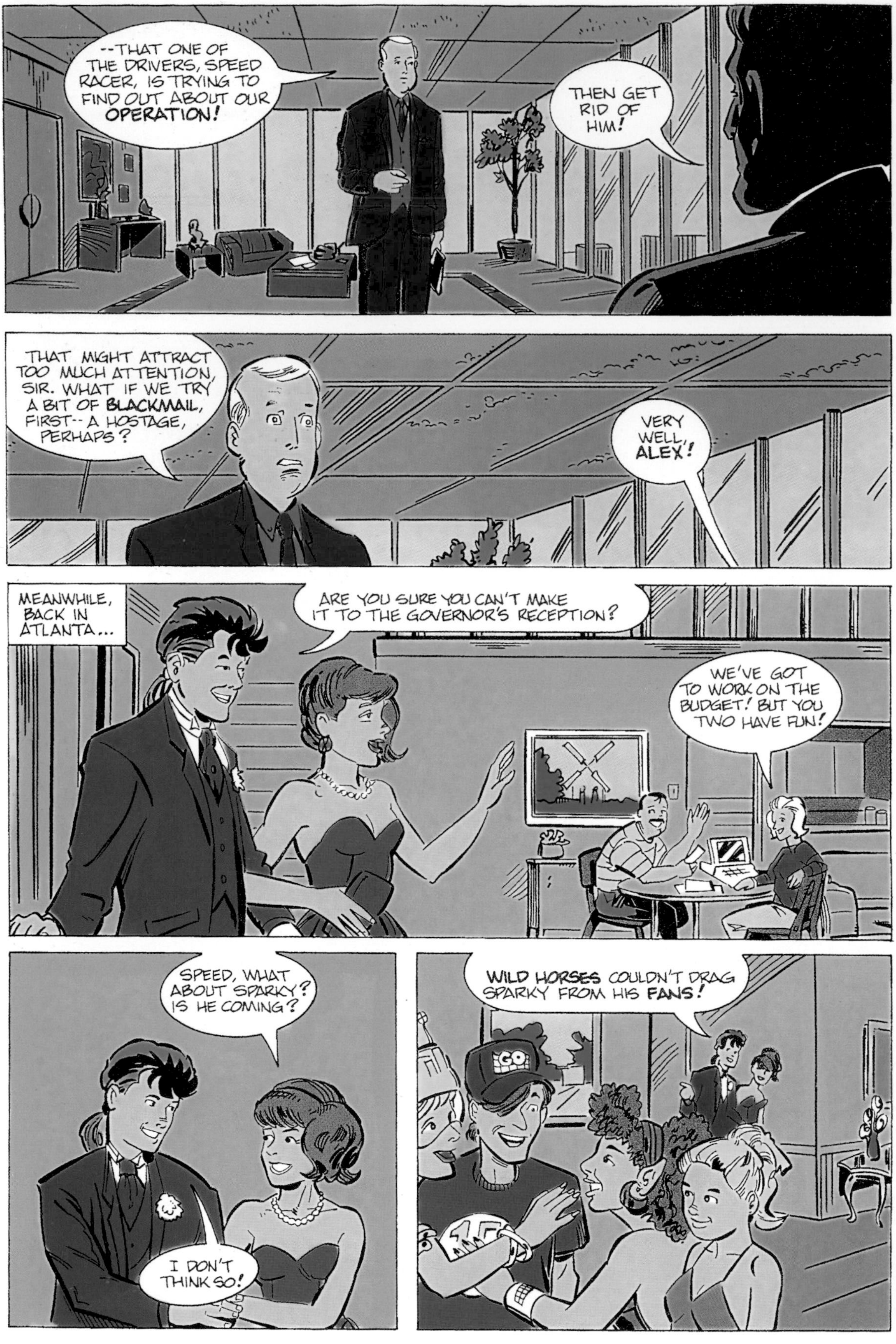
--THAT ONE OF THE DRIVERS, SPEED RACER, IS TRYING TO FIND OUT ABOUT OUR **OPERATION!**
THEN GET RID OF HIM!
THAT MIGHT ATTRACT TOO MUCH ATTENTION, SIR. WHAT IF WE TRY A BIT OF **BLACKMAIL**, FIRST-- A HOSTAGE, PERHAPS?
VERY WELL, **ALEX!**
MEANWHILE, BACK IN ATLANTA...
ARE YOU SURE YOU CAN'T MAKE IT TO THE GOVERNOR'S RECEPTION?
WE'VE GOT TO WORK ON THE BUDGET! BUT YOU TWO HAVE FUN!
SPEED, WHAT ABOUT SPARKY? IS HE COMING?
I DON'T THINK SO!
WILD HORSES COULDN'T DRAG SPARKY FROM HIS **FANS!**
GO

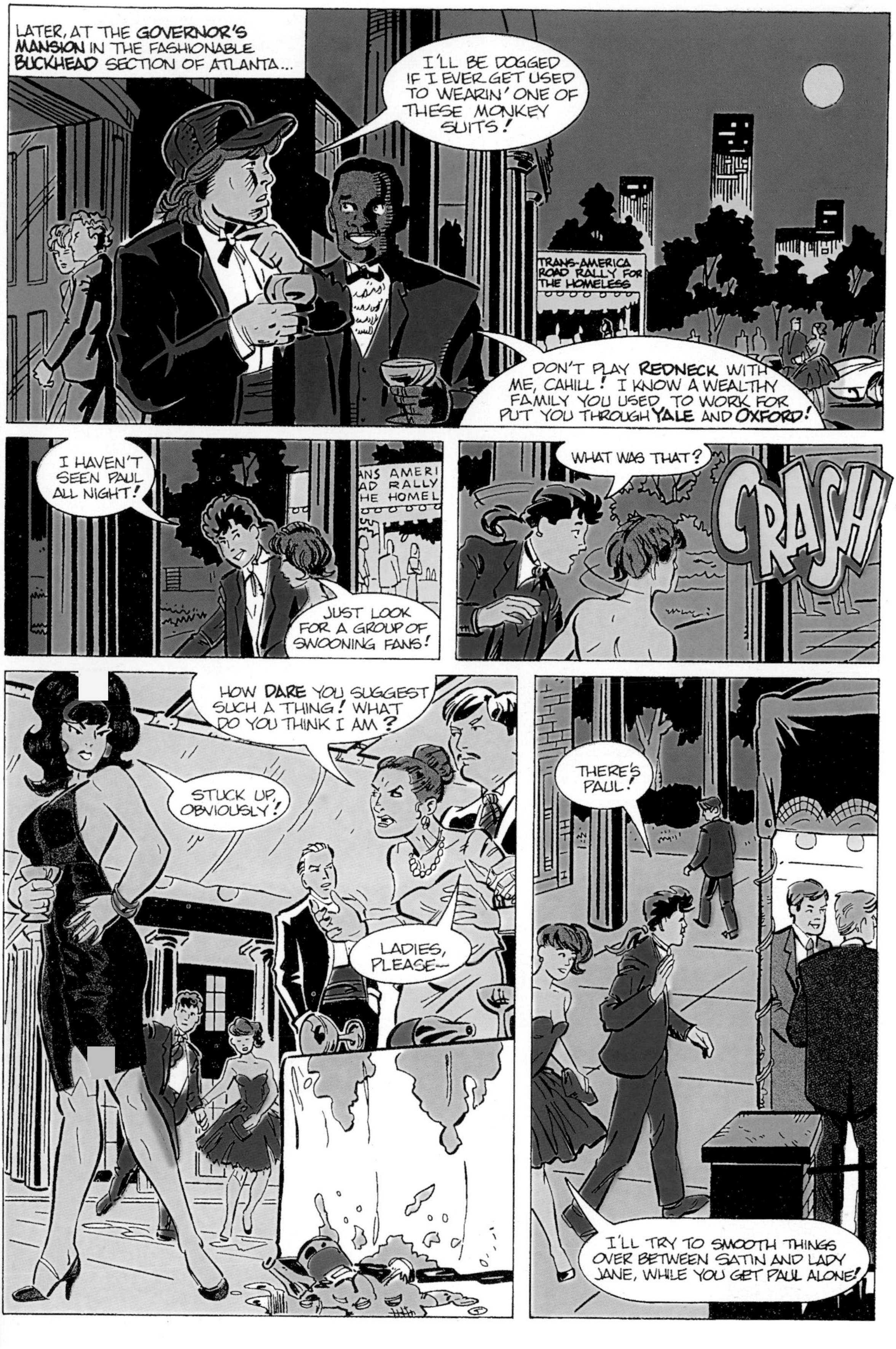
LATER, AT THE GOVERNOR'S MANSION IN THE FASHIONABLE BUCKHEAD SECTION OF ATLANTA...
I'LL BE DOGGED IF I EVER GET USED TO WEARIN' ONE OF THESE MONKEY SUITS!
TRANS-AMERICA ROAD RALLY FOR THE HOMELESS
DON'T PLAY REDNECK WITH ME, CAHILL! I KNOW A WEALTHY FAMILY YOU USED TO WORK FOR PUT YOU THROUGH YALE AND OXFORD!
I HAVEN'T SEEN PAUL ALL NIGHT!
JUST LOOK FOR A GROUP OF SWOONING FANS!
WHAT WAS THAT?
CRASH
HOW DARE YOU SUGGEST SUCH A THING! WHAT DO YOU THINK I AM?
STUCK UP, OBVIOUSLY!
LADIES, PLEASE--
THERE'S PAUL!
I'LL TRY TO SMOOTH THINGS OVER BETWEEN SATIN AND LADY JANE, WHILE YOU GET PAUL ALONE!

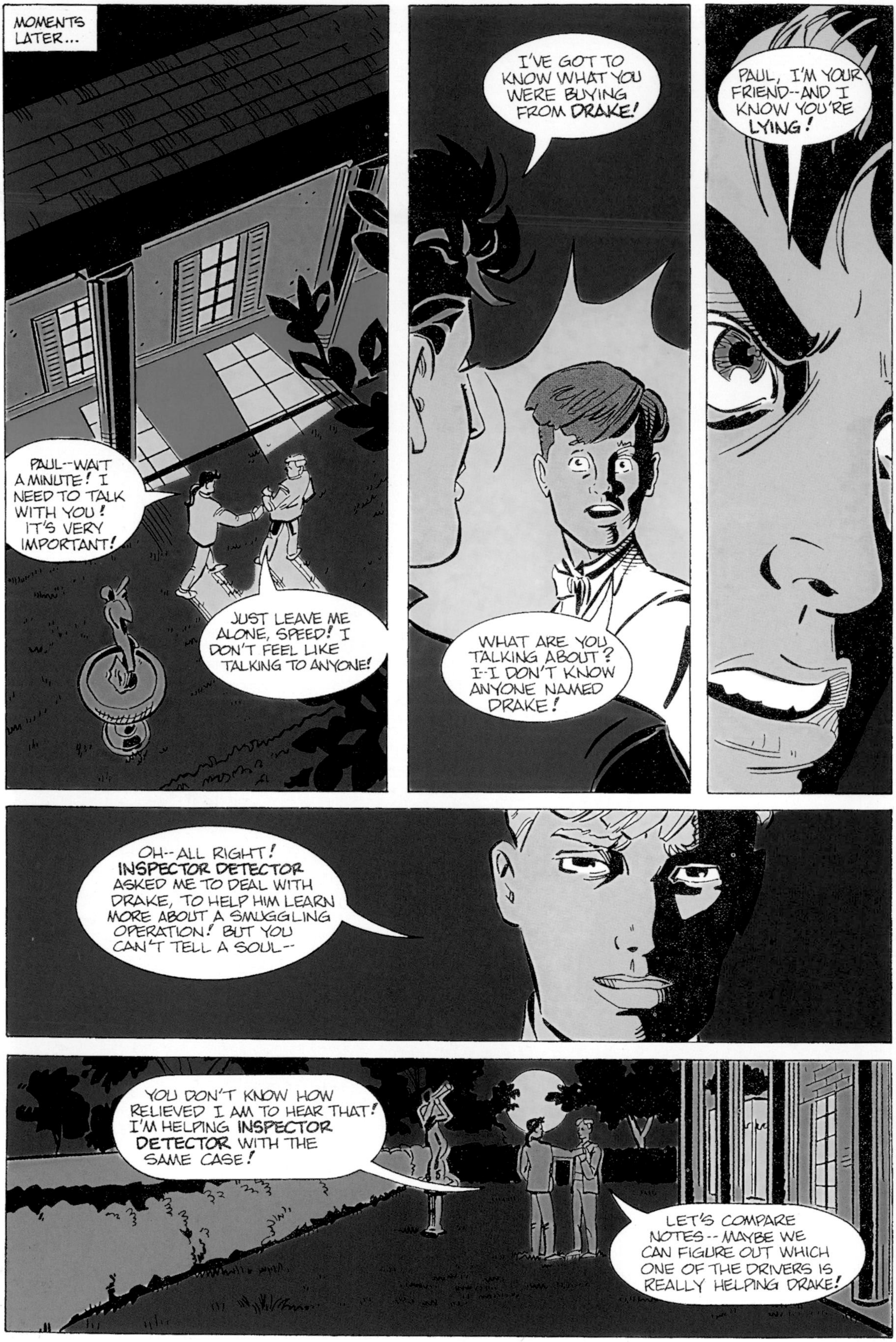
MOMENTS LATER...
PAUL--WAIT A MINUTE! I NEED TO TALK WITH YOU! IT'S VERY IMPORTANT!
JUST LEAVE ME ALONE, SPEED! I DON'T FEEL LIKE TALKING TO ANYONE!
I'VE GOT TO KNOW WHAT YOU WERE BUYING FROM DRAKE!
WHAT ARE YOU TALKING ABOUT? I--I DON'T KNOW ANYONE NAMED DRAKE!
PAUL, I'M YOUR FRIEND--AND I KNOW YOU'RE LYING!
OH--ALL RIGHT! INSPECTOR DETECTOR ASKED ME TO DEAL WITH DRAKE, TO HELP HIM LEARN MORE ABOUT A SMUGGLING OPERATION! BUT YOU CAN'T TELL A SOUL--
YOU DON'T KNOW HOW RELIEVED I AM TO HEAR THAT! I'M HELPING INSPECTOR DETECTOR WITH THE SAME CASE!
LET'S COMPARE NOTES--MAYBE WE CAN FIGURE OUT WHICH ONE OF THE DRIVERS IS REALLY HELPING DRAKE!

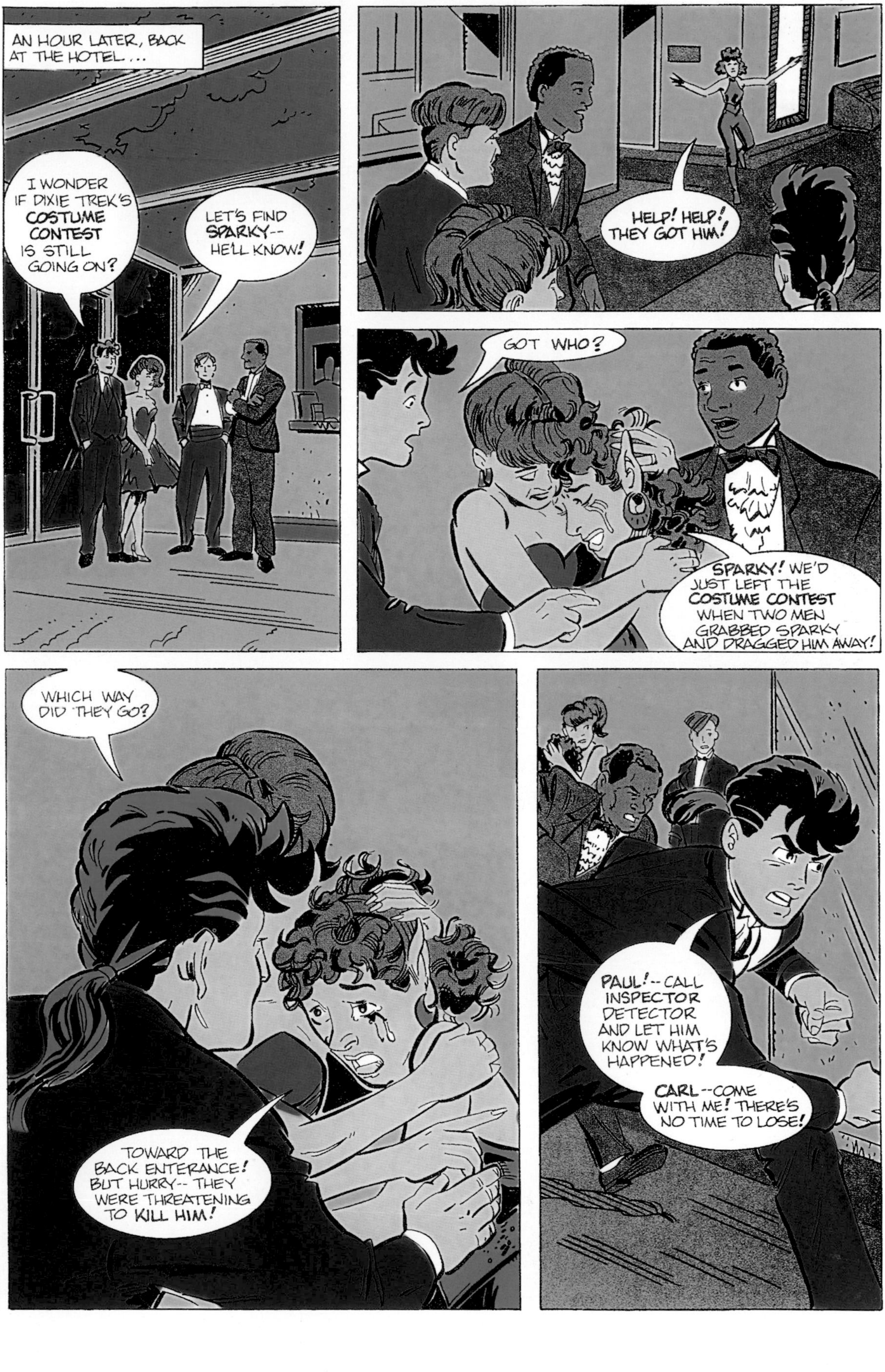
AN HOUR LATER, BACK AT THE HOTEL...
I WONDER IF DIXIE TREK'S **COSTUME CONTEST** IS STILL GOING ON?
LET'S FIND **SPARKY**-- HE'LL KNOW!
HELP! HELP! THEY GOT HIM!
GOT WHO?
SPARKY! WE'D JUST LEFT THE **COSTUME CONTEST** WHEN TWO MEN GRABBED SPARKY AND DRAGGED HIM AWAY!
WHICH WAY DID THEY GO?
TOWARD THE BACK ENTERANCE! BUT HURRY-- THEY WERE THREATENING TO **KILL HIM!**
PAUL!--CALL **INSPECTOR DETECTOR** AND LET HIM KNOW WHAT'S HAPPENED!
CARL--COME WITH ME! THERE'S NO TIME TO LOSE!

NO SIGN OF A STRUGGLE--

CARL! LOOK OUT!

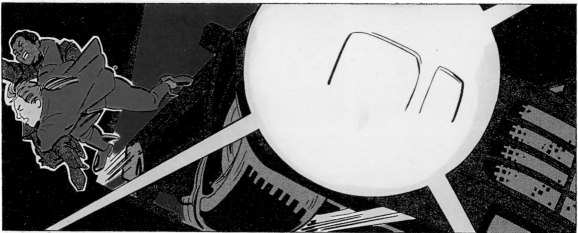

I'LL BET THEY'VE GOT SPARKY!

LET'S GET TO THE MACH 5!

GOOD! THEY'RE CAUGHT IN TRAFFIC!

BUT WE WILL BE TOO! IT'LL BE HARD TO CATCH UP TO THEM!

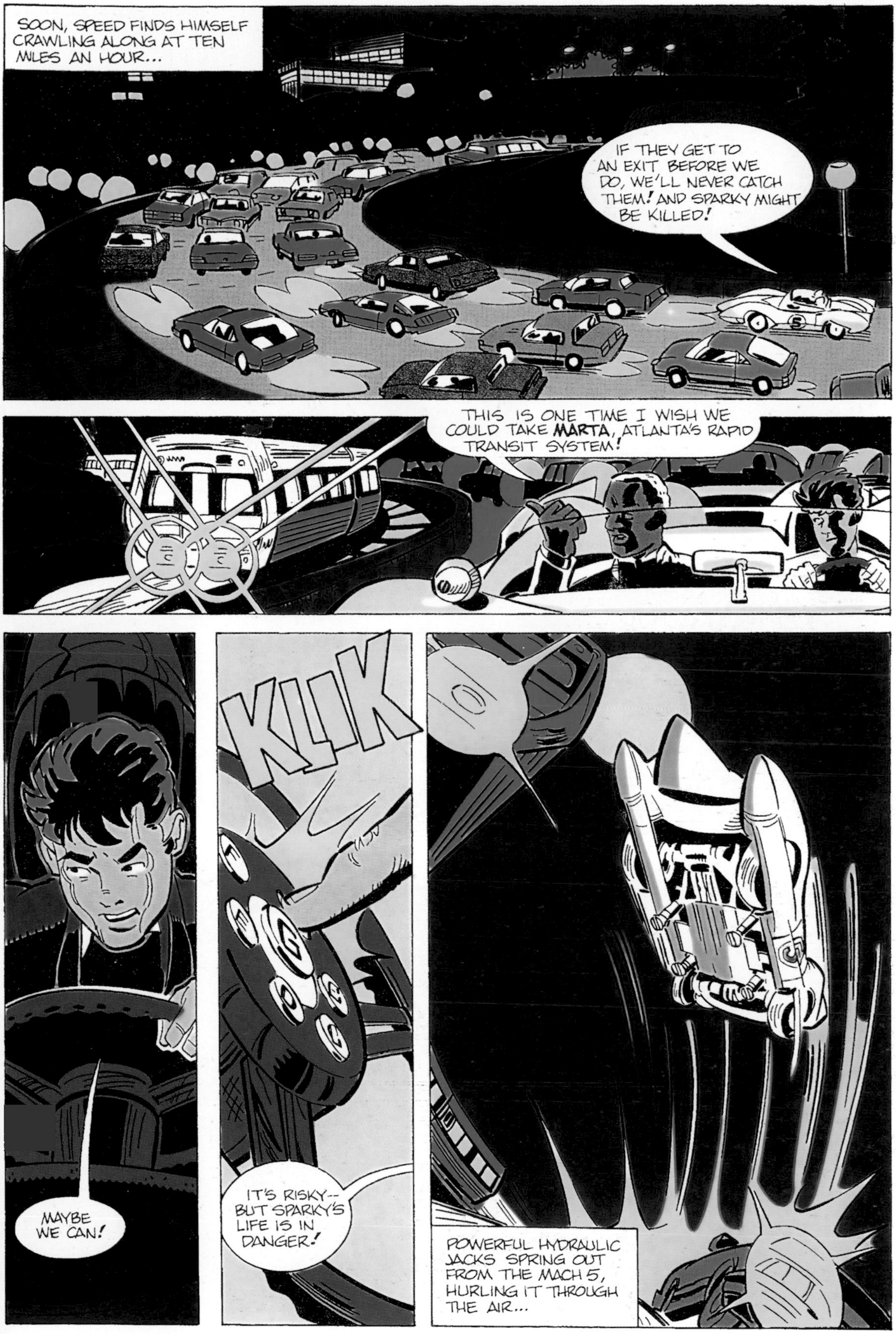

SOON, SPEED FINDS HIMSELF CRAWLING ALONG AT TEN MILES AN HOUR...
IF THEY GET TO AN EXIT BEFORE WE DO, WE'LL NEVER CATCH THEM! AND SPARKY MIGHT BE KILLED!
THIS IS ONE TIME I WISH WE COULD TAKE MARTA, ATLANTA'S RAPID TRANSIT SYSTEM!
MAYBE WE CAN!
KLIK
IT'S RISKY-- BUT SPARKY'S LIFE IS IN DANGER!
POWERFUL HYDRAULIC JACKS SPRING OUT FROM THE MACH 5, HURLING IT THROUGH THE AIR...

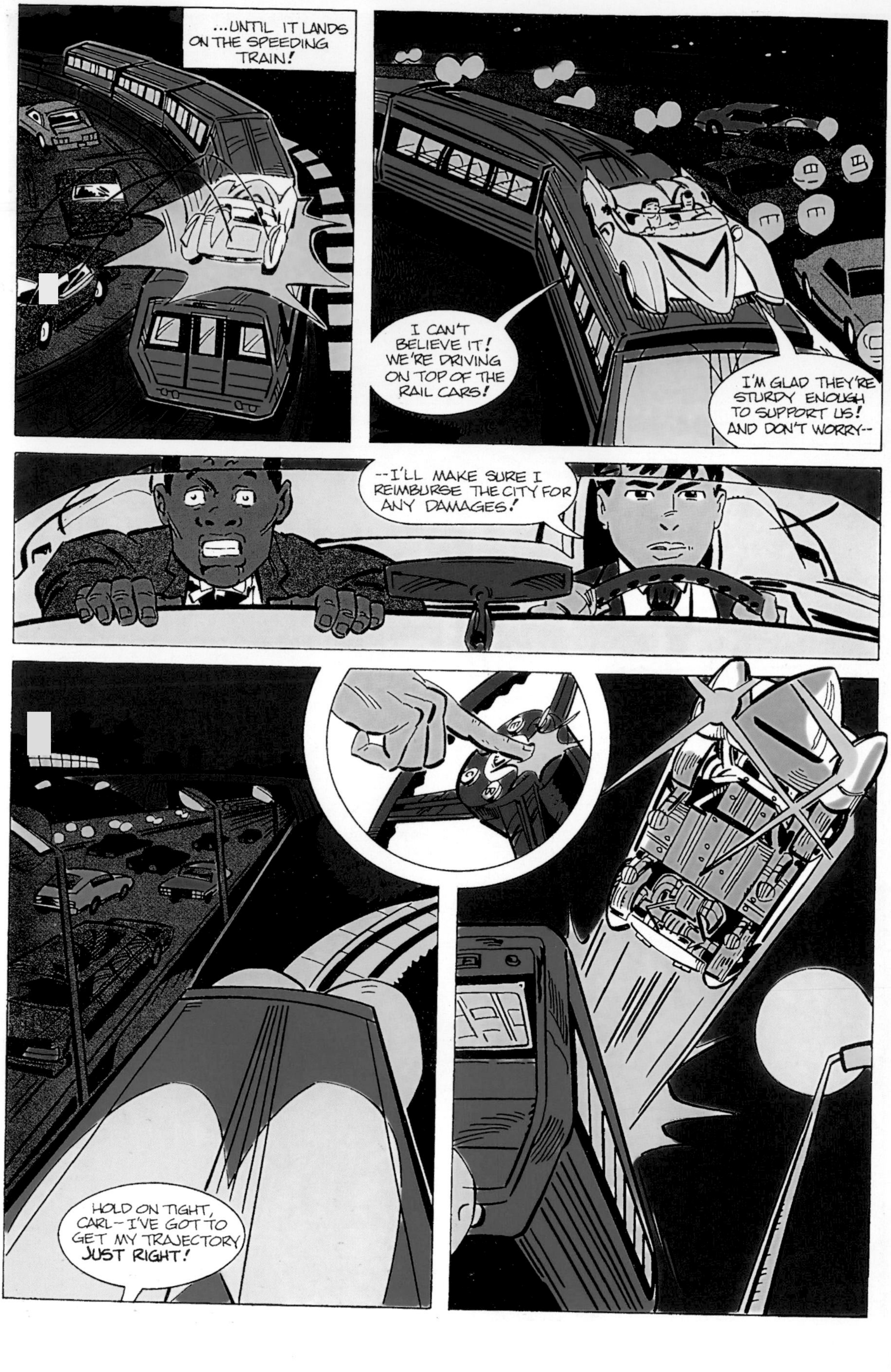
...UNTIL IT LANDS ON THE SPEEDING TRAIN!
I CAN'T BELIEVE IT! WE'RE DRIVING ON TOP OF THE RAIL CARS!
I'M GLAD THEY'RE STURDY ENOUGH TO SUPPORT US! AND DON'T WORRY--
--I'LL MAKE SURE I REIMBURSE THE CITY FOR ANY DAMAGES!
HOLD ON TIGHT, CARL-- I'VE GOT TO GET MY TRAJECTORY JUST RIGHT!

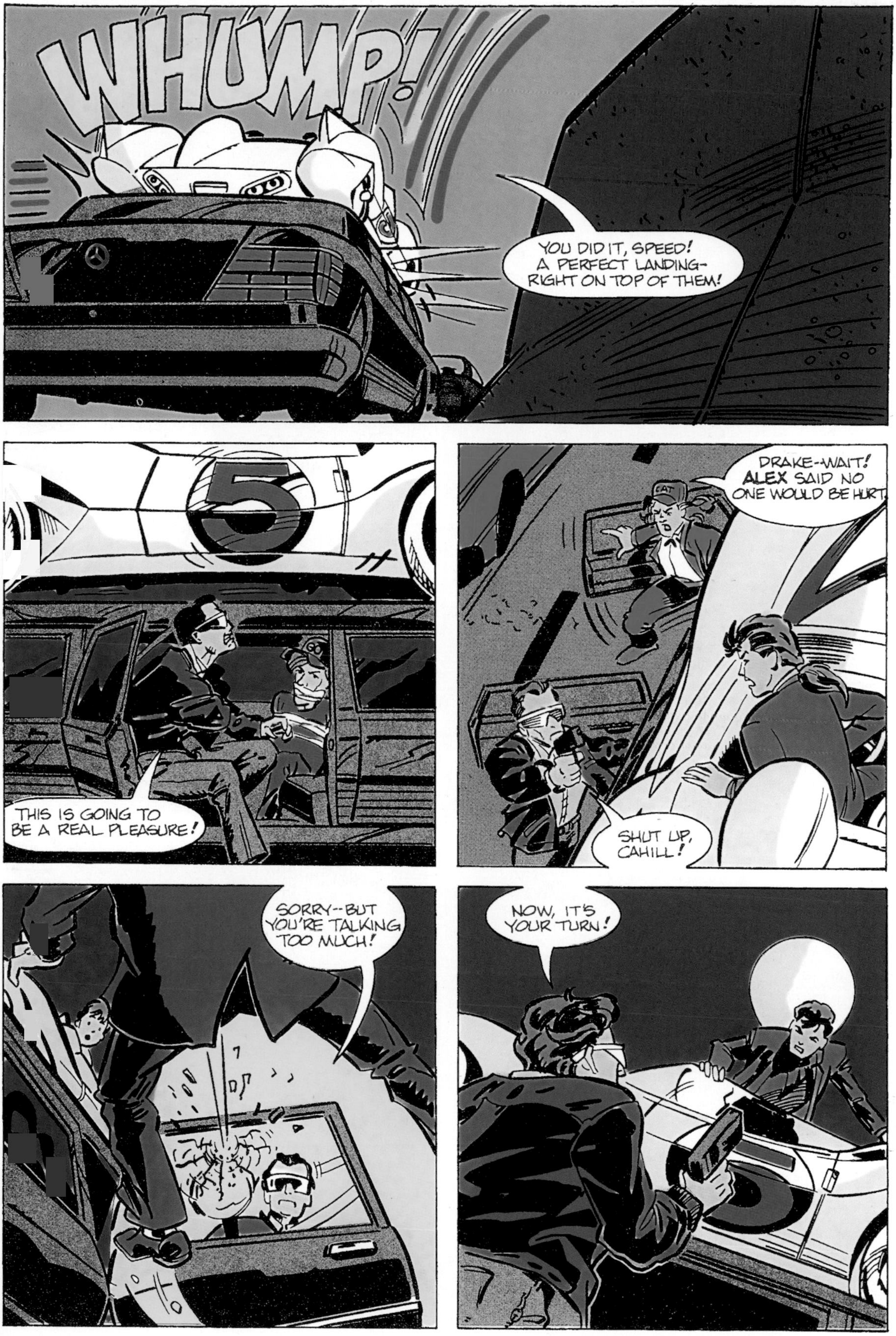
WHUMP!
YOU DID IT, SPEED! A PERFECT LANDING- RIGHT ON TOP OF THEM!
THIS IS GOING TO BE A REAL PLEASURE!
DRAKE--WAIT! ALEX SAID NO ONE WOULD BE HURT!
SHUT UP, CAHILL!
SORRY--BUT YOU'RE TALKING TOO MUCH!
NOW, IT'S YOUR TURN!

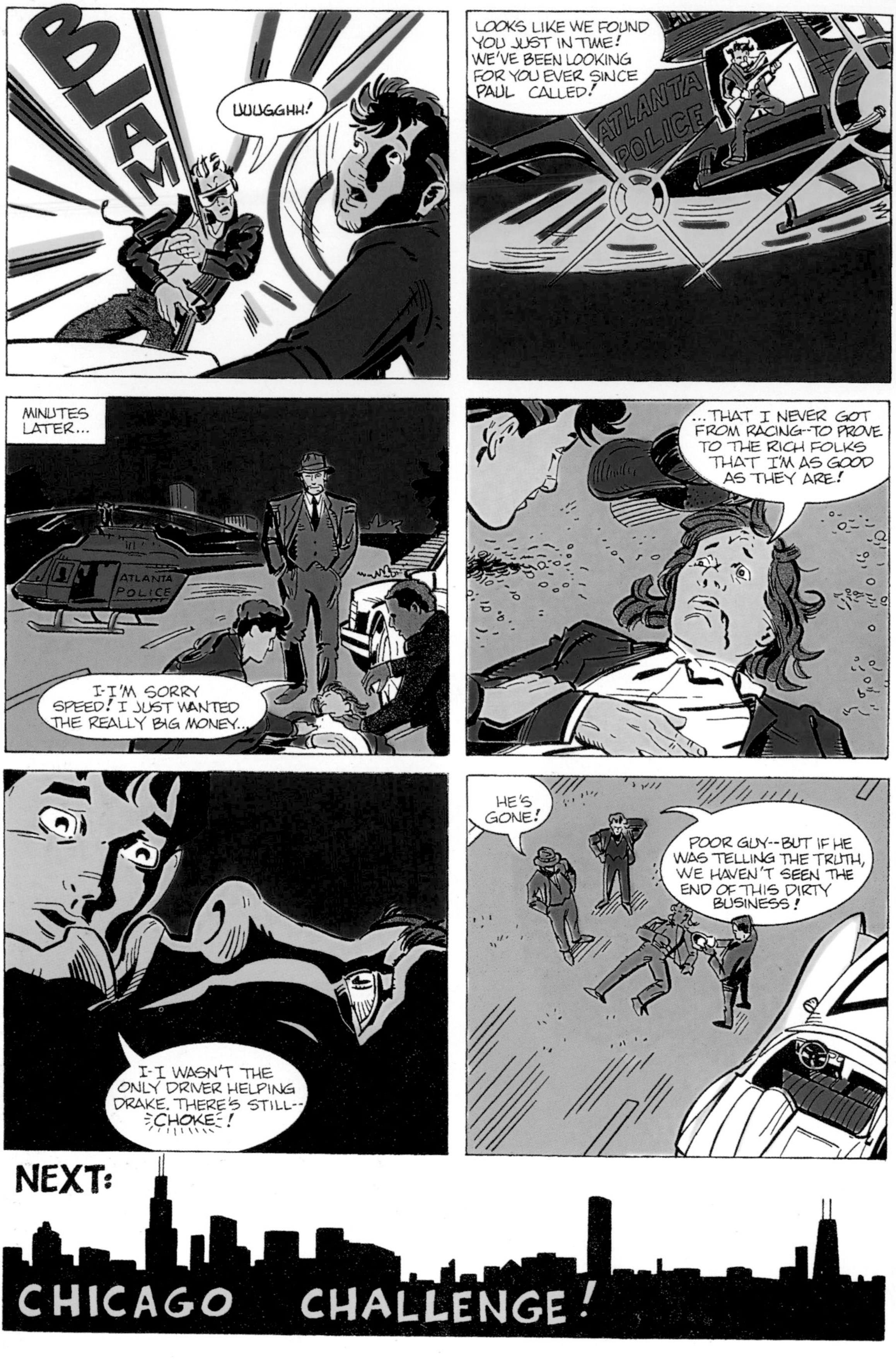
BLAM
UUUGGHH!
LOOKS LIKE WE FOUND YOU JUST IN TIME! WE'VE BEEN LOOKING FOR YOU EVER SINCE PAUL CALLED!
ATLANTA POLICE
MINUTES LATER...
ATLANTA POLICE
I-I'M SORRY SPEED! I JUST WANTED THE REALLY BIG MONEY...
...THAT I NEVER GOT FROM RACING--TO PROVE TO THE RICH FOLKS THAT I'M AS GOOD AS THEY ARE!
I-I WASN'T THE ONLY DRIVER HELPING DRAKE. THERE'S STILL-- CHOKE!
HE'S GONE!
POOR GUY--BUT IF HE WAS TELLING THE TRUTH, WE HAVEN'T SEEN THE END OF THIS DIRTY BUSINESS!
NEXT:
CHICAGO CHALLENGE!

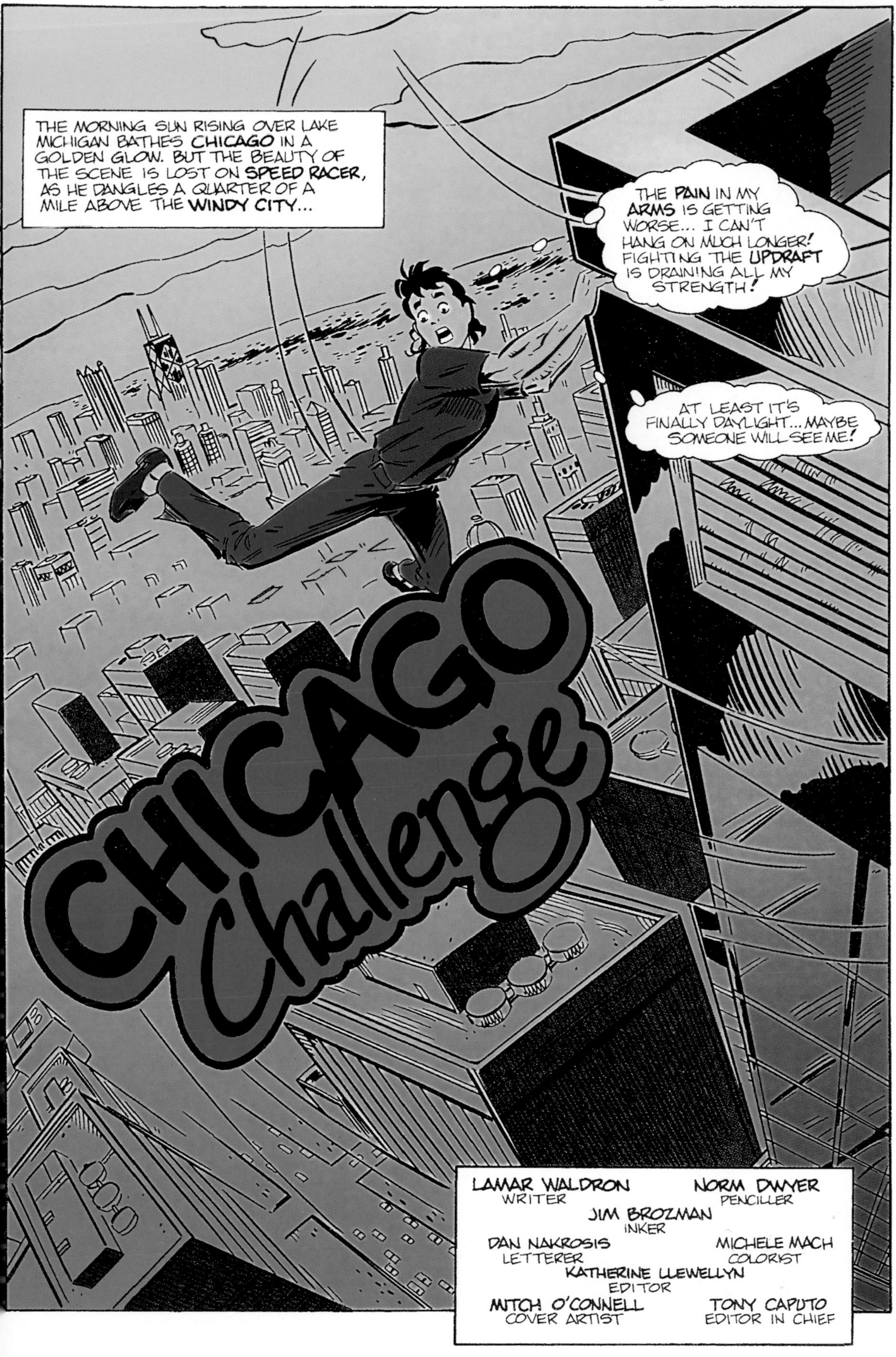
THE MORNING SUN RISING OVER LAKE MICHIGAN BATHES CHICAGO IN A GOLDEN GLOW. BUT THE BEAUTY OF THE SCENE IS LOST ON SPEED RACER, AS HE DANGLES A QUARTER OF A MILE ABOVE THE WINDY CITY...
THE PAIN IN MY ARMS IS GETTING WORSE... I CAN'T HANG ON MUCH LONGER! FIGHTING THE UPDRAFT IS DRAINING ALL MY STRENGTH!
AT LEAST IT'S FINALLY DAYLIGHT... MAYBE SOMEONE WILL SEE ME!
CHICAGO Challenge
LAMAR WALDRON WRITER
NORM DWYER PENCILLER
JIM BROZMAN INKER
DAN NAKROSIS LETTERER
MICHELE MACH COLORIST
KATHERINE LLEWELLYN EDITOR
MITCH O'CONNELL COVER ARTIST
TONY CAPUTO EDITOR IN CHIEF

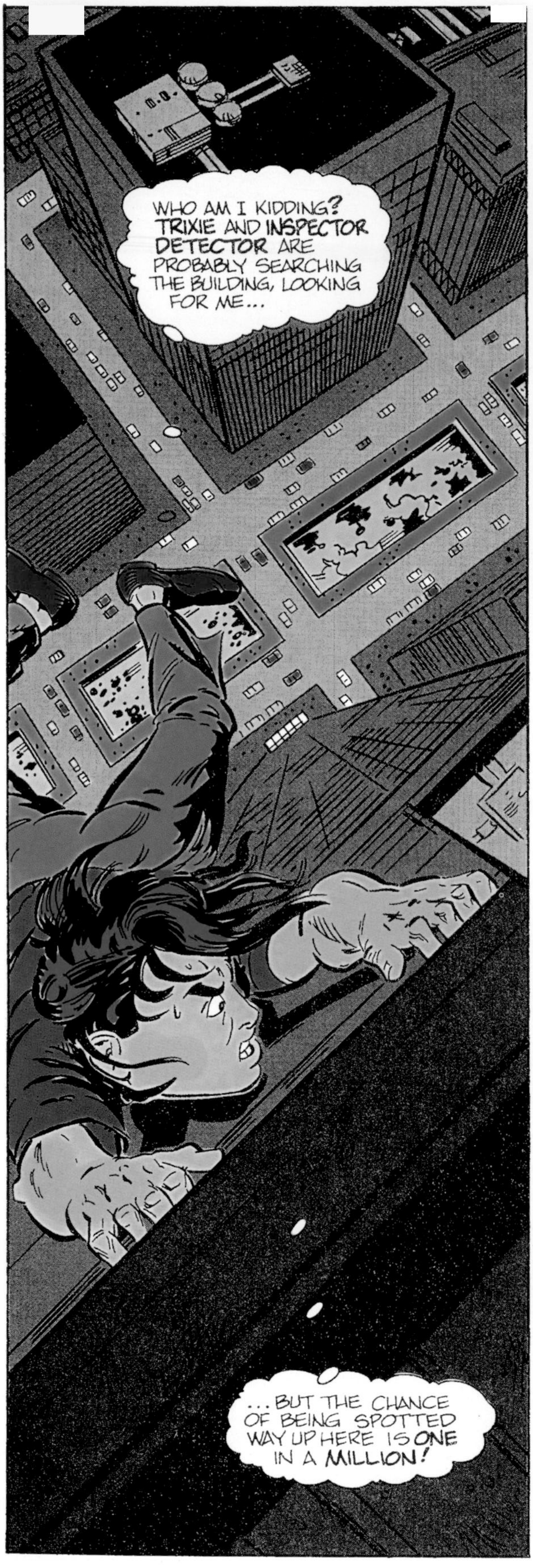
WHO AM I KIDDING? TRIXIE AND INSPECTOR DETECTOR ARE PROBABLY SEARCHING THE BUILDING, LOOKING FOR ME...
...BUT THE CHANCE OF BEING SPOTTED WAY UP HERE IS ONE IN A MILLION!

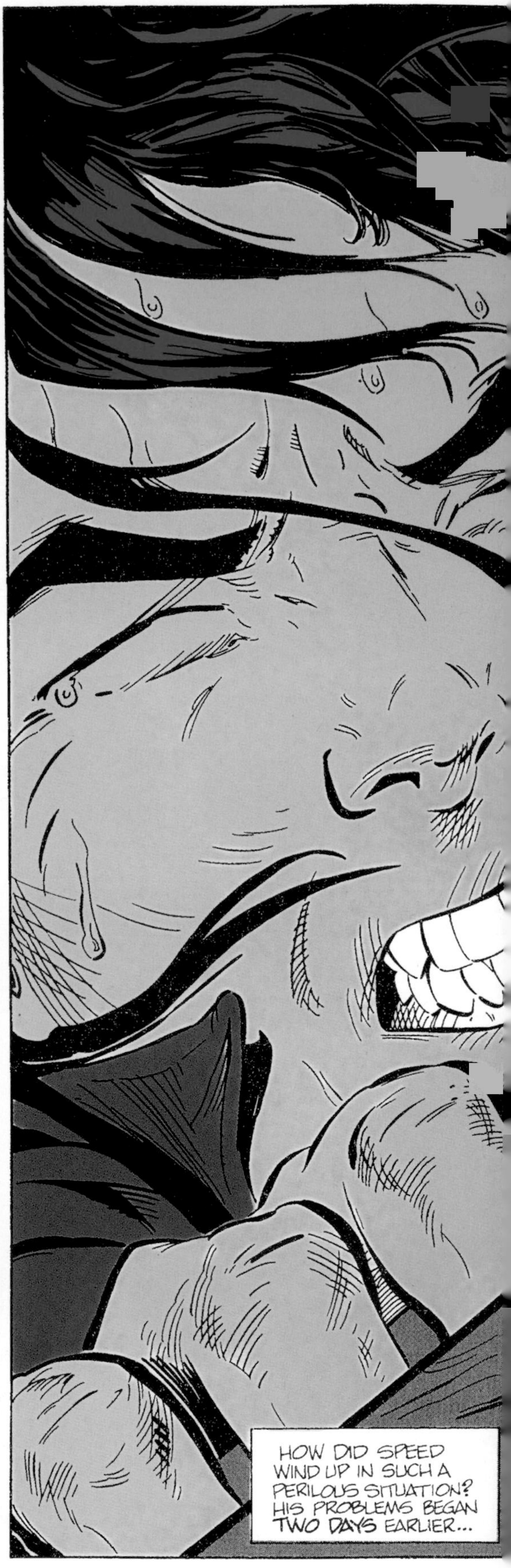
HOW DID SPEED WIND UP IN SUCH A PERILOUS SITUATION? HIS PROBLEMS BEGAN TWO DAYS EARLIER...

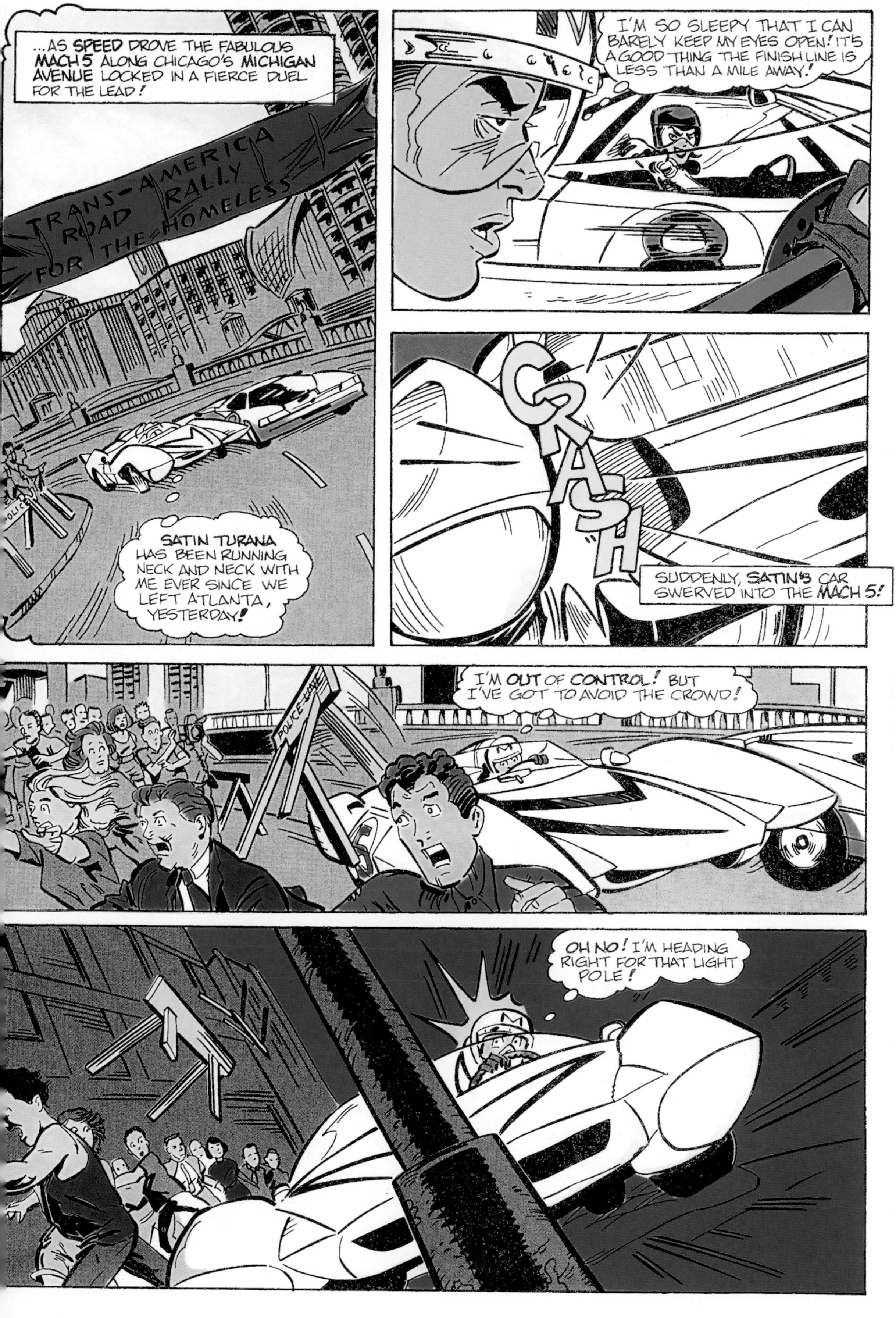
...AS SPEED DROVE THE FABULOUS MACH 5 ALONG CHICAGO'S MICHIGAN AVENUE LOCKED IN A FIERCE DUEL FOR THE LEAD!
TRANS-AMERICA ROAD RALLY FOR THE HOMELESS
SATIN TURANA HAS BEEN RUNNING NECK AND NECK WITH ME EVER SINCE WE LEFT ATLANTA, YESTERDAY!
I'M SO SLEEPY THAT I CAN BARELY KEEP MY EYES OPEN! IT'S A GOOD THING THE FINISH LINE IS LESS THAN A MILE AWAY!
CRASH
SUDDENLY, SATIN'S CAR SWERVED INTO THE MACH 5!
I'M OUT OF CONTROL! BUT I'VE GOT TO AVOID THE CROWD!
OH NO! I'M HEADING RIGHT FOR THAT LIGHT POLE!

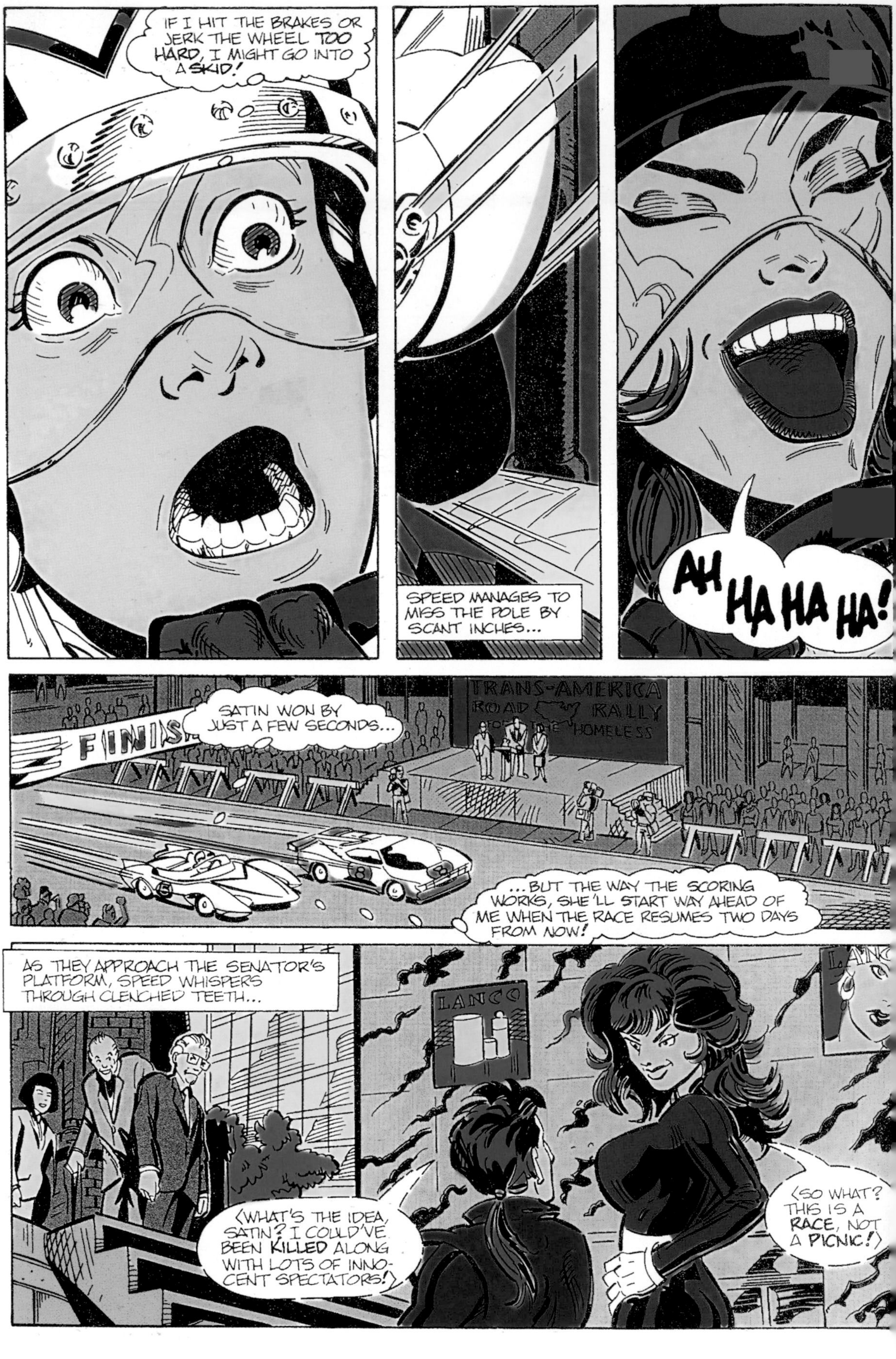
IF I HIT THE BRAKES OR JERK THE WHEEL TOO HARD, I MIGHT GO INTO A SKID!
SPEED MANAGES TO MISS THE POLE BY SCANT INCHES...
AH HA HA HA!
FINIS
TRANS-AMERICA ROAD RALLY FOR THE HOMELESS
SATIN WON BY JUST A FEW SECONDS...
...BUT THE WAY THE SCORING WORKS, SHE'LL START WAY AHEAD OF ME WHEN THE RACE RESUMES TWO DAYS FROM NOW!
AS THEY APPROACH THE SENATOR'S PLATFORM, SPEED WHISPERS THROUGH CLENCHED TEETH...
LANCO
<WHAT'S THE IDEA, SATIN? I COULD'VE BEEN KILLED ALONG WITH LOTS OF INNOCENT SPECTATORS!>
<SO WHAT? THIS IS A RACE, NOT A PICNIC!>

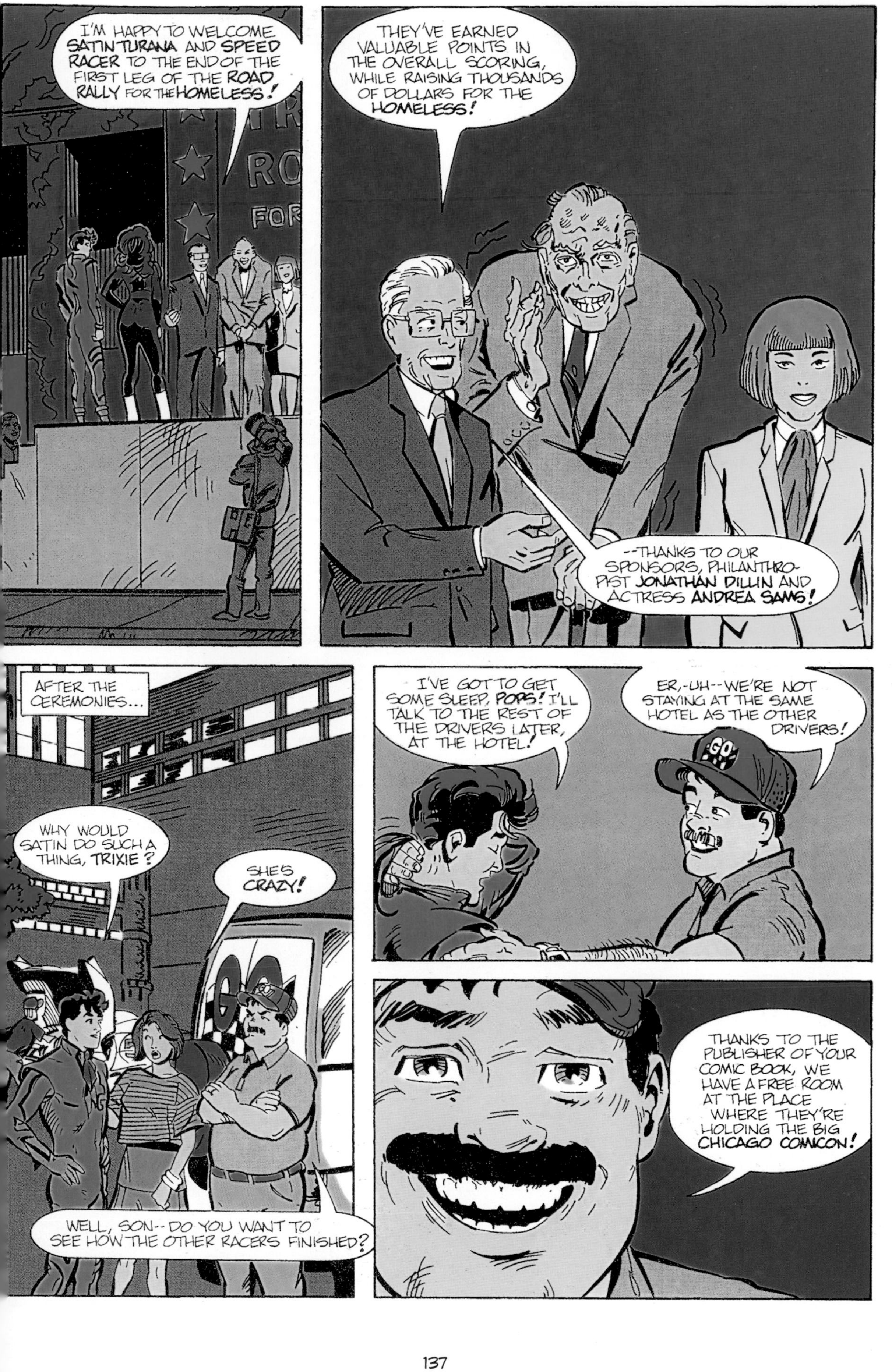
I'M HAPPY TO WELCOME SATIN TURANA AND SPEED RACER TO THE END OF THE FIRST LEG OF THE ROAD RALLY FOR THE HOMELESS!
THEY'VE EARNED VALUABLE POINTS IN THE OVERALL SCORING, WHILE RAISING THOUSANDS OF DOLLARS FOR THE HOMELESS!
--THANKS TO OUR SPONSORS, PHILANTHRO-PIST JONATHAN DILLIN AND ACTRESS ANDREA SAMS!
AFTER THE CEREMONIES...
WHY WOULD SATIN DO SUCH A THING, TRIXIE?
SHE'S CRAZY!
WELL, SON-- DO YOU WANT TO SEE HOW THE OTHER RACERS FINISHED?
I'VE GOT TO GET SOME SLEEP, POPS! I'LL TALK TO THE REST OF THE DRIVERS LATER, AT THE HOTEL!
ER,-UH--WE'RE NOT STAYING AT THE SAME HOTEL AS THE OTHER DRIVERS!
THANKS TO THE PUBLISHER OF YOUR COMIC BOOK, WE HAVE A FREE ROOM AT THE PLACE WHERE THEY'RE HOLDING THE BIG CHICAGO COMICON!

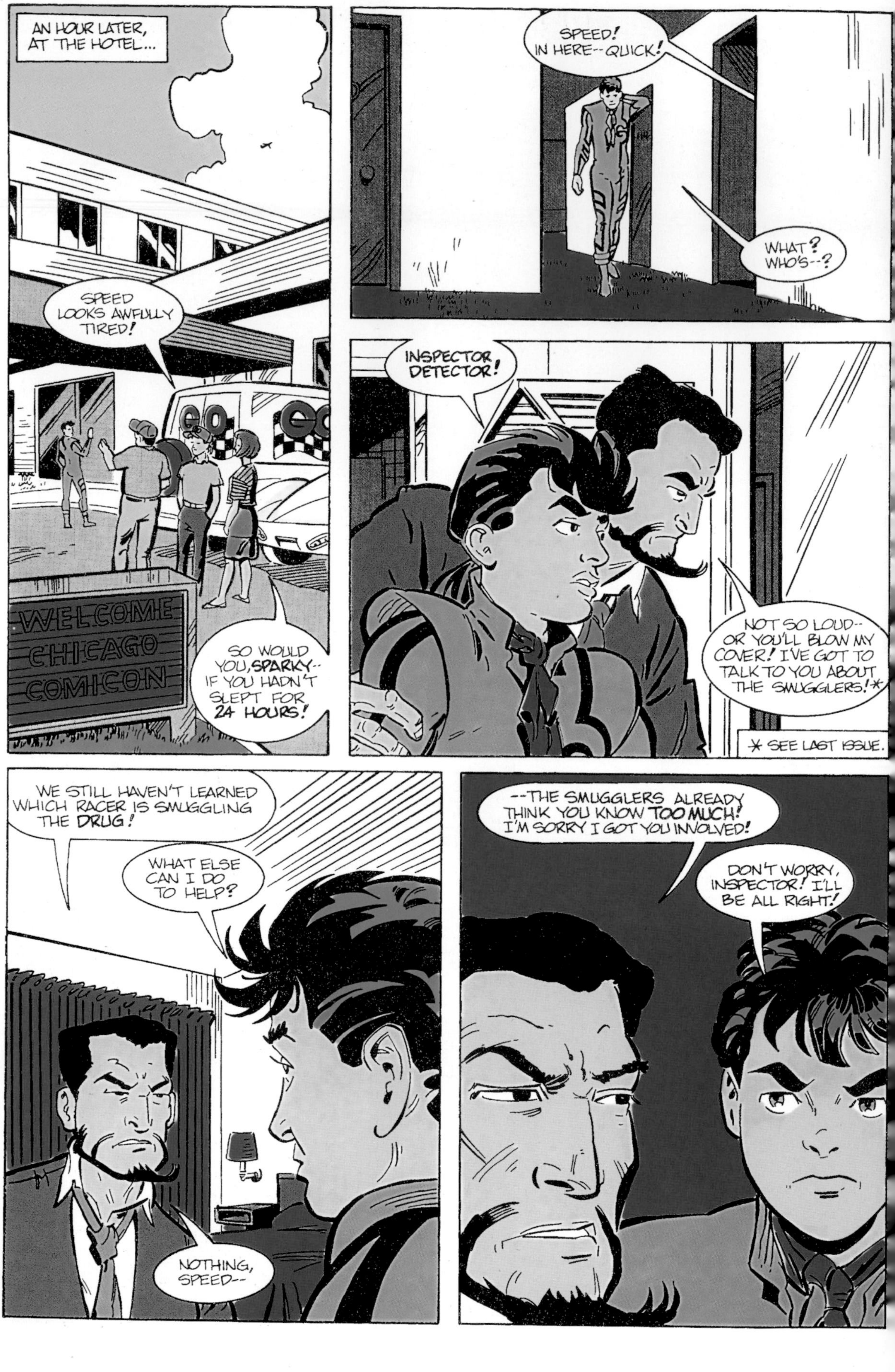
AN HOUR LATER, AT THE HOTEL...
SPEED LOOKS AWFULLY TIRED!
WELCOME CHICAGO COMICON
SO WOULD YOU, SPARKY-- IF YOU HADN'T SLEPT FOR 24 HOURS!
SPEED! IN HERE--QUICK!
WHAT? WHO'S--?
INSPECTOR DETECTOR!
NOT SO LOUD-- OR YOU'LL BLOW MY COVER! I'VE GOT TO TALK TO YOU ABOUT THE SMUGGLERS!*
* SEE LAST ISSUE.
WE STILL HAVEN'T LEARNED WHICH RACER IS SMUGGLING THE DRUG!
WHAT ELSE CAN I DO TO HELP?
NOTHING, SPEED--
--THE SMUGGLERS ALREADY THINK YOU KNOW TOO MUCH! I'M SORRY I GOT YOU INVOLVED!
DON'T WORRY, INSPECTOR! I'LL BE ALL RIGHT!

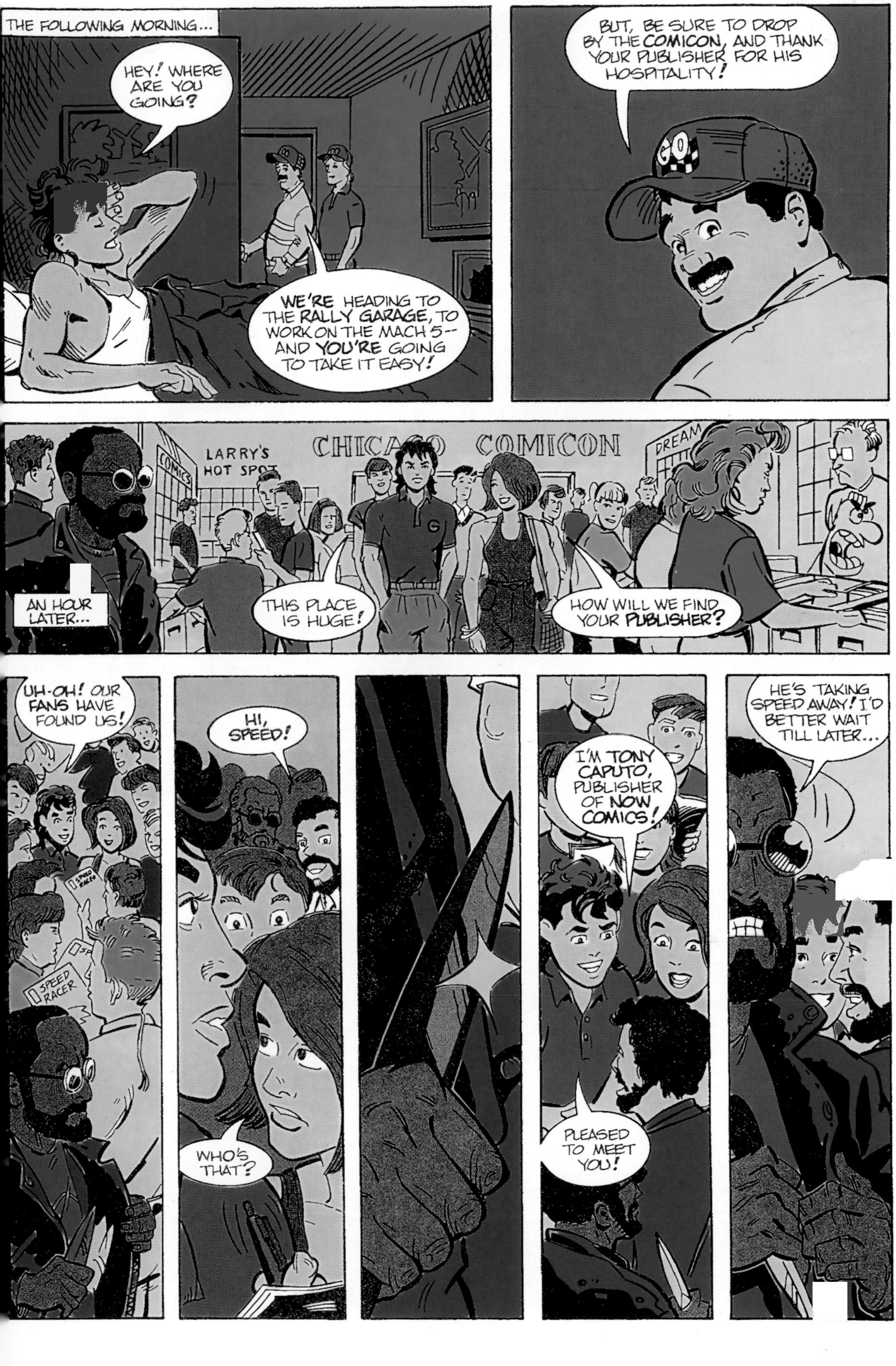
THE FOLLOWING MORNING...
HEY! WHERE ARE YOU GOING?
WE'RE HEADING TO THE RALLY GARAGE, TO WORK ON THE MACH 5-- AND YOU'RE GOING TO TAKE IT EASY!
BUT, BE SURE TO DROP BY THE COMICON, AND THANK YOUR PUBLISHER FOR HIS HOSPITALITY!
GO
CHICAGO COMICON
LARRY'S HOT SPOT
COMICS
DREAM
AN HOUR LATER...
THIS PLACE IS HUGE!
HOW WILL WE FIND YOUR PUBLISHER?
UH-OH! OUR FANS HAVE FOUND US!
SPEED RACER
HI, SPEED!
WHO'S THAT?
I'M TONY CAPUTO, PUBLISHER OF NOW COMICS!
PLEASED TO MEET YOU!
HE'S TAKING SPEED AWAY! I'D BETTER WAIT TILL LATER...

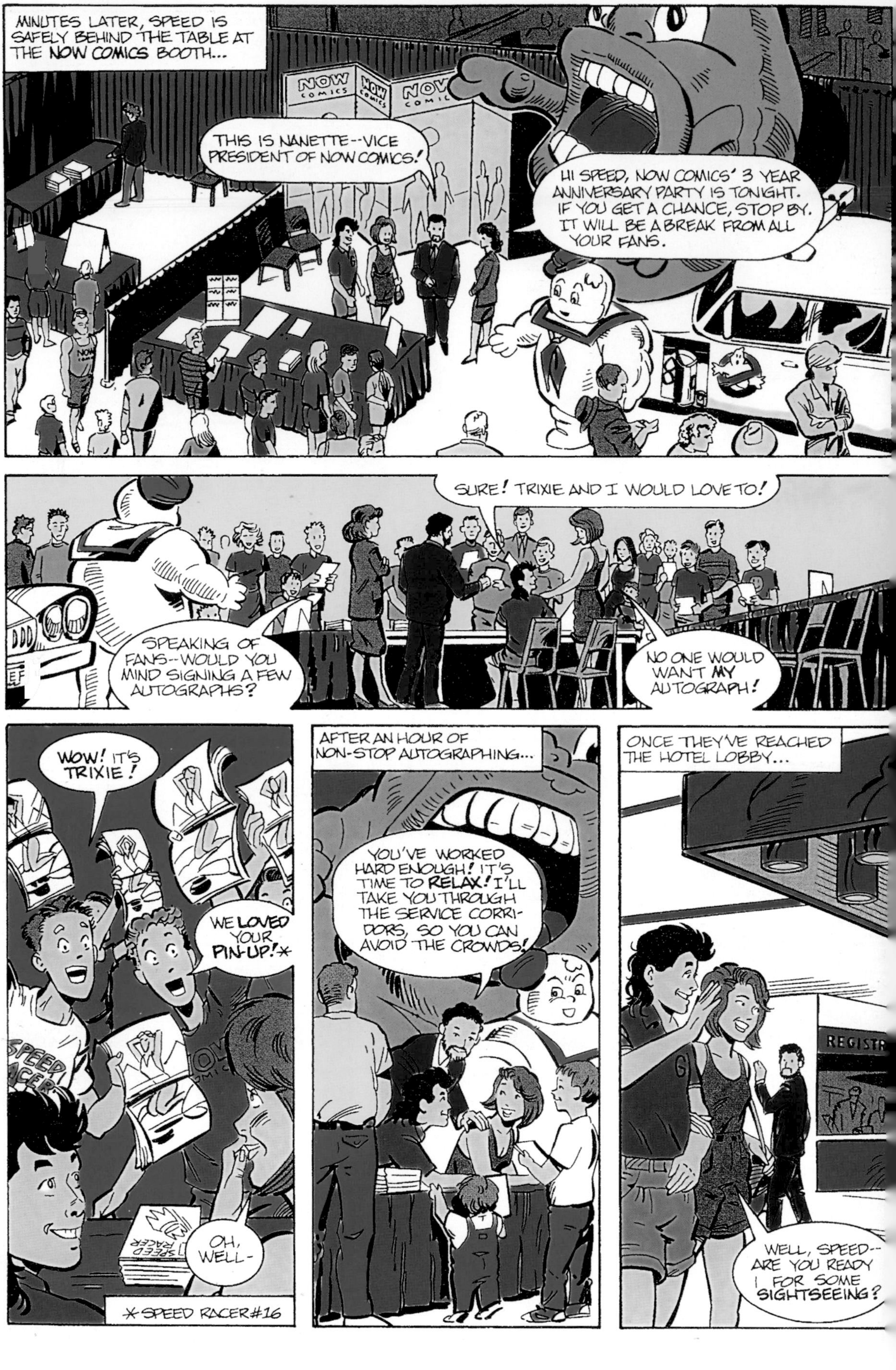

MINUTES LATER, SPEED IS SAFELY BEHIND THE TABLE AT THE NOW COMICS BOOTH...
NOW COMICS
THIS IS NANETTE--VICE PRESIDENT OF NOW COMICS!
HI SPEED, NOW COMICS' 3 YEAR ANNIVERSARY PARTY IS TONIGHT. IF YOU GET A CHANCE, STOP BY. IT WILL BE A BREAK FROM ALL YOUR FANS.
SURE! TRIXIE AND I WOULD LOVE TO!
SPEAKING OF FANS--WOULD YOU MIND SIGNING A FEW AUTOGRAPHS?
NO ONE WOULD WAN'T MY AUTOGRAPH!
WOW! IT'S TRIXIE!
WE LOVED YOUR PIN-UP!*
SPEED RACER
OH, WELL-
*SPEED RACER #16
AFTER AN HOUR OF NON-STOP AUTOGRAPHING...
YOU'VE WORKED HARD ENOUGH! IT'S TIME TO RELAX! I'LL TAKE YOU THROUGH THE SERVICE CORRI-DORS, SO YOU CAN AVOID THE CROWDS!
ONCE THEY'VE REACHED THE HOTEL LOBBY...
REGISTR
WELL, SPEED-- ARE YOU READY FOR SOME SIGHTSEEING?

I'D LIKE TO SEE THE FIELD MUSEUM OF NATURAL HISTORY AND THE FRANK LLOYD WRIGHT BUILDINGS IN OAK PARK!

SINCE POPS IS WORKING ON THE **MACH 5**, I'LL RENT A CAR SO WE CAN GET AROUND. WHAT WOULD YOU LIKE—A **MERCEDES**? A **BMW**?

OR I COULD RENT US A **LIMO** AND **DRIVER** TO TAKE US---

AW, TRIXIE DON'T BE SO **EXTRAVAGANT**!

IT REALLY **BUGS** ME WHEN YOU THROW YOUR MONEY AROUND!

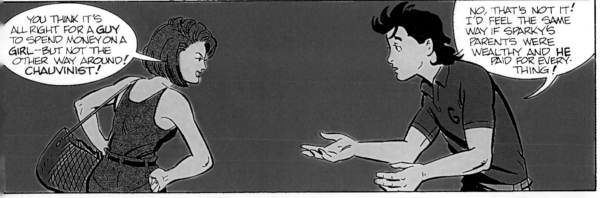

YOU THINK IT'S ALL RIGHT FOR A **GUY** TO SPEND MONEY ON A GIRL--BUT NOT THE OTHER WAY AROUND! CHAUVINIST!

NO, THAT'S NOT IT! I'D FEEL THE SAME WAY IF SPARKY'S PARENTS WERE WEALTHY AND **HE** PAID FOR EVERY-THING!

HERE'S AN IDEA-- LET'S TAKE THE BUS THIS AFTERNOON! AND TONIGHT, **YOU** CAN RENT US ANY CAR YOU WANT! DEAL?

DEAL!

THREE HOURS LATER, AFTER TOURING OAK PARK, THEY ARRIVE AT THE FIELD MUSEUM...

WE MADE IT JUST IN TIME! THEY'LL BE CLOSING IN A FEW MINUTES.

DON'T WORRY!

AFTER ALL, I'M THE ONE WHO INSISTED ON TAKING THE BUS!

IT'LL BE EASIER TO MAKE MY GETAWAY,

... IF SPEED'S DEATH LOOKS LIKE AN ACCIDENT!

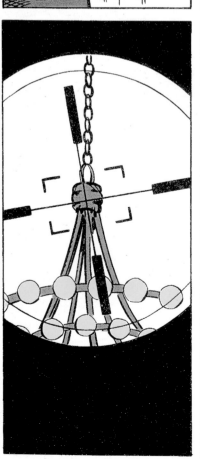

LOOK OVER THERE-- A PENNY ON THE FLOOR! FIND A PENNY, PICK IT UP, AND ALL THE DAY YOU'LL HAVE GOOD LUCK!

SUPERSTITIONS ARE A LOT OF NONSENSE! COME ON, LET'S---

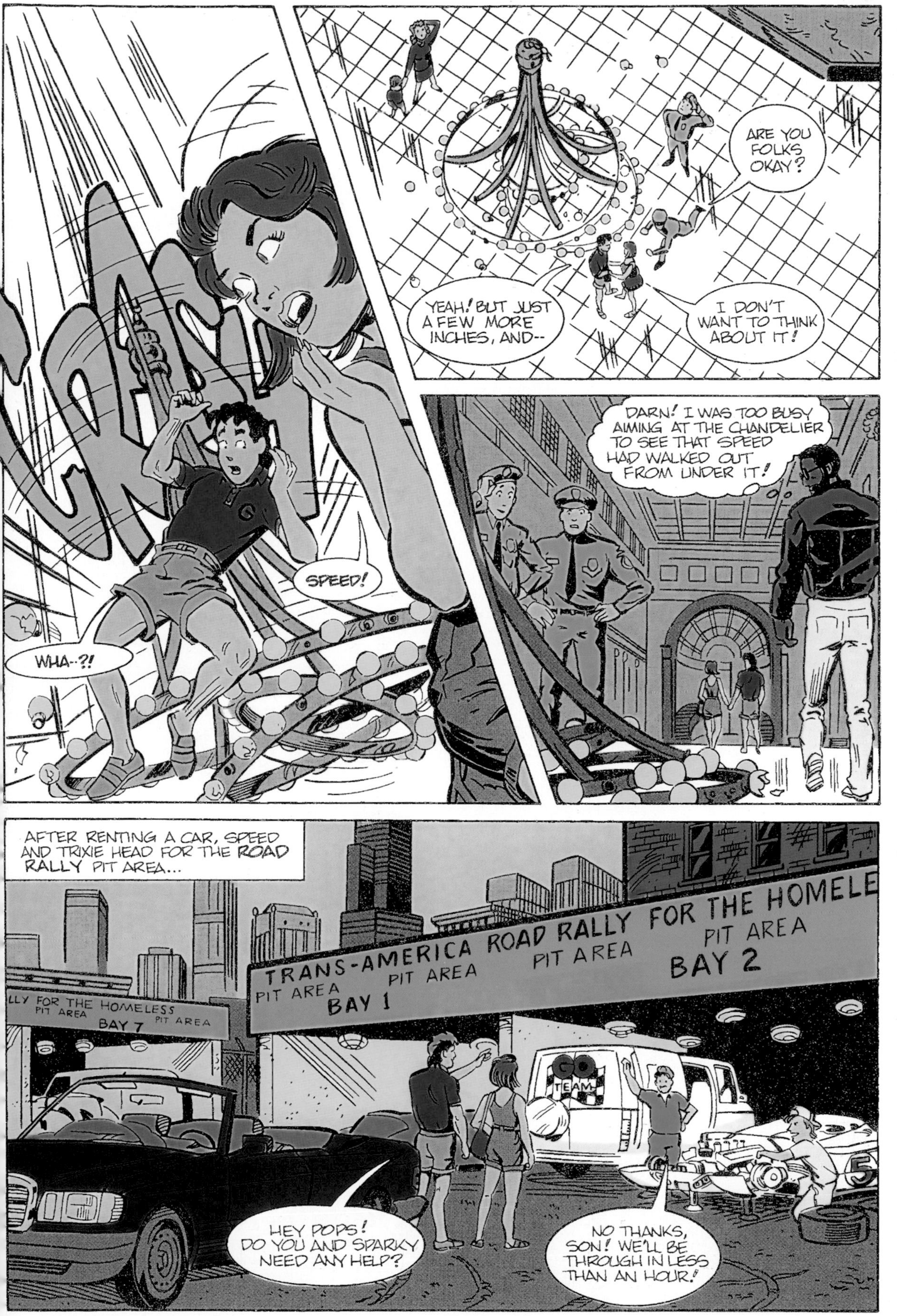
ARE YOU FOLKS OKAY?
YEAH! BUT JUST A FEW MORE INCHES, AND--
I DON'T WANT TO THINK ABOUT IT!
SPEED!
WHA--?!
DARN! I WAS TOO BUSY AIMING AT THE CHANDELIER TO SEE THAT SPEED HAD WALKED OUT FROM UNDER IT!
AFTER RENTING A CAR, SPEED AND TRIXIE HEAD FOR THE ROAD RALLY PIT AREA...
TRANS-AMERICA ROAD RALLY FOR THE HOMELE
PIT AREA
PIT AREA
PIT AREA
PIT AREA
BAY 1
BAY 2
LLY FOR THE HOMELESS
PIT AREA
BAY 7
PIT AREA
GO TEAM
HEY POPS! DO YOU AND SPARKY NEED ANY HELP?
NO THANKS, SON! WE'LL BE THROUGH IN LESS THAN AN HOUR!

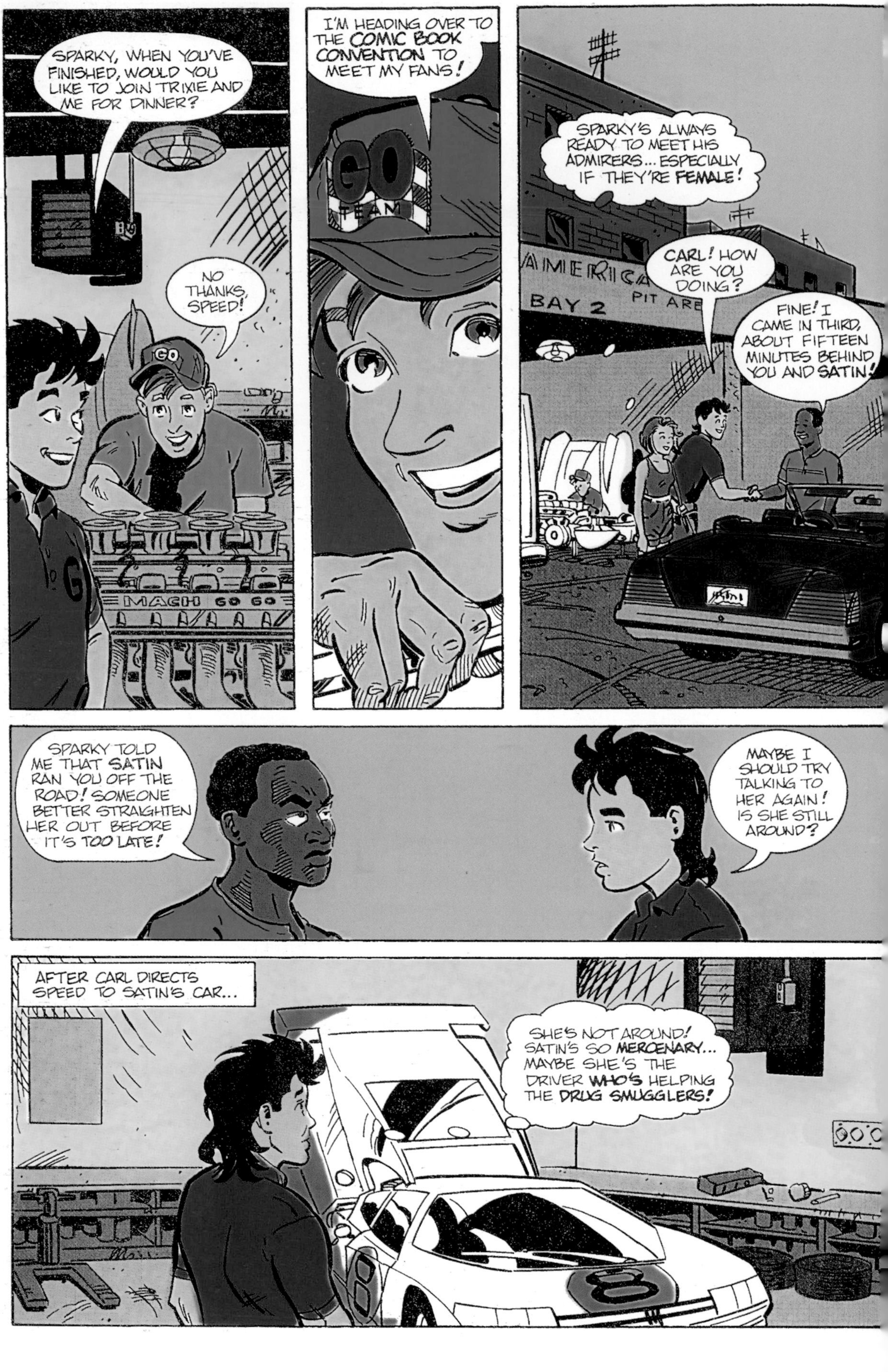

SPARKY, WHEN YOU'VE FINISHED, WOULD YOU LIKE TO JOIN TRIXIE AND ME FOR DINNER?
NO THANKS, SPEED!
MACH GO GO
I'M HEADING OVER TO THE COMIC BOOK CONVENTION TO MEET MY FANS!
SPARKY'S ALWAYS READY TO MEET HIS ADMIRERS... ESPECIALLY IF THEY'RE FEMALE!
BAY 2
CARL! HOW ARE YOU DOING?
FINE! I CAME IN THIRD, ABOUT FIFTEEN MINUTES BEHIND YOU AND SATIN!
SPARKY TOLD ME THAT SATIN RAN YOU OFF THE ROAD! SOMEONE BETTER STRAIGHTEN HER OUT BEFORE IT'S TOO LATE!
MAYBE I SHOULD TRY TALKING TO HER AGAIN! IS SHE STILL AROUND?
AFTER CARL DIRECTS SPEED TO SATIN'S CAR...
SHE'S NOT AROUND! SATIN'S SO MERCENARY... MAYBE SHE'S THE DRIVER WHO'S HELPING THE DRUG SMUGGLERS!

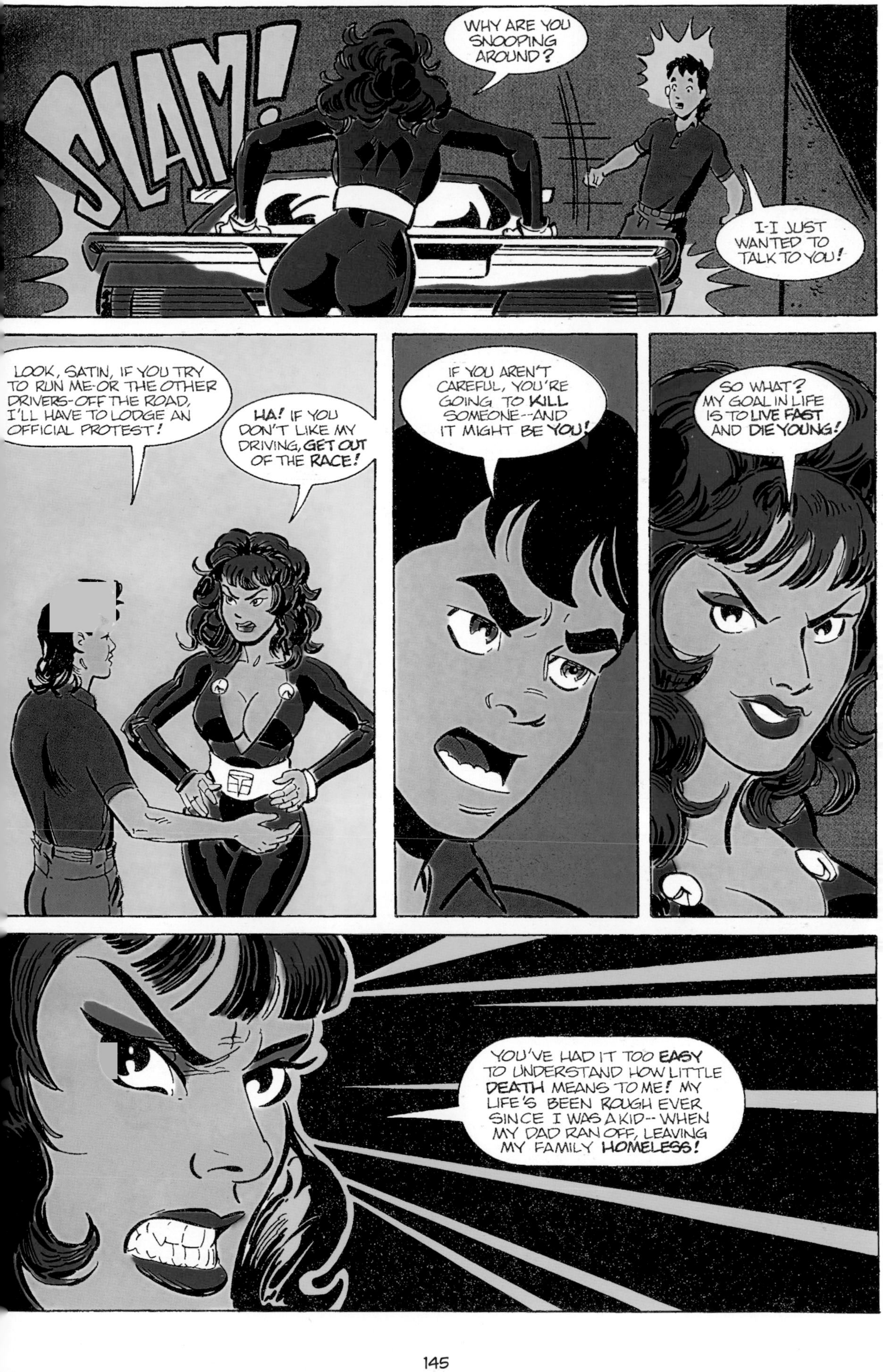
SLAM!
WHY ARE YOU SNOOPING AROUND?
I-I JUST WANTED TO TALK TO YOU!
LOOK, SATIN, IF YOU TRY TO RUN ME-OR THE OTHER DRIVERS-OFF THE ROAD, I'LL HAVE TO LODGE AN OFFICIAL PROTEST!
HA! IF YOU DON'T LIKE MY DRIVING, GET OUT OF THE RACE!
IF YOU AREN'T CAREFUL, YOU'RE GOING TO KILL SOMEONE--AND IT MIGHT BE YOU!
SO WHAT? MY GOAL IN LIFE IS TO LIVE FAST AND DIE YOUNG!
YOU'VE HAD IT TOO EASY TO UNDERSTAND HOW LITTLE DEATH MEANS TO ME! MY LIFE'S BEEN ROUGH EVER SINCE I WAS A KID-- WHEN MY DAD RAN OFF, LEAVING MY FAMILY HOMELESS!

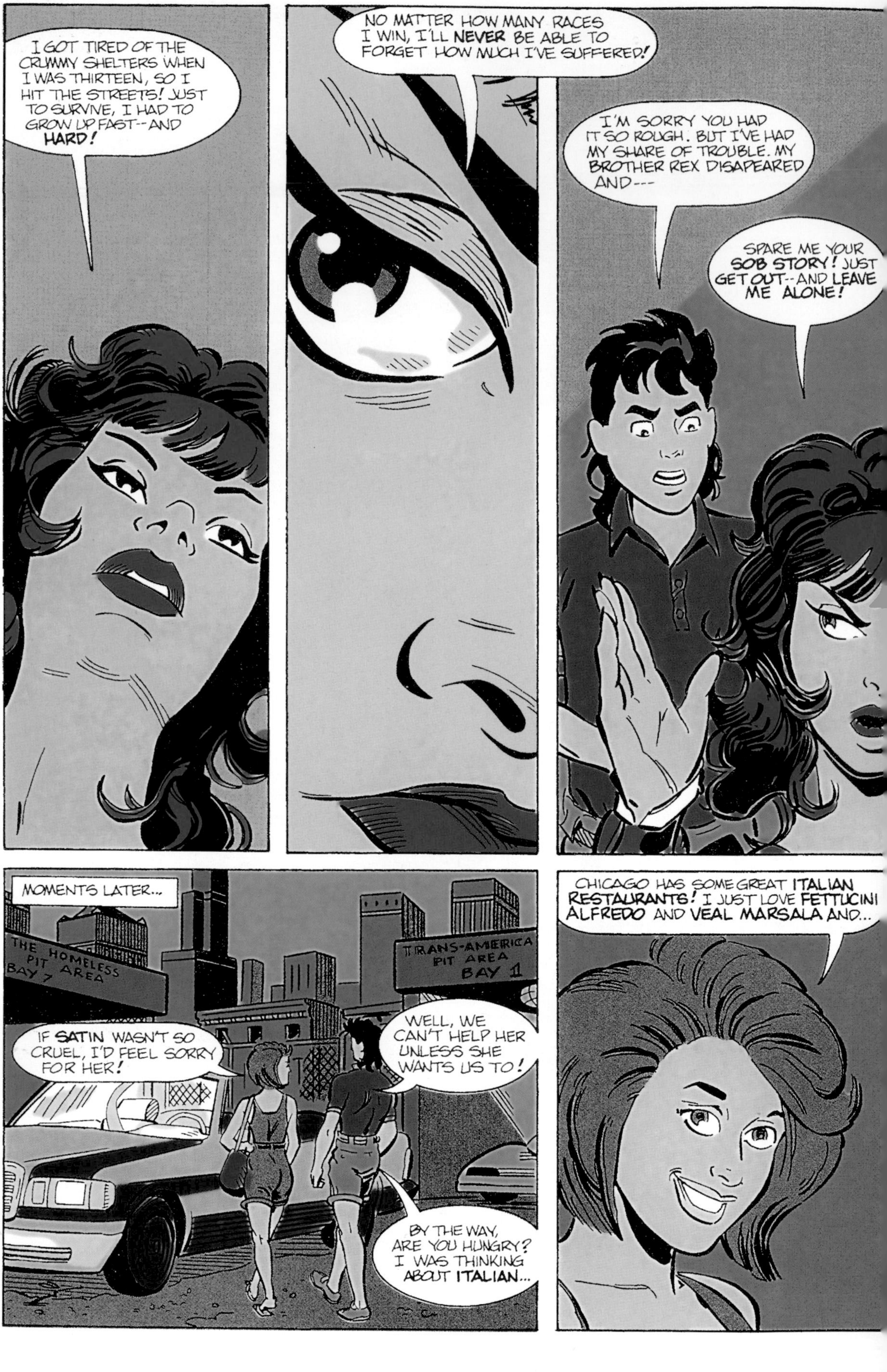
I GOT TIRED OF THE CRUMMY SHELTERS WHEN I WAS THIRTEEN, SO I HIT THE STREETS! JUST TO SURVIVE, I HAD TO GROW UP FAST--AND **HARD!**
NO MATTER HOW MANY RACES I WIN, I'LL **NEVER** BE ABLE TO FORGET HOW MUCH I'VE SUFFERED!
I'M SORRY YOU HAD IT SO ROUGH. BUT I'VE HAD MY SHARE OF TROUBLE. MY BROTHER REX DISAPEARED AND---
SPARE ME YOUR **SOB STORY!** JUST GET OUT--AND **LEAVE ME ALONE!**
MOMENTS LATER...
THE HOMELESS PIT AREA BAY 7
TRANS-AMERICA PIT AREA BAY 1
IF **SATIN** WASN'T SO CRUEL, I'D FEEL SORRY FOR HER!
WELL, WE CAN'T HELP HER UNLESS SHE WANTS US TO!
BY THE WAY, ARE YOU HUNGRY? I WAS THINKING ABOUT **ITALIAN**...
CHICAGO HAS SOME GREAT **ITALIAN RESTAURANTS!** I JUST LOVE **FETTUCINI ALFREDO** AND **VEAL MARSALA** AND...

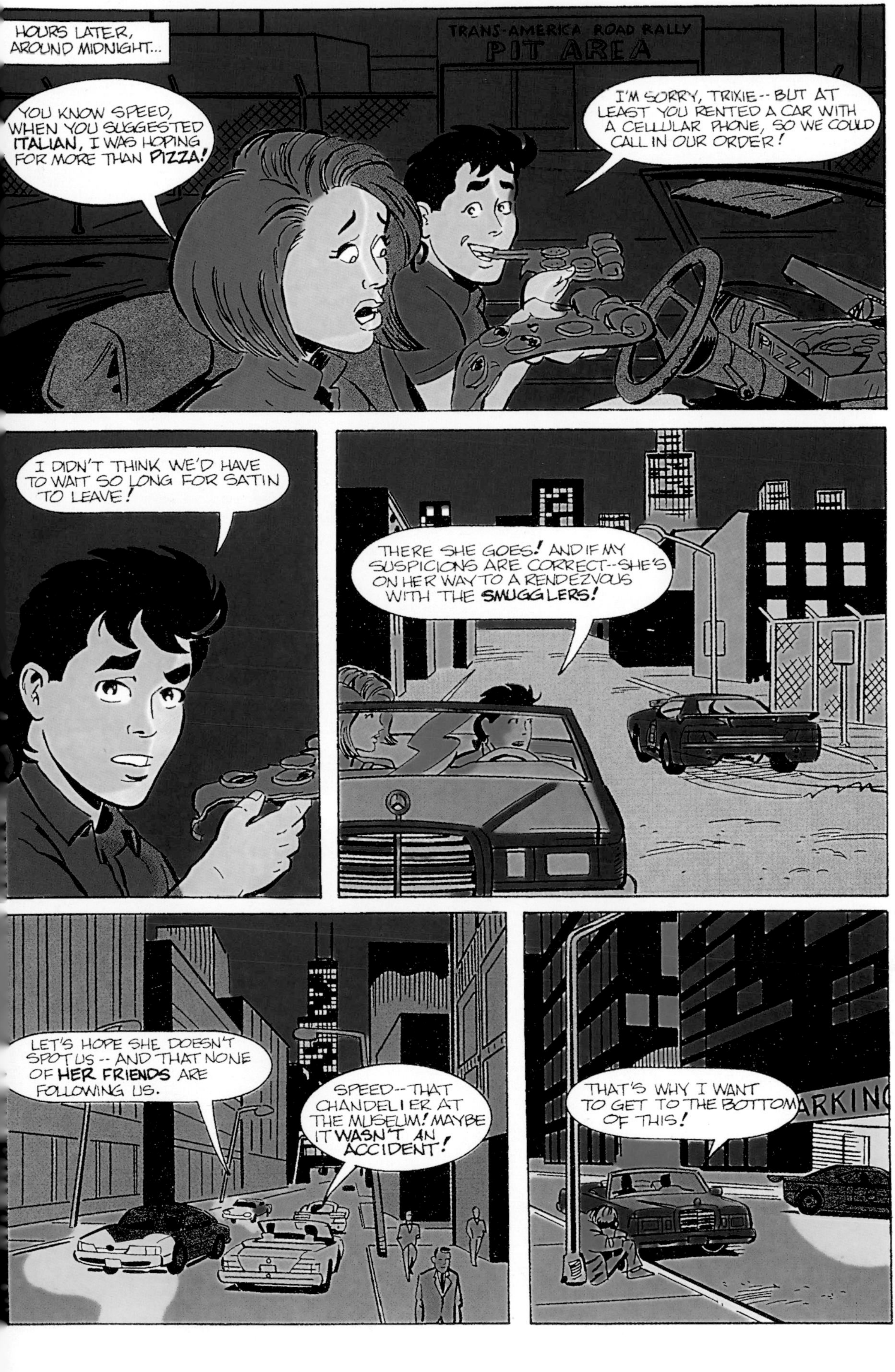
HOURS LATER, AROUND MIDNIGHT...
TRANS-AMERICA ROAD RALLY
PIT AREA
YOU KNOW SPEED, WHEN YOU SUGGESTED **ITALIAN**, I WAS HOPING FOR MORE THAN **PIZZA**!
I'M SORRY, TRIXIE-- BUT AT LEAST YOU RENTED A CAR WITH A CELLULAR PHONE, SO WE COULD CALL IN OUR ORDER!
PIZZA
I DIDN'T THINK WE'D HAVE TO WAIT SO LONG FOR SATIN TO LEAVE!
THERE SHE GOES! AND IF MY SUSPICIONS ARE CORRECT--SHE'S ON HER WAY TO A RENDEZVOUS WITH THE **SMUGGLERS**!
LET'S HOPE SHE DOESN'T SPOT US -- AND THAT NONE OF **HER FRIENDS** ARE FOLLOWING US.
SPEED--THAT CHANDELIER AT THE MUSEUM! MAYBE IT **WASN'T** AN **ACCIDENT**!
THAT'S WHY I WANT TO GET TO THE BOTTOM OF THIS!
ARKING

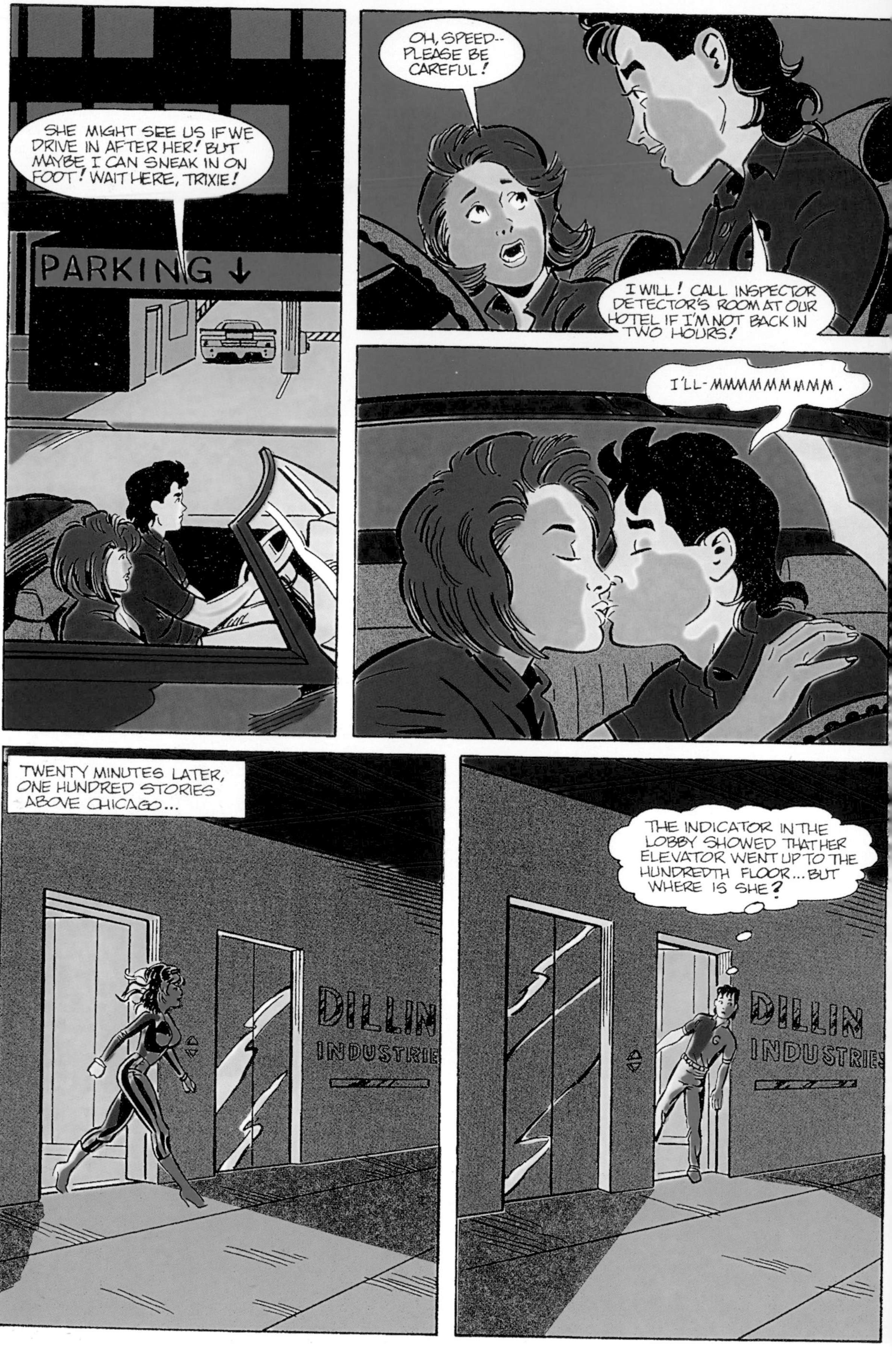
SHE MIGHT SEE US IF WE DRIVE IN AFTER HER! BUT MAYBE I CAN SNEAK IN ON FOOT! WAIT HERE, TRIXIE!
PARKING ↓
OH, SPEED-- PLEASE BE CAREFUL!
I WILL! CALL INSPECTOR DETECTOR'S ROOM AT OUR HOTEL IF I'M NOT BACK IN TWO HOURS!
I'LL-MMMMMMMMM.
TWENTY MINUTES LATER, ONE HUNDRED STORIES ABOVE CHICAGO...
DILLIN INDUSTRIES
THE INDICATOR IN THE LOBBY SHOWED THAT HER ELEVATOR WENT UP TO THE HUNDREDTH FLOOR... BUT WHERE IS SHE?
DILLIN INDUSTRIES

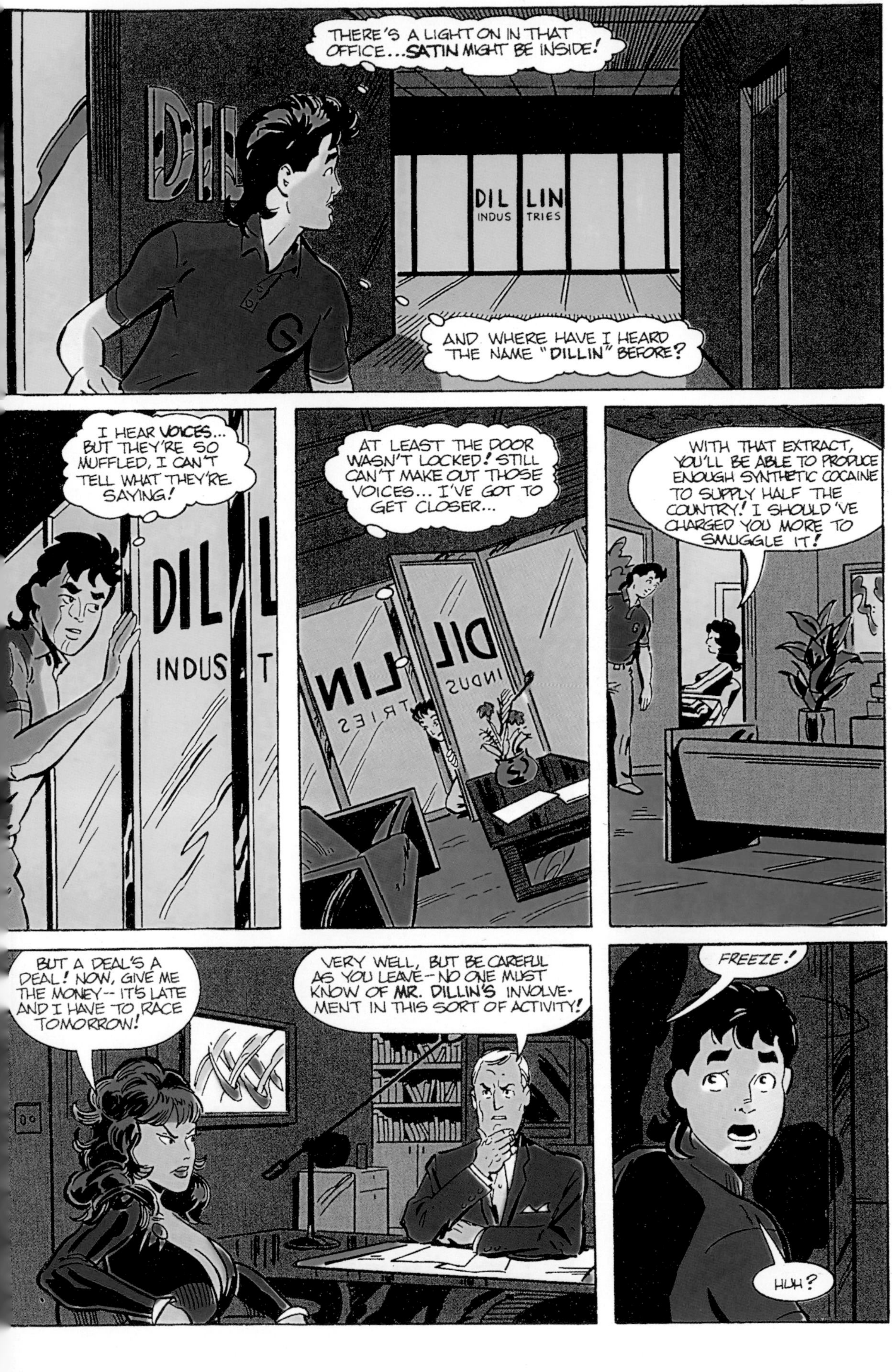
THERE'S A LIGHT ON IN THAT OFFICE... SATIN MIGHT BE INSIDE!
DILLIN INDUSTRIES
AND WHERE HAVE I HEARD THE NAME "DILLIN" BEFORE?
I HEAR VOICES... BUT THEY'RE SO MUFFLED, I CAN'T TELL WHAT THEY'RE SAYING!
AT LEAST THE DOOR WASN'T LOCKED! STILL CAN'T MAKE OUT THOSE VOICES... I'VE GOT TO GET CLOSER...
WITH THAT EXTRACT, YOU'LL BE ABLE TO PRODUCE ENOUGH SYNTHETIC COCAINE TO SUPPLY HALF THE COUNTRY! I SHOULD'VE CHARGED YOU MORE TO SMUGGLE IT!
BUT A DEAL'S A DEAL! NOW, GIVE ME THE MONEY-- IT'S LATE AND I HAVE TO RACE TOMORROW!
VERY WELL, BUT BE CAREFUL AS YOU LEAVE-- NO ONE MUST KNOW OF MR. DILLIN'S INVOLVEMENT IN THIS SORT OF ACTIVITY!
FREEZE!
HUH?

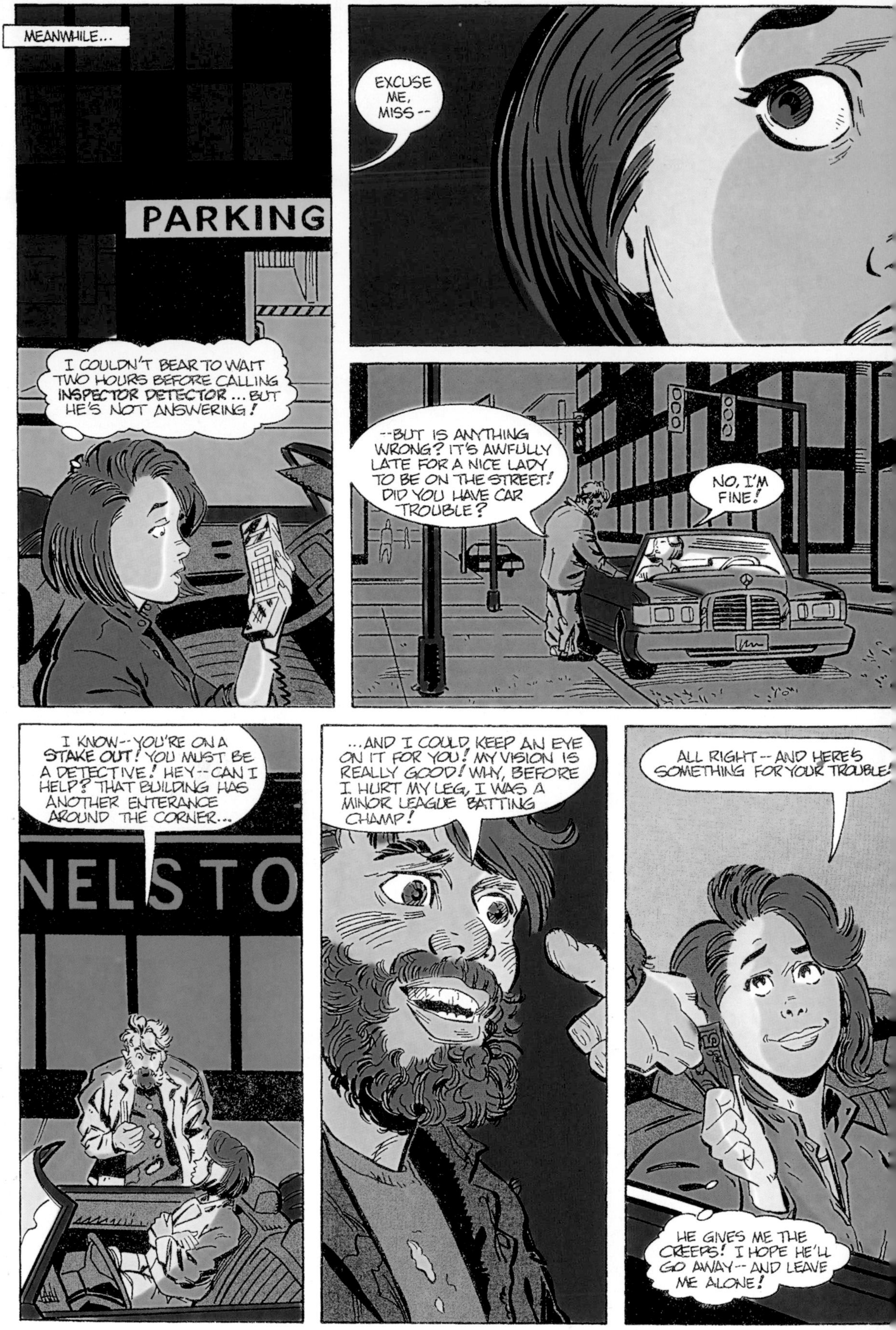
MEANWHILE...
PARKING
I COULDN'T BEAR TO WAIT TWO HOURS BEFORE CALLING INSPECTOR DETECTOR ... BUT HE'S NOT ANSWERING!
EXCUSE ME, MISS --
--BUT IS ANYTHING WRONG? IT'S AWFULLY LATE FOR A NICE LADY TO BE ON THE STREET! DID YOU HAVE CAR TROUBLE?
NO, I'M FINE!
I KNOW--YOU'RE ON A STAKE OUT! YOU MUST BE A DETECTIVE! HEY--CAN I HELP? THAT BUILDING HAS ANOTHER ENTERANCE AROUND THE CORNER...
NELSTO
...AND I COULD KEEP AN EYE ON IT FOR YOU! MY VISION IS REALLY GOOD! WHY, BEFORE I HURT MY LEG, I WAS A MINOR LEAGUE BATTING CHAMP!
ALL RIGHT--AND HERE'S SOMETHING FOR YOUR TROUBLE!
HE GIVES ME THE CREEPS! I HOPE HE'LL GO AWAY--AND LEAVE ME ALONE!

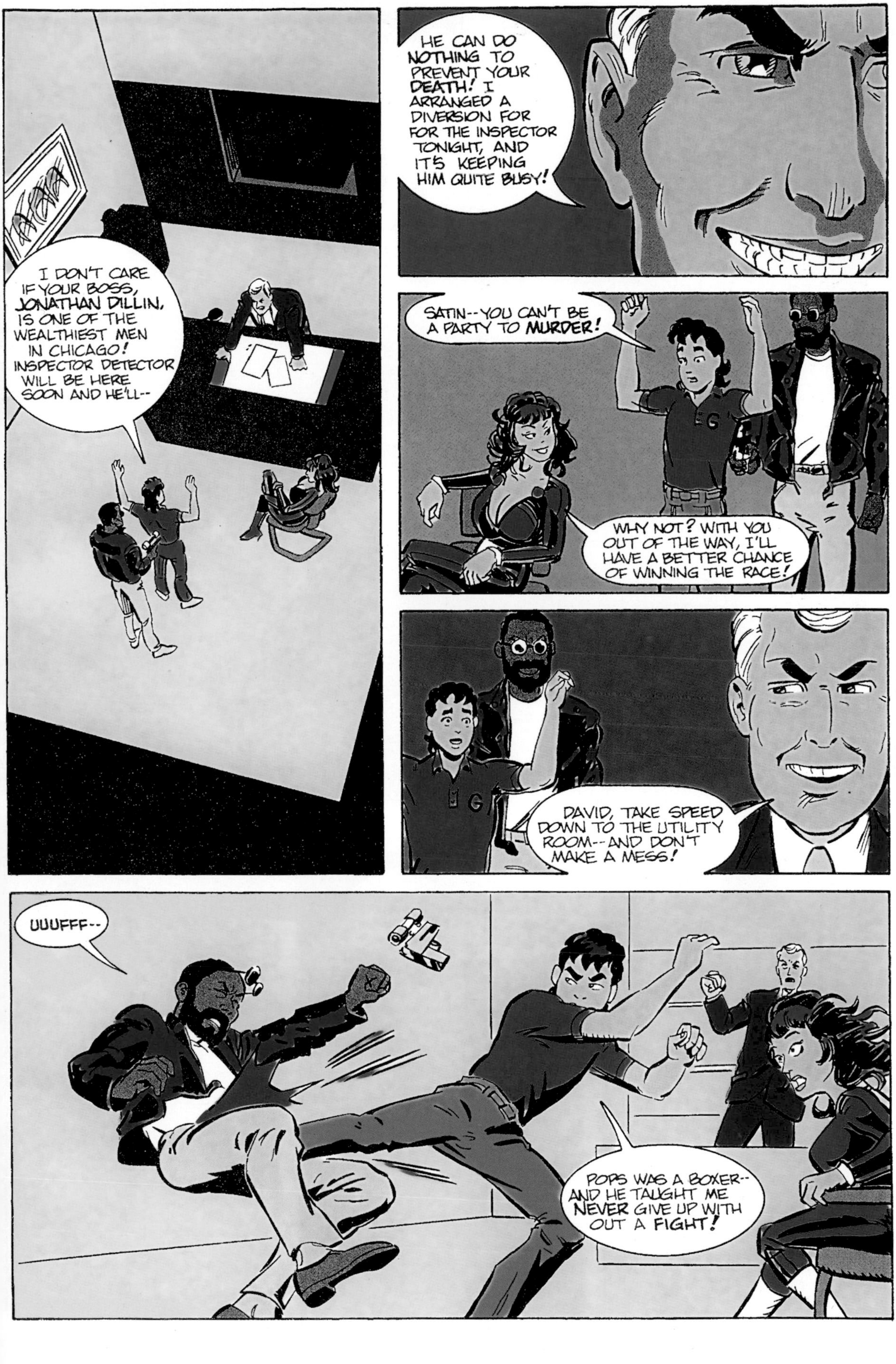
I DON'T CARE IF YOUR BOSS, JONATHAN DILLIN, IS ONE OF THE WEALTHIEST MEN IN CHICAGO! INSPECTOR DETECTOR WILL BE HERE SOON AND HE'LL--
HE CAN DO NOTHING TO PREVENT YOUR DEATH! I ARRANGED A DIVERSION FOR FOR THE INSPECTOR TONIGHT, AND IT'S KEEPING HIM QUITE BUSY!
SATIN--YOU CAN'T BE A PARTY TO MURDER!
WHY NOT? WITH YOU OUT OF THE WAY, I'LL HAVE A BETTER CHANCE OF WINNING THE RACE!
DAVID, TAKE SPEED DOWN TO THE UTILITY ROOM--AND DON'T MAKE A MESS!
UUUFFF--
POPS WAS A BOXER--AND HE TAUGHT ME NEVER GIVE UP WITH OUT A FIGHT!

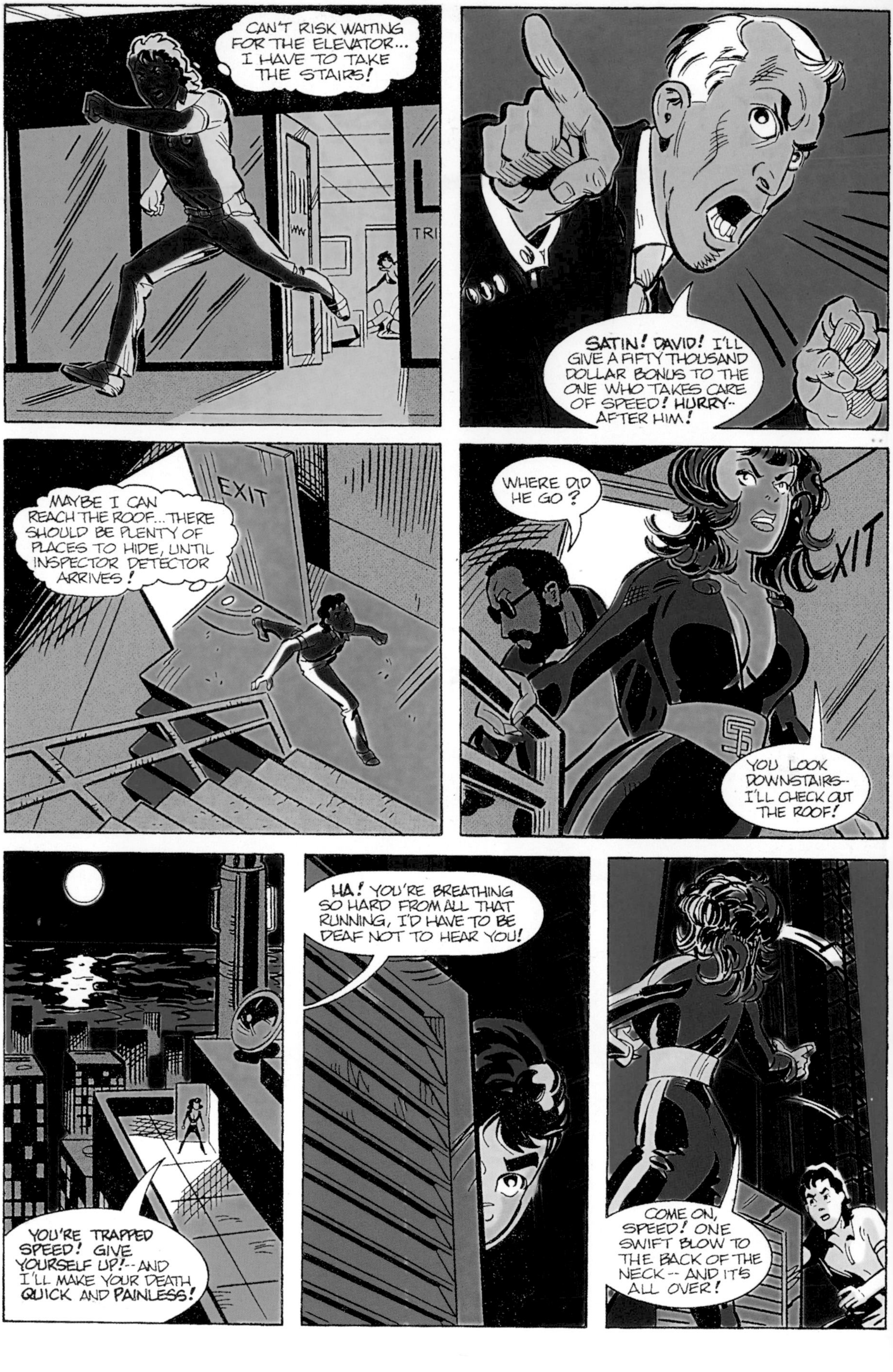
CAN'T RISK WAITING FOR THE ELEVATOR... I HAVE TO TAKE THE STAIRS!
SATIN! DAVID! I'LL GIVE A FIFTY THOUSAND DOLLAR BONUS TO THE ONE WHO TAKES CARE OF SPEED! HURRY-- AFTER HIM!
EXIT
MAYBE I CAN REACH THE ROOF... THERE SHOULD BE PLENTY OF PLACES TO HIDE, UNTIL INSPECTOR DETECTOR ARRIVES!
WHERE DID HE GO?
XIT
YOU LOOK DOWNSTAIRS-- I'LL CHECK OUT THE ROOF!
YOU'RE TRAPPED SPEED! GIVE YOURSELF UP!--AND I'LL MAKE YOUR DEATH QUICK AND PAINLESS!
HA! YOU'RE BREATHING SO HARD FROM ALL THAT RUNNING, I'D HAVE TO BE DEAF NOT TO HEAR YOU!
COME ON, SPEED! ONE SWIFT BLOW TO THE BACK OF THE NECK -- AND IT'S ALL OVER!

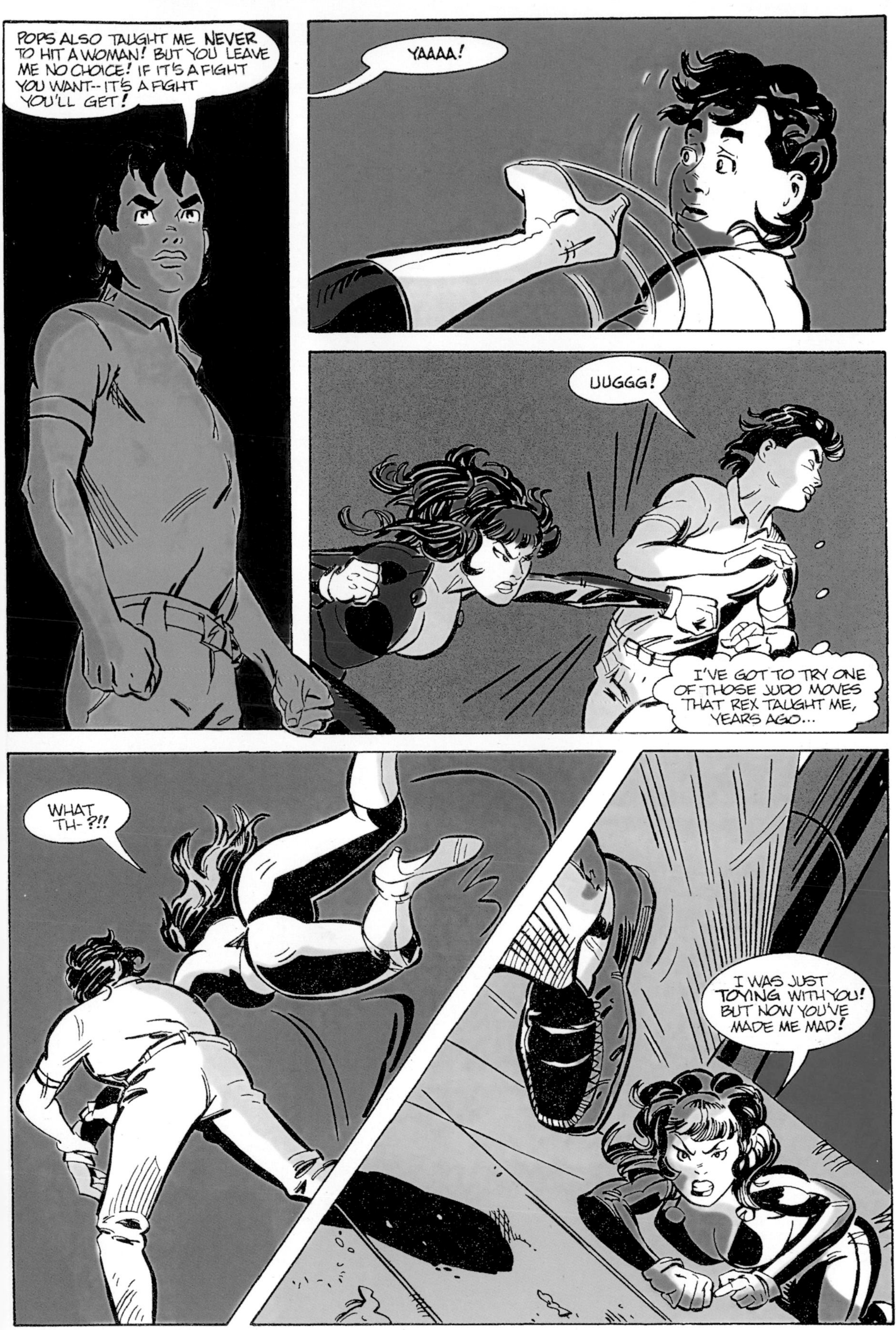
POPS ALSO TAUGHT ME NEVER TO HIT A WOMAN! BUT YOU LEAVE ME NO CHOICE! IF IT'S A FIGHT YOU WANT-- IT'S A FIGHT YOU'LL GET!
YAAAA!
UUGGG!
I'VE GOT TO TRY ONE OF THOSE JUDO MOVES THAT REX TAUGHT ME, YEARS AGO...
WHAT TH-?!!
I WAS JUST TOYING WITH YOU! BUT NOW YOU'VE MADE ME MAD!

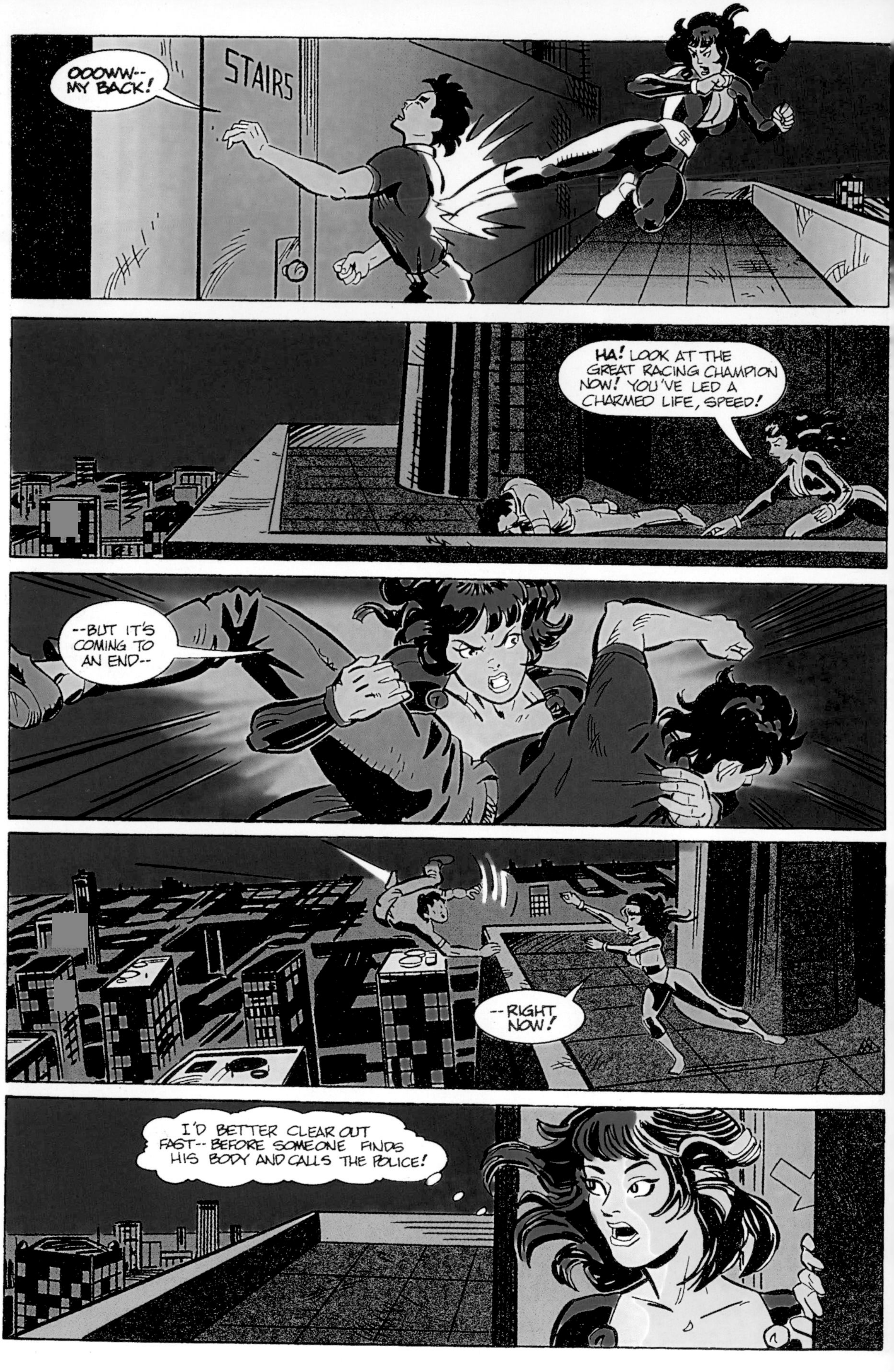
OOOWW-- MY BACK!
STAIRS
HA! LOOK AT THE GREAT RACING CHAMPION NOW! YOU'VE LED A CHARMED LIFE, SPEED!
--BUT IT'S COMING TO AN END--
--RIGHT NOW!
I'D BETTER CLEAR OUT FAST-- BEFORE SOMEONE FINDS HIS BODY AND CALLS THE POLICE!

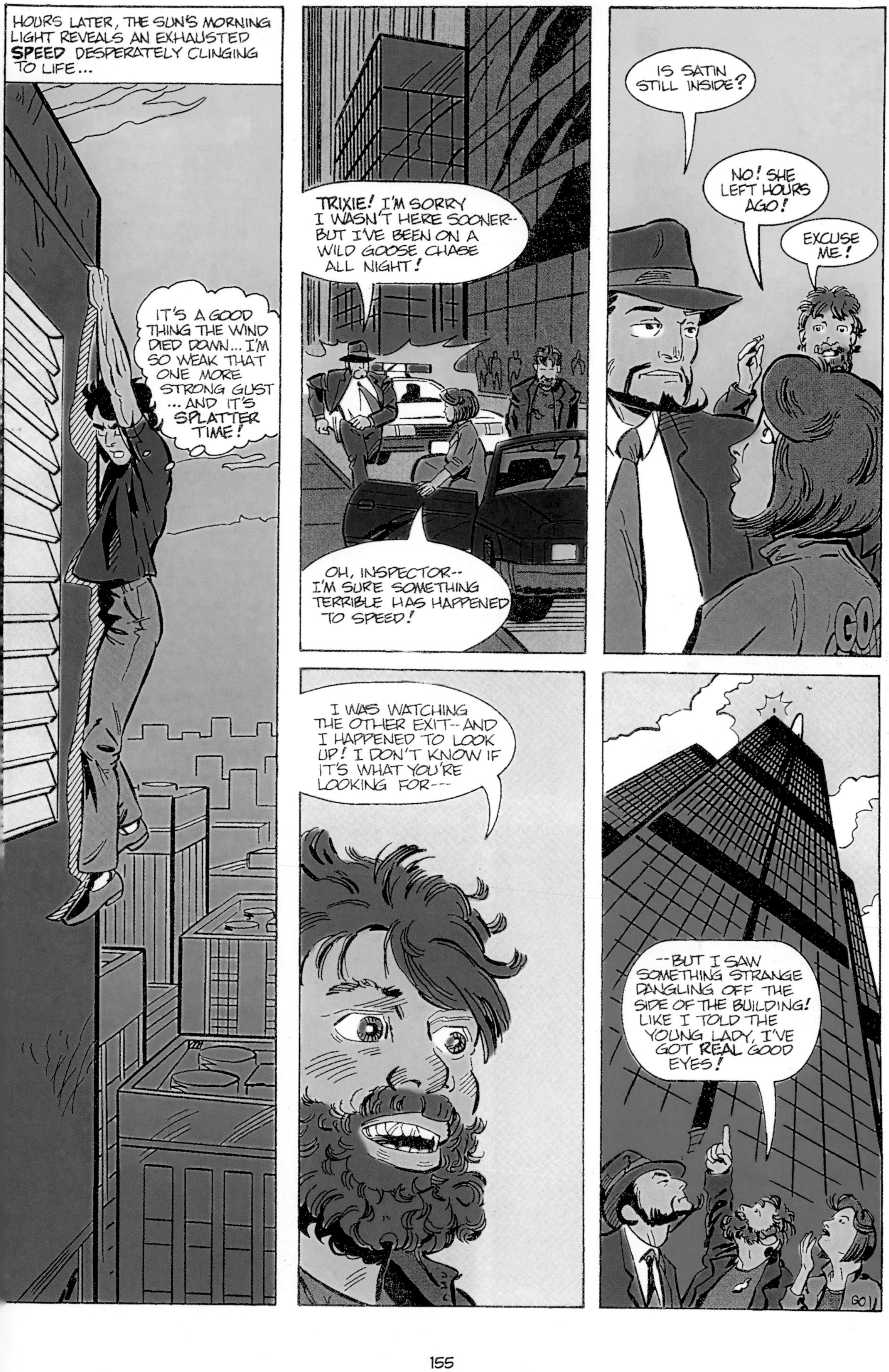
HOURS LATER, THE SUN'S MORNING LIGHT REVEALS AN EXHAUSTED **SPEED** DESPERATELY CLINGING TO LIFE...
IT'S A GOOD THING THE WIND DIED DOWN... I'M SO WEAK THAT ONE MORE STRONG GUST ...AND IT'S SPLATTER TIME!
TRIXIE! I'M SORRY I WASN'T HERE SOONER-- BUT I'VE BEEN ON A WILD GOOSE CHASE ALL NIGHT!
OH, INSPECTOR-- I'M SURE SOMETHING TERRIBLE HAS HAPPENED TO SPEED!
IS SATIN STILL INSIDE?
NO! SHE LEFT HOURS AGO!
EXCUSE ME!
I WAS WATCHING THE OTHER EXIT--AND I HAPPENED TO LOOK UP! I DON'T KNOW IF IT'S WHAT YOU'RE LOOKING FOR---
--BUT I SAW SOMETHING STRANGE DANGLING OFF THE SIDE OF THE BUILDING! LIKE I TOLD THE YOUNG LADY, I'VE GOT REAL GOOD EYES!

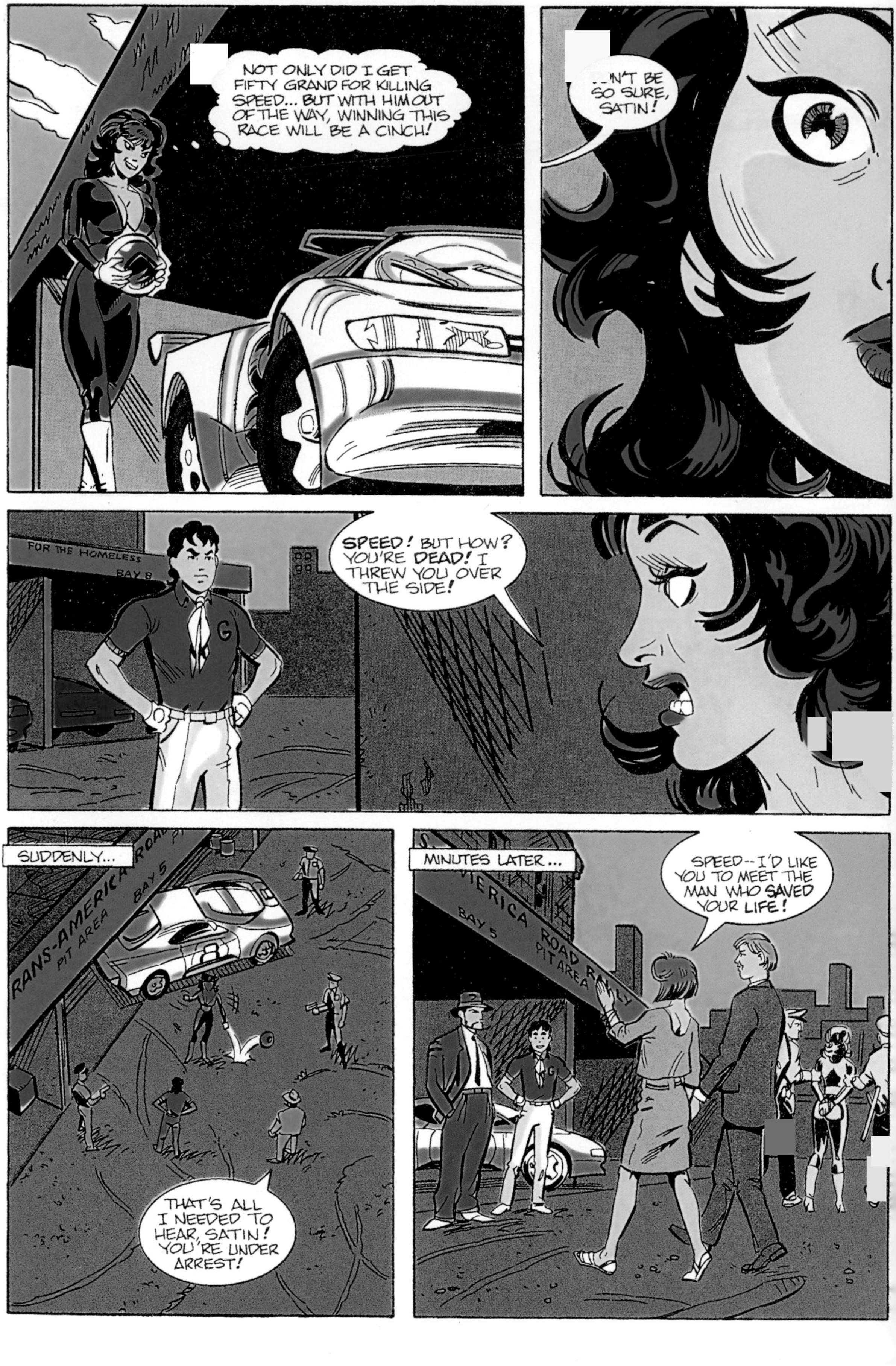
NOT ONLY DID I GET FIFTY GRAND FOR KILLING SPEED... BUT WITH HIM OUT OF THE WAY, WINNING THIS RACE WILL BE A CINCH!
N'T BE SO SURE, SATIN!
FOR THE HOMELESS
BAY 8
SPEED! BUT HOW? YOU'RE DEAD! I THREW YOU OVER THE SIDE!
SUDDENLY...
PIT AREA
BAY 5
THAT'S ALL I NEEDED TO HEAR, SATIN! YOU'RE UNDER ARREST!
MINUTES LATER...
BAY 5
PIT AREA
SPEED--I'D LIKE YOU TO MEET THE MAN WHO SAVED YOUR LIFE!

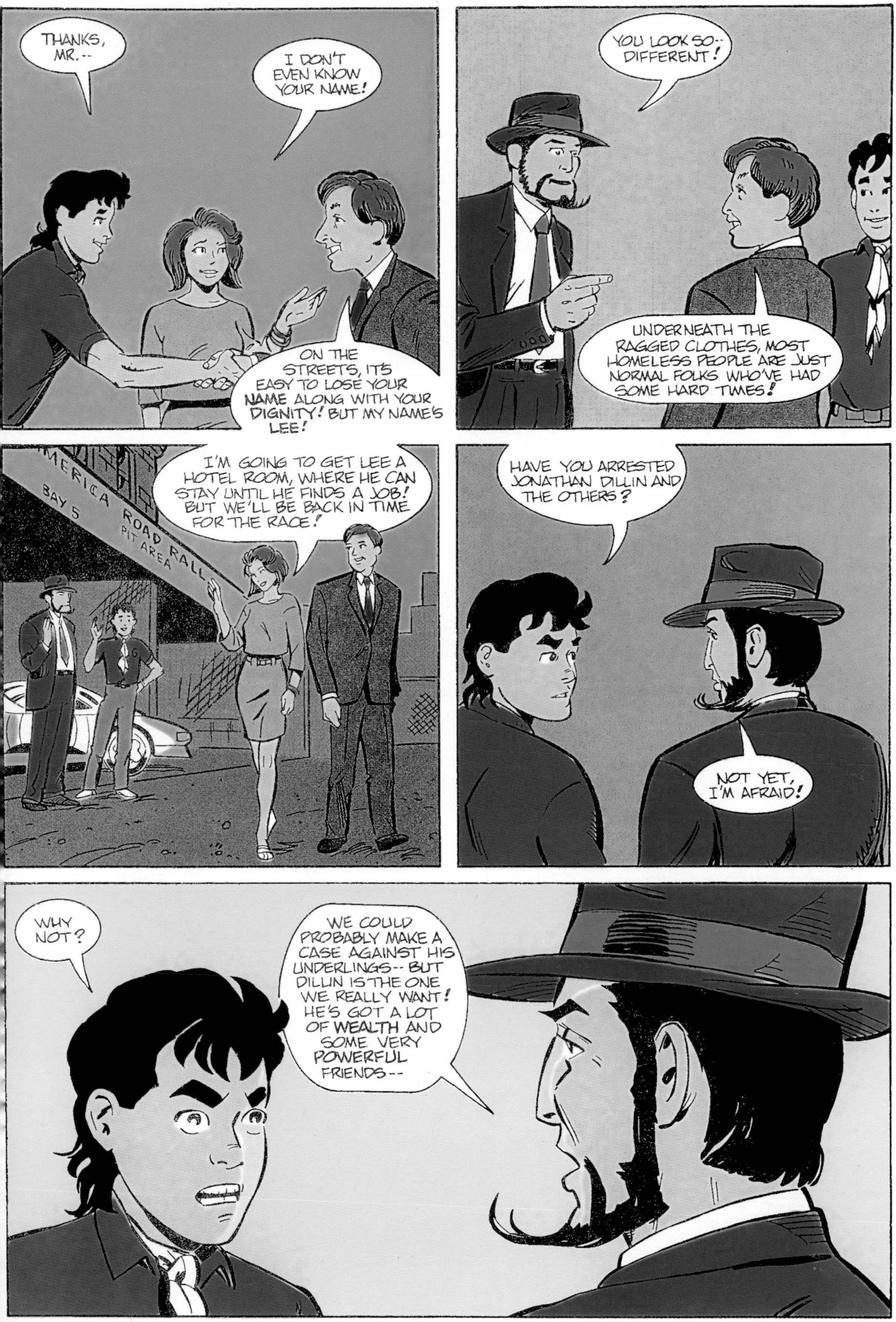

THANKS, MR.--
I DON'T EVEN KNOW YOUR NAME!
ON THE STREETS, IT'S EASY TO LOSE YOUR NAME ALONG WITH YOUR DIGNITY! BUT MY NAME'S LEE!
YOU LOOK SO-- DIFFERENT!
UNDERNEATH THE RAGGED CLOTHES, MOST HOMELESS PEOPLE ARE JUST NORMAL FOLKS WHO'VE HAD SOME HARD TIMES!
I'M GOING TO GET LEE A HOTEL ROOM, WHERE HE CAN STAY UNTIL HE FINDS A JOB! BUT WE'LL BE BACK IN TIME FOR THE RACE!
MERICA ROAD RALL
BAY 5
PIT AREA
HAVE YOU ARRESTED JONATHAN DILLIN AND THE OTHERS?
NOT YET, I'M AFRAID!
WHY NOT?
WE COULD PROBABLY MAKE A CASE AGAINST HIS UNDERLINGS-- BUT DILLIN IS THE ONE WE REALLY WANT! HE'S GOT A LOT OF WEALTH AND SOME VERY POWERFUL FRIENDS--

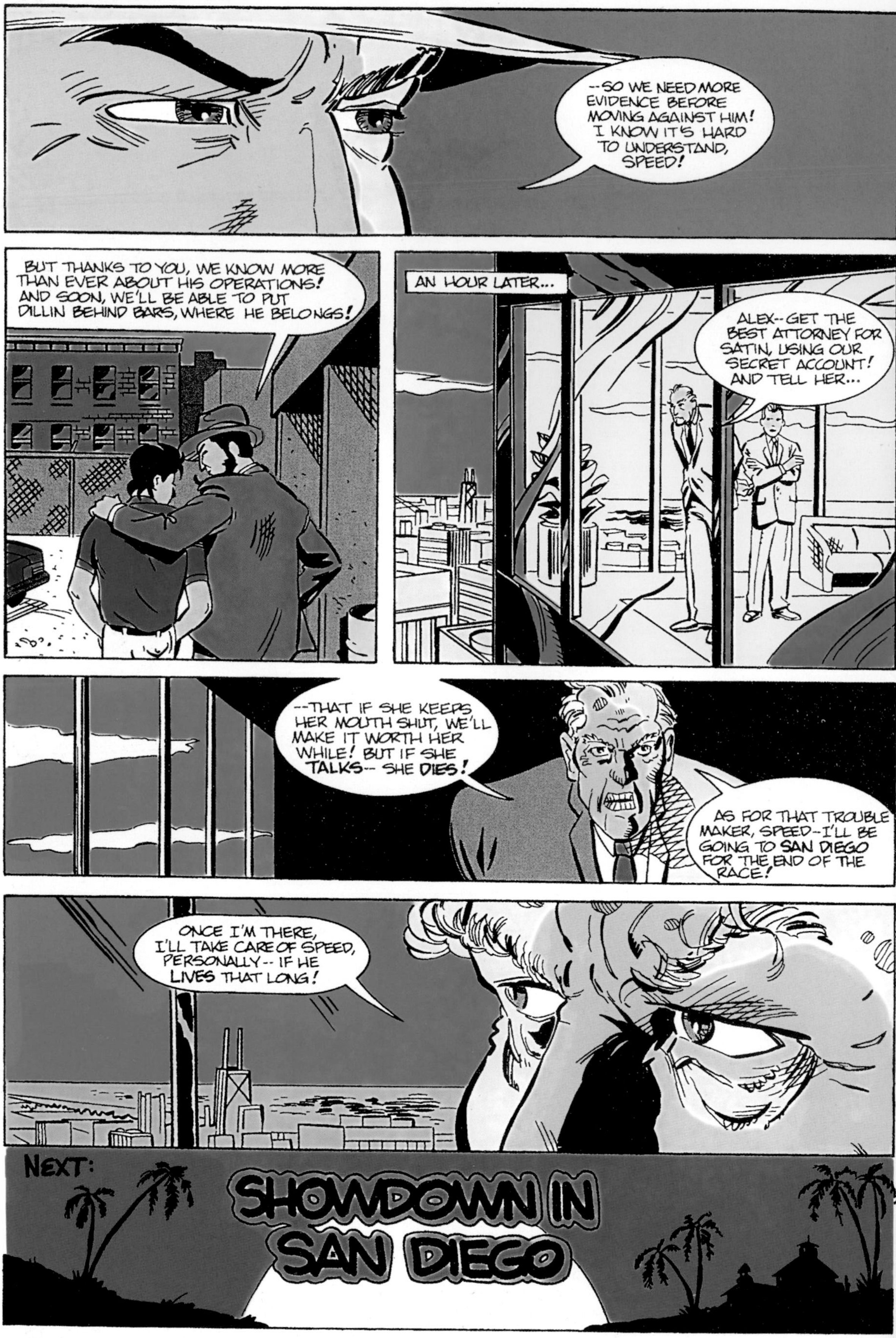
--SO WE NEED MORE EVIDENCE BEFORE MOVING AGAINST HIM! I KNOW IT'S HARD TO UNDERSTAND, SPEED!
BUT THANKS TO YOU, WE KNOW MORE THAN EVER ABOUT HIS OPERATIONS! AND SOON, WE'LL BE ABLE TO PUT DILLIN BEHIND BARS, WHERE HE BELONGS!
AN HOUR LATER...
ALEX--GET THE BEST ATTORNEY FOR SATIN, USING OUR SECRET ACCOUNT! AND TELL HER...
--THAT IF SHE KEEPS HER MOUTH SHUT, WE'LL MAKE IT WORTH HER WHILE! BUT IF SHE TALKS-- SHE DIES!
AS FOR THAT TROUBLE MAKER, SPEED--I'LL BE GOING TO SAN DIEGO FOR THE END OF THE RACE!
ONCE I'M THERE, I'LL TAKE CARE OF SPEED, PERSONALLY-- IF HE LIVES THAT LONG!
NEXT:
SHOWDOWN IN SAN DIEGO

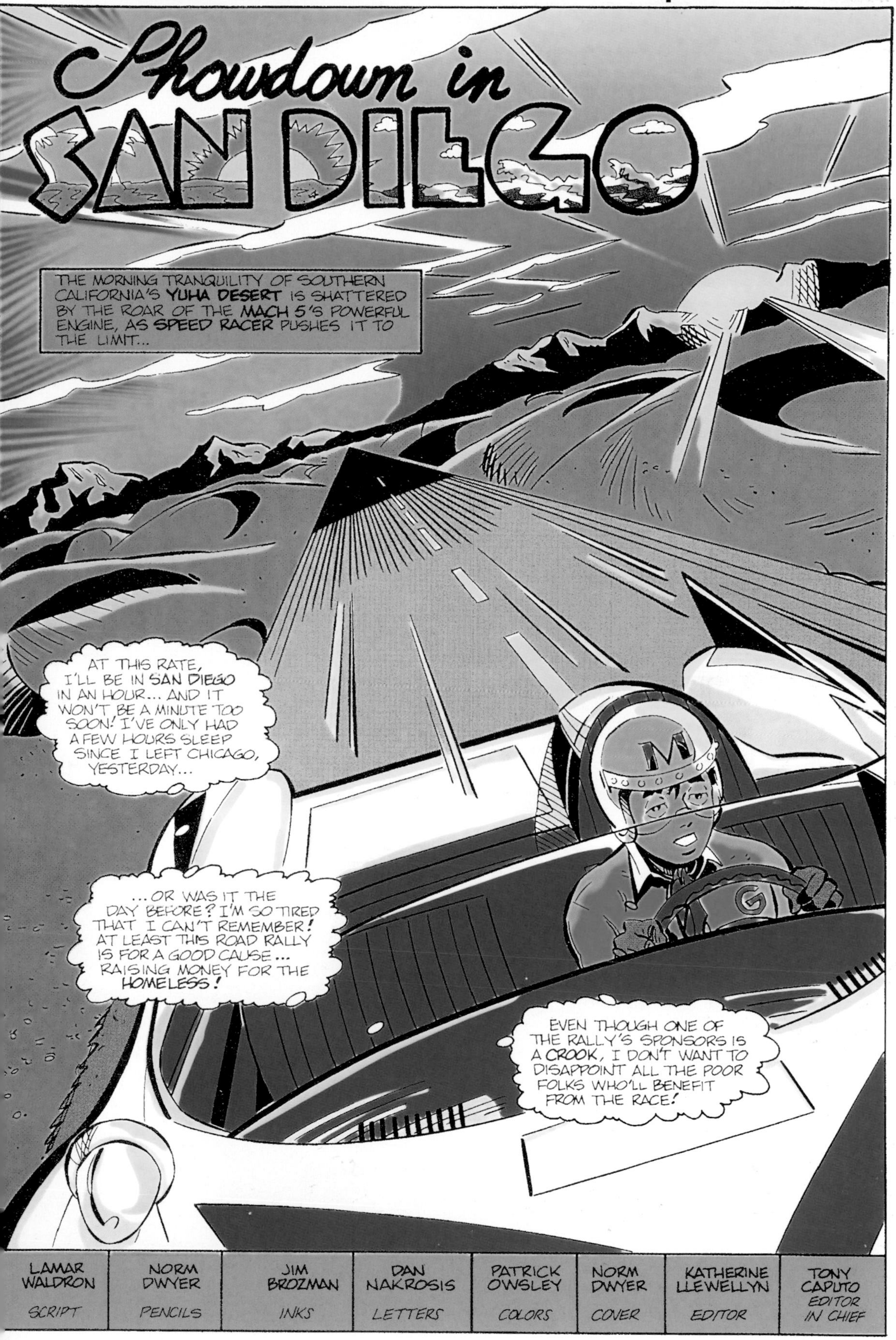
Showdown in
SAN DIEGO
THE MORNING TRANQUILITY OF SOUTHERN CALIFORNIA'S YUHA DESERT IS SHATTERED BY THE ROAR OF THE MACH 5'S POWERFUL ENGINE, AS SPEED RACER PUSHES IT TO THE LIMIT...
AT THIS RATE, I'LL BE IN SAN DIEGO IN AN HOUR... AND IT WON'T BE A MINUTE TOO SOON! I'VE ONLY HAD A FEW HOURS SLEEP SINCE I LEFT CHICAGO, YESTERDAY...
...OR WAS IT THE DAY BEFORE? I'M SO TIRED THAT I CAN'T REMEMBER! AT LEAST THIS ROAD RALLY IS FOR A GOOD CAUSE... RAISING MONEY FOR THE HOMELESS!
EVEN THOUGH ONE OF THE RALLY'S SPONSORS IS A CROOK, I DON'T WANT TO DISAPPOINT ALL THE POOR FOLKS WHO'LL BENEFIT FROM THE RACE!

LAMAR WALDRON	NORM DWYER	JIM BROZMAN	DAN NAKROSIS	PATRICK OWSLEY	NORM DWYER	KATHERINE LLEWELLYN	TONY CAPUTO
SCRIPT	PENCILS	INKS	LETTERS	COLORS	COVER	EDITOR	EDITOR IN CHIEF

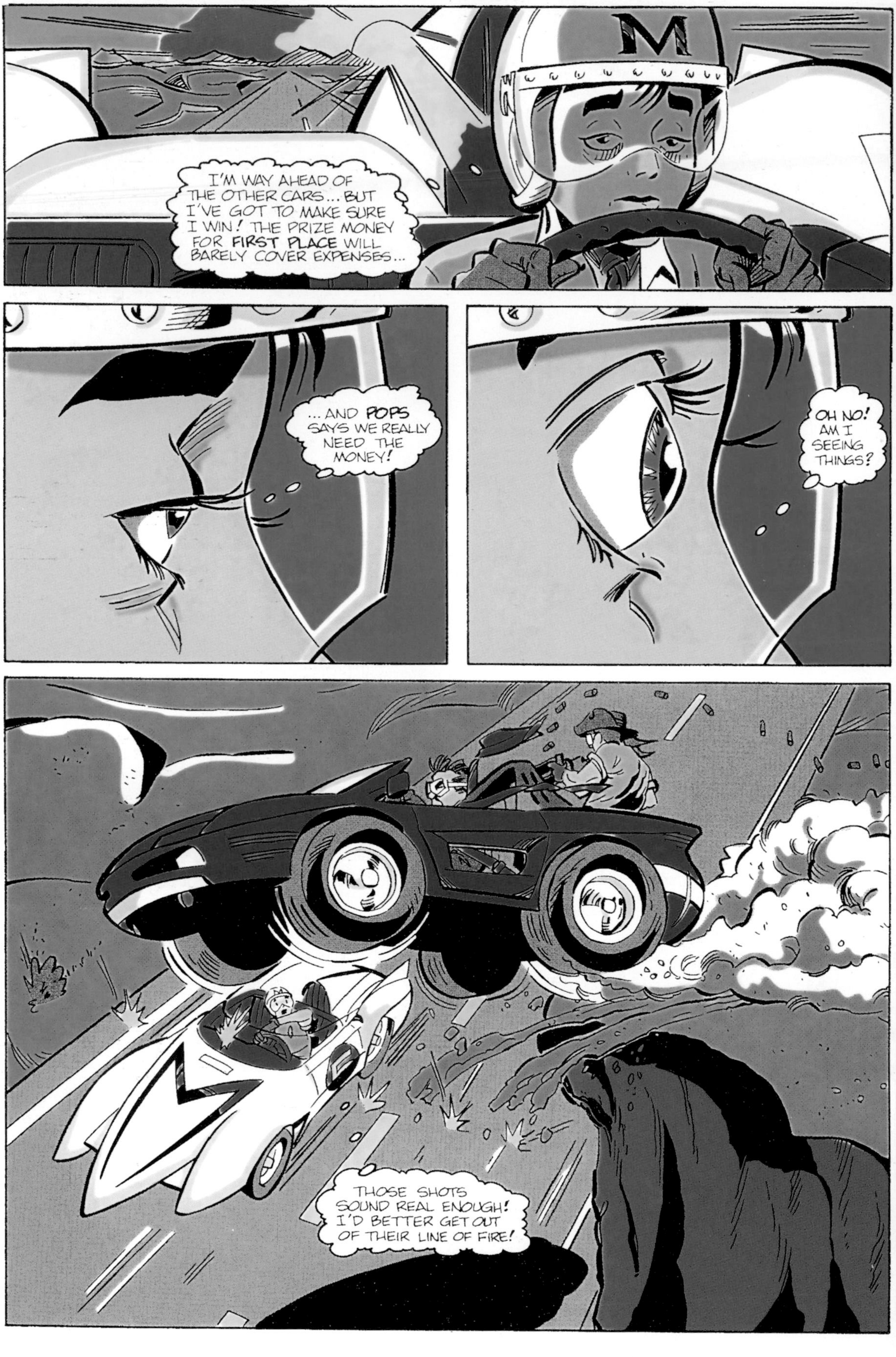
I'M WAY AHEAD OF THE OTHER CARS... BUT I'VE GOT TO MAKE SURE I WIN! THE PRIZE MONEY FOR FIRST PLACE WILL BARELY COVER EXPENSES...
...AND POPS SAYS WE REALLY NEED THE MONEY!
OH NO! AM I SEEING THINGS?
THOSE SHOTS SOUND REAL ENOUGH! I'D BETTER GET OUT OF THEIR LINE OF FIRE!

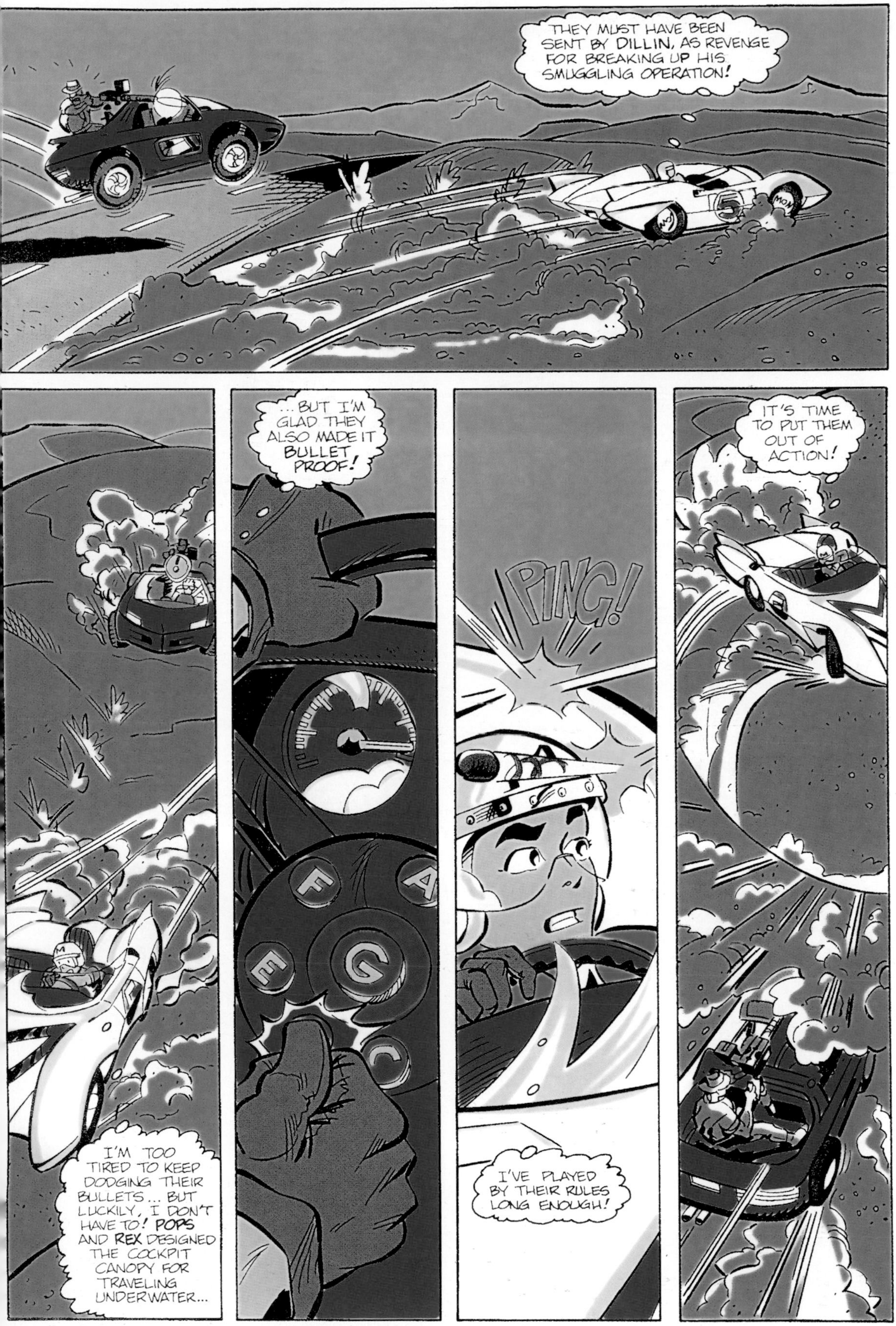
THEY MUST HAVE BEEN SENT BY DILLIN, AS REVENGE FOR BREAKING UP HIS SMUGGLING OPERATION!
I'M TOO TIRED TO KEEP DODGING THEIR BULLETS... BUT LUCKILY, I DON'T HAVE TO! POPS AND REX DESIGNED THE COCKPIT CANOPY FOR TRAVELING UNDERWATER...
...BUT I'M GLAD THEY ALSO MADE IT BULLET PROOF!
PING!
I'VE PLAYED BY THEIR RULES LONG ENOUGH!
IT'S TIME TO PUT THEM OUT OF ACTION!

SPEED HITS ANOTHER BUTTON ON THE STEERING WHEEL...

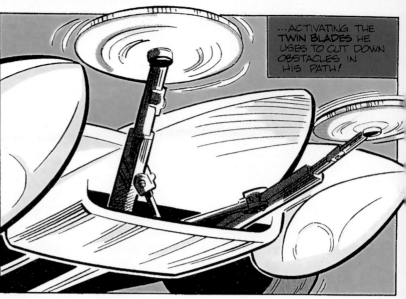

...ACTIVATING THE **TWIN BLADES** HE USES TO CUT DOWN OBSTACLES IN HIS PATH!

HAVE TO GET THE ANGLE JUST RIGHT...

RIP!

THAT OUGHT TO SLOW THEM DOWN!

I'D LOVE TO SEE THE LOOK ON **DILLIN'S** FACE WHEN HE FIND'S OUT I'VE BEATEN HIM **AGAIN!**

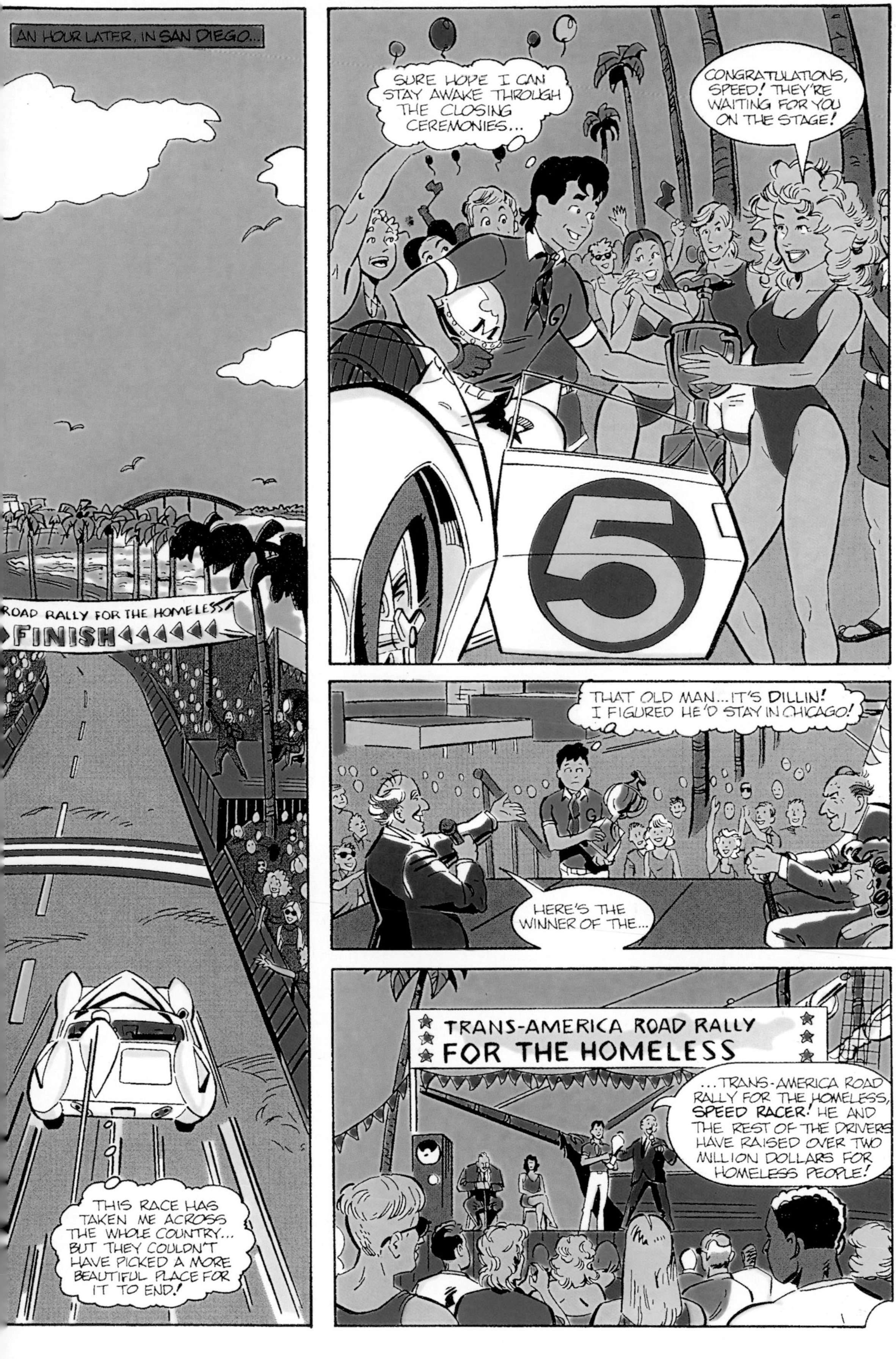
AN HOUR LATER, IN SAN DIEGO...
ROAD RALLY FOR THE HOMELESS
FINISH
THIS RACE HAS TAKEN ME ACROSS THE WHOLE COUNTRY... BUT THEY COULDN'T HAVE PICKED A MORE BEAUTIFUL PLACE FOR IT TO END!
SURE HOPE I CAN STAY AWAKE THROUGH THE CLOSING CEREMONIES...
CONGRATULATIONS, SPEED! THEY'RE WAITING FOR YOU ON THE STAGE!
5
THAT OLD MAN... IT'S DILLIN! I FIGURED HE'D STAY IN CHICAGO!
HERE'S THE WINNER OF THE...
TRANS-AMERICA ROAD RALLY FOR THE HOMELESS
...TRANS-AMERICA ROAD RALLY FOR THE HOMELESS, SPEED RACER! HE AND THE REST OF THE DRIVERS HAVE RAISED OVER TWO MILLION DOLLARS FOR HOMELESS PEOPLE!

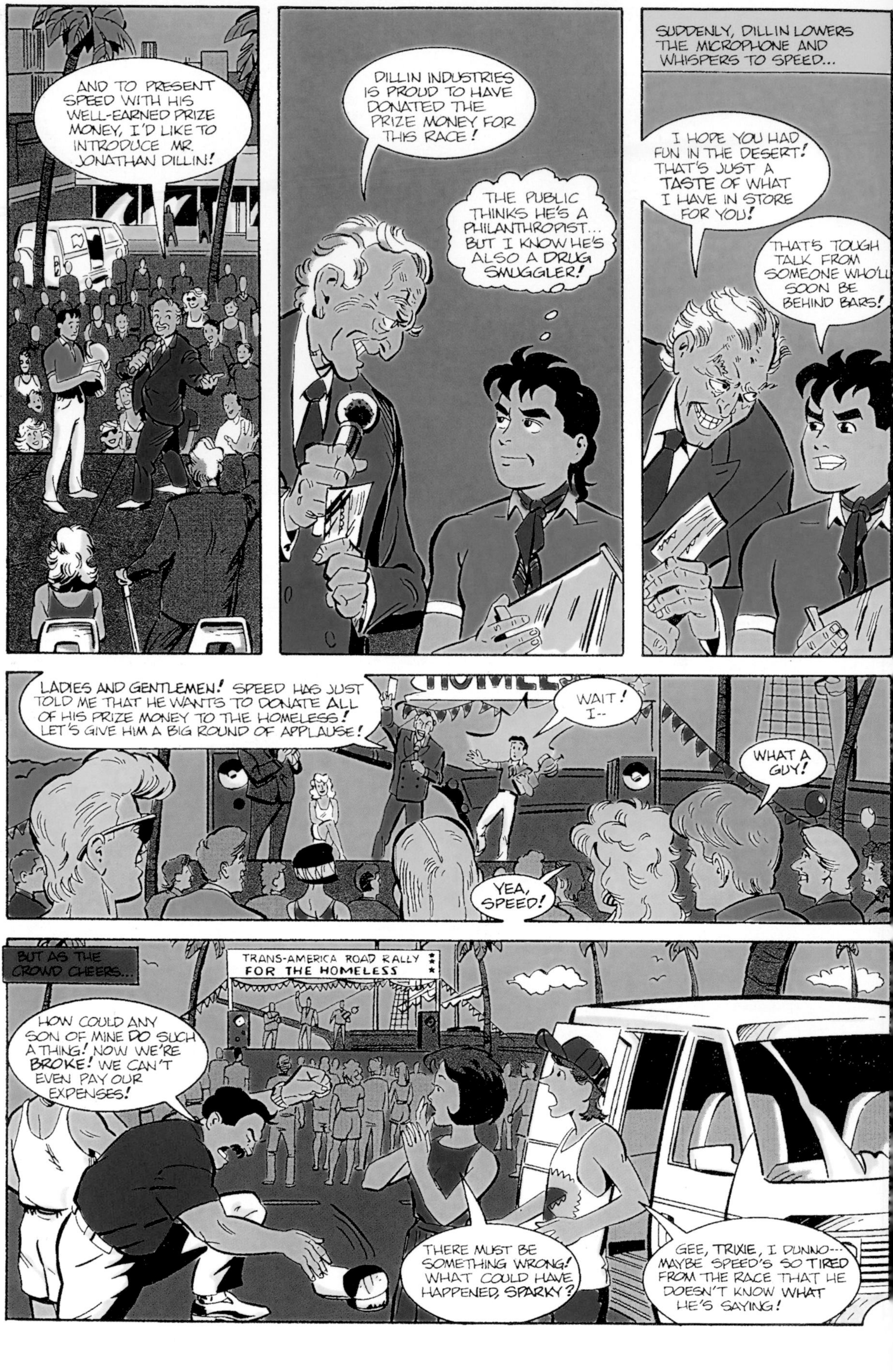
AND TO PRESENT SPEED WITH HIS WELL-EARNED PRIZE MONEY, I'D LIKE TO INTRODUCE MR. JONATHAN DILLIN!
DILLIN INDUSTRIES IS PROUD TO HAVE DONATED THE PRIZE MONEY FOR THIS RACE!
THE PUBLIC THINKS HE'S A PHILANTHROPIST... BUT I KNOW HE'S ALSO A DRUG SMUGGLER!
SUDDENLY, DILLIN LOWERS THE MICROPHONE AND WHISPERS TO SPEED...
I HOPE YOU HAD FUN IN THE DESERT! THAT'S JUST A TASTE OF WHAT I HAVE IN STORE FOR YOU!
THAT'S TOUGH TALK FROM SOMEONE WHO'LL SOON BE BEHIND BARS!
LADIES AND GENTLEMEN! SPEED HAS JUST TOLD ME THAT HE WANTS TO DONATE ALL OF HIS PRIZE MONEY TO THE HOMELESS! LET'S GIVE HIM A BIG ROUND OF APPLAUSE!
WAIT! I--
WHAT A GUY!
YEA, SPEED!
BUT AS THE CROWD CHEERS...
TRANS-AMERICA ROAD RALLY FOR THE HOMELESS
HOW COULD ANY SON OF MINE DO SUCH A THING! NOW WE'RE BROKE! WE CAN'T EVEN PAY OUR EXPENSES!
THERE MUST BE SOMETHING WRONG! WHAT COULD HAVE HAPPENED, SPARKY?
GEE, TRIXIE, I DUNNO--- MAYBE SPEED'S SO TIRED FROM THE RACE THAT HE DOESN'T KNOW WHAT HE'S SAYING!

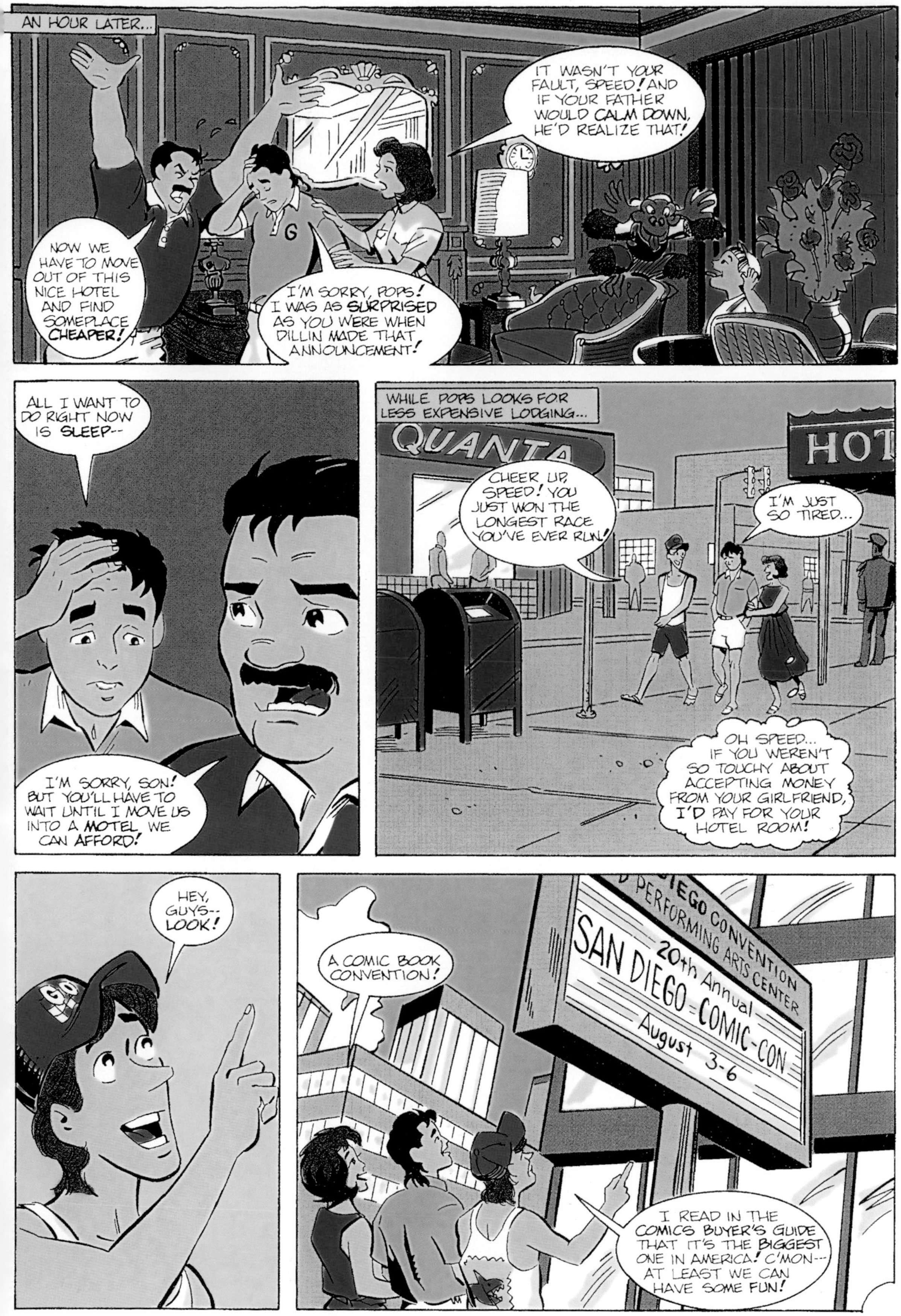
AN HOUR LATER...
IT WASN'T YOUR FAULT, SPEED! AND IF YOUR FATHER WOULD CALM DOWN, HE'D REALIZE THAT!
NOW WE HAVE TO MOVE OUT OF THIS NICE HOTEL AND FIND SOMEPLACE CHEAPER!
I'M SORRY, POPS! I WAS AS SURPRISED AS YOU WERE WHEN DILLIN MADE THAT ANNOUNCEMENT!
ALL I WANT TO DO RIGHT NOW IS SLEEP--
I'M SORRY, SON! BUT YOU'LL HAVE TO WAIT UNTIL I MOVE US INTO A MOTEL WE CAN AFFORD!
WHILE POPS LOOKS FOR LESS EXPENSIVE LODGING...
QUANTA
HOT
CHEER UP, SPEED! YOU JUST WON THE LONGEST RACE YOU'VE EVER RUN!
I'M JUST SO TIRED...
OH SPEED... IF YOU WEREN'T SO TOUCHY ABOUT ACCEPTING MONEY FROM YOUR GIRLFRIEND, I'D PAY FOR YOUR HOTEL ROOM!
HEY, GUYS-- LOOK!
A COMIC BOOK CONVENTION!
DIEGO CONVENTION
D PERFORMING ARTS CENTER
20th Annual
SAN DIEGO COMIC-CON
August 3-6
I READ IN THE COMICS BUYER'S GUIDE THAT IT'S THE BIGGEST ONE IN AMERICA! C'MON--- AT LEAST WE CAN HAVE SOME FUN!

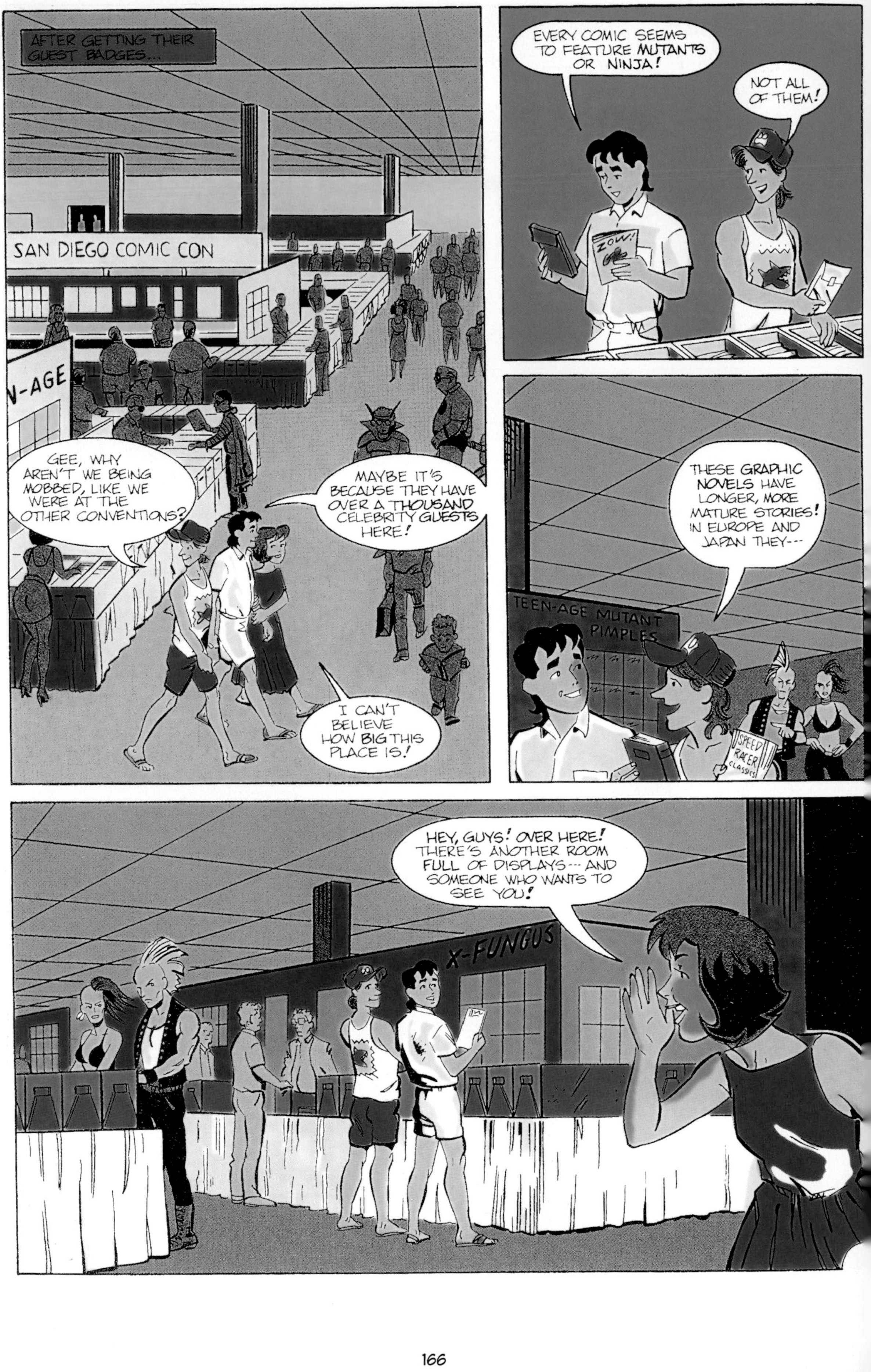
AFTER GETTING THEIR GUEST BADGES...
SAN DIEGO COMIC CON
N-AGE
GEE, WHY AREN'T WE BEING MOBBED, LIKE WE WERE AT THE OTHER CONVENTIONS?
MAYBE IT'S BECAUSE THEY HAVE OVER A THOUSAND CELEBRITY GUESTS HERE!
I CAN'T BELIEVE HOW BIG THIS PLACE IS!
EVERY COMIC SEEMS TO FEATURE MUTANTS OR NINJA!
NOT ALL OF THEM!
ZOW!
THESE GRAPHIC NOVELS HAVE LONGER, MORE MATURE STORIES! IN EUROPE AND JAPAN THEY---
TEEN-AGE MUTANT PIMPLES
SPEED RACER CLASSICS
HEY, GUYS! OVER HERE! THERE'S ANOTHER ROOM FULL OF DISPLAYS--- AND SOMEONE WHO WANTS TO SEE YOU!
X-FUNGUS

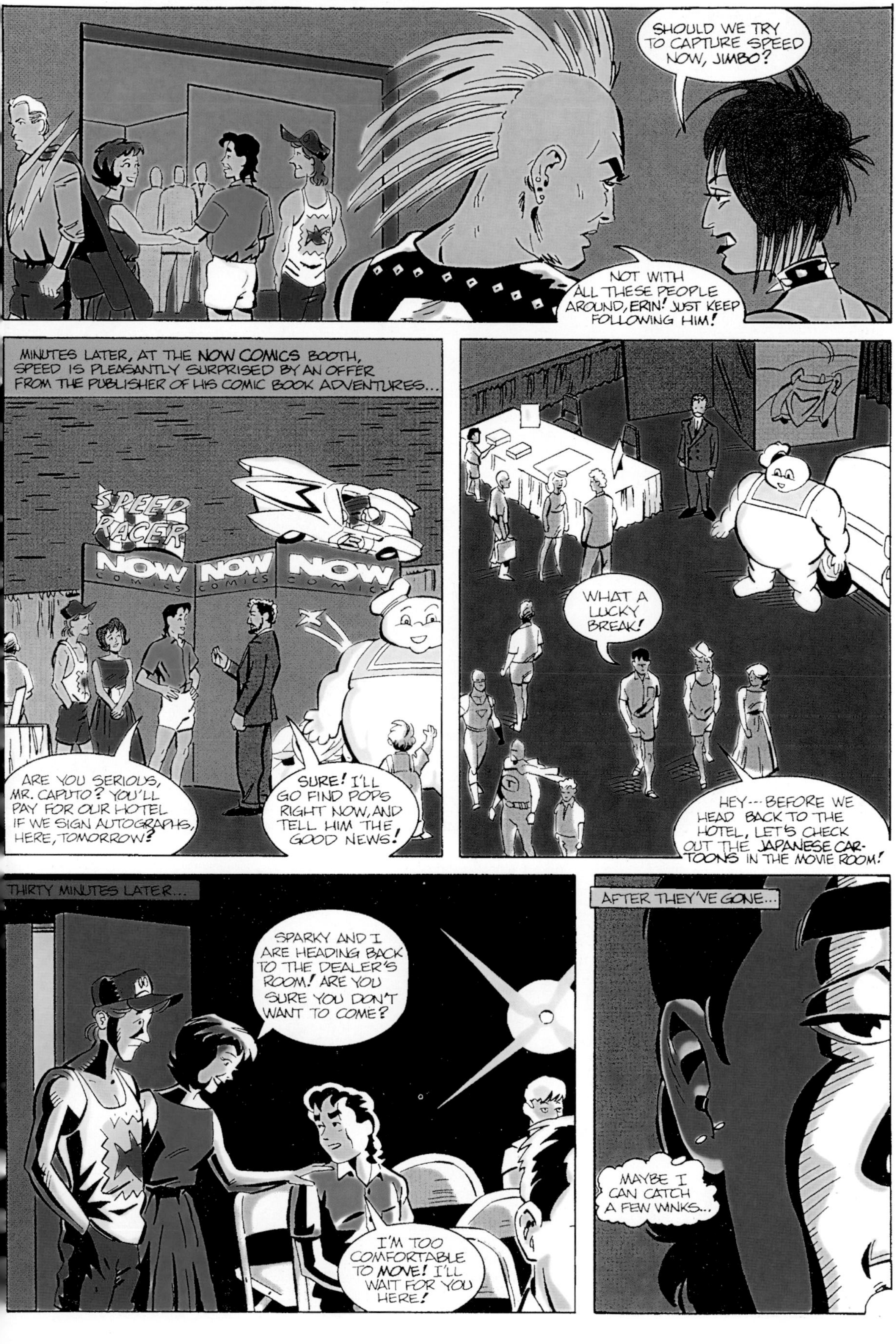
SHOULD WE TRY TO CAPTURE SPEED NOW, JIMBO?
NOT WITH ALL THESE PEOPLE AROUND, ERIN! JUST KEEP FOLLOWING HIM!
MINUTES LATER, AT THE NOW COMICS BOOTH, SPEED IS PLEASANTLY SURPRISED BY AN OFFER FROM THE PUBLISHER OF HIS COMIC BOOK ADVENTURES...
SPEED RACER
NOW COMICS
ARE YOU SERIOUS, MR. CAPUTO? YOU'LL PAY FOR OUR HOTEL IF WE SIGN AUTOGRAPHS, HERE, TOMORROW?
SURE! I'LL GO FIND POPS RIGHT NOW, AND TELL HIM THE GOOD NEWS!
WHAT A LUCKY BREAK!
HEY---BEFORE WE HEAD BACK TO THE HOTEL, LET'S CHECK OUT THE JAPANESE CAR-TOONS IN THE MOVIE ROOM!
THIRTY MINUTES LATER...
SPARKY AND I ARE HEADING BACK TO THE DEALER'S ROOM! ARE YOU SURE YOU DON'T WANT TO COME?
I'M TOO COMFORTABLE TO MOVE! I'LL WAIT FOR YOU HERE!
AFTER THEY'VE GONE...
MAYBE I CAN CATCH A FEW WINKS...

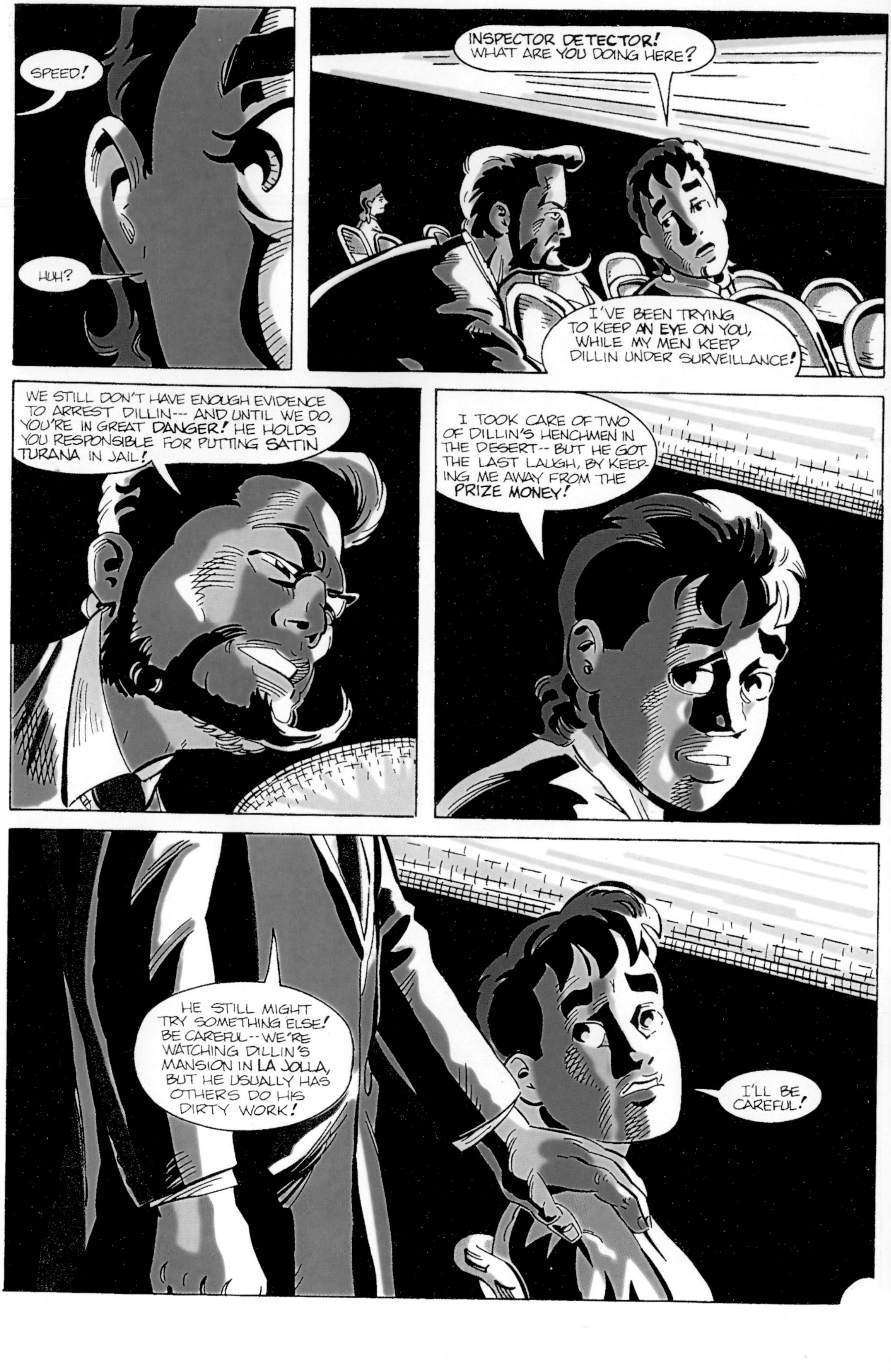
SPEED!
HUH?
INSPECTOR DETECTOR! WHAT ARE YOU DOING HERE?
I'VE BEEN TRYING TO KEEP AN EYE ON YOU, WHILE MY MEN KEEP DILLIN UNDER SURVEILLANCE!
WE STILL DON'T HAVE ENOUGH EVIDENCE TO ARREST DILLIN--- AND UNTIL WE DO, YOU'RE IN GREAT DANGER! HE HOLDS YOU RESPONSIBLE FOR PUTTING SATIN TURANA IN JAIL!
I TOOK CARE OF TWO OF DILLIN'S HENCHMEN IN THE DESERT-- BUT HE GOT THE LAST LAUGH, BY KEEPING ME AWAY FROM THE PRIZE MONEY!
HE STILL MIGHT TRY SOMETHING ELSE! BE CAREFUL--WE'RE WATCHING DILLIN'S MANSION IN LA JOLLA, BUT HE USUALLY HAS OTHERS DO HIS DIRTY WORK!
I'LL BE CAREFUL!

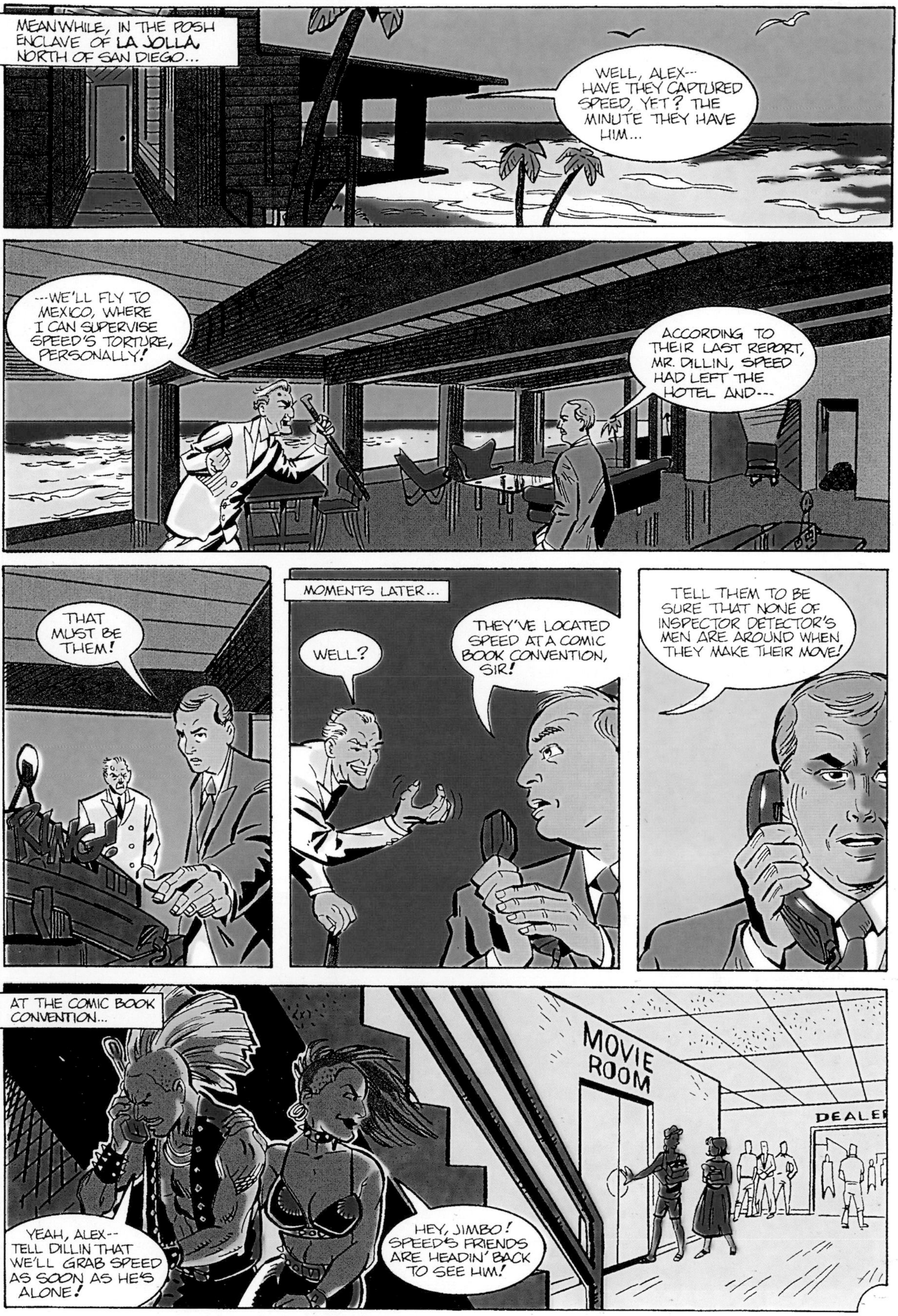
MEANWHILE, IN THE POSH ENCLAVE OF LA JOLLA, NORTH OF SAN DIEGO...
WELL, ALEX-- HAVE THEY CAPTURED SPEED, YET? THE MINUTE THEY HAVE HIM...
--WE'LL FLY TO MEXICO, WHERE I CAN SUPERVISE SPEED'S TORTURE, PERSONALLY!
ACCORDING TO THEIR LAST REPORT, MR. DILLIN, SPEED HAD LEFT THE HOTEL AND---
THAT MUST BE THEM!
RING!
MOMENTS LATER...
WELL?
THEY'VE LOCATED SPEED AT A COMIC BOOK CONVENTION, SIR!
TELL THEM TO BE SURE THAT NONE OF INSPECTOR DETECTOR'S MEN ARE AROUND WHEN THEY MAKE THEIR MOVE!
AT THE COMIC BOOK CONVENTION...
MOVIE ROOM
DEALER
YEAH, ALEX-- TELL DILLIN THAT WE'LL GRAB SPEED AS SOON AS HE'S ALONE!
HEY, JIMBO! SPEED'S FRIENDS ARE HEADIN' BACK TO SEE HIM!

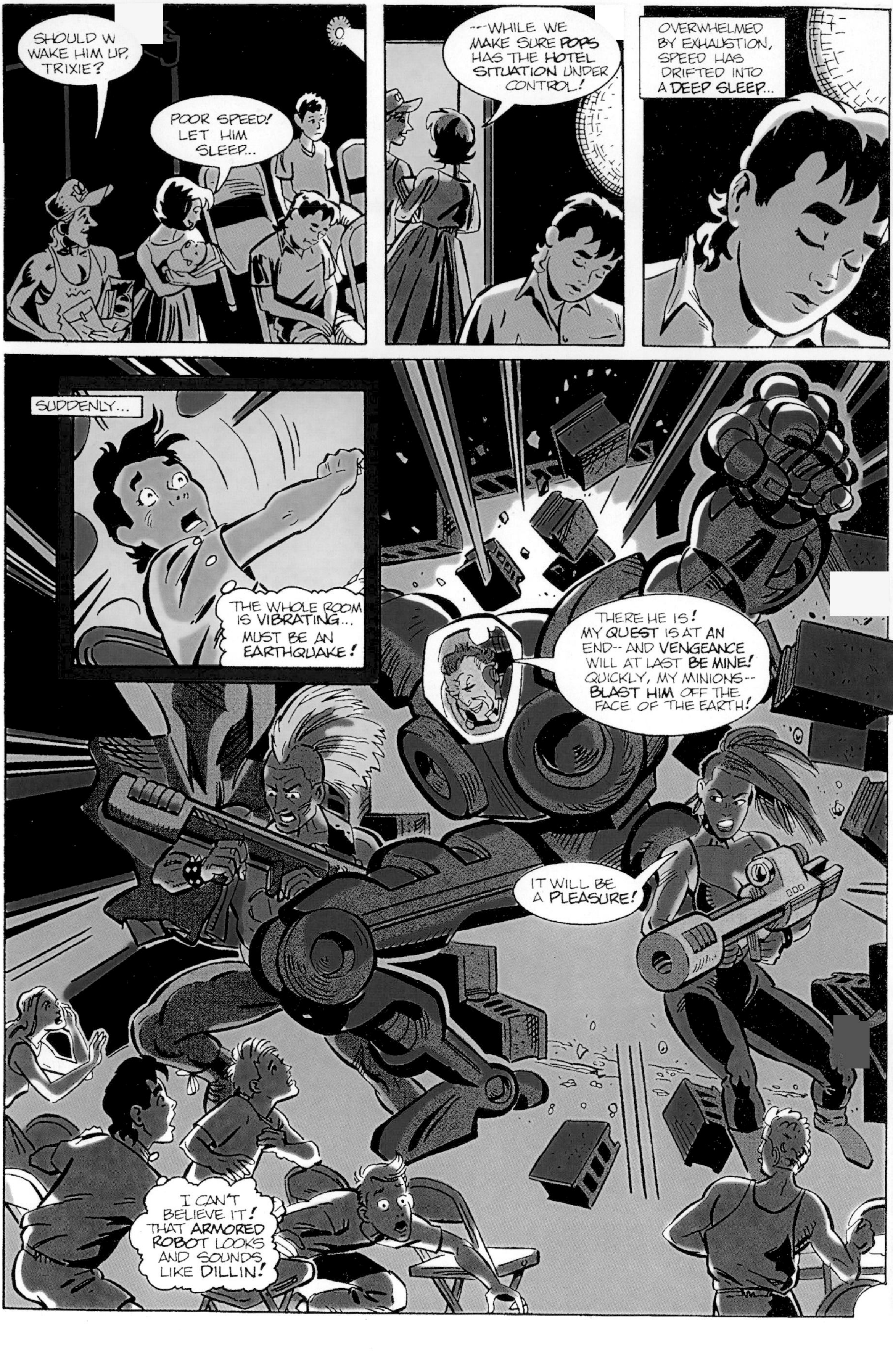

SHOULD W
WAKE HIM UP, TRIXIE?
POOR SPEED! LET HIM SLEEP...
---WHILE WE MAKE SURE POPS HAS THE HOTEL SITUATION UNDER CONTROL!
OVERWHELMED BY EXHAUSTION, SPEED HAS DRIFTED INTO A DEEP SLEEP...
SUDDENLY...
THE WHOLE ROOM IS VIBRATING... MUST BE AN EARTHQUAKE!
THERE HE IS! MY QUEST IS AT AN END-- AND VENGEANCE WILL AT LAST BE MINE! QUICKLY, MY MINIONS-- BLAST HIM OFF THE FACE OF THE EARTH!
IT WILL BE A PLEASURE!
I CAN'T BELIEVE IT! THAT ARMORED ROBOT LOOKS AND SOUNDS LIKE DILLIN!

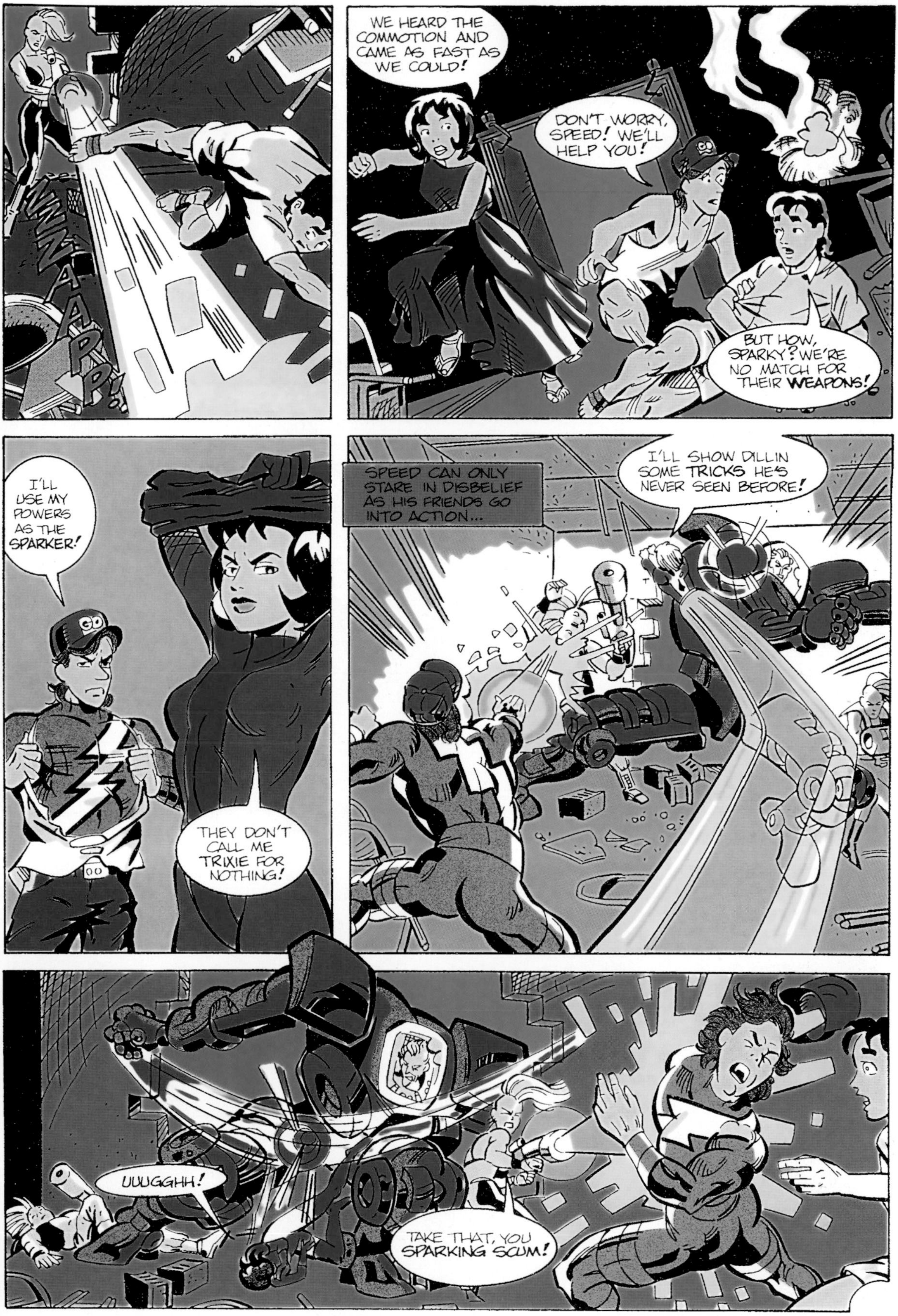
ZZZAAPP!
WE HEARD THE COMMOTION AND CAME AS FAST AS WE COULD!
DON'T WORRY, SPEED! WE'LL HELP YOU!
BUT HOW, SPARKY? WE'RE NO MATCH FOR THEIR **WEAPONS**!
I'LL USE MY POWERS AS THE **SPARKER**!
THEY DON'T CALL ME **TRIXIE** FOR NOTHING!
SPEED CAN ONLY STARE IN DISBELIEF AS HIS FRIENDS GO INTO ACTION...
I'LL SHOW DILLIN SOME **TRICKS** HE'S NEVER SEEN BEFORE!
UUUGGHH!
TAKE THAT, YOU **SPARKING SCUM**!

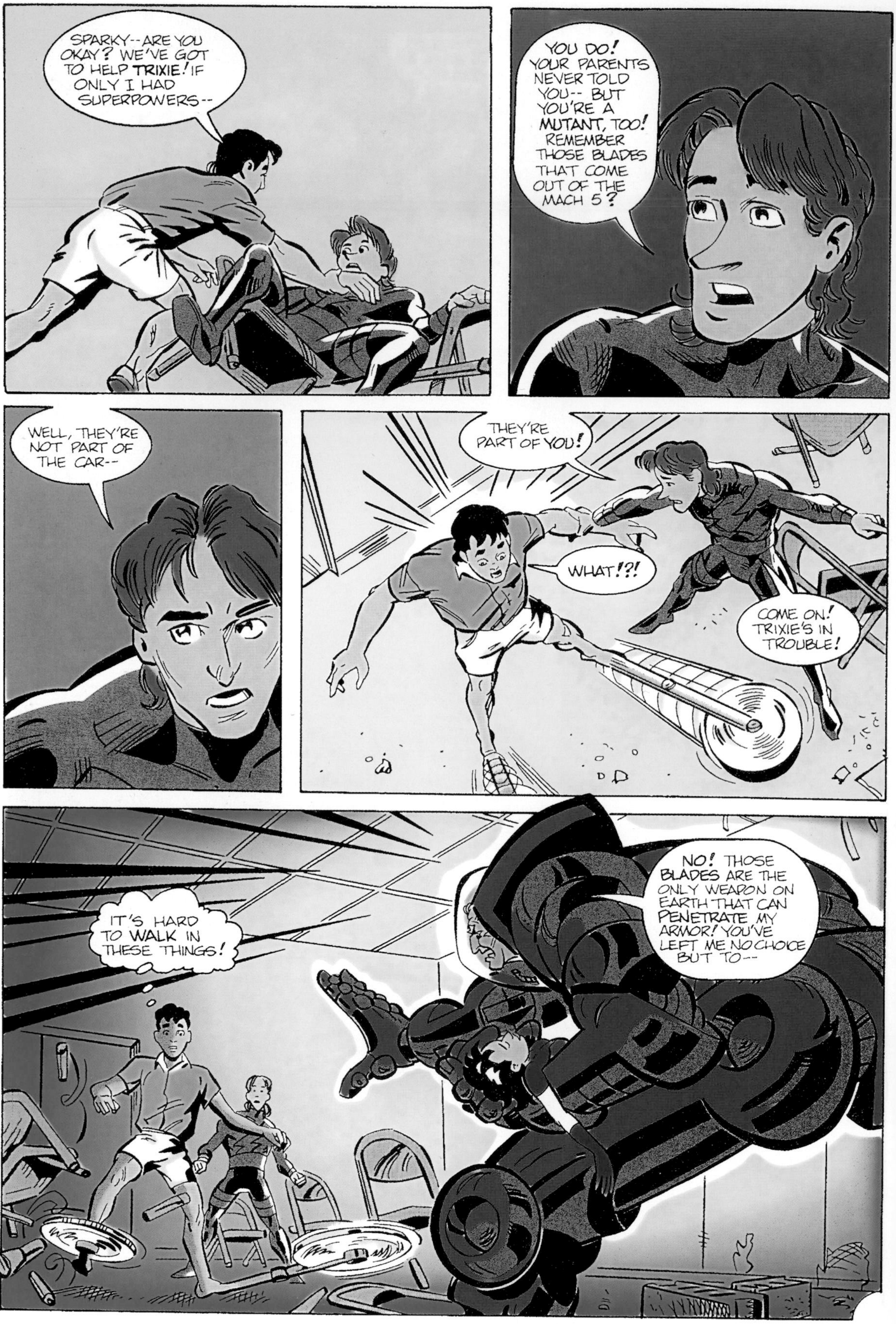
SPARKY--ARE YOU OKAY? WE'VE GOT TO HELP TRIXIE! IF ONLY I HAD SUPERPOWERS--
YOU DO! YOUR PARENTS NEVER TOLD YOU-- BUT YOU'RE A MUTANT, TOO! REMEMBER THOSE BLADES THAT COME OUT OF THE MACH 5?
WELL, THEY'RE NOT PART OF THE CAR--
THEY'RE PART OF YOU!
WHAT!?!
COME ON! TRIXIE'S IN TROUBLE!
IT'S HARD TO WALK IN THESE THINGS!
NO! THOSE BLADES ARE THE ONLY WEAPON ON EARTH THAT CAN PENETRATE MY ARMOR! YOU'VE LEFT ME NO CHOICE BUT TO--

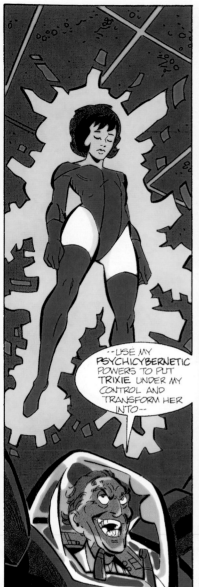

--USE MY PSYCHICYBERNETIC POWERS TO PUT TRIXIE UNDER MY CONTROL AND TRANSFORM HER INTO--

DARK TRIXIE!

QUICKLY, NOW--- SLAY SPEED AND THE SPARKER! THEY DARE TO THREATEN YOUR MASTER!

YEOW! THERE GO MY BLADES!

WE'VE GOT TO GET AWAY--- UNTIL WE CAN FIND A WAY TO DEFEAT DARK TRIXIE WITHOUT HARMING HER!

WHATEVER YOU SAY! JUST DON'T DROP ME!

THIS IS ALL SO INCREDIBLE! I CAN'T BELIEVE IT'S REALLY HAPPENING...

SAN DIEGO ZOO REPTILE A

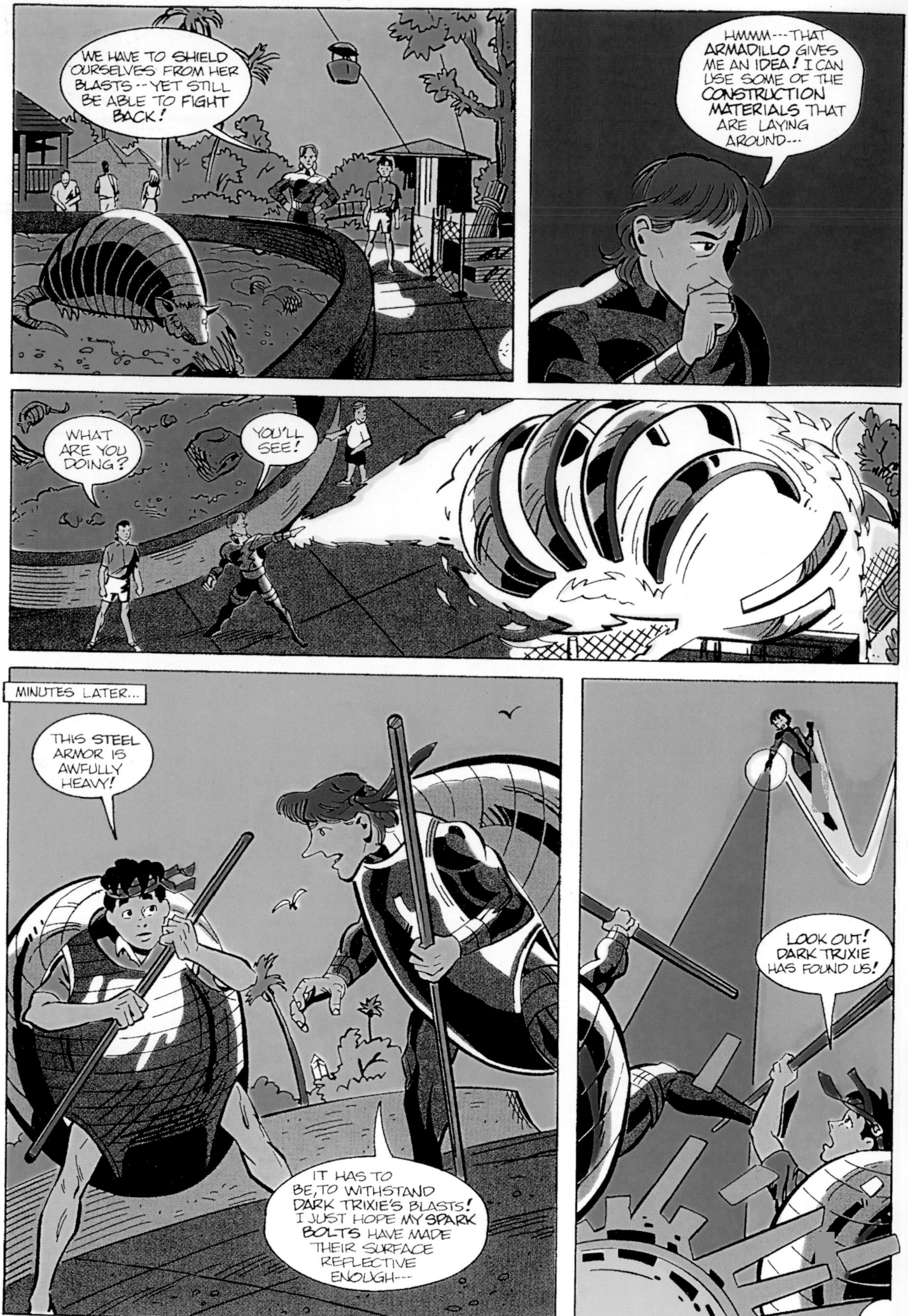

WE HAVE TO SHIELD OURSELVES FROM HER BLASTS -- YET STILL BE ABLE TO FIGHT BACK!
HMMM---THAT ARMADILLO GIVES ME AN IDEA! I CAN USE SOME OF THE CONSTRUCTION MATERIALS THAT ARE LAYING AROUND---
WHAT ARE YOU DOING?
YOU'LL SEE!
MINUTES LATER...
THIS STEEL ARMOR IS AWFULLY HEAVY!
IT HAS TO BE, TO WITHSTAND DARK TRIXIE'S BLASTS! I JUST HOPE MY SPARK BOLTS HAVE MADE THEIR SURFACE REFLECTIVE ENOUGH---
LOOK OUT! DARK TRIXIE HAS FOUND US!

THAT WAS CLOSE!

THE NEXT TIME SHE FIRES---

---PULL YOUR ARMS, LEGS, AND HEAD INSIDE YOUR SHELL!

ARE YOU CRAZY? WE'LL BE KILLED!

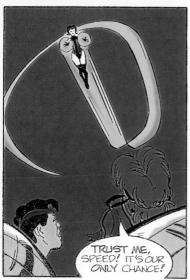

TRUST ME, SPEED! IT'S OUR ONLY CHANCE!

THE MASTER SAYS YOU MUST DIE!

BUT AS DARK TRIXIE'S BLASTS STRIKE THE SHINY SURFACE OF THE ARMOR...

...THEY'RE REFLECTED BACK AT HER!

HOW--HOW DID I GET HERE? FEEL DIZZY---GOING TO PASS OUT--

UGHH!

THE FEEDBACK CAUSED TRIXIE TO REVERT TO HER TRUE NATURE! BUT I'LL STILL HAVE MY REVENGE!

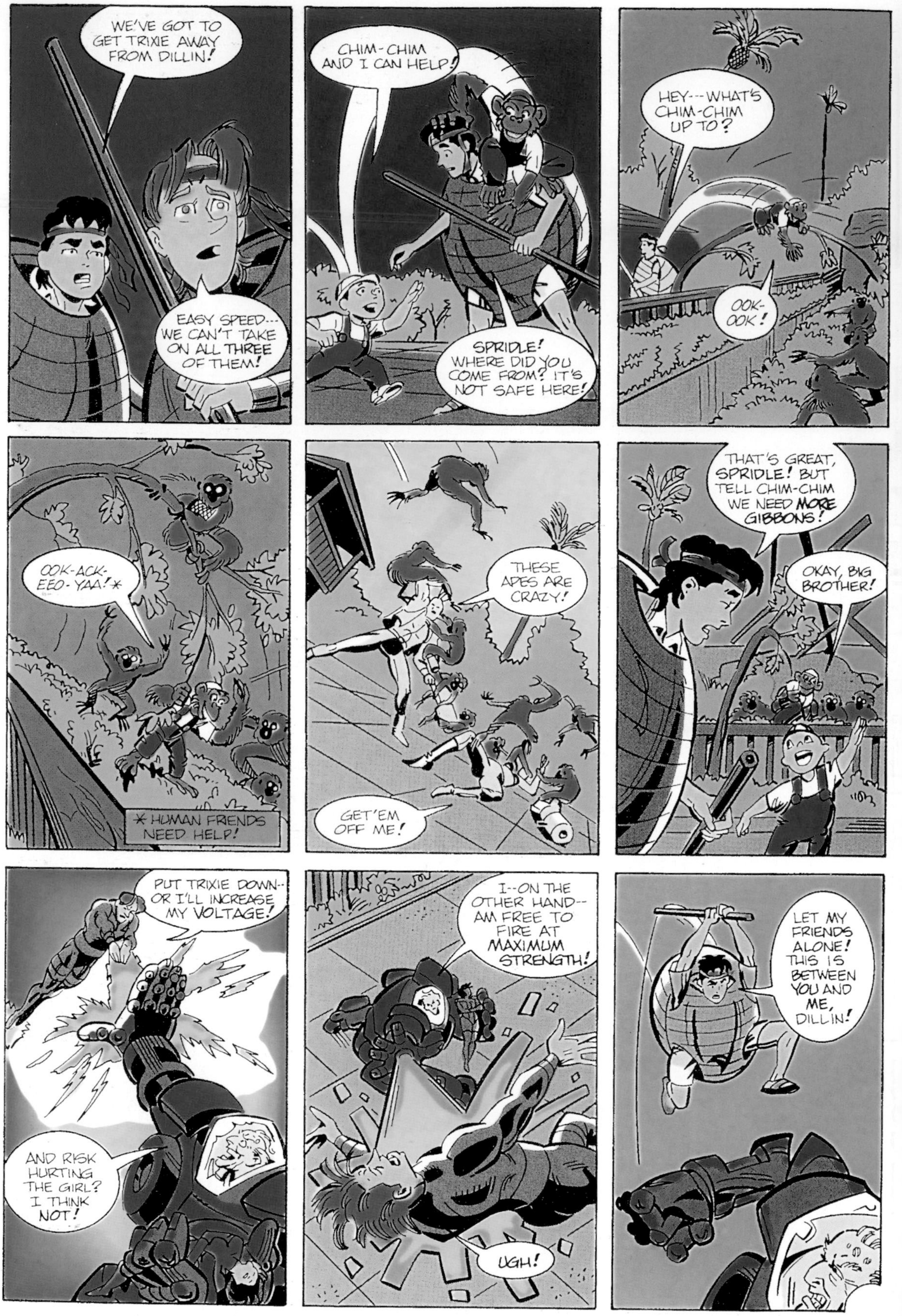
WE'VE GOT TO GET TRIXIE AWAY FROM DILLIN!
EASY SPEED--- WE CAN'T TAKE ON ALL THREE OF THEM!
CHIM-CHIM AND I CAN HELP!
SPRIDLE! WHERE DID YOU COME FROM? IT'S NOT SAFE HERE!
HEY---WHAT'S CHIM-CHIM UP TO?
OOK-OOK!
OOK-ACK-EEO-YAA!*
* HUMAN FRIENDS NEED HELP!
THESE APES ARE CRAZY!
GET'EM OFF ME!
THAT'S GREAT, SPRIDLE! BUT TELL CHIM-CHIM WE NEED MORE GIBBONS!
OKAY, BIG BROTHER!
PUT TRIXIE DOWN--OR I'LL INCREASE MY VOLTAGE!
AND RISK HURTING THE GIRL? I THINK NOT!
I--ON THE OTHER HAND--AM FREE TO FIRE AT MAXIMUM STRENGTH!
UGH!
LET MY FRIENDS ALONE! THIS IS BETWEEN YOU AND ME, DILLIN!

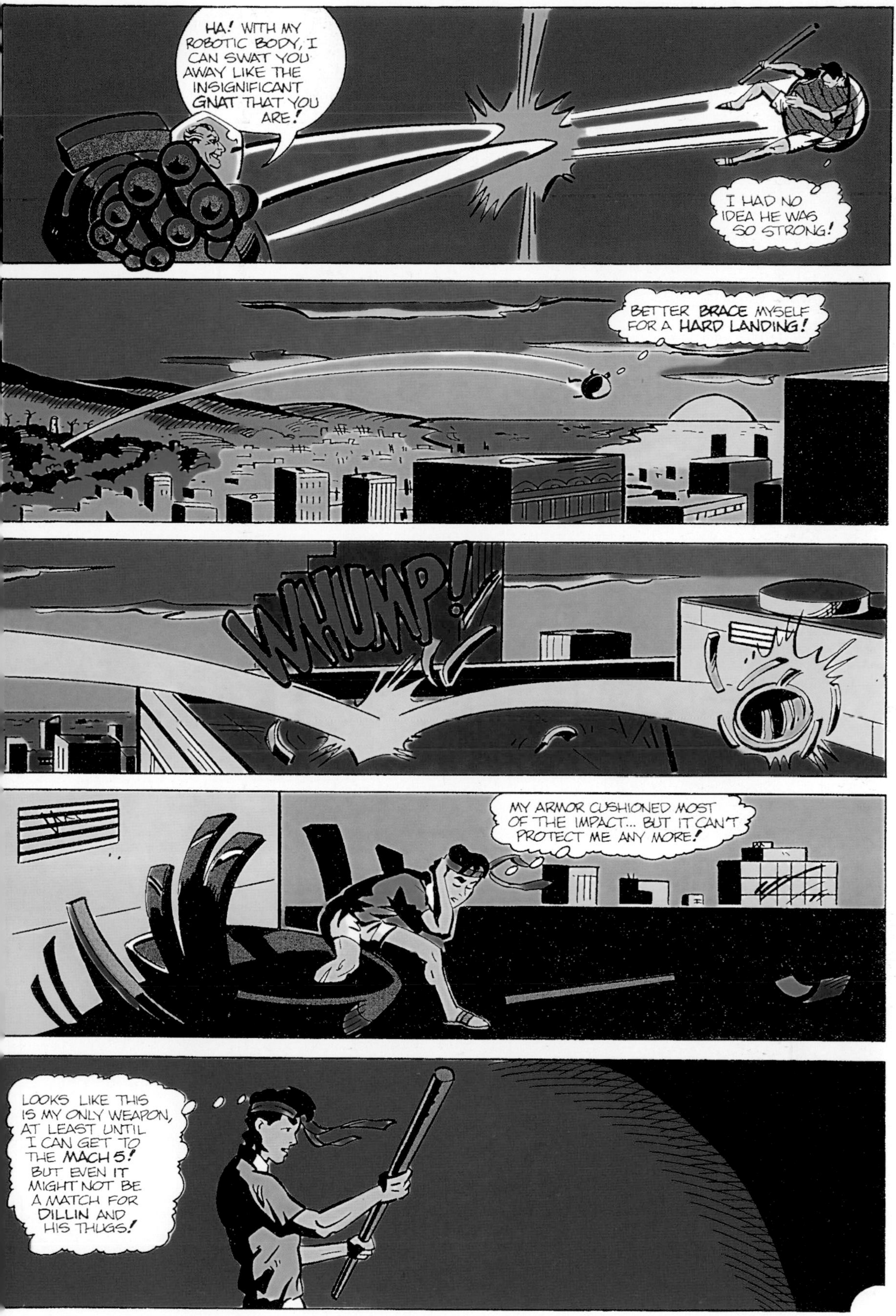

HA! WITH MY ROBOTIC BODY, I CAN SWAT YOU AWAY LIKE THE INSIGNIFICANT GNAT THAT YOU ARE!
I HAD NO IDEA HE WAS SO STRONG!
BETTER BRACE MYSELF FOR A HARD LANDING!
WHUMP!
MY ARMOR CUSHIONED MOST OF THE IMPACT... BUT IT CAN'T PROTECT ME ANY MORE!
LOOKS LIKE THIS IS MY ONLY WEAPON, AT LEAST UNTIL I CAN GET TO THE MACH 5! BUT EVEN IT MIGHT NOT BE A MATCH FOR DILLIN AND HIS THUGS!

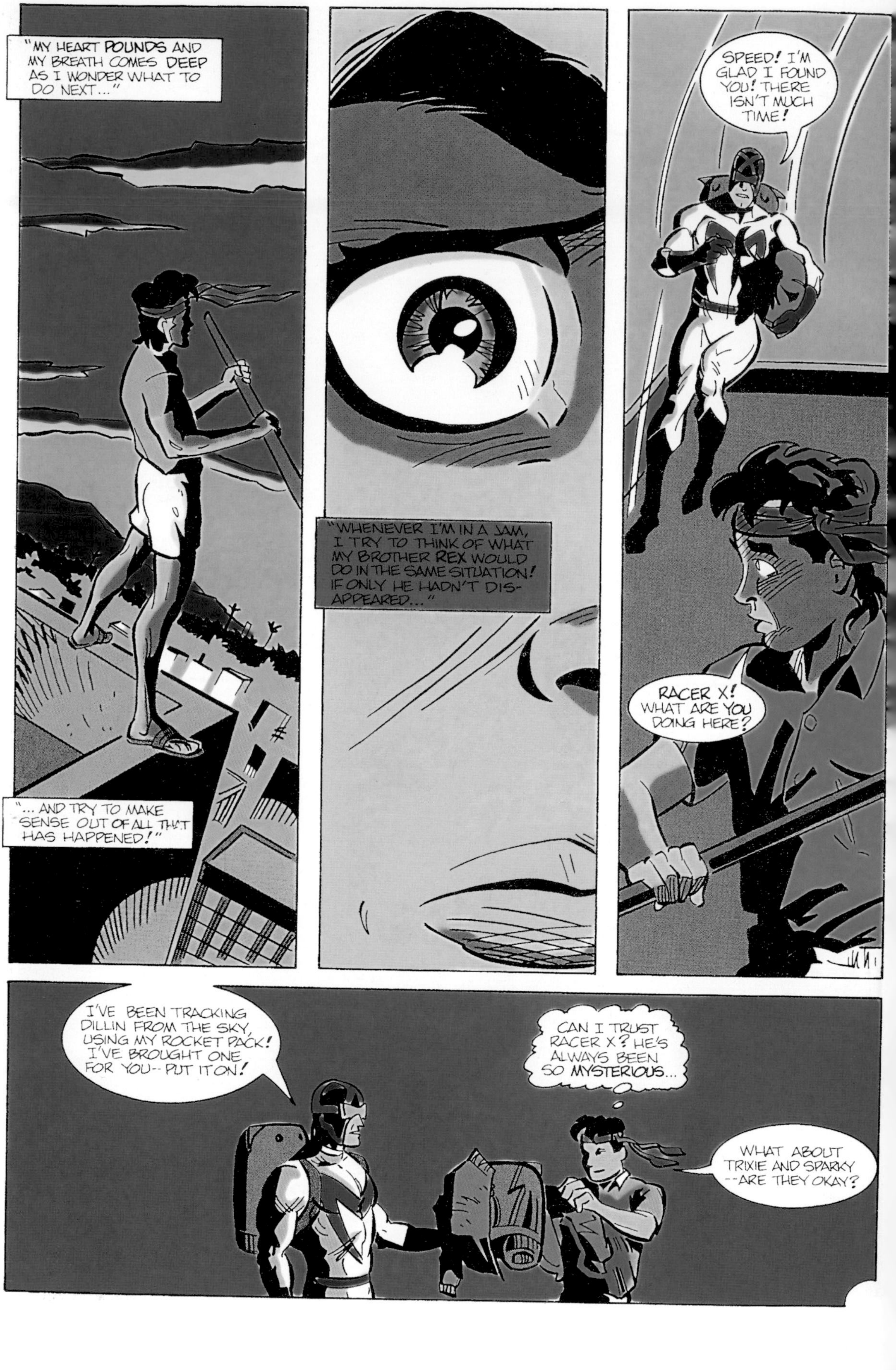
"MY HEART POUNDS AND MY BREATH COMES DEEP AS I WONDER WHAT TO DO NEXT..."
"... AND TRY TO MAKE SENSE OUT OF ALL THAT HAS HAPPENED!"
"WHENEVER I'M IN A JAM, I TRY TO THINK OF WHAT MY BROTHER REX WOULD DO IN THE SAME SITUATION! IF ONLY HE HADN'T DIS-APPEARED..."
SPEED! I'M GLAD I FOUND YOU! THERE ISN'T MUCH TIME!
RACER X! WHAT ARE YOU DOING HERE?
I'VE BEEN TRACKING DILLIN FROM THE SKY, USING MY ROCKET PACK! I'VE BROUGHT ONE FOR YOU-- PUT IT ON!
CAN I TRUST RACER X? HE'S ALWAYS BEEN SO MYSTERIOUS...
WHAT ABOUT TRIXIE AND SPARKY --ARE THEY OKAY?

FOR THE MOMENT! BUT DILLIN IS GETTING READY TO FLY THEM ACROSS THE BORDER, INTO MEXICO! WE'VE GOT TO STOP HIM!

THAT'S THE HANGAR WHERE DILLIN KEEPS HIS COLLECTION OF ANTIQUE PLANES!

DILLON AIRCRAFT

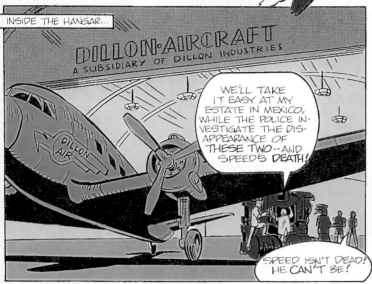

INSIDE THE HANGAR...

DILLON·AIRCRAFT
A SUBSIDIARY OF DILLON INDUSTRIES

DILLON AIR

WE'LL TAKE IT EASY AT MY ESTATE IN MEXICO, WHILE THE POLICE INVESTIGATE THE DISAPPEARANCE OF THESE TWO--AND SPEED'S DEATH!

SPEED ISN'T DEAD! HE CAN'T BE!

AND WHEN HE FINDS YOU---

IT WILL BE TOO LATE FOR HIM TO DO ANYTHING, MY DEAR!

WE WILL BE IN ANOTHER COUNTRY--- AND YOU WILL BE MY NEW BRIDE! HA! HA! HA!

GET TRIXIE DRESSED FOR OUR WEDDING! I WANT THE CEREMONY TO START AS SOON AS WE REACH TAMPICO!

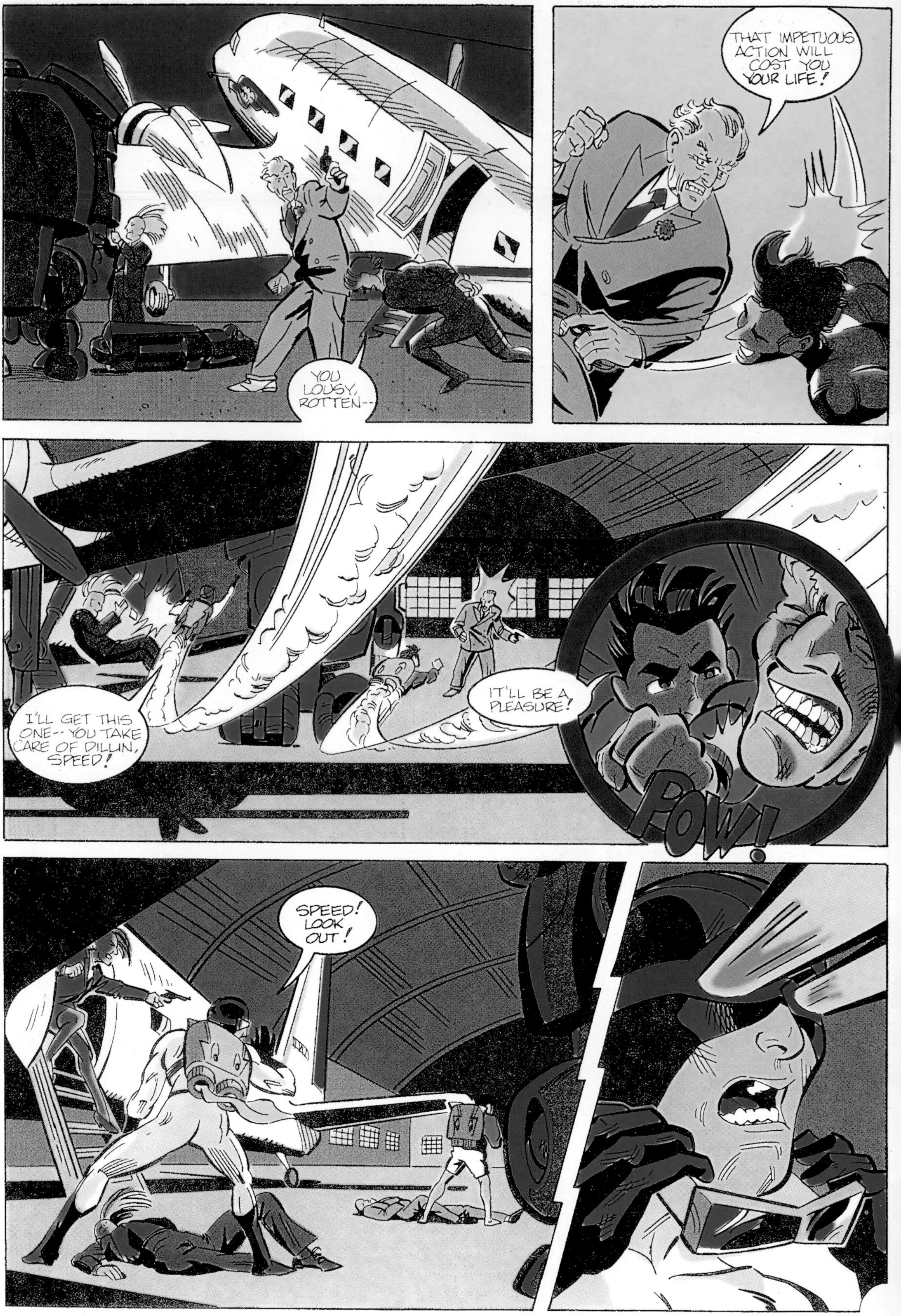
YOU LOUSY, ROTTEN--
THAT IMPETUOUS ACTION WILL COST YOU YOUR LIFE!
I'LL GET THIS ONE-- YOU TAKE CARE OF DILLIN, SPEED!
IT'LL BE A PLEASURE!
POW!
SPEED! LOOK OUT!

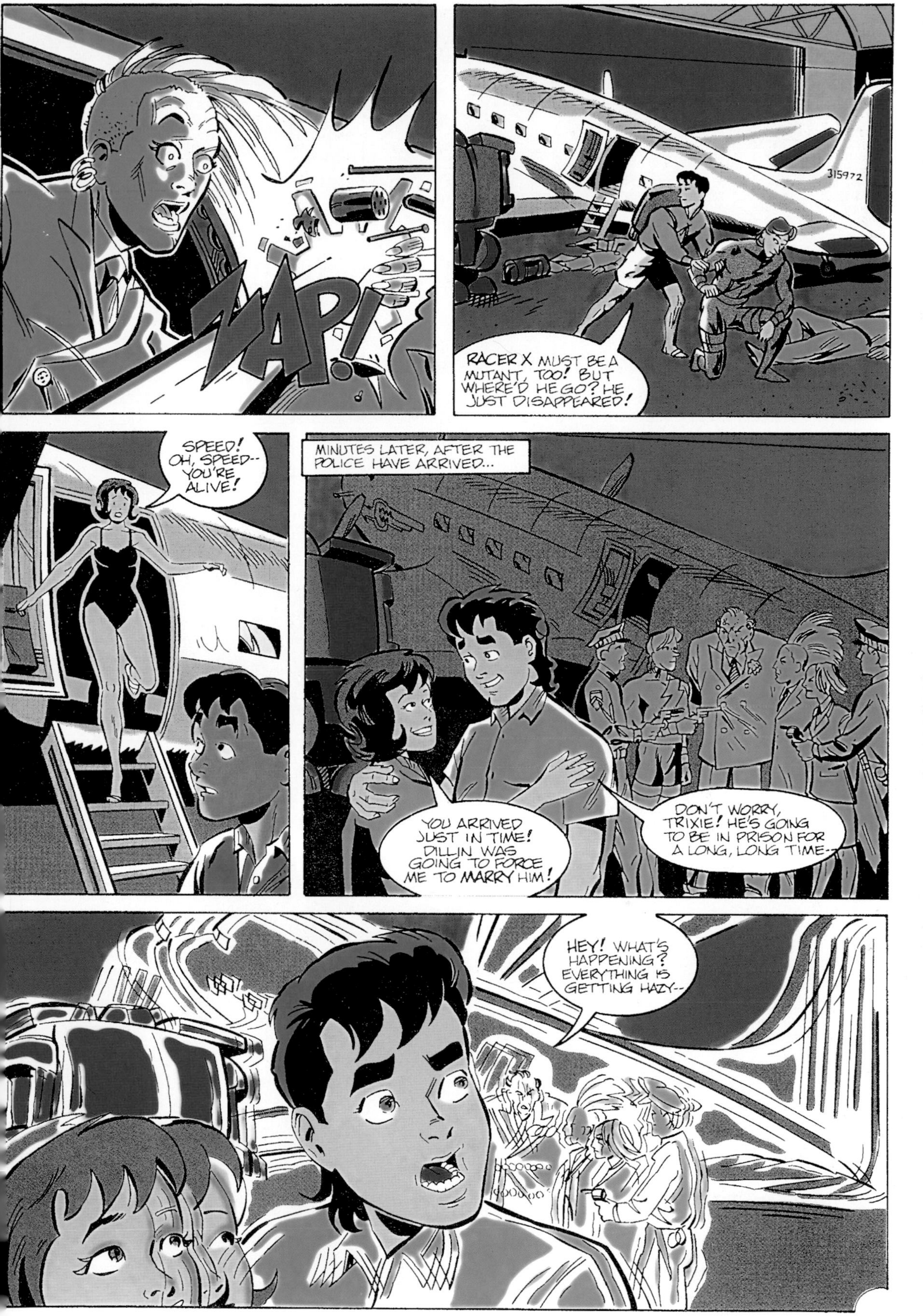
ZAP!
315972
RACER X MUST BE A MUTANT, TOO! BUT WHERE'D HE GO? HE JUST DISAPPEARED!
SPEED! OH, SPEED-- YOU'RE ALIVE!
MINUTES LATER, AFTER THE POLICE HAVE ARRIVED...
YOU ARRIVED JUST IN TIME! DILLIN WAS GOING TO FORCE ME TO MARRY HIM!
DON'T WORRY, TRIXIE! HE'S GOING TO BE IN PRISON FOR A LONG, LONG TIME--
HEY! WHAT'S HAPPENING? EVERYTHING IS GETTING HAZY--

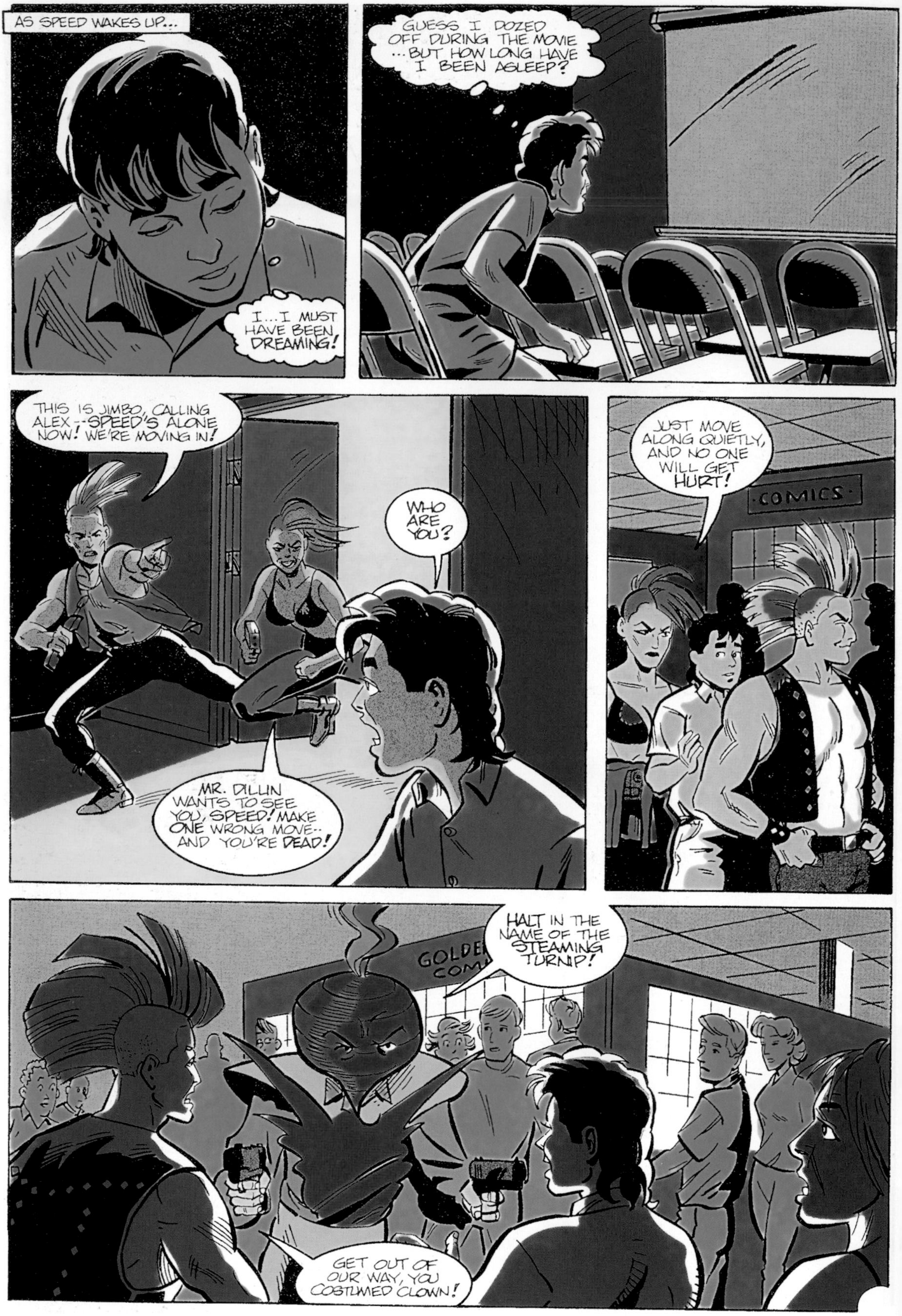
AS SPEED WAKES UP...
I... I MUST HAVE BEEN DREAMING!
GUESS I DOZED OFF DURING THE MOVIE ...BUT HOW LONG HAVE I BEEN ASLEEP?
THIS IS JIMBO, CALLING ALEX--SPEED'S ALONE NOW! WE'RE MOVING IN!
WHO ARE YOU?
MR. DILLIN WANTS TO SEE YOU, SPEED! MAKE ONE WRONG MOVE.. AND YOU'RE DEAD!
JUST MOVE ALONG QUIETLY, AND NO ONE WILL GET HURT!
COMICS
HALT IN THE NAME OF THE STEAMING TURNIP!
GET OUT OF OUR WAY, YOU COSTUMED CLOWN!

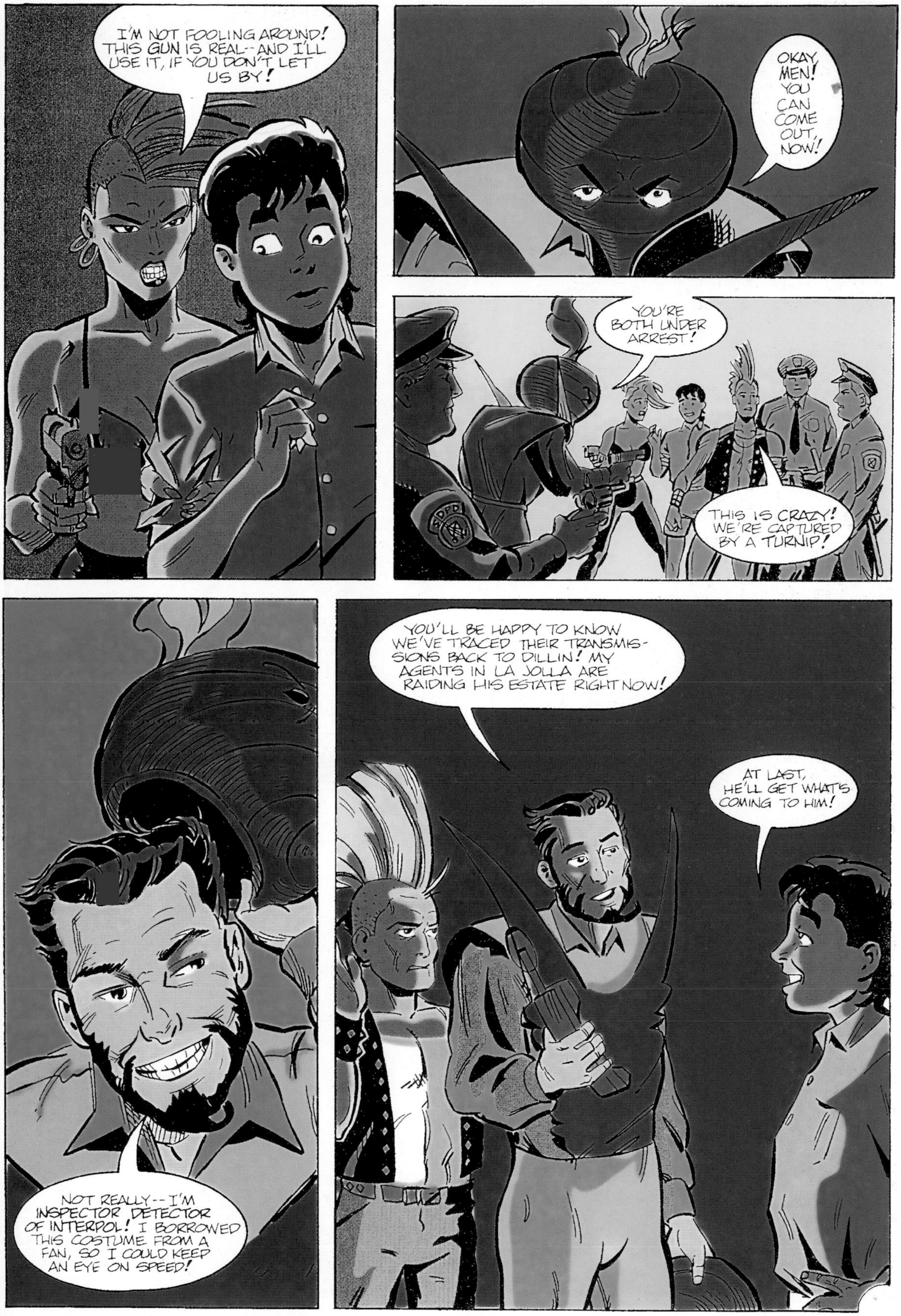
I'M NOT FOOLING AROUND! THIS GUN IS REAL--AND I'LL USE IT, IF YOU DON'T LET US BY!
OKAY, MEN! YOU CAN COME OUT, NOW!
YOU'RE BOTH UNDER ARREST!
THIS IS CRAZY! WE'RE CAPTURED BY A TURNIP!
NOT REALLY--I'M INSPECTOR DETECTOR OF INTERPOL! I BORROWED THIS COSTUME FROM A FAN, SO I COULD KEEP AN EYE ON SPEED!
YOU'LL BE HAPPY TO KNOW WE'VE TRACED THEIR TRANSMISSIONS BACK TO DILLIN! MY AGENTS IN LA JOLLA ARE RAIDING HIS ESTATE RIGHT NOW!
AT LAST, HE'LL GET WHAT'S COMING TO HIM!

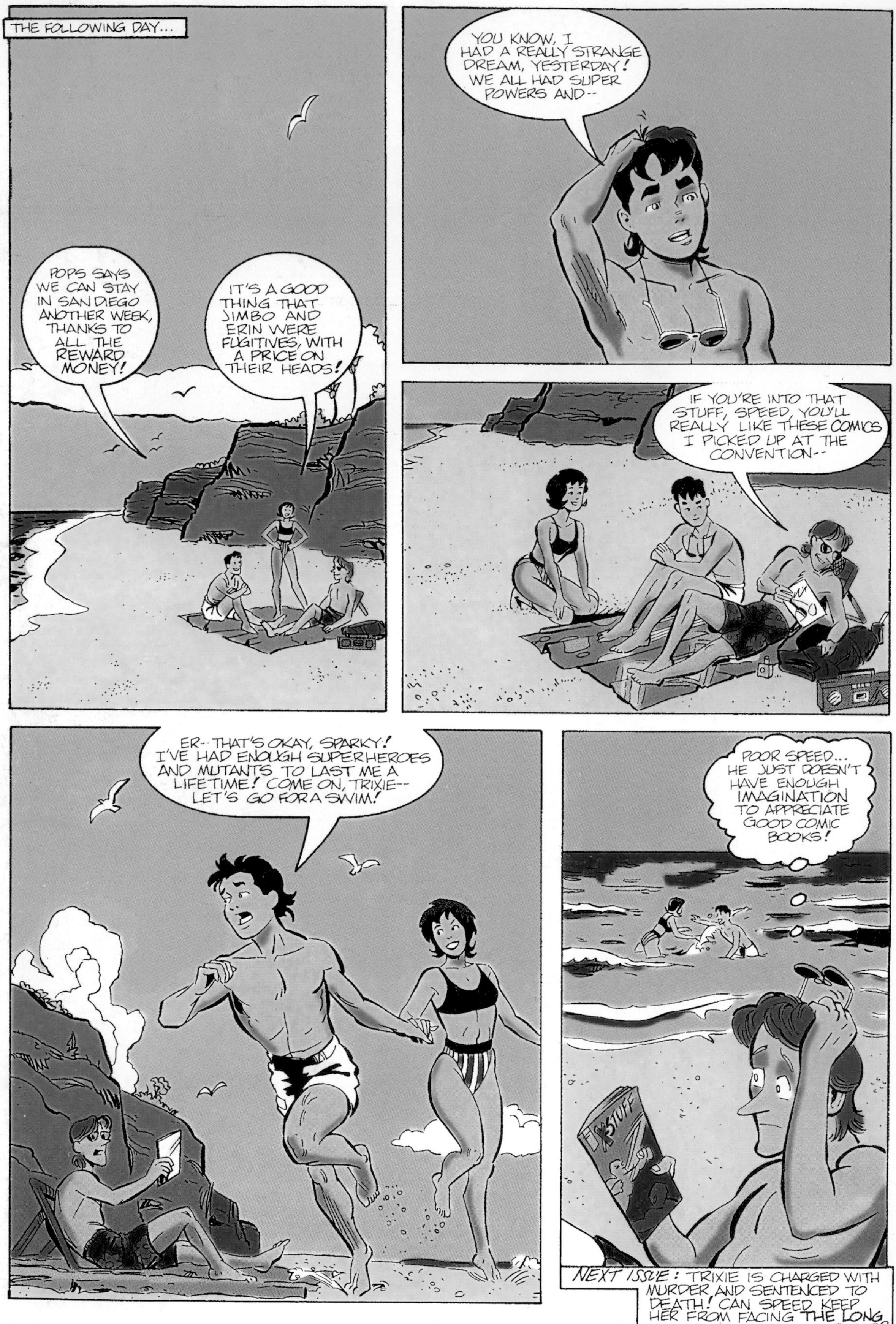
THE FOLLOWING DAY...
YOU KNOW, I HAD A REALLY STRANGE DREAM, YESTERDAY! WE ALL HAD SUPER POWERS AND--
POPS SAYS WE CAN STAY IN SAN DIEGO ANOTHER WEEK, THANKS TO ALL THE REWARD MONEY!
IT'S A GOOD THING THAT JIMBO AND ERIN WERE FUGITIVES, WITH A PRICE ON THEIR HEADS!
IF YOU'RE INTO THAT STUFF, SPEED, YOU'LL REALLY LIKE THESE COMICS I PICKED UP AT THE CONVENTION--
ER--THAT'S OKAY, SPARKY! I'VE HAD ENOUGH SUPERHEROES AND MUTANTS TO LAST ME A LIFETIME! COME ON, TRIXIE-- LET'S GO FOR A SWIM!
POOR SPEED... HE JUST DOESN'T HAVE ENOUGH IMAGINATION TO APPRECIATE GOOD COMIC BOOKS!
NEXT ISSUE: TRIXIE IS CHARGED WITH MURDER AND SENTENCED TO DEATH! CAN SPEED KEEP HER FROM FACING THE LONG SLEEP?